lost and found in history

FIRST
ENCOUNTERS

lost and found in history

FIRST
ENCOUNTERS

Epic true stories of cultural collision and conquest

Joseph Cummins

PIER **9**

CONTENTS

PART 4

THE GREAT SOUTHERN OCEAN

PART 5

FATEFUL ENCOUNTERS IN THE HEART OF AFRICA

PART 6

FIRST CONTACT IN THE TWENTIETH CENTURY

INTRODUCTION

The Maori were peacefully gathering clams in a New Zealand bay so quiet it was called 'Gentle as a Young Girl', when the white goblins showed up on a floating island. The inhabitants of the Yucatan Peninsula were going about their business of trading and farming when floating mountains, peopled by men wearing what looked like little frying pans for hats, appeared off their eastern shores. In the 1930s in the New Guinea highlands, native tribes had the astonishing experience of seeing their dead return to them, transformed but recognisable.

For a long time, many cultures and peoples in the world thought they were alone. Hundreds of thousands of people in Mesoamerica and Oceania—including New Zealand, Tasmania and mainland Australia—developed myths, legends, religions and customs based on the fact that they were the only ones who existed—the supreme ones. In fact, most of the names for their groups meant simply 'the People'.

And then one fine day others began sailing up in outlandish vessels—white people with an odd smell to them, frightful weapons and an offensive way of seeming to take over immediately. These white people, because of their trading experience and superior technology, which meant they had travelled over wider areas, were less surprised at the existence of the people they encountered, although when these people were not mere primitives, the white men reacted with astonishment (Cortés's men thought they were hallucinating on first viewing the fine Mexica city of Tenochtitlán).

Strangely enough, despite their utter amazement, the indigenous peoples were, at first, more accepting of the strangers, assigning them roles as gods, as the returning dead—a common theme—or, as historian Charles Mann has written, merely as 'unusual people' with possible superhuman powers. Their polytheistic religions tended to allow for this, unlike the Judeo-Christian backgrounds of the Europeans they encountered.

But, very soon, it would all go bad. While, from 1492 on, there were numerous well-meaning white people who sought to protect indigenous peoples, the Age of Discovery was the Age of Conquest. As soon as native peoples realised this, first encounters turned violent. And in fact—as with the Indians of certain tribes in the Amazon Basin today, or the small groups inhabiting one or two of the Indian Ocean's Andaman Islands—only fiercely hostile displays from the moment of contact had any hope of keeping the intruders away.

Despite this sordid history, there is something fascinating about first contact. The most powerful moments in history occur when two peoples, previously unknown to each other, come together for the first time. 'Surprises crackle, like electric arcs', writes historian Robert Hughes, when cultures collide. *First Encounters: Epic true stories of collision and conquest* is a book that captures first-contact moments drawn from the written records of human history, beginning with Carthaginians circumnavigating Africa and ending in 2008 with reports of uncontacted tribes in the Amazon. While the book unavoidably contains a great deal of the violence and bloodshed that attended first contact, it also captures the moments of awe and wonder—the African women surrounding eighteenth century explorer Mungo Park and exclaiming that he must have been dipped in milk at birth for his skin to be so white, or the small New Guinean boy who saw white men for the first time when Jack Hides's patrol approached his village and many years later, as an old man, would tell an anthropologist: 'We jumped. No one had ever seen anything like this before or knew what it was … these must be spirit people coming openly, in plain sight.'

First encounters are full of possibility if human beings are able to realise that they are not meeting spirits—or noble primitives, or gods—but themselves, in a different guise.

The village of Kamalia, as depicted in Mungo Park's Travels in the Interior Districts of Africa, *an account of his explorations in 1795–97.*

PART 1

FABLED ENCOUNTERS IN THE OLD WORLD

Hanno of Carthage sailed down the west coast of Africa and encountered many strange creatures, including gorillas he believed were 'hairy men'.

SEARCHING FOR LOST WORLDS

Beginning encounters

A long time ago, people believed in the vanished island of Atlantis and its counterpart in the Pacific, Lemuria, sometimes called Mu. We first learned about Atlantis from Plato who, writing in the fourth century BC, described it as a kingdom populated by beautiful and sophisticated people, an island 'full of marvellous beauty and inexhaustible profusion' that disappeared 'in a single day and night of misfortune'. When the Age of Exploration dawned, people searched for Atlantis everywhere. Fifty different sites throughout the Mediterranean and Caribbean were ballyhooed as the real Atlantis, while, by the end of the twentieth century, some two thousand volumes had been written about this magical place, which some claim is not just an island, but a continent.

Lemuria has a later genesis. In the nineteenth century it was thought that lemurs lived only in Madagascar, Africa and Southeast Asia. This strange spread of the animal (actually not true, since remains of prehistoric lemurs have since been found in America and Europe) caused certain highly serious but imaginative nineteenth and early twentieth century writers to claim the existence of a land bridge that connected India and South Africa via Madagascar some seventy-five million years ago. In the 1920s, an English writer named George Churchward published a book called *The Lost Continent of Mu*, in which he claimed to have found the remains of the civilisation of Lemuria on Pacific Islands ranging from the Marianas to Easter Island. Mu, Churchward wrote, was 'an earthly paradise' where, 'over the cool rivers, gaudy-winged butterflies hovered in the shade of trees, rising and falling in fairy-like movements'. The people who lived there (some sixty-four million strong) 'were highly civilized and enlightened'. It was too bad massive earthquakes destroyed the entire place, just as it was a shame Atlantis was demolished by a tsunami of record proportions.

The Phoenicians: seafarers

Humankind has spent many decades seeking paradises—one reason first encounters occur—but simple commerce is another reason. Five thousand years ago, the eastern end of the Mediterranean basin saw the rise of the civilisations of Egypt and Sumer, to be followed by those of Assyria and Greece. Finally, about 1400 BC, came the Phoenicians, an extraordinary seafaring people who used the comparative calm of the Mediterranean to perfect their sailing skills as the premier merchants of the ancient world. By 600 BC their single-masted, many-oared ships were ubiquitous, bringing livestock, cloth, slaves and gold to markets along the shores. The Phoenicians also sailed deep into the Nile and the Red Sea; according to the Old Testament prophet Ezekiel, they may even have reached the shores of India.

The Phoenicians were the great voyagers of antiquity, sailing as far north as Britain and perhaps even circumnavigating Africa in c. 600 BC.

THOR HEYERDAHL'S
LONG JOURNEY

Thor Heyerdahl was the kind of man most isolationist scientists—those who believe that cultures across the world developed alone, without contact with one another—loved to hate. Born in 1914, he was a Norwegian ethnographer, archaeologist and explorer who set out to prove the so-called diffusionist point of view—and particularly that the culture of the Pacific Islands evolved because of westward journeys by peoples from Peru. This, of course, flies in the face of accepted theory, which holds that the Pacific was settled by Polynesians originating in Southeast Asia. But Heyerdahl pointed out that the sweet potato— a staple in South America but unknown in Southeast Asia—thrived in the Pacific Islands at the time the first European explorers arrived there, and he believed that it came from Peru.

It was his theory, backed up by numerous Incan myths and legends, that South American Indians on primitive rafts settled the Pacific Islands, using the prevailing winds and currents near the Equator—winds and currents that the Polynesians would have had to fight against to get to South America. He did not dispute that Polynesians made their long journeys, just that they came later in time.

Naturally, the scientific establishment laughed at the idea of a flimsy Indian raft sailing across the Pacific, so Heyerdahl decided to prove them wrong. In 1947, he constructed a balsa-wood raft that he dubbed Kon-Tiki, and he sailed across the Pacific on it in company with four other adventurers. The balsa wood turned out to be remarkably buoyant. Fish swam up between the loose logs, providing ready nourishment for the voyagers as well as a source of moisture. Finally, Heyerdahl reached the Polynesian atoll of Raroia, having been at sea for 101 days. 'I crawled up on dry sand and counted the men around me. That feeling can never be matched. We had really made it and we were all alive.'

Heyerdahl was to make numerous other adventurous voyages, including one across the Atlantic from Africa to South America in a papyrus boat such as the Egyptians used. Heyerdahl's voyages did not prove that South American Indians reached the Pacific Islands or that Egyptians found their way to Brazil—only that such voyages were possible. And, indeed, they are.

The first recorded voyage of exploration by the Phoenicians comes to us from the pen of the Greek historian Herodotus and seems to have taken place around 600 BC. The ambitious Egyptian King Necho, who ruled from 610 to 595 BC, sent the Phoenicians—who often acted as seagoing intermediaries for the Egyptians, who hated the ocean—to travel through the Red Sea into the Indian Ocean, and on a journey that circumnavigated Africa. Herodotus claims that the Phoenicians provided enough food for the voyage simply by taking along plenty of seed:

> *When autumn came they went ashore, wherever they might happen to be and, having sown a tract of land with corn, waited until the grain was fit to cut. Having reaped it they again set sail; and thus it came to pass that two whole years went by, and it was not until the third year that they doubled the Pillars of Hercules [Strait of Gibraltar] and made good their voyage home.*

Hanno the Navigator

Herodotus did not describe the epic voyage around Africa in great detail and there is some doubt as to whether it really happened. However, a hundred years later Phoenicians made a voyage down the west coast of Africa and had hair-raising first encounter experiences. This voyage was led by Hanno, a prince of the North African city-state of Carthage, which would become the Phoenicians' most powerful colony and would, by the third century BC, supersede the cities of Phoenicia and challenge the Romans for supremacy of the known world.

Hanno, who became known to history as Hanno the Navigator, tells us in the account he left behind that the Phoenicians took thirty thousand men and women with them in seventy-oared galleys. This was to be a journey of colonisation, a way to spread the power of Carthage to unknown lands. After passing through the Pillars of Hercules, the wayfarers headed west and south down the coast of Africa until they came to 'a lake not far from the sea, full of reeds, many and large. In it were elephants, and other beasts of all kinds, feeding'.

Hanno wrote that he and his colonists here discovered a race of men called 'Aethiopians [who were] altogether inhospitable, inhabiting a country abounding in wild beasts and intersected by great mountains'. Not only that, but 'round the mountains dwell men of strange shape, called Troglodytes', whom the Carthaginians did not meet, but of whom they heard horrifying tales— enough to get them to push off again and set sail south and now east, entering the Gulf of Guinea. Reaching shore once again, they sailed through a tributary into a 'great lake', which contained three large islands. At the far shore of this lake, which was bounded by high mountains, Hanno and his Carthaginians were met by 'wild men clad in the skins of beasts, who cast stones and drove us off, preventing us from landing'.

They continued on to another wide river and sailed down it until the pilot of Hanno's ship was killed by a crocodile, at which point they hastily returned to the sea. Sailing farther south, they passed a heavily wooded island. They saw no people there, but at night numerous fires blazed and the Carthaginians heard 'the sounds of flutes and cymbals, and the beating of drums and an immense shouting … Fear therefore seized us, and the soothsayers bade us take our leave …'

Hanno's voyage into the unknown had become a voyage of terror. Farther south, they passed by 'a burning country … and from it huge streams of fire flowed into the sea'. In the midst of the land 'was a lofty fire, greater than the rest and seeming to touch the stars. This by day appeared a vast mountain [which the Carthaginians called] Theon Ochema [Chariot of the Gods]'. They had obviously passed an erupting volcano, which some historians think is Mount Cameroon, in present-day Cameroon. However, other historians place it as Mount Kukulima, in modern Guinea. (There is difficulty in reckoning exactly how far south the Carthaginians sailed because they, like their Phoenician forebears, were extremely cagey about revealing navigational details of their discoveries.)

However, after passing these fiery streams Hanno and his ships came upon another large island. When the Carthaginians landed, they found it:

> *... full of savages, of whom by far the greater number were women with rough, hairy bodies, whom the interpreters called Gorillas. We gave chase to the men but could not catch any, for they scampered up the cliffs and held us off by throwing stones ... But we took three women who bit and scratched those who led them and would not follow. So we killed them and flayed them and took their skins [and] we sailed no farther.*

Pytheas and the 'Tiu Islands'

This last Carthaginian encounter was almost certainly not with humans, but with apes, possibly chimpanzees or baboons—had the Carthaginians really tangled with gorillas (so-named by American missionary Thomas Savage, recalling Hanno's story, in the 1850s) they would have suffered more than a few hurled stones. Nonetheless, legends grew about the wilds of Africa and the savage people who lived there, legends that were believed into the nineteenth century, even as European explorers began to penetrate farther into the interior.

The Carthaginians had set up seven or eight colonies on Africa's west coast, colonies that lasted until the Romans destroyed Carthage in the second century BC. It is probable that Carthaginian sailors also explored north from the Pillars of Hercules— they certainly colonised Spain and may even have

reached Britain. But the first account we have of a real voyage of exploration into northern waters is that of Pytheas, whose fourth century BC adventures helped inspire Rome's invasion of Britain several hundred years later (see page 20). Pytheas was an extraordinary adventurer, navigator and writer from Massalia (modern Marseilles), a Greek colony. In about 325 BC, he set out on his voyage of discovery. Although some historians believe that Carthage had by this time placed a blockade around the Pillars of Hercules, trying to keep other countries from exploiting the riches of Africa and the Iberian Peninsula, it appears that Massalia, a powerful colony, had made a separate peace with Carthage that would have allowed Pytheas to pass unmolested into the Atlantic.

Once there, he probably sailed along the coast of the continent until he reached the English Channel, and then he set off across it, landing first in Land's End, Cornwall. There he met the Britons, a race whom he described as 'unusually hospitable', at least to visitors (clans warred against each other). Their main occupation was tin-mining—leading Pytheas to call the British Isles the 'Tin Islands'— which provided them opportunity for ample trade with the continent. After leaving Cornwall, Pytheas headed north up the east coast of England and probably rounded the tip of Scotland. He made note of the wild swing of the spring tides (quite different from the almost tideless Mediterranean) and even heard about a land he called Thule, which was 'the sleeping-place of the sun' and which was surrounded by a frozen sea.

Some historians believe that Thule is Iceland, and that Pytheas actually made his way there 'six days' sail' north of Britain, where he found a 'solidified sea' and a midnight sun. However, it may be that he actually travelled to Norway instead. If that is the case, his return voyage took him down the coast of northern France and back through the Straits of Gibraltar to Massalia; otherwise, after

ERICH VON DANIKEN:
VISITORS FROM BEYOND

Perhaps the ultimate believer in first contact between cultures is the Swiss writer Erich von Daniken, who has written in numerous books, most notably Chariots of the Gods *(published in 1968), that aliens from outer space visited Earth aeons before Asians, Europeans or Polynesians began to spread their culture.*

Von Daniken believes that extraterrestrial beings landed on Earth in humanoid form and mated with humans, thus passing on their genes to all the peoples of Earth. He points to what he considers to be numerous signs of alien presence on Earth—in India an iron pillar that never rusts, in Central America a depiction of a Mayan nobleman sitting on what von Daniken says is the seat of a rocket, and in the Yucatan Peninsula limestone holes that he claims are pits left by alien spaceships blasting off. His most controversial theories are that the still-mysterious line figures drawn on the plains of Nazca, Peru, were created to point the way for landing alien spaceships.

Naturally, von Daniken does not get much credence from mainstream scholars. The iron pillar in India does indeed rust, the Mayan nobleman is merely sitting on his throne, not a rocket seat, and the limestone holes in the Yucatan are natural sinkholes often found in such porous rock. The Nazca lines (and others like them found elsewhere in the Americas) are indeed mysterious. They represent giant figures of monkeys, birds and other animals (many of them only found in the high Andes, a great distance away from Nazca) that on the ground appear to be simply long lines rutted into the brown earth. But once the aeroplane was invented, they were revealed as deliberately created human designs. Many scientists think they were designed in tribute to gods who lived in the sky or mountains; some scholars believe that the lines are 'walking temples', in which people for centuries trod the same paths as a mode of worship; but no one thinks they are actually airstrips to vector in extraterrestrial vehicles.

leaving Iceland, he probably circumnavigated Britain and then crossed the Channel again.

St Brendan and Bishop Eric

Pytheas's voyage was much debated and mainly debunked by ancient historians, who believed it impossible to have seen the things that he had seen, but his forays into northern waters were harbingers of the future. Well after Rome had invaded and finally settled Britain in the first century AD, the

hardy inhabitants of Britain were using it as a springboard for exploration. One of the earliest explorers was St Brendan, the sixth century Irish monk and holy man whose fabled exploits were chronicled in the *Navigatio Sancti Brendani*, which was written perhaps two hundred years after Brendan's adventures and which enjoyed a wide readership for centuries in Europe.

Brendan was a combination of mystic and activist (and a bit of a con man), who founded two

The Irish monk St Brendan supposedly mistook the back of a whale for land on one of his voyages in the Atlantic.

monasteries in Ireland and organised voyages of monks and fellow believers to the Hebrides and other northern places. But his main voyage occurred in the mid-sixth century when he and seventeen fellow monks set out from Ireland in a *currach*—a skin-covered boat powered by both oars and sails—to seek out the 'Land Promised to the Saints' by God. During this seven-year voyage through the Atlantic Ocean, they supposedly landed on the back of a whale, which they had mistaken for solid land, and saw numerous mythical sea monsters. But some of their other claims can possibly be taken more seriously. The 'crystal columns' they saw in the sea may have been icebergs; the 'rugged island covered with slag' was possibly Iceland; the area of crystal clear waters with brightly coloured fish might have been the Bahamas; and the land glimpsed through banks of fog could easily have been Newfoundland.

No one will ever quite know what people, if any, Brendan met on his voyages, but those with a more fanciful bent believe that he may have found his way to the Americas, there to figure in the myths of Indians whom Europeans would meet in centuries to come. According to some theorists, Brendan may be the figure upon whom the Aztec god Quetzalcóatl is based—the white man who came from the east in a ship with curved prow (see page 53). Others think this person might be Bishop Eric of Greenland. In 1121, about a century after the last Norse attempt to colonise North America failed (see page 30), a scribe made a notation in the medieval *Icelandic Annals* that read simply: 'Bishop Eric went to visit Vinland'. After this, no more was heard of the matter until, over a decade later, he was presumed dead and the Greenlanders petitioned the pope for a new bishop, who was eventually appointed.

It is tempting to wonder what happened to Eric. Could he (or stories of him) possibly have made it as far south as the budding Aztec civilisation?

'We have set eyes on barbarian regions'

The lands of Mexico, Central America and South America were unknown to Europeans before Columbus's discovery in 1492, but they may not have been unknown to the Chinese of past centuries. The Chavin culture, which dominated what is now Peru from about 850 to 200 BC, produced exotic, mysterious and sometimes frightening religious art that closely echoes that of the Shang Dynasty in China, right down to animal eyebrows depicted as snakes, horned cats and strange dragon-like creatures with scaled tails. Both the Chinese and the Chavin people raised 'toy' dogs to be sacrificed or eaten. It takes a leap of the imagination, but it is possible that the Chinese made a landfall on Peru's northern coast.

There are some archaeologists and historians who go even further to say that the prevalence of Asiatic-influenced design in Mexico and Central America—not limited to the above-mentioned statuary, but also found in coins, textiles, mirrors and clay stamps—are signs of a steady trans-Pacific trade between China and Central and South America that lasted for a millennium but died out, for reasons unknown, around 1000 AD. (Although there are interesting reports that an expedition led by Francisco Coronado in 1540 saw unusual ships, with prows shaped like golden pelicans, on the Colorado River, and that a Franciscan monk in the sixteenth century saw a fleet of 'exotic ships' off the Pacific coast of Mexico.)

Certainly, of all the people of ancient times, the Chinese were capable of such a voyage. Their ability to understand celestial navigation and build ships had led them to voyage as far as Madagascar by the sixth century BC. They had invented the compass by the fourth century AD, well before the Europeans, and by the seventh century they owned the sea trade in the Indian Ocean, trading fine silk and porcelain.

The most famous voyages of the Chinese, however, took place in the early fifteenth century, when the eunuch admiral Zheng He made a series of seven journeys with his fleet of massive treasure ships. By the time political considerations back home had ended his voyages, Zheng He's treasure vessels had reached as far as Mombasa, on the coast of present-day Kenya. There the Chinese met people with rolled hair who lived in brick houses, traded beautiful amber of a deep, golden colour, and whose land was filled with strange and wondrous animals—the *qilin*, or giraffe, as well as ostriches, lions and leopards, all of which the Chinese brought back home with them for the emperor's edification. Zheng He was to write, at the end of his voyages:

We have traversed more than one hundred thousand li *of immense water spaces and have beheld in the ocean huge waves like mountains rising sky high, and we have set eyes upon barbarian regions far away hidden in a blue transparency of light vapours ...*

The 'barbarian regions' always remembered the Chinese—when the East Africans made first contact with Portuguese explorers almost a century later they spoke of the massive ships and the 'white ghosts' who captained them—but the Chinese were not to become great colonisers, in the main because of their tradition of cultural superiority. As the historian Zvi Dor-Ner writes: 'What could barbarians possibly have to offer the Chinese emperors, who considered themselves the 'Sons of Heaven'?'

DNA in chicken bones

The Chinese may not have been colonisers, but the Polynesians were. These surprising people, originating from Southeast Asia and the South China Sea, sailed out into the Pacific Ocean in outrigger canoes. In the first millennium BC they settled islands such as Vanuatu, Fiji and Tahiti.

Around 100 BC they journeyed from Tahiti to Hawaii, and they probably reached Easter Island by around 1200 AD, if not earlier.

Extraordinary recent evidence—contained in the bones of a humble chicken—may prove what many archaeologists have long contended: that Polynesians, probably from Easter Island, found their way to South America. The chicken bone in question was found in an archaeological site on the central coast of Chile in 2007 by a team of scholars from New Zealand, Australia and Chile. Carbon dating suggested the bone was buried anytime from 1320 to 1410 AD.

The DNA extracted from the bone showed the chicken was of Polynesian stock, because it had genetic mutations not seen in the European strains of chickens brought to America by explorers from around Columbus's time (previously, many scholars thought chickens were a European introduction to the New World).

Since it is impossible for a chicken to fly across such an expanse of ocean, the only way for a Polynesian chicken to make it to Chile at that time would have been on a Polynesian vessel (researchers are now waiting to discover the remains of Polynesian rats in South America, since these animals found their way to every single island the Polynesians reached). Scholars believe that Polynesian voyages to South America stopped around 1450, for reasons unknown—perhaps a change in weather patterns that made it more difficult to reach these eastern lands. With Chinese voyages east also at an end, it is no wonder that when the Spanish arrived in the Americas they had no idea that other ocean-going peoples had arrived there before them.

'No savagery on the face of the earth'

Before we head off into the realm of known history, beginning with blue-painted Britons staring down from the cliffs of Dover on a sunny autumn day as ships full of Roman soldiers appear out of the blue horizon, it is good to remember the story of the people of the lost and imagined continent of Mu.

'There was no savagery on the face of the earth', wrote Churchward, poignantly, 'nor had there ever been'. All was perfect. Then natural catastrophes took place, this Garden of Eden was destroyed and all that was left was a handful of people—the ancestors of today's South Sea islanders—who found themselves on these remote atolls staring out into a rolling sea that hid their devastated civilisation. While the story is not a true one, the emotions are universal: first encounters occur because we are seeking what we have lost.

THE COUNTRY OF THE HEAVENLY SQUARE

During Zheng He's treasure ship voyages in the early fifteenth century, his captains made their way to a place they called 'The Country of the Heavenly Square', which was quite obviously Mecca. The visit was recorded by the Chinese scribe Ma Huan who, in 1433, wrote the Overall Survey of the Ocean's Shores, *a record of the treasure ship voyages.*

The people of this country are stalwart and fine-looking, and their limbs and faces are of a very dark purple colour', Ma Huan wrote. 'The menfolk bind up their heads; they wear long garments; and on their feet they put leather shoes. The women all wear a covering over their heads, and you cannot see their faces ... If you travel from here for a day and a half, you reach the Heavenly Hall mosque; the foreign name for this Hall is K'ai-a-pai.

This place is obviously Mecca, the Muslim holy city, and the Heavenly Square is the sacred Ka'bah. How the Chinese, as infidels, were able to visit is unknown, but Ma Huan certainly got his details right:

All around [Ka'bah] on the outside is a wall; this wall has 466 openings; on both sides of the openings are pillars all made of white jadestone ... The Hall is built with layers of five-colour stones; in shape it is square and flat-topped. Inside there are pillars formed of five great beams of sinking incense wood, and a shelf of yellow gold. Throughout the interior of the Hall, the walls are all formed of clay mixed with rosewater and ambergris, exhaling a perpetual fragrance. Over [the Hall] is a covering of black hemp-silk ...

These descriptions have been verified by numerous other travellers, attesting both to the accuracy of Ma Huan's depiction, and to the timeless nature of this holiest of Muslim shrines.

ROMAN MIGHT MEETS A MYTHIC LAND

Caesar's invasions of Britain, 55—54 BC

On a quiet late morning in mid-August of 55 BC, a group of Celtic tribesmen stood on a high cliff in southeastern Britain watching a ship course its way through the choppy waters of what later generations would call the English Channel. The small, fast vessel with high, curving prow, a square sail and a double-tier of rowers darted in toward the coastline numerous times, making as if to land, before setting back out to sea, its oar-splash sending glittering spray up into the sunlight. The tribesmen, riding horses or driving small chariots, followed the progress of the strange ship northward, up the coastline, before it finally veered east and headed off in the direction of Gaul.

The Celtic scouts, who had been trailing the vessel's progress for four days, watched it disappear and then turned and galloped back to their waiting chieftains. As they did so, the young Roman officer aboard the bireme warship, Gaius Volusenus,

composed his report for Julius Caesar on possible landing sites for the planned invasion of Britain. The stage was now set for one of history's epochal encounters, which would pit the inhabitants of a strange, isolated land against the soldiers of the most powerful empire on Earth.

On the ocean

The islands that constitute the British Isles first entered written history with the explorations of that extraordinary Greek astronomer and geographer Pytheas (see page 10), who circumnavigated the island around 350 BC. Returning to his home in Massalia (present-day Marseilles), he wrote a book about his adventures, entitled *On the Ocean*, which unfortunately does not survive but which was quoted by numerous ancient authors. These fragments provide a snapshot of the inhabitants of these northern lands: according to Pytheas, they were primitives who lived in mud and wattle huts, brewed a mead-like drink from corn and honey, and divided themselves into warlike clans ruled by kings.

Over the next couple of hundred years, however, more and more ancient authors began to doubt that Pytheas's journey—for which there was no first-hand evidence—had ever taken place. The story began to be seen as mythical and some even began to doubt the existence of Britain (the name derives from the term *Pretannike*, by which Pytheas called one of the Celtic tribes he encountered). Gradually, the island began to make its way into folklore as a land of shaggy monsters, a place of mists and fierce seas—a destination of dreams (or nightmares) only.

A rich, vibrant world

Of course, Britain was far from a mythical place. By the time Gaius Volusenus's little ship coursed the Kentish coastline scouting for harbours, it had been inhabited for some half a million years. Before the Egyptian pyramids were built, there were Neolithic villages in the British Isles, most notably in distant Orkney, Scotland; there, the tiny hamlet of Skara Brae, perfectly preserved for future archaeologists by sand dunes, featured the tidy homes of farmers and fishermen, complete with channels of running water that may have been used for indoor plumbing.

But as the Iron Age dawned in Britain, more and more tribes of Celtic origin began to migrate from the continent, and a fierce struggle developed for arable land. The ancient Britain of popular imagination, covered with forests, was in reality a place of tilled fields and open pastureland bounded by patches of wilderness. At the moment when the Romans and the Britons were about to collide, Celtic tribes in Britain had developed into warring clans, each with its own great hill fort, strongholds surrounded by rings of ditches, earthworks and timber palisades, to which the local population could retreat in times of trouble. Each clan had a

relatively sophisticated social system, including fierce warriors with long, flowing hair, artists who made extraordinarily fine gold jewellery and druidical priests. While the Britons were more civilised than the shaggy and rude creatures of Roman imagination, they did engage in some decidedly ill-tempered pursuits, among them was the practice of cutting off the heads of their enemies and nailing them in triumph to the doorposts of their homes.

And they were animists, believing themselves to be surrounded by spirits of the sky, forests and animals. The Druids were needed to help the ordinary person navigate a world filled with gods who could be both benign and malignant. Druidical services were held in groves of sacred trees and Druids did not hesitate to employ human sacrifice to satiate angry gods—victims were either burned to death or ritually drowned or strangled.

It was into this rich, vibrant pagan world that the Romans stumbled in 55 BC, mainly because of the ambitions of Julius Caesar.

Caesar's sideshow

A few weeks after Gaius Volusenus's scouting mission, just after midnight on 26 August 55 BC, Julius Caesar boarded a Roman bireme warship near the port of Gesoriacum (modern-day Boulogne, France), gave a signal and the ship splashed out into the dark waters of the English Channel, followed by eighty others carrying some ten thousand Roman legionaries. Some five hundred cavalry were leaving from a different port. Caesar stood quietly near the helmsman, conversing with Volusenus and his other officers. He was forty-five years old and in the prime of an energetic life: Caesar was a man who slept only four hours a night, who travelled with two private secretaries to whom he dictated accounts of his campaigns, who wrote poetry and had a fascination with science. But, above all, Caesar was a man who longed for power. Since 58 BC he

THE SECRETS OF SKARA BRAE

The tiny Neolithic seaside hamlet of Skara Brae slumbered under deep sand dunes in mainland Orkney, Scotland, until an unprecedented storm in 1850 blew away the earth covering the site and revealed the outlines of one of the most unprecedented archaeological finds in the world. Over the next few decades, as scientists literally dug the village up out of the past, they revealed a world, not of wild and savage tribesmen, but of settled domesticity.

Skara Brae, which came into existence about five thousand years ago and survived in the same place for about six hundred years, is a marvel of orderliness. There are perhaps a dozen houses built into the earth for warmth and insulation, many of which have the same layouts and even the same stone furniture—chair, bed and the characteristic large dressers that were always positioned in the same place: on the wall facing the door, so that they were the first thing a visitor saw when he or she entered. On these dressers were various objects—stone balls, clay pots and jars, and bone necklaces—that were obviously displayed prominently. They were conversation pieces, in other words.

Each of these houses even had a toilet, with a system of water channels for flushing waste from the homes. There was also a communal burial chamber, sealed with a huge stone plug, where the bodies of those who died in the community were placed. Sometime around 2500 BC, the climate began to change, becoming colder and wetter. Those who lived at Skara Brae finally abandoned their homes and migrated south, literally to greener pastures, but they left behind a snapshot of a world frozen in time, one of tranquil civilisation in the supposedly primitive outback of Britain.

had been engaged in conquering the Gauls over 800,000 square kilometres (300,000 square miles) of what is now Belgium, France, Luxembourg and Germany west of the Rhine. By 50 BC he would have completed the job and then gone on to invade Rome itself and seize power.

Now, at the midway point in that trajectory, he had decided to take on the Britons. Ostensibly this was because some British tribes were helping the Belgae, a Gallic tribe that had been warring against Caesar on the continent, but most modern-day historians feel that any aid given by British tribes to the Belgae was quite minimal. They also point out that the troops aboard Caesar's eighty warships

carried very little in the way of supplies, even for a punitive raid. It seems likely that Caesar wanted to further his reputation back in Rome by becoming the first Roman to invade this mysterious land and that this late-summer crossing was a publicity stunt of sorts, what the historian Simon Schama has called 'a nice little sideshow' in which the barbarians who inhabited Britain would surrender to Roman might and he would have a few more captives and trophies to parade back in Rome that winter.

'Amazingly great cliffs'
As dawn broke over the Channel the Roman fleet arrived off the southern coast of England and had

to shield their eyes from an astonishing sight—the luminescent white cliffs of Dover, which shone brilliantly in the early morning sun. (The next year the visiting politician Cicero would write that Britain was 'walled around with amazingly great cliffs'.) The Roman fleet followed the cliffs, searching for the harbour Gaius Volusenus had picked as a likely landing site, but now they saw that the cliff tops were crowded with watching British tribesmen—members of the Catuvellauni and Trinovantes tribes that inhabited the area and were easily the most aggressive clans nearby. The shouting of these warriors reached the Roman ships quite clearly, even over the pounding of the time-keepers, whose wooden mallets banged steadily on wooden blocks to keep the rowers in rhythm. The tribesmen were a bizarre sight to behold, their bare upper bodies and faces covered with swirls of blue-green plant dye, their wild hair streaming behind them in the wind on the cliff tops. They carried long flat-bladed swords, daggers and javelins, and they appeared to be everything the legionaries had ever heard about the Britons—untameable, feral in their intensity.

As the Roman troops fingered their short swords nervously, Caesar anchored his flagship off the small harbour chosen by Volusenus. He grimaced in disapproval. The site was a narrow beach surrounded by walls of high cliffs from which it would be easy for the Britons to hurl down stones and javelins on the disembarking Roman troops. Caesar decided not to land there, giving orders for the rest of the fleet to anchor offshore. It was about 9 a.m. He was waiting for his contingent of cavalry to arrive, unaware that these vessels had been delayed because of logistical and weather difficulties and had not yet even sailed.

Finally, as morning wore into afternoon, Caesar gave up on the cavalry and ordered his fleet up the coast, searching for a better landing spot. The crowds of Celtic warriors on the cliff tops followed, most of them on foot, but with horsemen and charioteers riding ahead. After travelling about eleven kilometres (seven miles), Caesar found what he was looking for—a long, flat beach between current-day Walmer Castle and Deal.

'At a nod and at the instant'

Before he undertook what he knew would be that most perilous of war experiences—an amphibious landing under hostile fire—Caesar gathered his commanders and told them in no uncertain terms that he would need them to obey his orders 'at the nod and at the instant'—meaning, without hesitation. He then sent the transport vessels carrying the crack troops of the Tenth Legion straight to shore. Unfortunately, the heavier transport vessels were forced to anchor in water up to the legionaries' chests and necks, so that one misstep in the water would cause the heavily armoured soldiers to drown. They hesitated, and in that moment of hesitation the Britons swarmed over the flat, sandy beach, riding their horses and chariots right into the shallows, brandishing their spears and shouting.

These Roman troops had not seen chariots—which had been out of style in combat for at least a century, although certain armies in Mesopotamia and India still employed them—and were amazed at how nimbly the Britons drove them. They were not the chariots of *Ben Hur* renown, with high, curving metal sides, but were instead flat platforms with wicker sides that seemed unstable—except that these nimble charioteers never lost their footing. There were two warriors to a chariot, one driver and one warrior—usually a nobleman—who could walk out along the centre pole that yoked the horses, shaking his fist and hurling insults in what was to the Romans a guttural and incomprehensible language.

Confronted with the deep water and the chariots, many of the Roman troops baulked at going over the side. Seeing this, Caesar sent his oared warships farther down the beach and told their helmsmen to drive them right up onto the sand. Now it was the Britons' turn to be afraid, for they had never seen oared ships like these and stopped in their advance to gape. The Roman warships carried auxiliary archers and slingers who leaped over the sides of the ships and sent a storm of stones and arrows into the flanks of the Britons, causing them to fall back, momentarily in disarray.

'Leap, fellow soldiers'

It was at this crucial moment that the Tenth Legion's *aquilifer*—the brave man chosen to carry its revered silver eagle standard, which each member of the legion had sworn to die to protect—jumped over the side of the boat, carrying the standard with him. Chest deep in the water, he waved the standard in the air. 'Leap, fellow soldiers,' Caesar reports him as shouting, 'unless you wish to betray your eagle to the enemy!'

And then he began, waves splashing into his face, to make his way to shore and the waiting Britons. The legionaries watched him for one, horrified moment of shocked and silent astonishment, but then, as one man, leaped into the water after him and the standard. When they arrived at the beach, they were met by Britons wading into the shallows, swinging their long, flat swords. The Britons' tactic was to isolate one tired and soggy legionary, hack him to pieces, and then turn on another. Here Caesar's battle-tested ingenuity came to the fore. He ordered the ships' small boats to be filled with soldiers and lowered, and these squads of men were rushed to wherever the Roman lines were the weakest. Gradually, the Roman soldiers, coalescing around their standards, formed up into ranks and drove the Britons back up the beach. All that was missing, Caesar wrote unhappily later, in his usual third person, was the Roman cavalry 'who had not been able to maintain their course at sea and reach the island. This alone was wanting to Caesar's accustomed success'.

'The very dread of their horses'

Still, the Britons were impressed by the brave and steady attacks of these men in their linked armour and they watched them as the Romans set up their usual marching camp just off the beach. Either out of genuine fear or from a desire to buy time—probably a little of both—the Britons sent envoys to Caesar's camp, asking for peace. This Caesar granted, although he insisted on taking hostages to make sure the truce held. He, too, was buying time, while awaiting his cavalry. But four days later, as the transports with his cavalrymen and horses finally left Gaul on a favourable wind, a storm arose and drove them back to shore. The same storm, accompanied by a high tide, drove Caesar's anchored ships to the beach, where they crashed into those that had been beached there. The resulting destruction meant that not one ship was seaworthy, and that Caesar was isolated in Britain.

Watching from the nearby hills, the Britons were heartened by this turn of events and decided that their best approach to dealing with the unwanted invaders was not peace, but protracted war. They were particularly interested to see how few supplies the Romans had in their camp: these intruders had not come ready to wage a long campaign. The Britons put out a call to numerous tribes in southeastern England, telling them that the invaders were alone and ill supplied. Alliances were formed, even between old enemies, and a trap was laid.

The Britons watched as Caesar detailed one group of soldiers to repair the ships, while another force went out into a wheat field to harvest grain for bread. Carefully trying to maintain a semblance of normality, British chieftains sent women and old men into the fields to perform their usual harvesting

THE TERRIBLE REVOLT
OF THE QUEEN

In 60 AD a rebellion against Roman rule took place in Britain. It would cost thousands of lives and was all the more tragic because it was avoidable.

King Prasutagus was the leader of the Iceni, one of the largest Briton tribes in southeastern England. He allied himself with the Romans, in return for protection from other tribes and trade privileges. So well did this arrangement work that Prasutagus made a point of leaving half his kingdom to the Emperor Nero and the other half to his two daughters and wife, Queen Boudicca. But an arrogant local Roman administrator decreed that this arrangement was an insult to Nero—the great emperor did not accept half of any vassal's kingdom. Thus, he had Queen Boudicca publicly flogged and her two daughters raped. He then seized the entire kingdom of the Iceni and declared it a slave province.

This turned out to be a serious mistake. Enraged, Boudicca gathered an army of twenty thousand about her. She was a forceful, almost mesmerising personality. Although numerous myths have grown up about her, she was apparently in her mid-thirties, red-haired and tall. 'The glance in her eye was most fierce', wrote a Roman historian. And she could wield a sword with the best of her male subjects, something not unusual in Celtic women.

In the fall of 60, while Suetonius Paulinus, the Roman governor of Britain, was off hunting Druids in the north of England, Boudicca and her forces marched toward the Roman city of Camulodunum (modern Colchester), burning settlements as she went. She was an avenging angel, in a mood to take no prisoners. The Britons burned the entire city of Camulodunum to the ground, killing every man, woman and child in what one modern-day architect calls an example of 'ethnic cleansing'. Literally no one was left alive. The same fate was met by Londinium (London) and Verulamium (St Alban's). An estimated seventy to eighty thousand people died. Finally, Suetonius Paulinus returned and was able to defeat Boudicca in battle, in part because the Britons, who had brought their families with them, were unable to manoeuvre against the Roman forces. Her forces wiped out, Boudicca drank poison, but she lived on in legend—a statue of her on her chariot rises majestically near Westminster Bridge in London, a symbol of brave British resistance against the oppressing Romans.

work—these even greeted the legionaries with a wave and a smile. But when the legionaries approached the last uncut patch of wheat, British warriors, hiding in a nearby wood, were ready for them. They charged out from the forest, screaming, and attacked the surprised legionaries, many of whom were holding scythes and wicker baskets full of wheat. Quickly forming up, they tried to stand their ground against the British onslaught. The Roman commanders could not help admiring the way the Celts used their chariots: ' ... they drive about in all directions', Caesar wrote, 'and break up the ranks of the enemy with the very dread of their horses and the noise of their wheels', before leaping from the chariots to engage in hand-to-hand combat.

The legionaries in the wheat field were so hard-pressed that they were 'scarcely able to stand their ground' as the Britons surrounded them. Had Caesar not seen a cloud of dust in the distance and raced off with two cohorts to investigate, they would certainly have been lost.

Escape from Britain

As it was, the fighting between the Britons and Romans went on for several days. Even after they were driven out of the wheat field, the new alliance of Celts attacked the Roman camp in waves, only to be beaten off by the legionaries, who locked their shields together in traditional fashion and advanced together in units to push the Britons back. Already, the difference in the two fighting forces

British warriors from the time of the Roman invasions, shown with Boudicca. At times Celtic warriors went into battle naked.

was evident, with the Britons wildly courageous but undisciplined, preferring individual combat to unit tactics. Finally, after the Romans burned every British hut in the surrounding area, the Britons approached Caesar to ask for peace once again. It was a truce that Caesar was only too happy to accept. His sideshow expedition to the mysterious isles of the north had been more costly, and less successful, than he could have dreamed.

However, in typical fashion, Caesar did two things. He put a good face on what had happened when reporting back to Rome, so much so that the Roman Senate decreed a thanksgiving celebration of twenty days' duration when they heard of his 'successes' with the British. The second thing Caesar did was vow to be back, bigger and better than ever.

54 BC: *The second invasion*

Determined not to make the mistake of again going to Britain unprepared, Caesar set sail for the island in the spring of 54 BC with a massive invasion force of eight hundred ships and forty thousand legionaries. A stickler for detail, he made sure *all* the vessels, transports or not, were oared so that they could be rowed close to the beach. Early the morning after sailing, when this massive fleet—the largest invasion fleet ever to approach Britain, including the Spanish Armada—reached the white cliffs of Dover, they were not met by hordes of barbarians. In fact, the shores and cliffs were eerily empty.

The Celts were there, however, watching in awe and astonishment as this amazing fleet materialised on the ocean, spreading everywhere. None of them had ever seen anything like it and they decided their best course of action was, quite literally, to head for the hills. The Romans landed and—always masters of supply and logistics—set up a massive beachhead camp and then fanned out into the countryside. By taking and grilling isolated British prisoners, they found out that the Britons had allied themselves under one king, Cassivellaunus, a move that shows the desperation the tribes felt, since Cassivellaunus was head of the Catuvellauni, who had—until the Roman invasion—attempted to subject most other tribes. 'At an earlier period', Caesar wrote, 'perpetual wars had taken place between [Cassivellaunus] and the other states; but, greatly alarmed by our arrival, the Britons had placed him over the whole war and the conduct of it'.

Not far from the shore, Caesar learned, a large force of Britons had occupied one of their hilltop strong points. 'The Britons call it an *oppidum* [town] when they have fortified thickly wooded places with a rampart and ditch, as a place to assemble in order to avoid the attacks of their enemy.' Certainly, neither Caesar nor his troops were bothered by such a fortification. Shortly after setting up his camp, Caesar roused four of his legions, along with 1700 cavalry, in the middle of the night and set them on the march toward his enemy. They arrived at the fort at dawn, surprising the Britons and trapping the main body of their men within. Then Caesar insouciantly sent only one legion to attack it, while the others simply formed up in ranks and watched the action. In a classic example of Roman siege-craft, the attacking soldiers locked their shields above their heads, forming what was known as the *testudo*, or 'tortoise', and swarmed to the base of the fortress walls. Thus protected from the stones and spears hurled down on their heads by the enraged Britons, the legionaries threw up dirt against the walls to form ramps and, after several hours of this, simply charged up the ramps and dropped over the palisades and into the fort.

It was a characteristic encounter between technology and a more primitive way of warfare, and the Britons could not find a way to counter it. They fled the hill fort, racing into the surrounding forests with the triumphant legionaries chasing them and running them through with swords if they stood to fight.

Fight for the Thames

Unfortunately for Caesar, another storm had sprung up in the Channel, destroying more of his beached vessels, and so he was forced to recall his troops before they could pursue the Britons further. Marching back to the coast, he secured his rear, rebuilt the ships, and then had them protected on the beaches by wooden walls that would keep the sea from reaching them. Within ten days, he was ready to march again. By this time, however, more Britons had joined Cassivellaunus, and the alliance of the tribes had become even stronger. And Cassivellaunus hatched a plan. The stronghold of the Catuvellauni tribe was north of the Thames River, in modern-day Hertfordshire. Cassivellaunus wanted to keep the Romans south of the Thames as long as possible, and he devised a way of doing this by sending infantry, horsemen and chariots to harass the Romans and delay them.

While all this was going on, Cassivellaunus was gathering a force of thousands of charioteers. When and if the Romans crossed the Thames, he would spring an ambush on them, descending on their flanks and destroying them once and for all. As Caesar forged his way toward the Thames, hard-hitting groups of British warriors struck at the Roman flanks and then disappeared into the woods, only to attack again with renewed ferocity a little later. One assault column of chariots and cavalry, slashing into a Roman column, almost stole its eagle standards. Caesar himself was trapped with a small group of officers in a marsh and nearly killed by blue-painted warriors, until a lone bodyguard fought them off, allowing the Roman leader and his staff to escape.

Still, Caesar's legions were able to cross the Thames (probably at the site of the future city of London) and head north, towards the stronghold of Cassivellaunus. But whenever the Roman cavalry rode too far from the main ranks of the Roman legions, charioteers attacked 'from the woods by all the well-known roads and paths, and to the great danger of our horsemen, engaged with them; and this source of fear hindered them from straggling very extensively', Caesar wrote. The result was, Caesar was forced to keep his horsemen as close as possible to his infantry. But Cassivellaunus's huge attack never materialised, probably because most of the allied tribes, seeing the power of the Romans, had melted away, back to their homes.

All that was left was for the Romans to attack Cassivellaunus's hilltop fort, which was probably in modern-day Wheathamstead. It was the largest fort the Romans had ever seen, surrounded by marshes and forests, with walls made of huge timbers enclosing a space of perhaps 40 hectares (100 acres), which held hundreds of Britons and their cattle. In an attempt to divert Caesar's attention, Cassivellaunus managed to convince Kentish warriors near the coast to attack the Roman base camp and attempt to destroy the ships. But the Roman rearguard easily defeated the tribesmen in Kent, killing many of them and taking others, including prominent chiefs, prisoner. Hearing this news, and looking out over the Roman troops preparing to attack, Cassivellaunus decided enough was enough. He sent emissaries to Caesar, calling for a parley.

Time and myth

Caesar and Cassivellaunus reached terms that allowed Cassivellaunus to stay in power as long as he paid tribute to Rome, and Caesar was at last able to leave Britain, taking with him a long train of prisoners to be sold as slaves in Gaul. There was no significant gold and silver to be found in Britain—in fact, as Cicero wrote haughtily to a friend, 'no booty apart from captives, and I fancy you won't be expecting them to be highly qualified in literature or music'. Caesar's expedition to the fog-enshrouded island of Britain came to be seen in the eyes of most Romans as a waste of time and it was quickly forgotten in the rush of momentous events of the ensuing years—the Roman civil war, Caesar's rise to power and his assassination, and finally the beginning of Imperial Rome as Augustus, Caesar's adopted son and successor, took power.

Aside from tribute (and it is not certain this was routinely collected) the Britons were left to their wild ways for nearly a hundred years. But in 43 AD the Emperor Claudius—attracted by the disarray of the squabbling British tribes and with a better idea of the riches that Britain *did* contain (tin and iron, bountiful grain and slaves)—decided to invade with a huge force and, in a ruthless and highly organised campaign, conquered the country. The Romans would occupy Britain for the next four centuries, beginning the process that would eventually lead to the creation of modern-day England, while at the same time attempting to eradicate any trace of the old, mythic land. Queen Boudicca and her tribe were destroyed and the Druids hunted down and killed, their sacred groves burned to the ground. By the end of the first century AD those wild blue faces that had peered over the edges of the white cliffs of Dover had disappeared into the mists of time and myth, once again.

The British king Cassivellaunus approaches Julius Caesar to sue for peace after the second Roman invasion of 54 BC.

CLASH OF DARING PEOPLES

The Vikings and skraelings
in the New World

There was land somewhere out to the west—anyone living in the isles of the North Atlantic with a sea eye knew it. Irish monks who had settled in the Faeroes Islands watched flocks of migrating birds flying from the northwest every autumn, heading south. But where had they summered? The answer came in the eighth century when these hardy hermit monks sailed out into the western ocean in their *currach*s, or skin-covered boats, looking for complete isolation. Blown by storms, or possibly led on by a shimmering mirage, they found a large, uninhabited island with a forbiddingly mountainous and icy interior, but one whose outer fringes held deep, fish-filled fjords and verdant pastureland.

The Norse

Arising out of Scandinavia in the mid-eighth century, Viking raiders quickly became the terrors of the pre-medieval world, swooping down on the British Isles, where they made it a particular specialty to pillage monasteries, but also roaming as far afield as France—where their descendants would include William the Conqueror—the Mediterranean and even Russia. However, a century later, the Vikings were less pirate raiders than invading farmers, seeking land on which to settle and raise their flocks. In 860, having heard about the island the Irish monks had settled, a Viking explorer named Floki Vilgerdarsson headed out from Norway in his *knarr*—the broad-beamed, single-sailed ship that was the mainstay of Viking travel at the time—and landed there.

Vilgerdarsson's arrival scared the sparse population of monks so much that they immediately hopped into their *currach*s and fled, presumably back to Ireland (the Vikings had by this time taken over the Faeroes). It was Vilgerdarsson who actually named the island Iceland—not a brilliant public relations stroke, but it did not matter. Land-hungry settlers soon began to arrive, and by 930 all the arable pasture was taken up by some twenty thousand inhabitants. This shortage of land leads directly to a scoundrel by the name of Eric the Red and thence, less directly, to the shores of North America.

Eric the Red and the Vinland Sagas

'There was a man called Thorvald, who was the father of Eric the Red. He and Eric left their home in Jaederen, in Norway, because of some killings and went to Iceland …' This is taken from the *Greenlanders' Saga*, one half—along with another tale called *Eric's Saga*—of the epic narrative known as the *Vinland Sagas*. Both were written down about two hundred years after the events described. Up until archaeological finds confirmed the Viking presence in the New World, these were all we had to go on when it came to the travels and travails of the likes of Eric the Red. 'Because of some killings' could have been shorthand for Eric's life, for his temper was always getting the better of him, at which point it would strike him as a good idea to pull out his sword and run someone through.

In the somewhat more settled Viking world of the tenth century, this was a no-no, and after slaying a man in Norway he was exiled and went with his father to Iceland, arriving around 960. But with all the rich land gone, he was forced to settle in the cold and inhospitable northwest part of the island.

A stroke of good luck brought Eric into marriage with a young woman with a wealthy father and put him in comfortable surroundings in the valley of Haukadale, but, never one to stand good fortune for very long, Eric got into a dispute and ended up killing two men. He was banished from Haukadale and then got in further trouble, so much so that he was declared an outlaw and sent packing from Iceland.

It would seem that Eric the Red was rapidly running out of room to run to but, although murderous, he was bold and he had come up with a solution. Around 900 or so, a Viking named Gunnbjorn Ulf-Krakasson had been blown off course west of Iceland and sighted, in the distance, a large, mountainous country, which he did not explore but whose existence was thereafter much speculated upon in Iceland. Eric decided now was as good a time as any to try to find the place. In the summer of 982, he set sail and discovered a large island some 300 kilometres (200 miles) west of Iceland. 'He found the land he was seeking', the sagas tell us, 'and sailed south down the coast to find out if the country were habitable there'.

'This land seems worthless to me'

The east coast of the island, dominated by huge glaciers, was icy and forbidding, but the west was much more inviting. For three summers, Eric the Red explored its inlets and fjords. The fourth summer, he returned to Iceland, announced that he had discovered a new land and that it was called Greenland—'for he said that people would be much more tempted to go there if it had an attractive name'. Eric was a far better PR specialist than Floki Vilgerdarsson, but Greenland was also a warmer place in the first millennium—it was not until three hundred years later that the climate became as frigid as it is today (or was until the onset of global warming).

Hundreds of land-hungry settlers followed Eric to this new island; one of them, arriving in 985, was Herjolf Herjolfsson, who sold his poor farm in Iceland hoping to better himself. He must have done it on the spur of the moment, for, shortly thereafter, his son Bjarni Herjolfsson, a merchant, sailed back home from a trip to Norway to find that his father had decamped. Extremely upset, Bjarni refused even to unload his *knarr* but instead convinced his crew to sail straight away to Greenland to find

Herjolf. The only problem was, the ship became lost. After sailing west for days, Bjarni sighted through the mist and fog a land that was 'well-wooded, with low hills'. This did not fit the description of Greenland, so Bjarni kept sailing. Twice more he sighted flat, forested land but refused his crew's pleadings to stop there. 'This land seems worthless to me', he told them. Finally, a gale blew Bjarni north and east, and he found himself off the shore of Greenland.

The sagas tell us that Bjarni found his father and gave up trading to become a farmer; this incurious gentleman had, however, become the first recorded European to spot North America.

ARCTIC MIRAGE: THE ICY ILLUSION

For a long time, most people have assumed that Irish and Viking discoveries in the North Atlantic were the result of chance (their ships, which did not do well in crosswinds, being blown off-course by storms) or the skill of early navigators in the use of dead reckoning. Certainly this may be part of the picture. But if so, how were these mariners able to return with such precision from Iceland to the Faeroes, for instance, or from Newfoundland to Greenland?

The answer may lie in a phenomenon of northern weather known as the arctic mirage. In certain unusually clear and sunny atmospheric conditions, light waves are refracted, as if through a prism, so that they bend with the curvature of the Earth, causing glaciers or mountains lying below distant horizons to be reflected upwards, even to rise over the horizon, something mariners call looming. These mountains also appear to be much closer than they really are. In one recorded instance, crewmen aboard a ship that in 1939 was sailing halfway between Greenland and Iceland saw the summit of an Icelandic glacier in crisp detail, as if it were 40 or 50 kilometres (25 or 30 miles) away instead of its actual distance of 550 kilometres (340 miles).

It is quite probable that Vikings in western Greenland were confident that land existed in what is now North America because of arctic mirages. Someone standing on a mountain peak in Greenland in the right conditions can easily see the mirage of the Cape Dyer Heights on Baffin Island, some 450 kilometres (280 miles) away. Being familiar with the phenomenon, the Vikings probably did not assume these heights were as close as they looked—just that they did exist and could be sailed to.

The Irish monks had at last found what they sought—remoteness—and lived there peacefully for more than a century, but word leaked out about the island (sometimes called Thule). Attractions included great fishing, the rich farmland, even the lengthy summers—one French chronicler of the era claimed that it was a place where, in midsummer, the sun was so bright at midnight you could easily pick lice out of your shirt.

Naturally, it was not long before the Vikings heard about the place.

Leif the Lucky

Some fifteen years now went by. Eric the Red had settled down. He got married again, raised livestock on a large farm and produced four children, one of whom was named Leif Ericsson. It seems, according to the sagas, that Leif was the chosen son, as his nickname, Leif the Lucky, might imply. He was 'tall and strong and very impressive in appearance', a man who sired a child by a noblewoman and who converted to Christianity when it arrived in Greenland (although he was unable to get Eric the Red to change his pagan ways).

Like Eric, Leif was restless. He had grown up hearing the tales that Bjarni Herjolfsson told about his three sightings of the strange land to the west, stories that fed Ericsson's wanderlust. And so, around 1000, he went to Bjarni and purchased the very boat that Herjolfsson had made his voyage in. Leif then gathered a crew of thirty-five about him and twisted his father's arm to get him to come on the voyage. But on the way to the ship on the morning of their departure, Eric the Red fell off his horse. He was unhurt, but Norse superstition claimed that a fall before a journey was unlucky, so Eric begged off, supposedly telling Leif, 'I am not meant to discover more countries than the one we now live in', although this has the feel of an addition by a saga-teller adjusting history to make it a little more portentous.

In any event, Leif sailed from the harbour of Brattahlid, in southwestern Greenland, and after an unremarkable voyage found himself off a barren coast with grey glaciers tumbling down into the sea. Ericsson landed there briefly but found nothing of interest and began sailing on, after naming his first landfall *Helluland*—'Slab Land'. He had probably landed on barren and forbidding Baffin Island. Undeterred, Leif and his crew sailed southeast along the North American coast and soon came to the wooded country that Bjarni Herjolfsson had seen, which was almost certainly Labrador, in eastern Canada, a place of low hills, thickly forested—and thus Ericsson called it *Markland*, or 'Forest Land'.

Up to this point there is little doubt in the minds of modern historians as to the path Leif's voyage had traced—the *Vinland Sagas*, while exaggerated in some ways, were accurate when it came to geographic details, as befits stories told by a seafaring people for whom correct landmarks often meant the difference between life and death. As Leif coursed farther south, he passed a glorious, 55-kilometre (35-mile) long stretch of yellow sand beach, with, behind it, a vast forest of black spruce spreading as far as the eye could see. This beach he dubbed *Wonderstrands* and it can still be seen today, on Labrador's coast.

Vinland the Good

Continuing on, Leif and his hardy companions sailed down the coast of North America, gazing at the profusion of trees and wondering at the vastness and silence of this land—for they had seen no sign of any human habitation at all. There is an almost *déjà vu*-like intensity to the sagas here, as if the land already existed in the dreams and imaginations of those who had ventured in search of it. Some days' sail from the wondrous yellow beaches, the tired Vikings came upon a country of temperate climate, a place where salmon filled a vast river and grass for livestock grew freely on the hills. The days and nights, the saga tells us, 'were of more even length than in either Greenland or Iceland'.

Here, in this place, on a wide point of land overlooking the sea, Ericsson and his companions landed and built rude huts in order to have winter quarters while they explored. The site of these huts—known to the Vikings as 'Leif's Houses'—has been identified with a reasonable degree of

FOLLOWING PAGES Leif Ericsson sights the coast of North America. He wintered that year in Newfoundland but encountered no inhabitants of the country.

certainty as L'Anse aux Meadows, at the very northern tip of Newfoundland. From there, Ericsson and his men roamed south during these relatively mild winter months and found grapevines growing in profusion (although they may have been North American gooseberries). They decided to call this place 'Vinland the Good'.

Spring came and still there was no sign of any inhabitants in this great, empty paradise. After exploring southward, the Vikings packed up their belongings, boarded their *knarr* and headed for home, retracing their route north along the coast. They had many tales to tell of this uninhabited wilderness rich in timber, grapes and pastureland. Little did they know that they had been watched all along.

'This will lead to my death'

Leif returned to Greenland that summer and, for reasons the sagas do not divulge, never again explored the new world he had found. But relatives of his would make it a kind of cottage industry to go to North America. The first was his brother Thorvald, who retraced Leif's steps to Vinland in the summer of 1004, taking with him a crew of thirty men. Thorvald and his men wintered at Leif's Houses, before going exploring that spring, heading southwest along the North American coast. Like Leif before them, they found attractive wooded country with rivers teeming with fish. Unlike Leif, however, they discovered one jarring sign of human habitation, what they took to be a 'wooden haystack cover' (probably the top of a grain-storage receptacle) on the beach of an island off the coast.

Thorvald and his men returned to overwinter at Leif's Houses once again and then set off for further exploration the next summer, this time sailing north, into Markland. They sailed until they came to a beautiful spot, a point of land that jutted out into the ocean, with deep, fish-filled fjords on either side of it. The Vikings landed and explored. Thorvald admired the view greatly and told his men he would like to build a home there. Then, walking along the beach on their way back to the ship, they found 'three skin-boats with three men under each of them', according to the sagas. Thorvald and his Vikings immediately set upon the men, killing eight of them. However, one escaped in his boat, paddling madly out to sea.

Thus, the first encounter between Europeans and North Americans was a bloody one and things would only get bloodier. Surprisingly, instead of leaving, the Vikings—'overcome by a heavy drowsiness'—fell asleep on the beach after their slaughter was done. When one of their number shouted an alarm and they woke up, they saw 'a great swarm of skin-boats … heading towards them down the fjord'. Thorvald told the men to race to their *knarr*, whose gunwales they ducked behind as the strange men attacked. Now realising his mistake in killing the men on the beach, Thorvald told his men to defend themselves as best they could, but 'fight back as little as possible'.

The enraged men from the skin-boats fired off arrow after arrow at the Vikings, who took cover behind their shields. Then, suddenly, the attack was over and the men paddled back up the fjord. Thorvald asked if anyone were injured. No one was but him—an arrow had pierced his side. 'This will lead to my death', he said. And he was right. After he died, his crew went back to Leif's Houses, where they overwintered once more before heading back to Greenland.

'They were small and evil-looking'

The Vikings called the men who had attacked them *skraelings*—*skraeling* means 'savage' or 'wretch' and is a contemptuous term for someone who appears scared and weak. These men, the saga records, 'were small and evil-looking, and their hair was coarse; they had large eyes and broad cheekbones'. Or so they appeared to the frightened Vikings—and there is no record of how these Scandinavians looked to the equally scared and surprised Indians. But who were these *skraelings*? The men Thorvald killed and who later killed him were probably the woodlands Indians later known as the Montaignais. They were Algonquian-speaking, paddled skin-boats that were forerunners of birch-bark canoes, shot stoned-tipped arrows and lived in conical skin huts. They were the descendants of those hardy people who had, aeons before, crossed the Bering land bridge from Asia into North America and spread out over the continent.

In this regard, they were every bit as bold and adventurous as the Vikings who faced them on that beach, but the two groups were divided by a yawning cultural chasm, and understanding each other would become a near-impossible task—killing each other, as it turned out, was much easier. When Thorvald's Vikings returned home, the news they brought was mixed.

The new land was indeed full of pastoral riches, but it was inhabited by *skraelings* who intended to fight when provoked. Therefore, the next and probably the last major party to decide to sail to Vinland would be a large one, capable of defending itself. The *Vinland Sagas* place the number at perhaps 160 men and, this time, women as well. 'Livestock of all kinds' was brought along, including, significantly, a bull. The party set sail about 1010, led by Thorfinn Karlsefni, who was married to Gudrid, widow of Leif Ericsson's younger brother Thorstein. Also present—at least according to *Eric's Saga*—was Leif's sister, the quite formidable Freydis.

'A hail of missiles'

This new group arrived safely at Leif's Houses in Newfoundland in early fall and overwintered without seeing any sign of *skraelings*. One day that spring, however, a group of Indians came out of the woods, carrying packs filled with furs. It seemed that their intention was peaceful trade but, according to the *Sagas*: 'The cattle were grazing near

by and the bull began to bellow and roar with great vehemence. This terrified the Skraelings and they fled … They made for Karlsefni's houses and tried to get inside, but Karlsefni had the door barred against them'.

Neither Vikings nor *skraelings* could understand each other, but finally both sides calmed down and began to trade. The *skraelings* were particularly interested in cow's milk, trading furs for long draughts of it and, as the *Sagas* tell it, 'happily went away with their purchases in their bellies'.

Despite the peaceful outcome of this incident, Karlsefni had a palisade erected around the camp but this did not deter the Indians from trading. When they returned the following year—for it appears doubtful that these Indians, who were Algonquian-speaking and possibly of the Micmac or Beothuk tribes, actually lived in the area—they simply threw their packs over the top of the fortification and lined up for cow's milk. By this time there had been born to Karlsefni and Gudrid a son named Snorri, the first European child born in the New World.

As related in the *Sagas*, Gudrid was rocking Snorri in his cradle when a woman appeared near the hearth. Startled, Gudrid asked her who she was and she said her name was Gudrid, too. Then there was a loud shout and a crashing sound, and the woman disappeared—it was apparent to Gudrid that she had been a ghost.

The clamour outside had been caused when an Indian tried to steal a weapon belonging to one of Karlsefni's men and the man had killed the Indian. The rest of the *skraelings* fled but soon returned in force and Karlsefni led his men out to do battle against them. The fight was fierce. According to the *Vinland Sagas*:

> … *a hail of missiles came flying over, for the Skraelings were using catapults. [The Vikings] saw them hoist a large sphere on a pole; it was dark*

L'ANSE AUX MEADOWS:
THE PIVOTAL DISCOVERY

One day in the summer of 1960, the Norwegian explorer Helge Ingstad and his wife, the archaeologist Anne Stine Ingstad, who had spent a decade attempting to find the spot Leif Ericsson called Vinland, were aboard a ship visiting tiny fishing villages on the coast of Newfoundland. Every chance they got, they spoke with fishermen and farmers, asking them if there were any old ruins around. Finally, one man took them to a place called L'Anse aux Meadows, pastureland overlooking the ocean on Newfoundland's northernmost coast. There, with growing excitement, Helge Ingstad found 'overgrown outlines in the ground [which] suggested the remains of very old dwellings'. Excavating those ruins the next year, Anne Stine Ingstad found a slate-lined ember pit identical to the ones the Vikings used in Greenland. For the first time, she and her husband felt strongly they were on the right track.

For well over a hundred years a debate had raged in the historical and scientific community as to whether or not the Vinland Sagas could be taken at face value; if so, where on the North American coastline was Vinland? Since the wild grapevines most people felt 'Vinland' referred to did not grow north of Maine, most scholars thought Vinland lay there or at some point south, but Helge Ingstad had a different idea: that the 'vin' in Vinland was being used in another Norse sense, to refer to pasture or grazing land. Accepting this hypothesis allowed him to place Vinland farther north, at a point Leif Ericsson and his men could easily reach by sailing down the North American coast from Baffin Island.

L'Anse aux Meadows fits the description of Vinland in other ways—pastureland running right down to the ocean and a flat beach on which the Viking knarrs could be easily drawn up. Carbon dating placed the iron fragments in the remains of a smithy at about the year 1060, give or take seventy years. Still, the Ingstads were not completely sure what they had found until, in the fourth year of excavation, Anne Stine Ingstad dug up a tiny spindle whorl, of the type used by Norse women to spin thread for weaving. Just three centimetres (one and a quarter inches) in diameter, it showed not only that the Vikings had been there, but that, just as the sagas had told, women were with them.

In nearly fifty years, L'Anse aux Meadows has been the only Viking settlement found in North America. There are still scholars with doubts as to whether it is Vinland—the sagas' references to 'vines' are always in the context of grapes and wine-making and thus do not appear to be talking about pastureland. But the discovery among the ruins of two whole butternuts, which are mentioned in the sagas and are not indigenous to Newfoundland but are found in New Brunswick and farther south, pointed scholars in an entirely different direction. In this hypothesis, L'Anse aux Meadows was merely a gateway site to an entire region called Vinland, an overwintering camp for the Vikings who had come from Greenland. With this camp as their base, the Vikings ranged much farther south—to the lands of butternuts and also of wild grapes—in search of hardwood to take back home, until it was decided that the risk of attack from skraelings was simply too great to justify the limited gains involved, and L'Anse aux Meadows was abandoned.

blue in colour. It came flying in over the heads of Karlsefni's men and made an ugly din when it struck the ground. This terrified Karlsefni and his men so much that their only thought was to flee.

In fact, this large sphere was probably a rock wrapped in skin and hurled from two poles—a favourite weapon of the Micmacs at the time—but it was enough to scatter the already frightened Vikings. The day would have been lost but for Freydis, according to the version of the story told in *Eric's Saga*. Freydis was pregnant and could not run away fast enough, so:

> . . . *she snatched up a sword and prepared to defend herself. When the Skraelings came rushing towards her, she pulled one of her breasts out of her bodice and slapped it with the sword. The Skraelings were terrified at the sight of this and fled back to their boats.*

Abandoning Vinland

Whether or not it really took the intervention of one of Freydis's apparently awe-inspiring breasts to scatter the *skraelings*, it was evident to the Norse that they could not ever comfortably settle Vinland. Before the Vikings arrived both Iceland and Greenland had had only small populations, of Irish monks and Inuit hunters, respectively. Both were easily scattered. These *skraelings* were another matter.

Karlsefni and his men and women returned to Greenland the next spring, carrying with them wild grapes, timber and stories of the savages who had plagued them. Theirs was the last large expedition to Vinland, although most archaeologists think it probable that numerous small parties of Norse found their way to North America from Greenland over the next three hundred years, trading and fishing in the more northerly regions of Canada. Vinland, however, was abandoned and a sad fate awaited Eric the Red's settlements in Greenland, as well.

By the mid-fourteenth century a drop in temperatures clogged the sea lanes around the large island with ice, cutting it off from frequent supply ships from Norway (whose population had, in any event, been decimated by the bubonic plague outbreak known as the Black Death). One by one, the settlers of Greenland died, of cold and exposure, until by the mid-fifteenth century there was no one left alive. Thereafter, the stories of the Norse, the *skraelings* and the verdant Vinland the Good would dim in memory, so much so that when Columbus sailed to what he thought were the Indies he discovered a land that he was certain no European had ever set foot in before.

PART 2

COLUMBUS
AND THOSE
WHO CAME
AFTER

*Christopher Columbus's landing on
the island of San Salvador in 1492
changed the world for the peoples of
the Old World as well as those they
now encountered.*

THE COMING OF
THE DRESSED PEOPLE

*Columbus arrives in the
Caribbean, 1492*

Between the time the last Norsemen left the shores of North America, probably about 1300 or so, and the morning in 1492 when three Spanish ships hove into view off a small cay in the Caribbean, there were almost certainly numerous, unrecorded first encounters between Europeans and the inhabitants of the vast New World. Between 1431 and 1486, Portugal sent at least eleven adventurous captains sailing west in search of rumoured lands, exotic and real, but records of these voyages were destroyed in a fire in 1775 and so are lost to history. Ships sailing from Bristol, in England, sought western land as early as 1480, while at the same time English fishermen (almost every historian now accepts) drew up bulging nets of cod in the rich fishing grounds within sight of Newfoundland. Surely, people of the New and Old Worlds met.

But the voyage of Christopher Columbus was to be dramatically different, both for Europeans and for the Taino Indians who stood that October morning on the beach of the island they called Guanahaní and watched boats row in from the ships with the billowing white sails with red crosses emblazoned on them. To begin with, Columbus had muscle behind him—he was backed by the sovereigns of a major European power, who intended to plunder and colonise any lands they found. Every bit as important, Columbus's voyage was documented, not just in the diaries of the great Admiral of the Ocean Sea himself, but by royal scribes who accompanied the *Niña*, *Pinta* and *Santa María* for just that purpose. Others would soon know about the voyage—not just those in Spain, but everyone in Europe as well. And that would mean a land rush such as the world has never seen, before or since. And for the naked Indians watching as the longboats ground to a halt in the shallows, it would mean the end, forever, of their way of life.

The Admiral of the Ocean Sea

Christopher Columbus was a stubborn and often misguided man, but a brilliant one nonetheless. Forty years old when he arrived in the azure waters of the Caribbean, he had been born in Genoa, Italy, a city famous for its sailors, and had probably gone to sea by the age of ten. Having become a prominent navigator, mainly in the employ of the Portuguese, he approached the King of Portugal, John II, with a proposition that he sail across the Western Ocean in order to find a new route to the Indies, whose silks and spices were in great demand in Europe. John II, intent on finding his own sea route around Africa, turned down Columbus. The Genoese then petitioned King Ferdinand and Queen Isabella of Spain, who approved and funded the expedition, right down to agreeing to name him 'the Admiral of the Ocean Sea' if he succeeded—a title Columbus's not inconsiderable vanity demanded.

Many people thought Columbus, who set sail from Palos in Spain on 3 August 1492 with ninety men in a little caravan of three ships, was crazy. If so, there was method in his madness. Despite the fact that the Atlantic—the Western Ocean, or the Ocean Sea, as it was called—was a great unknown, astute navigators like Columbus had already recognised that it had two different but unvarying wind systems. One, the northeast trade winds, would push a sailing vessel across the ocean from the latitudes of the Canary Islands. The other wind system, farther north, was the southwesterly trades, which presumably would blow a mariner back from the Indies.

For the first ten days of his voyage, Columbus made record time, with the trades blowing him along for 1160 nautical miles (a nautical mile is 1.85 kilometres or 1.15 miles). Since he had expected to reach land within two weeks, he was actually alarmed at this rate of progress and lied to his crew about the speed at which the vessels were carrying them into the unknown. However, by 25 September, the *Niña*, the *Pinta* and the *Santa María*—the latter was Columbus's flagship—were becalmed in the Sargasso Sea, a great watery meadow of green and yellow seaweed. Now, as the trades dropped, the crews became increasingly worried. False sightings of land occurred with some regularity and certain members of the crew vowed mutiny.

It was in this fraught atmosphere that, around 2 a.m. in the morning of 12 October, a lookout aboard the *Pinta* cried out *Tierra! Tierra!* With a distant white beach gleaming in the moonlight, Columbus tacked his ships back and forth and waited impatiently for dawn.

Guanahaní

After this remarkably uneventful crossing of the Atlantic, Columbus had brought his three small ships to an outlying island of the chain we now know as the Bahamas. There continues to be some dispute about which island it is—most historians believe that it is Watling Island, although a strong minority are convinced it is a nearby islet named Samana Cay—but Columbus named what he immediately thought of as *his* island—his and Spain's—San Salvador.

Meaning 'Holy Saviour', it was the first of a host of Christian names placed upon the New World in what one historian has called Columbus's 'frenzy' of naming, but the Taino Indians watching in wonder as the longboats ferried the great admiral and his crew to shore called the low, curving island Guanahaní, a word that, quite ironically, means 'welcome' in their Arawak language. Tainos had been living in the Caribbean for 1500 years by the time Columbus arrived. They had left the coast of northern South America and migrated to the Greater Antilles and points west, finding themselves in the Bahamas around 900 AD. Over the centuries, they had pushed out the original inhabitants of the Caribbean islands, the Guantahatabeys, or Ciboneys, who had probably arrived from the southeastern

United States but who, by the time Columbus landed, were few in number and living only in western Cuba.

At this time the Taino themselves were having trouble with the Carib Indians, who had also come from northeastern South America and who were driving them farther west. All told in 1492, there were about four million people—all of whom spoke some derivation of the Arawak language—living in the Caribbean, so Columbus had by no means found an unpopulated paradise, nor one that was in stasis. Nor, of course, had he found the Indies, although, as he spied the naked people on the beach, he thought he had, for he called them *Indios*, a name that stuck.

'And make them do as you wish'

When Columbus landed on Guanahaní, the Tainos who had been watching his progress gathered around him unabashedly and stared. Columbus simply ignored them. Carrying the royal banner (others in his party brandished green flags with the letters 'F' and 'Y', the initials of the Spanish king and queen, emblazoned on them), he fell to his knees, thanked God and took possession of the island in the name of Spain. Surrounded by the inhabitants of this strange and wondrous place, Columbus had decided to simply … confiscate it, the first but certainly not the last moment of supreme European arrogance in the New World.

Having performed these rites, and after erecting a cross, Columbus finally turned to observe the Tainos. 'All those that I saw were young people', he recorded, 'for none did I see of more than thirty years of age. They were all very well formed with handsome bodies and good faces. Their hair is coarse, almost like the tail of a horse—and short.

The New World of the sixteenth century: Central America, the islands of the Caribbean, and La Florida *to the north.*

They wear their hair down over their eyebrows except for a little in the back which they wear long and never cut'. Columbus was thrilled by the fact that the Tainos did not wear clothing. 'They all go around naked as their mothers bore them, and also the women', he wrote to his patrons, King Ferdinand and Queen Isabella of Spain, continuing in a gossipy tone, 'although I didn't see more than one really young girl'.

He was even more thrilled by what appeared to be the docility of these people. They were 'friendly and well-dispositioned', he wrote. They did not appear to be a threat because, 'they have no iron'. Thus, when Columbus and his men showed the Tainos their swords made of tempered Seville steel, 'they grasped them by the blade and cut themselves through ignorance'—although it was apparent that the Tainos had experience with warfare, since

 ## 'THE FEARSOME CARIBS'

After his first landfall, as he sailed through the glittering seas of the Caribbean isles, Columbus discovered very quickly that all was not well in paradise. The Tainos and Arawaks, he discovered, 'greatly fear the people of Caniba, or Canima, who they say live on the island of Bohio … they believe those of Bohio eat people'. In another journal entry, on 3 November, he wrote: 'These islands are inhabited by Canabilli, a wild, unconquered race which feeds on human flesh …'

The Canabilli, or Caribas, or Caribs, as they are now generally called, were recent arrivals in the Caribbean. They had paddled their dugout canoes from northeast South America less than a hundred years before Columbus's arrival and spread quickly through the Lesser Antilles islands, driving the Arawak and Taino Indians farther west. Were they cannibals? Supposedly, Columbus himself visited a hut full of human skulls and bones, which convinced him that, indeed, these Caribs were man-eaters, but there are several problems with these observations. Not a great deal is known about the Caribs, but the presence of human bones in their huts would not necessarily be a sign of cannibalism—many tribes in the Caribbean and Central and South America practised funeral rites that involved the bones of their revered relatives.

Secondly, the main evidence we have of the Caribs being man-eaters comes from their mortal enemies, the Tainos. According to crewmen of Columbus's ship, the Tainos led them to a supposed Carib hut where 'the neck of a man was found cooking in a pot' and later to another Carib dwelling place where there was 'a human arm ready for roasting on a spit'. But, of course, the Taino held a serious grudge against the Caribs and it would have benefited them to tell these powerful newcomers that their enemies were guilty of despicable crimes, when what the men were viewing could have been roasted monkey.

The jury is still out on Carib cannibalism, but almost certainly they did not deserve their now immortal reputation as canibales. In the end, being fearsome did them no good—they were destroyed, by Spanish steel and disease, as readily as the gentler Indians Columbus encountered during those early days.

their bodies bore wounds they had received, they told Columbus by sign language, they had been in warfare with neighbouring islands.

Despite this, the Tainos were gentle and relatively trusting people, and Columbus was already sensing that these men, women and children would make good servants. 'With fifty men you could subject everyone on [Guanahaní] and make them do as you wish.'

'People of high rank'

Of course, the Tainos were by no means the simpletons Columbus portrayed them as, for theirs was an old and highly developed civilisation. The Tainos were separated into various tribes run by chiefs, or *caciques*. In fact, the word Taino itself means 'people of high rank', and some archaeologists and historians believe that the Taino tribes themselves comprised elite ruling classes who contributed the *caciques*, warriors and shamans for the Arawak-speaking populations. The elite Tainos wore feathers and golden ornaments, were sometimes carried in litters and lived in their own compounds, in longhouses with conical roofs facing a large central plaza that was used for public ceremonies. Some of this lifestyle was borrowed from that of the Mesoamerican tribes, with whom the Taino had a good deal of cross-cultural contact. The Taino were experienced sailors, who sailed great dugout canoes, or pirogues, carrying as many as thirty people across what is now the Gulf of Mexico. Mexican iguanas (a favourite delicacy of the Taino) and gold jewellery for noses and ears were exchanged for tobacco and other Caribbean crops.

As in any multi-level society, some people were better off than others. The naked Indians Columbus first met on the beach of Guanahaní—an island that was probably used as a base for fishing, not for permanent habitation—were commoners, farmers or fishermen, and they may even have been the class of homeless and landless people known as Naboria, a group whom the Taino employed as servants. Whoever they were, Columbus had his eye on them. Writing in his journal, with an eye to it being read by King Ferdinand and Queen Isabella, Columbus said: 'Our Lord pleasing, I will carry off six of [the Tainos] at my departure, in order that they may learn to speak [Spanish]'.

Hunting for gold

Of course, despite the beauty of his surroundings, one thing Columbus was disappointed by was the lack of gold and other evidence that might hint that he was in the fabled Indies. Some of the Tainos wore little plugs of gold in their noses, but all they had to trade for the red caps and beads Columbus brought them were cotton and parrots.

On 15 October, taking six Tainos with him, Columbus left to explore a larger island to the south, 'where all these men that I am taking from San Salvador make signs that there is a lot of gold and that they wear it in bracelets on their arms and their legs and their ears and their chests ... I cannot fail with Our Lord's help to find out where it comes from'. The next island, which Columbus named Santa María de la Concepción, had no glittering yellow stones, nor did the next the Taino directed him to, nor the next. Columbus began to wonder whether the Indians were not simply moving him along to get rid of him, for he was beginning to understand that these supposedly 'simple' people were not so simple after all. The Taino instinctively had begun doing what tribes all over the Americas would in future generations do—try to get these persistent strangers to leave by telling them that riches lay elsewhere.

Despite himself, as he journeyed through the islands, Columbus was impressed by the beauty of his surroundings, by the virtual paradise he had stumbled into. 'Islands with lofty mountains, most beautiful and of a thousand shapes', he wrote. '[The islands] are filled with trees of many kinds and tall, and they seem to touch the sky. Some were flowering and some bearing fruit. And the nightingales were singing and other birds of a thousand kinds. There are six or eight kind of palms which are a wonder to behold ...' The fish, he wrote, 'are of the brightest colour in the world, blue, yellow, red, and of all colours, and painted in a thousand ways'.

At the same time that he was marvelling at the scenery, Columbus was becoming more and more callous toward the people who inhabited this Eden. At one juncture, he sent men ashore to capture: 'seven head of women, young ones and adults, and three small children'. It was an alarming sign that he thought of the Taino as cattle.

The fabled Cipangu

Columbus spent two weeks exploring the Bahamas, but he never found the scent of the Indies. However, he kept on hearing from the Taino he met of a place he thought they called Colba, or Cuba (in reality, the Taino were saying *Cubanacan*, which was a name for a place in the centre of what is now the island of Cuba). In his fervour to find gold, he thought they were referring to Cipangu, which was, as reported by Marco Polo, the Chinese name for the fabled island of Japan. Columbus said the Taino told him that the Cipangu had a huge harbour 'full of ships and sailors both many and great'.

Finally, on 28 October, led by Taino pilots, Columbus reached Cuba, only to be grievously disappointed. The bustling harbour contained only a single dog 'who couldn't bark', as Columbus wrote sardonically. They finally located a few people and asked them who their king was.

These Indians kept pointing around the coast to the west, and so Columbus sailed along Cuba's beautiful shoreline until he reached a harbour known today as Puerto Gibara. He anchored there and sent two men inland searching for the Great Khan of Cipangu. His sailors, in the meantime,

attempted to show a local inhabitant of the island how to sing the 'Ave Maria'. In a few days, his men returned, having found a large village of upwards of a thousand people, but no cities. They carried cotton back with them, and also some of the plant that the Indians rolled up 'to drink the smoke thereof', but nothing else.

It is difficult to know what the Tainos thought of this restless quest on the part of the Spanish. They were not acquisitive themselves. A Spanish friar who arrived in the Caribbean in 1594 studied their religion closely and found it to be one in which songs were sung to *zemis*, or gods, whose likenesses abounded in Taino huts, carved out of wood or stone. One *zemi* was Yocahu, 'the Being of Yucca', who was their great agricultural deity. The Tainos believed that they had arisen as a people from a womb in the heavens, from a celestial mother sometimes described as a 'Mother of Waters', combining the sea, lakes and rivers. They sang a great deal—songs called *areytos*, which were songs of worship, but also songs that celebrated great events in their past.

The Taino also placed great store in dreams. According to the Spanish friar who learned to converse in their language, shortly before Columbus arrived in 1492 two Taino *caciques*, after deliberately fasting for days, had a shared dream or vision in which Yocahu appeared and told them that they would 'enjoy their domain for only a brief time because dressed people, very different, will come to their land and will impose themselves' on the Taino.

These people, the Taino now realised, were the very Spanish who were restlessly coursing among their islands, searching for huge quantities of gold.

'Gold by candlelight'

The Tainos in Cuba, like those in the rest of the Caribbean, wanted to get rid of these unwelcome visitors and so told them of another island, named

'A SORT OF INTOXICATION'

Seeing the New World up close for the first time, Columbus wrote: 'All of the plants are as different from ours as day is from night'. One of these very different plants was the 'strange new leaf' known as 'tobacco', a plant that would very soon become extremely important in the history of the world.

Columbus noted in his diary on 6 November: 'On the way inland [in what is now Cuba], my two men found many people who were going to different villages, men and women, carrying firebrands in their hands and herbs to smoke, which they are in the habit of doing'. These herbs were tobacco; the Spanish friar Bartolomé de Las Casas describes its effect only fifty years later. Tobacco smoking, he said:

> ... causes a drowsiness and sort of intoxication, and according to [the Tainos'] accounts relieves them from the sensation of fatigue. These tubes [cigars rolled in broadleaves] they call by the name of 'tobacos'. I know many Spaniards in the island of Espaniola who were addicted to the use of them, and on being reproached with it as a bad habit, replied that they could not bring themselves to give it up.

Tobacco was spread quickly through Europe, both by the Spanish and by the English who colonised Virginia. One hundred years after Columbus sailed to North America, explorers entering Siberia found the native inhabitants smoking tobacco they had received in trade. There would be no idea for centuries to come how unhealthy the 'strange new leaf' was—only how profitable.

Babeque, where, Columbus wrote down, 'people gather gold by candlelight at night in the sand and then with hammers make bars of it'. Who could believe such a childish tale? But Columbus, in his greed, did. Twice that November he attempted to set sail from Cuba to find Babeque, but each time storms drove him back. In the meantime, however, the lightest vessel, the *Pinta*, captained by Martin Pinzón, abandoned Columbus and took off on its own in search of the golden island 'because of greed'. (Pinzón eventually found Babeque, thought to be the modern island of Great Inagua, but there was no gold there.)

However, yet another rumour now wafted to Columbus's ears—the tale of a beautiful island called Bohio, which supposedly teemed with treasure. At the beginning of December 1492, the *Niña* and *Santa María* set sail across the strait now known as the Windward Passage and found themselves at an island of great beauty, which Columbus called *La Isla Española* because it reminded him so much of Spain with its evergreen and oak trees, broad plains, high mountains and even weather, which was 'wintry like October in Castile'. We now know the island as Hispaniola, the island divided into Haiti and the Dominican Republic.

Here, too, Columbus began to feel that at last he was much closer to the Indies and to treasures of gold. On 20 December, he anchored his two ships in beautiful Acul Bay, on Hispaniola's northern coast, a harbour so big that it could hold, Columbus assured his journal, 'all the ships in Christendom'. The local inhabitants were initially shy of encountering the Spanish, but then Columbus met the local *cacique*, one Guacanagari, and assured him that not only did the Spanish have the best of intentions, but that they would be happy to protect the locals from their enemies, the Caribs. He told Guacanagari that the Spanish would capture the Caribs, have them 'all brought with their hands bound' and would kill them. In order to demonstrate his power, Columbus then ordered a cannon and a musket fired, causing the Indians to fall to the ground in terror.

When they rose, however, they began to bring Columbus gifts, including an ornate belt whose buckle was a mask 'with two large ears, a tongue, and a nose of hammered gold'. Not only that, but Columbus had sent a scouting party along the coastline and they returned with the news that, in the interior of the island, there was a place, perhaps a mine, called Cibao (Columbus's ears once again heard Cipangu) where there was a vast store of gold. So, on 24 December, after feasting all night with the Taino, Columbus set sail with his two vessels up the coastline. 'Our Lord in His mercy will direct me to find the gold mine', Columbus wrote. 'I have many people here who say they know where it is.'

By early Christmas Day, the two vessels were anchored off what is now Cape Hatien and Columbus decided to go to bed. ('I had not slept for two days and one night', he wrote, which gives one some indication of his exhausted and overheated state of mind.) No sooner did he fall asleep than he was awakened by a lookout's cries and a shudder that ran through the spine of the *Santa María*—it had run aground on a coral reef. Moving quickly,

Columbus ordered the ship's owner, Juan de la Cosa, to lower a ship's boat, tie off to the stern of the *Santa María* and tow her off the reef. But La Cosa, in a panic, rowed instead to the nearby *Niña*, and the *Santa María*, forced against the reef by the waves, burst its seams and sank, although all hands aboard were saved.

Columbus, now on the *Niña*, tried to make the best of the fact that he was now down to only one ship (for Pinzón had still not returned with the *Pinta*). 'I recognised that our Lord has caused me to run aground at this place', he wrote, 'so that I might establish a settlement here'.

Villa de la Navidad

And so, in this most beautiful, fertile and gold-bearing of islands, Columbus built a fort, stripping the *Santa María*'s timbers to help do so. In honour of the Christmas sinking, it was called the Villa de la Navidad and he left forty men behind in order to man it—men who fought for the opportunity. They would trade for gold with the Taino on the island; Guacanagari would organise the Indians' efforts, bringing the precious metal from the interior. It seemed like Providence had at last smiled on Christopher Columbus and he decided now to head for home. He had begun to suspect that the continued absence of Martin Pinzón meant that Pinzón had, in fact, begun to sail to Spain ahead of him, to claim all the glory as his own.

But before leaving his fort and men behind, Columbus decided that there should be one more demonstration of his power:

> For this purpose, I ordered one lombard [cannon] loaded and fired at the side of the Santa María, which was aground. The King [Guacanagari] saw how far the lombard shot reached and how it passed through the side of the ship ... I did all this so that the King would consider those I am leaving as friends, and also that he might fear them.

As Columbus sailed on 5 January, Martin Pinzón appeared on the *Pinta*. He told Columbus that he had, in fact, found Babeque, but that it had turned out to be devoid of gold, although he claimed to have found gold nuggets in exploring Hispaniola from the other side of the island. Columbus allowed Pinzón to join him on the return voyage. It was good to have two ships instead of one, but Columbus did not trust Pinzón, writing in his log: 'I do not know why he has been so disloyal and untrustworthy toward me. Even so, I am going to ignore these actions in order to prevent Satan from hindering this voyage, as he has done up until now'.

Even on his return voyage, Columbus chased down fables, stopping in northeastern Hispaniola to seek gold from Indians who may have been Caribs. They were armed with bows 'as large as those in France or England' and skirmished with the Spanish. After making one last side journey in search of an island populated only by women and visited seasonally by Carib warriors—naturally, he did not find it—Columbus sailed northeast in search of the southwesterly trades and then headed back to Spain. His journey back was as rough as his outward voyage had been easy—the *Niña* and *Pinta* were hit by two powerful storms that separated the ships—

Among the trophies Columbus brought back to Spain for Queen Isabella and King Ferdinand were green parrots, gold and Taino Indians.

51

but at last Columbus found himself back in Spain, being honoured in front of the king and queen. He brought back with him green parrots, gold baubles—and Taino Indians, who gazed in wonder at what was, to them, a strange new world.

The destruction of the Taino

This was the high point of Christopher Columbus's life. He was to make three more voyages to the Americas and, despite increasing evidence to the contrary, never gave up believing that he had found the Indies. He was incensed at the Spanish government's refusal to give him ten per cent of the gold found in the New World, and died in 1506 at the age of fifty-five, an embittered man. In the meantime, the Spanish swarmed to the Caribbean and ultimately to Mexico and Peru, where the true golden treasures were found.

The Taino people who had initially met Columbus became slaves to the first wave of Spanish settlers to set up plantations in Cuba, Puerto Rico, Hispaniola and other places. The 'dressed people' had taken over the Taino paradise and set about the process of turning it into hell. The Taino began to die off, either through starvation or through Old World diseases such as smallpox, for which they had

no immunity. The Spanish also murdered them, by the hundreds of thousands. The Spanish friar Bartolomé de Las Casas estimated that three million Taino had died by 1561. 'Who in future generations will believe this?' he asked plaintively.

Las Casas went on to describe the tortures the Indians were subjected to, from settlers who:

> ... made bets as to who would slit a man in two, or cut off his head at one blow; or they opened up his bowels. They tore the babes from their mother's breast by their feet, and dashed their heads against the rocks ... they spitted the bodies of other babes, together with their mothers and all who were before them, on their swords ... and by thirteens, in honour and reverence for our Redeemer and the twelve Apostles they put wood underneath and, with fire, they burned the Indians alive.

While historians dispute the total numbers, the docile and naked people who met Columbus on Guanahaní, the island of welcome, would become nearly extinct by the beginning of the seventeenth century. It was just a small taste of what awaited the inhabitants of the New World in the next three centuries.

'HE STRIKES
AT KINGS'

Cortés meets
Montezuma, 1519

*We were amazed and said that it was like
the enchantment they tell of the legend of
Amadis, on account of the great towers and
temples and buildings rising from the water, and
all built of masonry. And some of the soldiers even
asked whether the things they saw were not a dream
... There is so much to think over that I do not
know how to describe it, seeing things as we did
that had never been heard of or seen before, not
even dreamed about.*

The conquistador Bernal Díaz del Castillo tried to
describe his feelings, that day in 1519, when he stood
near the top of the active volcano Popocatepétl and
viewed the Mexica city of Tenochtitlán for the very
first time, along with Hernán Cortés and his small
band of conquistadors. We can hear the awe in his
voice, the striving to find the right words to depict
just what it was he was seeing. This was a man who
had seen the great cathedrals of Seville, yet he was
forced to turn to fiction—the fantastic medieval
legend of the Gallic knight Amadis—to find a
reference point.

For the first time in any encounter between Old
World and New, Europeans had come upon a
civilisation that rivalled, even surpassed, their own
in beauty and complexity. The people traditionally
called Aztecs but now more accurately referred to
as the Mexica (pronounced *Me-shee-ca*) had built a
shining, bustling metropolis on a lake island that
had at least thirty grand palaces and temples made
out of red volcanic rock and was populated by
250,000 inhabitants. These were not *skraelings*
frightened by a Norse bull or Taino Indians to be
placated with bits of red cloth. The powerful Mexica,
led by their Emperor Montezuma, could erase this
small band of Spaniards in half an afternoon—
could 'obliterate all memory of us', as Hernán

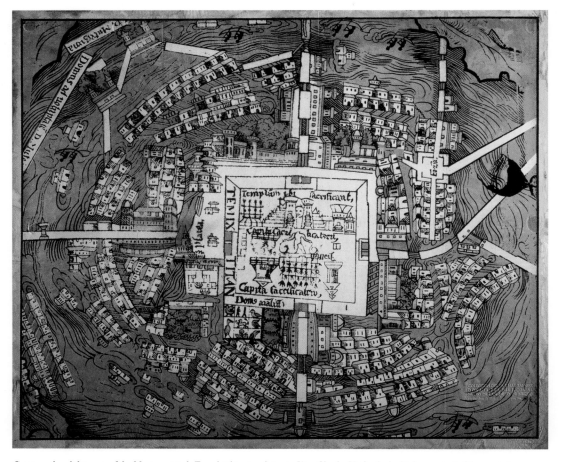

Cortés enclosed this map of the Mexica capital, Tenochtitlán, in a letter to King Charles V after he had taken control of the great city.

Cortés put it. The fact that they did not changed the entire history of the Americas.

The wandering people

The Mexica arose during the first millennium AD as a poor, wandering tribe from what is now northern Mexico. But after the great and still-mysterious civilisation of the Toltecs fell at the beginning of the thirteenth century (probably because of a prolonged drought followed by massive crop failure), the

Mexica moved south, along with numerous other tribes, into the Valley of Mexico in the central part of the country. In the early fifteenth century, led by King Itzcóatl, the man whom scholars now think of as the founder of the Mexica Empire, the Mexica began a campaign of conquest that saw them take over a territory stretching from the Gulf of Mexico to the Pacific Ocean and encompassing some 200,000 square kilometres (80,000 square miles). By the early sixteenth century, they ruled eight million people, divided into some fifty small nations, from the capital city of Tenochtitlán. And it was no wonder the Spanish stared when they saw the place. It was bigger than Paris, Constantinople or Naples, had three huge causeways that connected it to the mainland and was provided with fresh water by aqueducts, which carried sparkling stream water down from the snow-covered mountains around the city. Its broad streets were planted with flowers (botanical gardens dotted the city) and a thousand street cleaners were out in force every day, sweeping the gutters (something not seen in European towns).

The Mexica belief system was as complex and startling as their city on a lake. Their creation myth, revised and formulated by Itzcóatl's nephew and royal counsellor Tlacaelel, one of the most influential figures in Mexica history, foretold that the sun would eventually go dark. In order to keep this from happening—or at least delay it—the sun needed life-energy (*chalchihuatl*), which could only be furnished by blood offerings to the fearsome Mexica god of war, Huitzilopochtli. These offerings came in the form of human sacrifices, with the victims being either prisoners captured during battle or slaves ceremonially prepared for the occasion.

Despite all this power and civilisation, the Mexica had a flaw. They—and in particular their ruler Montezuma, who took power in 1502—were superstitious and believed their fates to be powerfully ruled by their myths and legends. One such legend, in particular, would be their undoing.

'A range of mountains on the sea'

After conquering much of the Caribbean after Columbus's first voyage in 1492, Spanish adventurers had begun to venture farther west, arriving at the Yucatan Peninsula and other points along the Mexican coast. It is probable that the Mexica began hearing about these strange, bearded white men around the time that Montezuma took power.

Little by little, odd rumours came to Montezuma's attention. Probably around 1512, a trunk washed ashore with contents so unusual—jewellery of an unknown type, a razor-sharp sword and several suits of alien clothing—that they were taken directly to Montezuma, who puzzled over them with his priests. Shortly afterward, a pictogram message arrived from the Yucatan, probably sent by a Mexica trader, showing what looked like three white temples floating on canoes—obviously, Spanish sailing ships. When Montezuma asked his priests what these were, they again had no answer, and so he had them punished.

But, little by little, he was beginning to worry. In the spring of 1518, a common labourer arrived at the Mexican capital—the man was, strangely enough, said to have no ears, thumbs or big toes—and brought the news that on the eastern coast there was 'a range of mountains, or some big hills, floating in the sea'. Montezuma immediately had him thrown in prison, to keep the rumour from spreading, but took the story seriously enough to send one of his chief advisors to the sea. The advisor and his retinue climbed a tree near the ocean and saw, to their surprise, that the labourer was right—there appeared to be white hills, sailing back and forth on the sea.

However, they also saw boats detach themselves from these objects, and men in these boats fishing in the sea with lines and hooks, so they knew the mountains were not mountains but enormous ships, the like of which no one in the Mexica Empire had ever seen. They returned to the capital and told Montezuma that some of the men 'had red handkerchiefs on their heads and others, scarlet hats, some of which were very big and round in the style of little frying pans'. The skin of these men was white, they told their ruler, and 'all of them have long beards and hair down to their ears'.

Montezuma secretly had presents made for these white men, including fine bracelets of gold and silver, and ordered his emissaries to go back to the coast and approach them. This the Mexica did. The bearded white men accepted the gifts, asked the Mexica who their ruler was, and in return gave them cheap bead necklaces, which the Mexica politely pretended to be enthusiastic about. When they were about to leave, the white men said: 'Go in peace. We at first go to Castile, but we shall not delay in returning to Mexico'.

The Mexica brought this news back to Montezuma, along with the beads. Seriously alarmed, the Mexica ruler ordered the beads buried and told the messengers that no one could speak of these strange happenings, under penalty of death.

The arrival of Cortés

While Montezuma puzzled about the implications of this strange contact, the demise of the Mexica, in the person of one Hernán Cortés, was moving closer and closer. Born in Medellín, Spain, in 1485, Cortés sailed for the Americas to seek his fortune, like many other ambitious young Spaniards of his era.

In 1511, he joined Diego Velázquez on his expedition to conquer Cuba. Afterward, he married Velázquez's sister, and seemed to be settling down in Cuba when he heard rumours about the great empire of the Mexica. Early in 1519, he convinced Velázquez to let him lead an expedition with eleven ships and five hundred men to explore the western shores of the Gulf of Mexico. As Cortés was about to set sail, Velázquez grew concerned about his lieutenant's ambition and ruthless nature and ordered him to relinquish the leadership of the expedition to a conquistador appointed by Velázquez. Cortés refused and sailed anyway. It was a typical move by a man who was, as one historian has put it, almost 'inhumanly determined' to have his own way. This stubbornness would make men hate him, but it would serve him well in the ordeal that awaited him.

In April of 1519, on Maundy Thursday, Cortés and his fleet arrived off the Mexican coast at what is now Veracruz. After giving thanks for his safe deliverance, he went ashore on Good Friday, where he was welcomed by Totonac Indians, who received him warmly—they were subject peoples of the Mexica and had no love of their masters. But the Mexica, with eyes everywhere, had heard of the coming (the second coming, as far as they were concerned) of these bearded white men, and one of Montezuma's emissaries, named Teudile, hurried to greet Cortés on Easter Sunday. It was the beginning of an elaborate diplomatic charade between Cortés and the Mexica leader. Teudile brought gifts for Cortés, including jewels and finely detailed featherwork capes, and even 'ate dirt' (dipped his finger in the ground and touched his lip with it) to indicate that he was subservient to Cortés. He also placed two thousand Mexica servants at Cortés's service—but their ranks were no doubt filled with spies to observe the comings and goings of these strange men.

Cortés, for his part, put on a show of force for the Mexica. He had his men ride their horses (which the Mexica still thought of as stags) up and down the beach, brandishing their superior swords made of shining Castilian steel (the swords of the Mexica were obsidian blades embedded in wood). He also had his gunners fire their cannons, the flashes and bangs of which made the Mexica fall to the ground in fear.

Even so, Teudile had his wits about him. He asked if Cortés would give him a metal helmet, which, he said, looked like one worn by a god in a temple painting in Tenochtitlán. He secretly wanted to bring it back to Montezuma, for him to examine—for Mexica gods were identifiable by their distinctive headdresses.

For his part, Cortés agreed only to *loan* him the helmet—on the condition that he return it full of gold dust.

'NO ONE TOOK CARE OF OTHERS ANY LONGER'

The arrival of Cortés marked the first contact for the Mexica not just with Europeans, but also with deadly European diseases, especially smallpox. A smallpox epidemic arose in Hispaniola in 1518, helping to complete the decimation of Taino Indians who had not died already from Spanish violence or starvation. By 1519 smallpox had spread to Cuba and thence to the Yucatan Peninsula. By September 1520 the disease had reached the Valley of Mexico.

The Mexica had absolutely no immunity to it. Town after town was emptied as people from all walks of life died (Montezuma's successor, Cuitlahuac, died of it). Because of their previous exposure to the disease and immunity, the disease spared most Spaniards while killing thousands of Mexica, naturally causing the Indians to decide that it was a visitation upon them by angry gods. And what a horrifying visitation it was. As the Franciscan missionary Bernardino de Sahagún (who carefully interviewed Mexica survivors and compiled their stories) wrote in 1575:

> Large bumps spread on people, some were entirely covered. They spread everywhere, on the face, the head, the chest, etc. ... [People] could no longer walk about, but lay in their dwellings and sleeping places, no longer able to move or stir ... The pustules that covered people caused great desolation; very many people died of them, and many just starved to death; starvation reigned and no one took care of others any longer.

The disease helped Cortés immensely in that the will and ability of the Mexica to resist was significantly weakened, and also because whenever a Mexica prince or lord died in the outlying regions controlled by the Spanish, Cortés was able to appoint his successor and thus make sure these important positions were filled by Mexica loyal to him. The effect on Mexica military power was such that most historians think that when Cortés finally attacked Tenochtitlán in May 1521, he would probably have lost had it not been for the losses inflicted on the Mexica warrior population by smallpox.

A century after Cortés landed, the population of Central Mexico had shrunk from about eight million (although some estimates have it at as high as twenty-five million) down to 750,000. Much of this was due to smallpox and its macabre twin, starvation. The population of Mexico would not reach its pre-conquest levels again until the mid-twentieth century.

'He strikes at kings'

Teudile and his men returned to Montezuma full of the astounding news of their encounter. The newcomers were indeed white. Their food, too, was white (meaning their bread) and tasted chalky. They were covered with iron from head to toe. The stags they rode on were 'as high as houses [and] they snort and bellow', the messengers told Montezuma. 'They sweat a very great deal, the sweat pours from their bodies in streams.' Montezuma was told about the Spanish war dogs, too, how horrifying they were, with fiery yellow eyes, drool slavering from their massive jaws and ribs showing through their flanks. They barked ferociously, unlike the tiny Mexica dogs (generally speaking, kept to be eaten), which gave only shrill yaps.

Worst of all, he was told that Cortés had asked Teudile what kind of man he, Montezuma, was. There was no human on Earth who would have the effrontery to ask such a question about the ruler of the Mexica, and this added to Montezuma's growing suspicions that he was dealing with a deity. In that regard, there were a number of possibilities. Perhaps Cortés was the god Huitzilopochtli, who, Mexica legend told, had led the Mexica into the Valley of Mexico, helped them establish their great city of Tenochtitlán and then left, travelling to the east, promising to return someday. Huitzilopochtli was a warrior god, to whom people were sacrificed every day in Tenochtitlán—a fearsome deity to find returning to Earth to claim his throne.

Another, perhaps stronger possibility from Montezuma's point of view, was that Cortés was the god Quetzalcóatl. The name means 'feather serpent', but Quetzalcóatl was a difficult god to define. Sometimes he was indeed a serpent, other times a humane god (he hated cannibalism and human sacrifice) with white skin who had sailed off to the east from Mexico on a raft made of serpents, promising to return. As far as Montezuma was concerned, Quetzalcóatl fit the bill much more

closely than Huitzilopochtli. Before Montezuma had become emperor, he had been a high priest and he knew Mexica mythology and the complicated Mexica calendar better than most. Thus he knew that Quetzalcóatl had been born in the year 1-Reed and had disappeared in the year 1-Reed. And now it was 1519, the year 1-Reed again. As Mexica legend had it:

> If he comes on 1-Crocodile, he strikes the old men, the old women;
>
> If on 1-Jaguar, 1-Deer, 1-Flower, he strikes at children;
>
> If on 1-Reed, he strikes at kings ...

'Allow me to end my days here'

Montezuma sent more even offerings to Cortés—monkeys and beautiful headdresses, golden bells, necklaces and statues of animals. He also sent gifts related to the legend of Quetzalcóatl—feathered plumes and jewelled serpents—and told his emissaries to closely watch Cortés, to see how he reacted.

He went further, tasking his messengers with preparing Mexica food and drink for Cortés. If he ate and drank readily, he might be Quetzalcóatl, because he would have a familiarity with his former people's mealtime customs. If, however, he would not eat the food, Montezuma told one ambassador, 'you should allow yourself to be eaten. I assure you that I will look after your wife, relations and children ...' Presumably if Cortés would eat human flesh, he was not Quetzalcóatl, so here was yet another test of the bearded man's identity. And—here the pathos of Montezuma echoes down through the centuries—if Cortés was indeed found to be Quetzalcóatl, the ambassador should deliver a message from Montezuma. 'Tell him to allow me to die. Tell him that after my death he will be welcome to come here and take possession of his kingdom ... But allow me to end my days here.'

Cortés, presumably, did not understand the full nature of what he was being offered or why he was being offered it, but his instincts were superb and they sensed weakness on the part of the Mexica and Montezuma. He began to bully the ambassadors. He told them that he had heard that they were fierce fighters and that he wanted to joust with them, at the same time firing off a cannon, which he knew frightened them out of their wits. He disparaged the gifts Montezuma sent him. 'Is this all?' he demanded of the messengers. 'Is this your gift of welcome? Is this how you greet people?' He then put some of the Mexica in irons and took them to his ships, where he kept them for a time as prisoners.

At the same time, he cajoled, telling Teudile, who had returned with Montezuma's presents, that he wanted to visit the great lord he had heard so much about, and his grand city. Despite the fact that Teudile tried to dissuade him, Cortés began to move inexorably toward Tenochtitlán, having first burned his own ships at harbour in Veracruz, in order to show his men that there would be no going back. As he started toward the mountains, he fought battles with several tribes whose territory he went through, including the Tlaxcala, who were great rivals of the Mexica and whose thousands of warriors, once defeated, became allies of Cortés.

As Hernán Cortés and his men came closer and closer to Tenochtitlán, Montezuma, more convinced than ever that he was dealing with Quetzalcóatl, began to despair. Mexica records say that he was 'filled with dread, as if swooning. His soul was sickened, his heart anguished'. He kept turning to his courtiers and saying, 'What will happen to us?' He stopped eating, and for a time appeared to be thinking of taking flight, perhaps to a sacred cave on the side of a nearby mountain. Apparently he even set out for it, but a priest spotted him and told him that he should not desert his people. Montezuma

did not retreat, but he grew increasingly distraught as reports of the Spanish progress toward Tenochtitlán kept arriving. According to Mexica memories later related to Spanish friars, the great king 'went out into the city and wept in public, abundantly, over the arrival of these foreigners. He begged the gods ... to have pity on the poor, the orphans, the aged, and those who would surely be made widows. He drew blood from his ears, arms and shins and offered it to the gods ...'

But the Mexica people began to feel deserted. Wild rumours spread among them of the impending arrival of these new people, who, it was said, were half-god and half-beast. None of the Mexica gods appeared to protect them, no matter how many sacrifices were made on the high altars of the temples of Tenochtitlán.

As Cortés approached the city, Montezuma made feeble, almost laughably transparent, attempts to stop him. He sent ambassadors to greet him warmly, but to tell him that Montezuma was ill and that he should not come. Cortés was warned that the roads were bad, that the Mexica people did not want him there. He was bribed—Montezuma told him that he would send huge tributes of gold to him every year, if only he would go away. But Cortés would not go away and, on 8 November 1519, he entered the great city.

'Are you Montezuma? Are you the king?'

As they approached the city, the four hundred Spanish conquistadors tried to hide the fact that they were in awe of Tenochtitlán—not only the high buildings and temples, but the hustle and bustle of the population, the hundreds of canoes plying their way over the water (some carrying as many as sixty people) and the broad causeways that stretched into the city. They were greeted at first by Mexica nobles, who placed their hands to the earth and then kissed their fingers, bowing

Montezuma welcomes Hernán Cortés to Tenochtitlán, one of the pivotal events in the history of the Americas.

low, not looking at these godlike creatures. At last Montezuma came forward—he had decided that it was better to meet these gods or men and provide them with hospitality. He was carried on an ornate litter that had a canopy of green feathers to match his green-feathered headdress. Montezuma also wore gold sandals decorated with precious stones, something that did not escape the notice of the Spanish.

When Cortés saw Montezuma, he dismounted from his horse, and Montezuma descended from his litter. Cortés tried to embrace the Mexica emperor, but the emperor's attendants would not allow this, so instead he shook his hand. Cortés said, through an interpreter: 'Are you Montezuma? Are you the king?'

To which Montezuma replied: 'Yes, I am he'.

Another version of this story, supplied by the Spanish friar Bernardino de Sahagún, who interviewed Mexica witnesses, has Montezuma replying more elaborately: 'Our lord, you are weary. The journey has tired you, but now you have arrived on Earth. You have come to your city, Mexico. You have come to sit on your throne'.

And with this, he took the hand of Quetzalcóatl and led him through the streets of Tenochtitlán. Bernal Díaz del Castillo describes the watching Mexica: 'Who could count the multitude of men, women and children which had come out on the roofs, in their boats on the canals, or in the streets to see us?' It was an amazing and transformative moment for both cultures. The Mexica saw their godlike king walking with a man who might well be the bearded white god Quetzalcóatl. The Spanish, for their part, saw their leader strolling with a strange being who wore gold lip and ear plugs and a huge feathered headdress and was surrounded by senior warriors clad in jaguar skins with the heads still attached.

This first night, all was well. The Spanish were taken to a grand palace with numerous rooms and fed tortillas and turkey and clear water. Montezuma left them, promising to return later, which he did. He then made a speech, whose contents were reported by most of those present (these include Bernal Díaz del Castilloand several other Spanish chroniclers, as well as Mexica who spoke later to Bernardino de Sahagún). In the speech, Montezuma—hopelessly conflicted about the identity of Cortés—apparently declared himself Cortés's vassal. There may have been some ceremonial aspect to this (just as bending and kissing the dirt was a formal, but not real, ritual of submission) but everyone present appears to have understood Montezuma to mean what he said. And Cortés replied: 'Have confidence, Montezuma. Fear nothing. We love you greatly'.

The teules

This capitulation on the part of the most powerful man in the Americas to a band of unwashed Castilians who were outnumbered thousands to one shows the power of first encounters when one participant is observing a magical reality that the other is not. Montezuma thought Cortés a returning god. Cortés thought Montezuma merely a figure to be manipulated. It was superstition against *Realpolitik*, and in such a contest pragmatism will always win out. In his book *1491*, Charles Mann writes: 'As a rule, Indians were theologically prepared for the existence of Europeans' because they were willing to believe that 'unusual people [existed who] might have qualities unlike those of ordinary men and women'. Europeans were far more consistently puzzled by Indians (right down to naming them after the people of a different continent) and often wondered how such people could have arisen and yet not be accounted for in the Bible.

The story of Montezuma and Cortés—and their two empires—essentially played itself out in a week's time. While Cortés was biding his time in Tenochtitlán, a group of Spanish soldiers he had left behind in Veracruz had been killed in a battle with Mexica when they tried to interfere with the usual Mexica habit of gathering yearly tribute from the Totonac Indians. One of the Spanish soldiers was captured alive and sacrificed, his head cut off and sent to Montezuma. Montezuma, horrified at what had transpired, apparently sent the head away quickly, but Cortés got wind of it and decided to use the incident as a pretext to strike at Montezuma.

On the night of 14 November, he requested an audience with the Mexica emperor and arrived in Montezuma's throne room with several Spanish soldiers. At first he joked with Montezuma but then suddenly turned the conversation to serious matters, accusing him of the murder of the Spanish soldier on the coast. He told Montezuma that he must accompany him to Spanish headquarters. If he went willingly, all would be well. But if he resisted ... well, Cortés gestured at his lieutenants, his implication being that they might run the Mexica king through with their swords.

Although he protested ('My person is not such as can be made a prisoner of') Montezuma finally went with them, having convinced his guards and advisors that the god Huitzilopochtli had told him it would be a good idea. At any point up until he was actually a prisoner of the Spanish, Montezuma could have called off this charade and had them killed, but he did not. And at this point his effectiveness as emperor was over. Both fearful of and fascinated by the Spanish, he may no longer have thought of them as gods, but they now controlled his life completely. The people of Tenochtitlán now ceased to pay any attention to the emperor, who was so obviously being controlled by Cortés. Montezuma

had been the centre of their universe. Now 'fear reigned', as the Mexica later related to Bernardino de Sahagún, 'as if everyone had lost heart. Even before it grew dark, everyone huddled in frightened, awed and thunderstruck groups'.

Cortés ruled Mexico through Montezuma until the spring of 1520, when he learned that Governor Velázquez was sending a force of Spanish conquistadors against him to bring him back to Cuba for disobeying orders. Cortés immediately marched east to meet and defeat this group and, while he was away, the lieutenant he had left in charge, one Pedro de Alvarado, massacred thousands of Mexica, inciting an uprising. Cortés returned to a Tenochtitlán in chaos and was forced to fight his way out, losing hundreds of conquistadors and several thousand Indian allies in the process. During the fighting, Montezuma was killed—stoned to death by his own people. He was then unceremoniously cremated by the Spanish. In a year's time, Cortés would return to Tenochtitlán and seize the city once and for all.

By the time of his death Montezuma had probably ceased to think of Cortés and his men as gods. However, the Mexica and Montezuma were right about the Spanish in one sense. They called Cortés and his men *teules*, which Bernal Díaz del Castillo translated as 'the name for both their gods and evil spirits'. Historian Hugh Thomas in his book *Conquest: Mexico, Cortés and the Fall of Old Mexico* says that the word *teules* is less a word to depict gods than to describe 'a notion of magical charging, possession of a vital fire, a sacred force'. It was perhaps this vital fire, most of all, that attracted Montezuma to the charismatic figure of Hernán Cortés.

THE GREAT WALK

Cabeza de Vaca encounters America, 1528–1536

In December of 1537, a small, grim-faced man could be seen haunting the court of King Charles V in Valladolid, Spain. Nearly fifty years old, he wore the fine clothing of a gallant soldier and royal appointee, which in fact he had been, but those who encountered him found his presence disturbing. The man seemed uncomfortable not just in his clothes, but in his very skin. He was extremely restless and hard to engage in conversation, yet sometimes he would not stop talking. He could be seen staring off into space or muttering to himself. He did not suffer those he considered to be fools patiently or gladly. *He*, however, had an important tale to tell, and he needed to tell it to King Charles himself.

The man's name was Álvar Núñez Cabeza de Vaca and that December he would get his chance to talk to the king. For despite his surly and off-putting manner, he had experienced something

no other Spaniard—or other European, for that matter—had experienced. Along with two other white men and one black slave, he had walked 4000 kilometres (2500 miles) across the unknown area the Spanish knew only as *La Florida*—the vast lands north and east of Mexico. In doing so, as the historian Andres Resendez writes, Cabeza de Vaca and his friends instituted 'an extraordinary instance of first contacts between peoples whose ancestors had remained apart for 12,000 years'.

This was not the type of contact that Hernán Cortés, Francisco Pizarro or Hernando de Soto fostered, marked by plundering and killing, but contact of an entirely different sort. For Cabeza de Vaca lived among the Indians he met in a number of guises—as supplicant, slave, trader, and finally healer and shaman. And he knew them not as people to be robbed of their treasures, or as chattel, but as human beings.

From our point of view, half a millennium later, Cabeza de Vaca's story is one of the few glimpses we have into cultures that were about to be destroyed forever. This is what makes his journey and the narrative he later wrote of it (his *Relación*) so valuable, even if, ultimately, King Charles V did not think so.

The young soldier

Álvar Núñez Cabeza de Vaca had a name that made some of his contemporaries snicker, since Cabeza de Vaca literally meant 'head of a cow'. But those who laughed were not aware of his illustrious forebears. He was born in the province of Andalusia, in a town called Jerez de la Frontera, about eighty kilometres (fifty miles) south of Seville—a place famous for the sweet wine the English called 'sherry'. Cabeza de Vaca's unusual name comes from a probably apocryphal tale: that a humble shepherd ancestor of Cabeza de Vaca's mother placed a cow's head at a mountain pass, thus guiding King Alfonso VIII of Castile to victory over the Moors at the battle of Las Navas de Tolosa in 1212. But Cabeza de Vaca did have a distinguished lineage. His grandfather, Pedro de Vera Mendoza, was one of the conquerors of the Canary Islands. Another relative was the famous musician Luis Cabeza de Vaca, who was a tutor to King Charles I (who later became Holy Roman Emperor and thus Charles V). Luis was probably the one who introduced the young Cabeza de Vaca to the Spanish court.

Despite these illustrious family members, Cabeza de Vaca had a difficult upbringing. Both his mother and father died while he was still a teenager and, with no inheritance, he turned to soldiering to make his way in life. He fought with gallantry with the Spanish forces in Italy from 1511 to 1513 and thereafter won favour with King Charles by helping put down a rebellion against the Spanish crown around 1520. By now, Cabeza de Vaca—short of stature, but highly ambitious—had married and needed more in life than the uncertain spoils of a

soldier. In 1527, through his connections at the Spanish court, he had himself appointed Royal Treasurer—essentially, second-in-command—of an expedition that was about to plunge into the unknown wilderness of the New World known as *La Florida*.

'On your royal conscience'

La Florida was essentially the entire Gulf Coast of America from Mexico—known as New Spain—to the current state of Florida. In the 1520s very few Europeans had visited this area. One of them was the Spanish explorer Ponce de León, who had sought the so-called 'Fountain of Youth' in a legendary land called Bimini, which supposedly existed north of the Bahamas. Ponce de León landed on the Atlantic coast of what is now Florida during Easter week—the so-called 'Flowery Festival' or *Pascua Florida*, which is how the area got its name.

Hernán Cortés had conquered Mexico in 1519–20 (see page 53) and found riches beyond belief there, and many Spaniards were certain that north of Mexico there would be another civilisation filled with gold and silver. There were any number of ambitious Spanish explorers who were ready to explore these lands, but few had any idea of what they were dealing with. All underestimated New World distances. Such vast expanses simply did not exist within the old, European world. Therefore, it was thought that the distance from the River of Palms (*Rio de las Palmas*) in eastern Mexico to Florida was only a matter of a few hundred kilometres. Instead, it was four thousand (2500 miles).

The one-eyed conquistador Pánfilo de Narváez, who headed the expedition (or *adelantamiento*) that Cabeza de Vaca joined, certainly believed this. Narváez is not one of history's most sympathetic figures. Cabeza de Vaca's exact contemporary, he had taken part in the conquest of Jamaica in 1509 and in 1520 was sent by Governor Diego Velázquez to halt the conquest of the Mexica by Cortés—

Velázquez had decided Cortés was taking too much of this rich pie for himself. As a reward for his efforts, Narváez lost an eye to the pike of one of Cortés's men and was imprisoned by Cortés in Mexico for three years.

Once he was allowed to return to Spain, he beseeched King Charles for an expedition of his own, claiming that he was really seeking the conversion of the Indians. He did not, he said, want it to 'weigh heavily on your royal conscience' if these poor pagans were not brought to the light of Christ. Of course, other considerations came into play, mainly the riches that might be gained by such an expedition, and in the end Charles allowed Narváez a huge land grant. He gave Cortés the southern half of Mexico, but bestowed all else north of the River of Palms and east to Florida on Narváez. By being successful in such an expedition, Narváez could outshine his old rival Cortés, as well as greatly increase the riches and lands of the kingdom of Spain.

It is doubtful that Narváez chose Cabeza de Vaca as his Royal Treasurer, since it was understood that a patent from the king included numerous royal appointees. Three other men who joined Narváez and who would help make history with Cabeza de Vaca were captains Alonso del Castillo and Andrés Dorantes, as well as Dorantes's North African slave, Estabancio.

'A colossal navigation mistake'

Narváez's fleet of five ships left Spain on 17 June 1527 with six hundred men. They arrived in Cuba in the early autumn, but a hurricane then devastated the fleet to such an extent that Narváez was forced to delay sailing from Cuba until April 1528. Finally, his ships set sail for *La Florida*. Here there occurred what one historian has called 'a colossal error in navigation' on the part of Narváez's navigator, Diego Miruelo. The actual destination of the expedition was the River of Palms, in northeastern Mexico (probably today's Rio Soto la Marina) on the *western* side of the Gulf of Mexico. But fighting contrary gales, their progress slowed by the Gulf Stream, which here runs from northwest to southeast, the little fleet was guided by Miruelo to the west coast of the Florida Peninsula, on the *eastern* side of the Gulf, an error of some 1500 kilometres (930 miles). The fleet landed, probably in the vicinity of modern-day Sarasota, in Tampa Bay, on Easter Sunday.

It is hard to understand, even with the rather primitive dead reckoning navigation of the day, how such a mistake could have been made, but when Narváez first set foot on the Florida coast and claimed it for Spain, he thought he was actually in northern Mexico, just a few hundred kilometres south of the River of Palms. All the disasters of the expedition followed from this one crucial mistake.

The first contact the Spanish had with the local Indians was uneasy. The first tribe they met made 'signs and threatening gestures' at the Spanish, as Cabeza de Vaca wrote in his *Relación*, but retreated when Narváez ordered the passengers aboard the ships to disembark. This horde of people—and horses, which the local Indians would not have seen before—frightened the Indians enough to make some flee, while the others agreed to trade with the Spanish. But, moving a little farther inland, a Spanish scouting expedition found a tribe in the possession of 'many crates belonging to Castilian merchants, and in each one of them was the body of a dead man, and the bodies were covered with painted deer hides'.

Along with the crates the Spanish found numerous Spanish items, such as shoes and pieces of iron. It was obvious a ship had been wrecked along this coast, probably a vessel heading east from Mexico, and that the Indians had treated the remains of the survivors almost worshipfully. But the priests who were along on the Spanish expedition thought that the way in which the bodies had been preserved

ESTABANCIO:
'LIKE A ST SEBASTIAN'

The Indians whom Cabeza de Vaca met were fascinated by white men but even more astonished by the black slave, known to us only as Estabancio (alternatively, Estavanico). Estabancio came from the Moroccan coastal town of Azamor, a place of some wealth whose inhabitants were mainly Arabic-speaking Muslims. In 1513, the town's abundance captured the eye of the Portuguese, who sent a powerful armada to attack it (one of the young sailors on the Portuguese fleet was Ferdinand Magellan). After seizing the town, the Portuguese began to take slaves, and one of the men they seized was Estabancio.

Estabancio was almost certainly a Muslim who was made to convert to Christianity. He was sold in the slave markets of Seville to Captain Andrés Dorantes, who then took him along on the Narváez expedition. Estabancio turned out to be a pretty good person to have along in the wilderness after he and the three Spaniards had escaped their captivity. He had a powerful facility with languages and was more outgoing than the others (who to some extent remained deliberately apart, so as to continue to seem godlike to the locals). Thus, Estabancio was able to find out which route they were taking, what villages lay ahead and what, if any, dangers lay in their path.

Estabancio was the only one of the four survivors to return to the rough country of northern Mexico and the southwest of North America, guiding another expedition that left Mexico City in 1538. A group of Franciscan friars accompanied this reconnaissance, the idea being that they would convert the Indians. The Indians whom Estabancio met recognised him and, remembering his powerful position as a healer, gave him young women and turquoise. This offended the Franciscans, who ordered him to stop sleeping with the women. Estabancio refused, instead moving on ahead at some distance from the friars, away from their prying eyes. One day he ran into an unknown group of Indians and told them he was the emissary of a group of white men, following behind, who 'were coming to instruct them about things divine'.

Estabancio also demanded women of these men but, not having heard of his reputation, the Indians turned on him and shot him so full of arrows he looked 'like a St Sebastian', according to the friars who later found his body. His remarkable journey from North Africa was finally over.

smacked of 'idolatry' and so ordered them, and the crates, to be burned, much to the displeasure of the Indians. When the Spanish then asked the Indians, who possessed a few pieces of gold, where they could get more of the precious metal, the Indians were only too happy to point them northward, claiming there was another tribe, 'in a province called Apalachee', who owned all the treasure the Spanish could hope for. (Hernando de Soto would end up having far more extensive dealings with the Apalachee—see page 91.)

The Bay of Horses

Narváez now called a conference of his captains, who included Cabeza de Vaca, as well as Alonso del Castillo and Andrés Dorantes. He told them that Miruelo had assured him that the River of Palms was only a few hundred kilometres distant, to the north, and that therefore he had decided to split up his force. His ships would sail up the coast with his sailors and settlers, while the military contingent of the expedition, some three hundred men strong, would go overland, keeping to the coast, to discover this gold-laden land of the Apalachee. Cabeza de Vaca protested greatly against this decision, telling Narváez 'by no means should he leave the ships as [the pilots] … did not know where they were' and that the army would be 'travelling mute, that is, without interpreters [through] a land about which we had no information'. At least, he says he did— there were no survivors to contradict him when he finally put his story down in writing in his *Relación* in 1542. But there is a record of others protesting—a woman who was along on the expedition gave a dire warning to Narváez that, in the end, went unheeded. He was the leader of the *adelantamiento* and his word would be obeyed.

It was the second fateful—and fatal—error of the expedition. Narváez's ships sailed off, planning to rendezvous with him farther up the coast, while Narváez led his men overland. Perhaps something

might still have been salvaged from the expedition had he actually kept to the coastline, but he turned his men much farther inland and they soon found themselves struggling through the Florida swamps with little to eat, sweltering in the heat. Cabeza de Vaca, Castillo and Dorantes begged Narváez to turn back to the coast or at least to send scouts westward to establish contact with the ships but, intent on the imagined trail of the Apalachee, Narváez refused.

An Indian of Florida. The Indians Narváez met used guile and harassment to speed him out of their territory.

For over a month they wandered, capturing Indians to use as guides. They finally came to the land of the Apalachee, where they battled the Indians, only to find a poor, threadbare land, with no gold or other precious metals. Not only that, but the Indians were natural guerrilla fighters, shooting arrows with deadly accuracy from their long bows, killing any conquistador who ventured out alone, before melting away into the woods.

For three months, the Spanish marched and countermarched through the countryside, seeking larger and more prosperous Apalachee villages (these did exist, but much farther north). Fifty men died, of Indian arrows, starvation and disease. Finally, Narváez could take it no more and decided that they had to make their way back to the sea. Arriving near the coast, they found themselves in a land of shallow estuaries, near a muddy bay that was only waist deep. There were no ships in sight. (In fact, the mariners of the fleet, pushed farther out to sea by shallow water and unable to find the River of Palms, had finally realised their error in assuming Florida was Mexico. After searching fruitlessly for Narváez and his men, they returned to Cuba.)

When Narváez realised that help was not forthcoming, he decided that he and his men needed to save themselves. Stranded in what they called the Bay of Horses, because they had to kill a horse every third day just to stay alive, the starving conquistadors desperately built five rafts from pine or cypress trees, caulking them with resin and tying them together with sinews from the legs of their horses. They stitched together sails made from deer skins. Each raft was about ten metres (thirty-three feet) long and rode only about twenty centimetres (eight inches) above the water when fully loaded with fifty men and supplies. Yet, 'so greatly can necessity prevail', wrote Cabeza de Vaca, 'that it made us risk going in this manner and placing ourselves in a sea so treacherous,

and without any one of us ... having any knowledge of the art of navigation'.

The rafts pushed off on 22 September 1528.

'Like giants'

Keeping as close to the coastline as possible, the five rafts sailed for about a month along the Gulf of Mexico. In their weakened state, the Spanish tried to avoid landing, but soon they began to run out of water, since the water bags they had fashioned out of the hollowed legs of horses had begun to rot. Men dehydrated quickly in the hot sun. Some began to drink seawater and died. Finally, the rafts encountered canoes with Indians, who guided them to shore and fed them, but then turned on them in the night, attacking and killing several men.

The Spaniards managed to set the rafts afloat again and escape, but as they journeyed westward they were again attacked by hostile Indians when they tried to land. At last they reached the broad mouth of the Mississippi River, whose powerful current sent fresh water kilometres out to sea so the Spanish were able to slake their thirsts. But no sooner had they relaxed than a powerful storm arose, separating the rafts. After several days, Cabeza de Vaca spotted another raft on the horizon and ordered his men to row for it. This raft turned out to be Narváez's, which was sailing far more strongly than Cabeza de Vaca's own vessel. Cabeza de Vaca begged Narváez to throw him a line and tow him toward shore, but Narváez refused, claiming he had now relinquished command of the expedition and that it was every man for himself.

Narváez then sailed off, leaving Cabeza de Vaca and his men to fend for themselves. Narváez's fate and that of most of the other conquistadors was to be a dire one, but after a day more at sea, with his companions near death, Cabeza de Vaca heard the sound of surf breaking and saw land about five kilometres (three miles) away. The men who could still move frantically rowed for land and the raft was finally tossed upon the beach by a large wave. The men left the raft 'half-walking, half-crawling'. Huddled under a sandy bluff, they drank rainwater, built a fire and roasted some cornmeal they had with them. Cabeza de Vaca sent out one man, Lope de Oviedo, to climb a nearby tree and take their bearings. He came back with the news that they were on a long and narrow island. (Scholars have long debated just which island this is, but most now agree that it was an island off the coast of the present-day state of Texas, just south of Galveston Island.) He claimed that 'the land was rutted in a way that it usually is when cattle roam', which meant to the Spanish that Christians inhabited the island.

This hope was dashed when Oviedo ventured forth again and found himself being followed by three Indians with bows and arrows. Very soon, the

 ## THE FIVE RAFTS

Of the five rafts that set sail across the Gulf of Mexico, heading for Mexico, two, carrying Cabeza de Vaca and his fellows, were cast up on the shores south of Galveston Island. But what happened to the other three? Over the next few years, Cabeza de Vaca discovered their fate.

The raft that got the farthest found its way perhaps as far as Mustang or Padre Island off the coast of Texas, outsailing Cabeza de Vaca by some 250 kilometres (155 miles). But the men were in such a weakened condition when they came ashore that they immediately fell prey to an Indian tribe known as the Camones. The Spaniards, according to Cabeza de Vaca, 'were so skinny that even though they were being killed they could not defend themselves'. Another raft, which carried the friars who had accompanied the group as well as several officers of the expedition, broke up just as it landed near the San Bernard River. Its survivors attempted to walk along the coast, having a difficult time in marshy country, eating crabs and seaweed. After some distance, they came upon the crew of the raft of Pánfilo de Narváez. When Cabeza de Vaca had last seen the expedition commander, he was floating off across the ocean, having told his second-in-command to save himself. His raft had apparently landed on the Gulf shore near what is now Matagorda Bay.

The two groups, at first happy to see each other, soon began to fight over scarce resources and the fact that they had only one raft—Narváez's—which could carry only half of the eighty men who had survived. In order to protect the raft, and probably to keep himself safe from Indians, Narváez began sleeping on it as it was moored out at sea, with only a helmsman and a servant. This turned out to be a mistake, as the raft was caught in a storm one night and blown out to sea. They were never seen again.

The men left behind continued their journey along the coast but were caught in the same harsh winter Cabeza de Vaca experienced on his Malhado. Without Indians around to whom they could even enslave themselves to survive, the men resorted to cannibalism to live. 'They were people beyond hope and all died that winter of hunger and cold, eating one another', wrote Cabeza de Vaca in his Relación.

castaways were surrounded by a hundred Indians, all with bows and arrows. 'Whether or not they were of great stature', Cabeza de Vaca later wrote, 'our fear made them seem like giants'.

Tossed ashore, away from all that was, to them, civilisation, without arms, armour or horses, Cabeza de Vaca and his companions were at last meeting, face to face, the inhabitants of the North American continent. It was 6 November 1528.

The slaves

The Indians that the Spanish met were either from the Han or Capoques tribe, both of which used the island as their winter habitation. At first, they displayed extraordinary generosity to Cabeza de Vaca and his fellows, bringing them food in the form of roots and fish. Still, their presence made the Spanish nervous (the Indians were, in fact, over 1.8 metres (6 feet) tall, with powerful physiques) and they made an attempt to sail off the island, taking off their clothes as they pushed the raft into the water. Unfortunately, the raft capsized, with the loss of two men, and the Spanish, now naked, were cast ashore. When the Indians returned the next day and saw them in such a miserable state, they began weeping at their plight. Novembers in the region are frigid and were even more so at a time when the climate was cooler than it is today; they knew the Spanish were going to be in trouble.

The Indians literally carried the white men to large fires they had made and allowed them to warm themselves. Although at first Cabeza de Vaca and his men did not realise it, the raft that carried Andrés Dorantes and Alonso del Castillo, which Cabeza de Vaca had not seen since the storm arose near the mouth of the Mississippi, had landed on the opposite side of the island and the men aboard it also found themselves being cared for by Indians. But in a short time this situation changed. The winter of 1528–29 was to be one of the harshest the

region had ever experienced, food was scarce, and the Han or Capoques (for it is not clear which tribe took in which group of Spaniards) could not be expected to feed these strangers forever, particularly when their own diets consisted of little more than roots and what fish they could catch.

Of the eighty Spaniards in the two groups that had arrived on the island—which they began to call *Malhado*, or the Island of Doom—only fifteen survived as spring came on. And those who did survive had become slaves. This did not happen in the organised way that Europeans enslaved people but came about little by little. Certain Spaniards, afraid of being victims of the type of human sacrifice that existed among the Mexica (but not these tribes), chose to live by themselves on the beach but were eventually so desperate with hunger that they began to eat their dead. This horrified the Indians, who never practised cannibalism, and it seems to have dehumanised the Europeans in their eyes. The Indians also caught a disease, probably dysentery, from the Spanish. Probably half of the four hundred or so Indians on the island died of this disease, a tragedy of epic proportions. In their great rage, the survivors nearly killed the remaining Spaniards, but instead decided to enslave them.

Escape from Malhado

Cabeza de Vaca's slavery was harsh. The Han or Capoques forced him to carry heavy loads and to wander completely naked through swamps digging for roots. The slightest offence would earn him a slap across the face or a beating with a stick. The Indians could be as harsh as they had been generous, killing three Spanish because they had ventured to another house without permission. Another man was clubbed to death because a woman had had a bad dream about him. Yet during this period of slavery, Cabeza de Vaca loosed the bonds that had held him to European ways and began to assimilate into the Indian way of life, one of the first Europeans to do so. His observations are worthy of an ethnologist. He noted that his captors slept on animal skins, that in the spring they went from the island to the mainland to pick blackberries, and that when a child died, 'the parents and the relatives and all the rest of the people weep. And the weeping lasts a whole year, that is, each day in the morning before sunrise, first the parents begin to weep, and after this the whole community weeps'.

At a time when half of this community had died of Spanish disease, there must have been wholesale mourning going on. Cabeza de Vaca also noticed how ineffective the Indian doctors were—their main cure consisted of placing hot stones on the abdomens of those who were ill and then blowing on the sick person to 'expel the disease from him'. Cabeza de Vaca and the others derided this approach, but then the Indians took their food away until the Spanish agreed to try to become healers. And of all the Spanish, it seems that Cabeza de Vaca was the most successful. His practice was to whisper prayers, make the sign of the cross and blow gently on the patient's forehead and about his body.

Apparently, this worked, or worked enough for the Indians to keep Cabeza de Vaca alive, despite the fact that he himself suffered from a severe illness and nearly died. For the next year, he was taken back and forth from the island to the mainland with the nomadic Indians. Much to his chagrin, those Spanish remaining in the group led by Dorantes and Castillo had been allowed to leave their captors and travel west along the coast, while Cabeza de Vaca and one other Spaniard, Lope de Oviedo, remained enslaved. Finally, Cabeza de Vaca escaped and made his way 'to those who live in the forests on the mainland', a tribe called the Charrucos, whom he had met while wandering with his Indian captors. He began working among them as an itinerant trader, which made him a valuable person, although also one whose life was precarious because the various Indian tribes he travelled among were almost always at war with each other.

Yet here, too, he learned a great deal about Indian cultures. Travelling for about 150 kilometres (95 miles) up the coast, he carried the items that the Indians valued—red ochre paint, the hearts of animals, seashells, pearls, flints, glue and hard cane for making arrows. For the next two years, he plied his trade, happy because 'practising it, I had the freedom to go wherever I wanted'. In fact, the only reason he did not start off for Mexico was that Oviedo remained behind on Malhado and would not leave. But finally, in the spring of 1533, Oviedo agreed to go with him.

'Three men like us'

Travelling along the Gulf coast, Cabeza de Vaca and Lope de Oviedo encountered an Indian tribe who told them, much to their astonishment, that 'three men like us' were alive farther up the coast, near the lower part of what is now the state of Texas's Guadalupe River. However, the Indians who told them this also taunted the Spanish, pointing arrows at them and telling them that other white men had also been alive but had been killed merely on a whim of their captors.

This information was so frightening to Oviedo that he insisted on returning to Malhado with some Indian women he met, and thus he vanishes from history. But Cabeza de Vaca continued onward and, much to his surprise and joy, met up with Alonso del Castillo and Andrés Dorantes, along with Dorantes's North African slave, Estabancio. These men were slaves of two different Indian tribes who had gathered on the banks of the Guadalupe to pick the wild pecans that grew in great abundance.

FOLLOWING PAGES Spanish explorers encounter local Indians on the coast of Florida (detail from a map of 1564).

Prom Gallicum

F

sinum.

These Spaniards were amazed to see Cabeza de Vaca alive and agreed that they would find a way to escape together. In the meantime, Cabeza de Vaca was given as a slave to the Mariames Indians, who owned Dorantes; the other two men were owned by a neighbouring tribe called the Yguazes.

Children of the sun

The Indians with whom the Spaniards lived moved nomadically from the pecan harvests along the Guadalupe about 150 kilometres (95 miles) south to the Nueces River, where they feasted on prickly pears. The Spanish secretly agreed that at the next prickly pear festival they would escape, join up and make their way to New Spain. Cabeza de Vaca anxiously awaited this moment, but also captured mental snapshots of life in the American southwest as it had been going on for hundreds of years—the hunts where Indian men, beating wooden clappers, drove deer into the water, the vast herds of bison (Cabeza de Vaca and his friends were the first Europeans to see them), and the drunken feasts of the Mariames, who loved to dance and also to tell tall tales.

After six months, the Spaniards arrived in the land of the prickly pears, but they were unable to effect their escape because the tribes they belonged to got into a dispute and went off in different directions. Much to his horror, Cabeza de Vaca now had to wait another six months. Dorantes was

 THE WOMEN WITH NARVÁEZ

The Narváez expedition was not just a raid or reconnaissance in force, as were those of Cortés and Pizarro. Instead, Narváez intended to settle Florida. Because of this, he brought ten women along. There were any number of good reasons why an adventurous young woman might choose the path of going to the New World. Women outnumbered men in Spain of the 1520s, mainly because of migration of men to the Americas, but also because of the deaths of Spanish soldiers in war. As a result, according to one foreign observer, the city of Seville was 'very nearly under the control of women', who performed such traditionally male tasks as bricklaying and roofing.

The New World held promise because there the ratio was reversed and women were greatly sought after by the lonely settlers of Cuba and the other islands. On the Narváez expedition, which was admittedly riskier than going to a settled colony, most of the women were already married to members of the expedition. As such, they were a united voice raised against the idea of separating Narváez's men from his ships, since they were certain that this would end in disaster. One woman even told Narváez that before she had left Spain a Moorish fortune-teller had told her that, if the men did separate to venture through this strange country by land, 'those who escaped would be few or none at all'.

Narváez refused to listen to her and ordered his ships to set sail with the ten women on board. Immediately, the woman who had warned him told the other women that they should give their men up for dead and find protectors among the sailors. A harsh edict, but she turned out to be correct.

now with another tribe and Cabeza de Vaca was alone. 'During this time I endured a very bad life', he wrote in his *Relación*, 'as much because of my great hunger as because of the bad treatment I received from the Indians, which was such that I had to flee three times'.

Finally, in the autumn of 1531, the Spanish reunited again, and this time they made good their escape. They found another, less hostile, tribe and were allowed to live among them as free men that winter before they headed off in the general direction of what they thought was New Spain. Gradually, the Spanish began to work as healers again, Cabeza de Vaca prominent among them. It is difficult to know why they had the success that they did—perhaps there were Indians afflicted with psychosomatic diseases, or perhaps they were suggestible to placebo, or maybe Cabeza de Vaca had some real cures up his sleeve.

Whatever happened, the men began to gain a following of Indians, who called the Spanish 'children of the sun'. Cabeza de Vaca writes: 'Among all these people it was taken for certain that we came from the sky, because all the things that they do not have or do not know the origin of, they say come from the sky'.

The Indians would creep into the Spanish campsites at dawn, with their fingers pointing to the sky. Then they rubbed their hands, with some astonishment, over the bodies of the Spanish, before bringing their sick to be cured. Gradually, the Spanish developed a method, almost as if they were doctors in a modern medical practice together. Estabancio acted as the receptionist/nurse, screening patients and finding out what ailed them. Dorantes, Castillo and Cabeza de Vaca held themselves deliberately aloof, so as to increase their mystique, before seeing their patients. They generally cured their patients by making the sign of the cross or praying over them, but also by blowing on them. Once Cabeza de Vaca even successfully performed

surgery, using a knife to remove an arrowhead from a man's chest. The healers took their payment in food and also, probably, women, although in a manuscript subject to censorship by the Inquisition, Cabeza de Vaca does not explicitly state this.

Thus the healers trekked from Indian group to Indian group as they made their way in a southwesterly direction, across the Rio Grande and into northern Mexico. They began to meet trading caravans, large groups of a hundred or so Indians carrying copper and woollen goods. Everywhere the Europeans went, they were followed by a permanent band of men and women, who acted as their disciples. The Spanish started down the Mexican peninsula on the Gulf side but were dissuaded by the Indians who followed them, because they said that 'bad Indians' lived there. So, instead, Cabeza de Vaca and his men followed a meandering semi-circle through northern Mexico before heading south again, on the Pacific side of New Spain.

Then, one day, Cabeza de Vaca saw an Indian wearing an amulet that was made from the belt buckle of a sword scabbard. Through the buckle was a horseshoe nail. It was the first sign of anything Spanish he had seen in eight years.

'American by experience'

One day in the spring of 1536, in what is now the northern Mexican state of Sonora, a group of Spanish slavers rode out to capture Indians—an easy task, for the natives could never outrun their horses. These slavers saw a band of about a dozen Indians moving across the plain and raced toward them, expecting them to flee. But these Indians were different. Instead of running, they turned toward the Spanish and approached them. One of the Indians, a short, dark man with hair down to his waist and a beard that hung almost to his belt, shocked the slavers by greeting them in perfect Spanish. The men 'remained looking at me for a long time', Cabeza de Vaca later wrote, 'so astonished that they neither talked to me nor managed to ask me anything'.

Cabeza de Vaca was finally able to explain who he and his companions were, and shocked the slavers even more by refusing to allow them to take the Indians as prisoners. This infuriated the Spanish, who through an interpreter told the Indians that Cabeza de Vaca and his fellows were Christians like themselves—implying, ironically enough, that they were just as cruel and rapacious. But the Indians did not believe this—a great testament to Cabeza de Vaca and his friends, who who were probably the only Europeans on the North American continent who did not try to convert the Indians.

When Cabeza de Vaca left his little band behind, they were weeping. He and his companions entered Mexico City on 23 July 1536, to a heroes welcome. About a year later, Cabeza de Vaca arrived home, where he immediately began to beseech King Charles to give him a patent to explore the lands he had just wandered through. But despite the fact that Cabeza de Vaca seems to have hinted that there was treasure to be found in *La Florida*—he may have done this to make himself more valuable—Charles had already decided to grant the patent to Hernando de Soto. Finally, in 1540, he made Cabeza de Vaca governor of the area of the Rio de Plata in South America, but there, because he refused to allow the Indians to be enslaved and because he was increasingly difficult to get along with, he alienated his men and was shipped back to Spain on corruption charges, which were almost certainly trumped up.

Cabeza de Vaca spent much of the rest of his life disentangling himself from this mess and restoring his reputation, which he was finally able to do. He died in 1559, having penned his Relación, in which he no longer pretended that there was treasure to be found in the lands he had wandered through. Instead, he simply told his tale as he knew it, one of the most amazing first encounter stories in North American history. Cabeza de Vaca and his comrades were, as Andres Resendez writes, forced to 'find a middle ground' each time they came upon a new native group. They could not rely on force of arms. They were, as Resendez also writes, 'European and African by birth, but becoming American by experience'.

'THE INCA
REMAINED STILL'

Conquest of the Land of
Four Quarters, 1532

After their difficult trek through the mountains, the contingent of Spanish conquistadors arrived in the valley of Cajamarca, altitude some 2700 metres (9000 feet), and lodged themselves in the town of the same name, a place of whitewashed buildings surrounding a broad inner square. It was hailing and the tiny pellets bounced off the armour of the conquistadors with metallic pings. The Spanish were exhausted and frightened. Looking from the outskirts of the town, they could see, just a short distance away, what appeared to be an entire hillside billowing in white.

The white billows were, in fact, the tents of the army belonging to the Inca king Atahualpa, whom Francisco Pizarro, along with 168 conquistadors as well as a priest and assorted black slaves and Indian translators, had come to destroy, although naturally he pretended otherwise, sending messengers ahead to Atahualpa seeking a meeting.

Atahualpa knew the Spanish were there but did not react to their presence, and so in the late afternoon, as the weather cleared, Pizarro sent his aggressive young captain Hernando de Soto to suggest to the mighty Inca that he might come to greet the Spanish. Soto, who would in eight years lead the first major expedition through North America (see page 91), did not even blink at the order to take fifteen horsemen into the heart of the Inca camp. Arriving at the site of the billowing tents, he and his men rode for six kilometres (almost four miles) through lines of silent, watching Inca infantrymen, who stood outside their tents with their lances thrust into the ground in front of them, looking strangely like medieval pages in their knee-length tunics. The Spanish crossed two streams. After splashing through the second, Soto instructed his men to stay behind, except for two trusted lieutenants and an Indian interpreter

Francisco Pizarro, the Spanish conquistador who overcame the Incan Empire and founded the city of Lima.

named Martin. They then advanced toward what Soto later described as 'a pleasure palace', a building with two towers and a central courtyard that contained a bath fed by stone pipes from surrounding streams, one a natural hot spring, the other clear and icy cold.

As they rode into the courtyard, Soto saw the great Inca Atahualpa himself, surprisingly 'seated on a small stool, very low on the ground, as the Turks and Moors are accustomed to sit'. He was surrounded by his guards, his noblemen and his women. Despite the sound the horses' iron shoes must have made on the hard-packed dirt of the courtyard, Atahualpa did not look up, but instead stared straight down at the earth at his feet. Recognising gamesmanship when he saw it, Soto rode his horse straight up to the powerful leader of an empire of ten million people, arriving so close

'that the horse's nostrils stirred the fringe [of the headband] on the Inca's forehead', as another observer put it. 'But the Inca remained still, he never moved.'

Rebels and upstarts

Thus, on this puzzling note—aggression versus passive-aggression—two empires officially met. One was the faraway kingdom of Spain, the other the land of the Inca, which stretched down the east coast of South America, covering most of modern-day Ecuador, Peru and northern Chile, from the high Andes to the Pacific Ocean. On the face of it, these two empires had little in common, separated by thousands of kilometres and an even wider chasm of culture. The Spanish had steel, books, guns, horses and, it turned out, lethal diseases. Although there was some iron-ore mining in the country, the Inca were essentially in the Bronze Age, had not found the wheel, had no explosive weapons or printed books and depended on their own fleet feet for transport—unless one was lucky enough to be Atahualpa or one of his nobles, in which case one was carried on a litter.

But Hernando de Soto and his armour-clad conquistadors and Atahualpa and his Indians in their tunics were alike in the sense that they were upstarts, people who had decided to rock the given social order and seize the chance to enrich themselves. The Inca had only ruled their land for a little over three generations, since 1450, taking it by force in a series of empire-building moves and essentially turning the entire country—some 4000 square kilometres (2500 square miles)—into a huge collective farm in which a massive workforce laboured for food and clothing (a single set per person per year, handed out from government store houses). And Atahualpa himself, at this crucial moment when the Spanish met up with him, was in the process of winning a chaotic and bloody civil war against his own brother.

As for the Spanish, their kingdom was out for all it could grab in the New World its mariner Christopher Columbus had discovered only thirty years before. The sweaty, bearded, armoured men rising almost three metres (ten feet) high on horses above Atahualpa's low figure were the point men of this conquest—greedy, brave, extraordinarily arrogant, racist and cruel. Just over a decade before, a contingent about the size of this one had defeated the mighty Mexica (or Aztec) Emperor Montezuma, using kidnapping and murder as their primary tool. That expedition had been led by Hernán Cortés, a kinsman of Francisco Pizarro; Cortés's astounding triumph had given Pizarro a blueprint on how to proceed as he faced thousands of Inca soldiers and an elaborate and sophisticated civilisation. And on that November day in 1532, as he waited anxiously back in camp for word from Soto, Pizarro was already calculating how to put the plan into effect.

A hardscrabble beginning

Francisco Pizarro was fifty-four years old in 1532, quite long in the tooth to be a conquistador—his second cousin Cortés had conquered Mexico while still in his thirties. Still, Pizarro was a determined man. He had been born into poverty in an area of western Spain, part of the Kingdom of Castile, called Extremadura, a poor, backcountry region where most people lived hard, hand-to-mouth existences. Interestingly, it was from Extremadura that other Spanish explorers of the time also came, including Ponce de León, who discovered Florida, Vasco Nùñez de Balboa, who was the first European to sight the Pacific, and Hernando de Soto. The area had a reputation for turning out toughened, amoral warriors who would let nothing stop them as they fought to improve their lot in life.

Pizarro was illegitimate, the son of an infantry captain and a maid who also worked as a prostitute, and he grew to become an illiterate teenage swineherd—not an auspicious beginning for a man who would one day have an entire kingdom at his beck and call. But as a harsh young man from a harsh place, he was a survivor. He hired himself out as a common soldier and, in 1502, set sail for Hispaniola, where, within seven years, he had risen to the rank of lieutenant in the employ of the governor. Not a great deal is known of Pizarro's activities at this time, but he apparently specialised in fighting rebellious Indians, a grisly business. Soon enough, further adventures beckoned. Pizarro was with Balboa in 1512 in Panama when Balboa crossed the isthmus and discovered the Pacific. He stayed on in Panama to become a well-to-do landowner (he even had his own private island with 150 Indian slaves) but found himself growing older and not getting a great deal wealthier. Cortés's astonishing coup in Mexico in the early 1520s had turned him into a fabulously wealthy man and Pizarro wondered if the same fate could be his.

It was why he pricked up his ears when he began hearing stories of a fabled empire to the south, variously called *Viru* or *Biru* or *Piru*.

'Their share of it'

After the discovery and conquest of Mexico there were numerous stories of indigenous nations filled with gold and treasure out in the unexplored hinterlands of the New World—it was rumours of these places that sent conquistadors like Ponce de León and Hernando de Soto thrashing through dismal wildernesses. In 1522, a Spanish explorer named Pascual de Andagoya sailed several hundred kilometres south from Panama City and returned with the exciting news of a great land that was ruled by a divine king, a place where gold was used to sheath brick walls.

When Pizarro heard, he joined forces with two other men—his friend and sometimes rival Diego de Almagro and a priest named Hernando de Luque, who was a front man for another, wealthy backer of the expedition—and bought Andagoya's ship. Pizarro and Almagro set sail south in November 1524, but their first expedition was a failure, ending in Almagro losing an eye during fighting with Indians near the mouth of the San Juan River, in modern-day Nicaragua, and the whole expedition party nearly starving to death. In 1526, the conquistadors tried again. While sailing south down the coastline, they met and captured a large balsa-wood raft with cotton sails—obviously the work of a sophisticated people, as were the many goods found on the raft, which was on a trading mission. The Spanish captured members of the crew (more escaped by leaping over the side of the raft and swimming for shore) and kept them to train as interpreters, a tactic borrowed from Cortés.

Still, this mission too ended with men wretched and dying from hunger, and finally Pizarro was forced to abandon it. It was not until 1528 that Pizarro and Almagro literally and figuratively struck paydirt. Entering the Gulf of Guayaquil in northern Peru, they came upon the Inca city of Tumbes. Here, instead of stinking jungle and grass shacks, they discovered real civilisation. Tumbes was a place of whitewashed, cube-shaped houses, of orderly streets, of prosperous people with gold and silver jewellery. Even more: a landing party for Pizarro noted that the walls of some temples were 'of gold and silver sheets' and that the women were very comely. The people were, in fact, quite friendly and curious about the Spanish. One man, dressed in a better quality cotton tunic than the rest and wearing wooden plugs in his ears (a sign of Inca nobility that led the Spanish to call nobles *orejones*, or 'big ears') approached the Spanish in a state of excitement, making hand gestures, since they had no other way to communicate, to indicate that he wanted to know who they were and where they came from.

Pizarro gave him a couple of pigs and an iron axe; the latter 'strangely pleased [the *orejon*], who esteemed it more than if they had given one

hundred times more gold than it weighed', a sign of the value of iron in a Bronze Age society. Eventually Pizarro left, but not before claiming this land for Spain. He and his men were quite pleased with Peru, as they began calling it, and hoped 'with God's help to enjoy their share of it'.

Tawatinsuyu

Having visited a tiny portion of a huge empire and claimed it for himself and his country, Pizarro sailed back to Panama and from there to Spain, where he convinced King Charles V to back an expedition to conquer Peru. Naturally, the Inca were unaware of this. Had they been, they would have ignored Pizarro as they might have a buzzing insect. Much more momentous things were happening in their world, which was known in their Quechuan language as *Tawatinsuyu,* or 'The Land of Four Quarters', because the Inca had divided Peru into four different administrative districts, all under the control of the Inca (in Quechuan, 'the lord' or 'royal person'). Their civilisation was in some ways more remarkable than that of the Mexica, for the Inca were organisational geniuses who today could be employed to good effect as time-management consultants to corporations. Since they had taken control of this vast swathe of territory, this once tiny tribe from the area of Lake Titicaca had put in 40,000 kilometres (25,000 miles) of stone roads, some of them carved out of the sides of mountains. Collective agriculture was practised and government works projects—building huge terraces to hold crop fields in the high mountains and to husband water resources in the dry plains— employed everyone.

Ensconced in his remarkable city of Cuzco, situated high above a broad plain with a ring of mountains surrounding it, the Inca himself was an ineffably fabulous presence, a living god-man so worshipped that most courtiers spoke to him only

THE CREATURE WITH
SILVER FEET

The captain advanced so close that the horse's nostrils stirred the fringe on the Inca's forehead. But the Inca remained still, he never moved.

Although there are numerous moments in the history of the conquest of Peru that stand out, Hernando de Soto's encounter with Atahualpa on the night before the history of the Incas changed forever stands out because it was not only a first encounter between a European and the Inca ruler, but also an initial meeting of horse and Inca. Although Atahualpa was not frightened of the big, snorting animal blowing onto his sacred fringe, many of his men shied away from it—so much so that the Inca had them executed for showing fear. Actually, as Atahualpa later confessed to Francisco Pizarro and Soto, he made immediate plans to steal the horse from the Spanish (once he destroyed Pizarro's little expedition), breed the animals and make himself even more powerful as ruler of the land.

Some Incas saw the horse as a mythic creature—in fact, Atahualpa's own nephew later told the Spanish how the people were frightened by the conquistadors riding 'giant animals which had feet of silver', by which they meant metal horseshoes. But Atahualpa was too cool and good a commander for that. His plan to become master of the horses never materialised, of course, because Pizarro outwitted him—in part through the shock caused by thirty-seven charging horses in the plaza at Cajamarca. The Inca simply had no protection against the horse. They could not outrun it, nor could they adequately defend themselves when faced with a Spaniard with a razor sharp sword swinging down on them from above, or spearing them from a distance with a lance.

Inca rebels did take measures to fight the horse. They would dig holes and pits, disguise them, and then try to lure Spanish riders over them. The best weapon they finally mustered against the horse was the bolo, three rocks tied at the ends of interconnecting strands of tough llama tendons, which they hurled at the legs of horses, entangling them enough to bring them up short so that Inca warriors could race in and try to kill the creatures while their Spanish riders fought ferociously to save the animals. And with good reason— without his horse and with little hope of getting a new one, a Spanish cavalryman became a foot soldier, and the odds of dying in battle against the Inca increased greatly.

KHIPU: THE TALKING KNOTS

When Atahualpa pushed away the Spanish friar's book in the market square of Cajamarca, it was partly because he did not recognise it as a book. Unlike the Aztecs, the Inca did not have written language—the main reason why, aside from isolated accounts like that of Atahualpa's nephew, the history of the demise of their empire is told only from the point of view of the Spanish.

But the Inca did have something quite extraordinary and ingenious in its own way: the khipu. Khipu were rows of string in which the number of knots and the way they were tied (as well as the colour of the string) were used for counting and record-keeping. A special class of men, called quipucamayocs, were able to create and read the khipu, which were also used for census-taking, for recording crop yields and for the yearly listing of every single possession the mighty Inca rulers owned. The khipu were also used for storytelling. It is not known quite how this worked—possibly the knots functioned as mnemonic devices reminding the storyteller of important parts of his tale, since they were used as part of a tradition of oral storytelling.

There are only a few hundred khipu still in existence and archaeologists are still trying to decipher their secrets. If they are able to, we may find another, entirely different version of the conquest stories.

through a screen, and his waste, right down to his fingernail clippings, was collected and ritually burned once a year. When the Inca died, he was mummified but never considered quite dead—his mummy lived in its own palace and could and did issue directives through numerous aides and loyal followers.

Although not as superstitiously inclined to believing in portents as the Mexica (the land the Inca lived in was far too harsh for them to spend overly much time worrying about what the portents might be on any given day), the Inca did suffer from one of the same flaws: a top-heavy system of government, dependent on the worship of a single man who, in fact, was not a god but a mere human. And as mere humans, the Inca were quite vulnerable. A few years before Pizarro and his fellows arrived at Tumbes in 1528, the civilisation was reaching its height under a grand Inca named

Huayna Capac, who had been fighting wars in the north, in present-day Ecuador, to subjugate the Indians there. Then, people began dying of a mysterious disease—their skin burst into boils and sores and shortly thereafter they dropped dead. This was almost certainly smallpox brought by Europeans, part of the outbreak that began in Hispaniola, found its way to Central America, spread north to Mexico in 1521 (thus creating the outbreak that helped Cortés destroy the Mexica) and then wound its deadly way south to Peru.

Although Huayna Capac secluded himself upon hearing of this pestilence, it did no good. The very human Inca died in 1525, but not before naming his son Ninan Cuyoche as heir. Unfortunately, Ninan died shortly after Huayna, also of smallpox, and a civil war then broke out as two other sons, half-brothers Huascar and Atahualpa, engaged in a deadly power struggle that lasted for four years.

The battle raged between Huascar's headquarters in Cuzco, in the south, and Atahualpa's centre of power in Quito, in the north.

In 1532, just as Pizarro's new expedition landed in Peru, Atahualpa's generals stormed Cuzco and defeated Huascar's forces, capturing Huascar and holding him captive while slaughtering his wives and children. They immediately sent relay runners to inform Atahualpa of his triumph, and he began to proceed south from Quito to make his triumphant entry into Cuzco. Along the way, however, he decided to stop at Cajamarca to deal with this small band of bearded white men of whom he had been hearing strange reports.

'Most serene Inca!'

When Hernando de Soto was unable to get the Inca Atahualpa to react by threatening him with the physical presence of his horse, he cantered back a few paces and, through his interpreter Martin, made a speech, prepared beforehand, which began 'Most serene Inca!' and focused on the fact that the Spaniards had come to bring the word of God to the Inca. It was long and flowery and it is doubtful Atahualpa understood much of it, mainly because Martin was a captured Indian who knew as little fancy Spanish as the royal Quechuan language. The Inca, in any event, continued to stare at the ground, and one of his nobles finally explained to Soto that Atahualpa was on the last day of a ceremonial fast and was not, strictly speaking, accepting visitors. The man presumably did not have the words to explain to Soto that his sheer effrontery in approaching the Inca, even looking at him, was nothing short of astonishing.

At this juncture, another Spaniard, Hernando Pizarro, rode into the square. Hernando was sent by his brother Francisco to discover what was taking Soto so long and somehow it was communicated to Atahualpa that Hernando was the blood relation of the Spanish leader. When he understood this, the Inca looked up for the first time and the Spanish were able to appraise him. He was later described as being about thirty years old, with 'a large face, handsome and fierce, and bloodshot eyes'. He spoke 'with much gravity' in a dignified voice, and this is what he told the Spanish: 'A captain that I have on the river of Zuricara sent to tell me that you mistreated the chiefs and put them in chains, and he sent me an iron collar [as evidence] and he says that he killed three [Europeans] and a horse'.

Hernando Pizarro and Soto were astonished at Atahualpa's accurate information. The incident in question had, in fact, happened four months before, as the Spanish entered Peru. The Spanish response to the deaths of their men was to kidnap a local chief and his nobles and burn them alive. And the Inca ruler, hundreds of kilometres away, knew all about this. Uneasy, Hernando told Atahualpa that this chief of his was a liar and a scoundrel, but the Inca was obviously not fooled. Changing the subject, he told Hernando that he had some subjects who were disloyal to him—could the Spanish accompany his men to help destroy these subjects?

Feeling on safer ground, Hernando told Atahualpa that 'you don't need to send any of your men'. Ten Christians alone would be enough to do the job, he bragged. Atahualpa said nothing but, according to Hernando, 'smiled like a man who did not think so much of us'. Obviously, the Inca, as yet unfamiliar with the power of Spanish conquistadors at war, thought this man was making a foolish boast. In any event, as the sky darkened, the Spanish extended Francisco Pizarro's invitation to the Inca to come to Cajamarca the next day. The Inca, perhaps amused at being invited to visit a town in his own kingdom, accepted.

'A fearsome sight'

Francisco Pizarro eagerly awaited the return of his brother and Soto in Cajamarca, for he knew that quite soon would be the defining moment for his expedition—whether it would be successful and, in fact, whether they all would live or die. When he had again landed at Tumbes, four months earlier, he had been surprised: the neat, orderly little town had been in ruins, houses had tumbled down and the bodies of Indians were hanging from trees in the nearby forests. The locals had told him of the great civil war between the two Inca brothers and Pizarro had immediately realised that in the discord of this nation stood his greatest opportunity. There would have been no chance for him to approach the great Inca had Atahualpa not been marching with his army, had not extraordinary events brought the Inca out from behind his grand walls.

Now, Francisco Pizarro was determined to take advantage of the proximity of the Inca ruler. When Soto and Hernando returned, Francisco called a meeting in one of the buildings facing the town square. Late into the night, the Spanish pondered their options. Many of the conquistadors were quite frightened. Hernando Pizarro had told them that the Inca army numbered forty thousand men (he privately informed Francisco that the number was more than twice that) and this seemed like enormous odds. They were several weeks out of Tumbes, where lay their ships and avenues of escape. They were high in the mountains where they would be easily trapped and surrounded by thousands of warriors of a strange and savage empire. How could they possibly win a victory here?

Francisco knew. Using the blueprint that had been handed down by Cortés's action in Mexico, he told them that the only reasonable way to proceed was to kidnap the Inca himself. He was making an assumption that, like Cortés with Montezuma, he would be able to control the Inca through their ruler. However, he had no proof that this was going to be the case and his men were still 'full of fear', as Miguel de Estete, a notary who was present, wrote. They could see the campfires of the Inca army. 'It was a fearsome sight as most [of the fires] were on a hillside and close to one another … [It looked] like a brilliant, star-studded sky.'

Attempting to overcome his men's trepidation, Francisco proposed a plan. He would hide all of his men within the confines of the buildings that looked out on the Cajamarca town square, a space 180 metres (600 feet) square. Three groups of roughly twenty horsemen would be placed in buildings on three sides of the square, with infantry in between. In a building on the fourth side, Francisco positioned his artillery captain, Pedro de Candia, and his harquebusiers. Each of these buildings had numerous doorways, so that the conquistadors would be able to charge out from hiding almost simultaneously.

As dawn approached, Francisco hid his men carefully. He told them that he would wait until the last minute before deciding what he was going to do—ally himself with the Inca, negotiate, attempt to retreat, or capture Atahualpa himself. If he decided to do the latter, he would shout for Candia to fire and then the others must charge with all their might into the square. In the melee that would surely follow, Francisco himself and a handpicked group of men would seize the godlike ruler of this vast land and hold him, literally for dear life.

'Where are they?'

In the Inca camp that night, Atahualpa was planning a very different fate for the Spanish. As he later told Pizarro and Soto, what he was really interested in were their horses, for he saw right away that these creatures would make him the most powerful Inca who ever lived. His plan was to attack the Spaniards after visiting them in the square. Those who did not die he would castrate and use as eunuchs to guard his harem. Then he would take away their magnificent animals and breed them.

The next day, the Spanish anxiously watched the Inca camp, but they saw no sign of movement. Morning wore on into early afternoon, and the

Father Valverde confronts the Inca ruler Atahualpa before the battle at Cajamarca, with which the Spanish began their conquest of Peru.

'THE CREATOR OF ALL THINGS'

A great difference between the Inca and the Spanish lay in their weaponry. The Spanish were all about steel—steel blades and lances, steel armour and helmets. The Indians carried clubs rather than swords, and even though these were often studded with blades or spikes of copper or stone, they were weapons meant to crush rather than to stab or slice through. But even the mightiest Inca club could not penetrate or shatter a Spanish helmet, although it might make the wearer of said helmet's ears ring for some time.

In fact, after battle most Spaniards in armour must have walked away vibrating. Another favoured weapon of the Inca—perhaps their best weapon—was the sling, usually made of llama wool, into which a rock was fitted before the warrior twirled it over his head numerous times and let fly. Spanish sources describe a rock launched in such a way as able to cut a sword in half at thirty metres (one hundred feet). It was just such a rock that killed Juan Pizarro, Francisco's brother, at Cuzco. But these, too, were unable to penetrate armour, and they bounced off the Spanish rather like small calibre bullets rebounding off the hide of a tank.

The Spanish did have harquebuses and small cannon, which they valued for their shock effect on the enemy, but in fact their main weapon was the sword. Spanish sources describe Pizarro's men spending hours sharpening their weapons to a razor's edge before the attack on Atahualpa at Cajamarca. The result was a blade that could quite easily, almost effortlessly, slice off arms, legs and heads. The Inca had no response to it.

Finally, the most effective weapon of the Spanish was their aggressiveness. They understood that, outnumbered vastly, the only tactic that really worked was simply to take the battle to the enemy, never to let the Inca gain the upper hand. And these strange white warriors were a fearsome sight to the Inca, as Atahualpa's nephew Titu Cusi later told a Spanish friar. He said that they seemed like viracochas—'the name that we gave in ancient times to the creator of all things'—when they charged, hoofs pounding, through a valley. There was simply nothing like it in the Inca view of the world and they had no answer to it.

Spanish began to worry. What could Atahualpa be planning? In fact, the Inca had just finished a fast and was feasting and celebrating the victory of his forces at Cuzco. He was taking his time and relaxing before he dealt with what was, after all, a small matter—a mere curiosity.

The Spanish, increasingly nervous, sent an emissary to Atahualpa inviting him to come and,

finally, Atahualpa decided it was time to deal with these men. Late in the afternoon, his entire army began to march towards Cajamarca. One Spanish observer wrote: 'In a short while the entire plain was full of men, rearranging themselves at every step, waiting for [Atahualpa] to emerge from the camp'. As the Inca warriors approached the town square, the Spanish who were able to watch (most were in hiding) saw an extraordinary sight, one Europeans had literally never seen before. Atahualpa had decided to awe the Spanish with his presence and thus came with all the pomp and glory of an Inca king. After stopping for a time in a meadow outside the town, he entered the town square as the sun was beginning to set.

At the front of the procession was 'a squadron of Indians wearing a livery of chequered colours, like a chessboard. As these advanced, they removed straws from the ground and swept the roadway'. These men were also singing. Next the square began to fill with 'many men wearing armour, thin metal plates, and crowns of gold and silver. Among [these nobles] travelled Atahualpa in a litter lined with multi-coloured macaw feathers and adorned with plates of gold and silver'. Behind all these, Inca soldiers crowded into the square until it was filled with men standing shoulder to shoulder, perhaps five to six thousand in all. Significantly, these men were unarmed except for small battle-axes and their slings. As the square filled literally to overflowing with Inca warriors, the hidden Spanish soldiers became truly fearful. Pedro Pizarro, another brother of Francisco, wrote that he saw 'many Spaniards urinate without noticing it out of pure terror'.

Atahualpa stopped his litter now and looked around the square. There were no Spanish in sight. Atahualpa, according to at least one account, had sent spies earlier in the day to see what the bearded strangers were up to and these spies had reported that they were hiding in the buildings around the square. That made sense to Atahualpa. Naturally these men were afraid of him and were cowering inside their quarters. As silence fell over the square, an Inca officer left the ranks of the army and, walking ahead, rammed a lance with a banner attached to it into the ground. This was Atahualpa's royal standard, which went wherever he did.

Atahualpa now rose in his litter and called out in Quechuan: 'Where are they?'

'Come out, Christians!'

From the shadows of one of the buildings emerged the Dominican friar Vicente de Valverde, the expedition's chaplain. He carried a cross and his breviary high and he walked slowly through the Inca soldiers toward Atahualpa's litter. Alongside him was the interpreter, Martin. Here, too, was another first encounter—the initial meeting between a representative of Christianity and the very symbol of the pagan ways of the Inca.

The priest, who was no doubt sent by Francisco Pizarro, first invited Atahualpa into one of the buildings to meet Pizarro, but Atahualpa dismissed this suggestion for the foolishness that it was. He told Valverde peremptorily that he wanted the Spanish to return to him everything they had stolen along their line of march to Cajamarca. Since he emphasised that this included food the Spanish had eaten, it was clearly impossible and he may have been attempting to incite them in order that the Inca might attack.

Valverde ignored this and began speaking to Atahualpa. He said that he had been sent by the King of Spain to read to the Inca a document known as the *requiriemento*, or 'requirement', which the king had stipulated be read to all people about to be conquered. The requirement made the case that the Christian God had created the world and the pope was His representative on Earth. Since the pope had granted all lands in the New World to Charles and his country, Spain, it would therefore behove the Inca to become subjects of Spain as well as to accept baptism. If they refused, well, anything that happened to them was their own fault.

Valverde began to speak aloud this neat little piece of justification for genocide while Atahualpa listened. That the Inca understood little of what was being said was apparent from the puzzled look on his face. Valverde stopped and told him that all he needed to know was contained in his breviary, which the great Inca asked to see. Valverde handed it to him, but there ensued a tense moment when Atahualpa was unable to get the book open. Valverde reached up to help him and Atahualpa swatted his hand away in irritation. He finally got the book open and paged through it, but then suddenly, his face bright red, he threw it to the ground. He said to the friar: 'I know well how you have behaved on the road, how you treated the chiefs'.

Atahualpa had instinctively recognised the hypocrisy of the Spanish religion—their words about God did not jibe well with burning Indians alive. But his action in throwing the holy book aside horrified Valverde, who ran back to the Spanish hidden in the buildings, yelling: 'Come out! Come out, Christians! Come out at these enemy dogs who reject the things of God!'

At the same time, according to some sources, Atahualpa rose in his litter and shouted at his men. He may have been giving a signal for them to attack, but he was too late, for Pizarro raised his hand and dropped it, suddenly. At this signal, the artilleryman Candia discharged his cannon and harquebuses, and all hell broke loose.

Santiago!

Candia was only able to get two of his four cannons to fire, but these, along with the harquebuses, had a devastating effect on the closely packed crowd of Inca soldiers, blowing bloody holes in their ranks. The Inca were not familiar with firearms and the thunderous explosions coupled with bodies falling around them would have been a nightmarish and surreal experience. But worse was to come. For at the discharge of the guns, the Spanish cavalry charged from their hiding places, spurring their horses through the doors with a fury born of desperation. Shouting *Santiago!* (their battle cry to *Sant Iago*, Saint James, one of the twelve apostles), they burst through into the Inca. The conquistadors had tied rattles to their horses so they would make a great deal of noise. Coupled with the gunshots, the shouts and the screaming of the wounded, the sounds rose to a fever pitch and the crowd panicked, racing for the exit from the square.

The Spanish horsemen plunged through the Inca, chopping and stabbing with their razor-sharp swords (which many had spent much of the night sharpening) and causing arms, hands and heads to go flying, sending gouts of blood spurting across the plaza. Without weapons, the Inca soldiers were defenceless. 'They were so filled with fear that they climbed on top of one another', wrote one Spaniard, 'to such an extent that they formed mounds and suffocated each other'. In the meantime, Francisco Pizarro, with a special flying squad of twenty men, raced right at the Inca's litter, which heaved and swayed in the rolling crowd like a ship on the waves. It was held aloft by eight noblemen, and Pizarro and his men hacked at their hands and arms, cutting them off—and still, astonishingly, the Inca held onto their ruler's litter, resting it on their shoulders until they were stabbed to the ground.

Pizarro at one point got close enough to Atahualpa to grab his arm but the litter was too high and he could not keep his grip. Finally, however, a group of Spanish horsemen spurred their way over and used the brute force of their steeds to tip the litter over, trampling the Inca nobles underfoot, and Atahualpa was pulled into Spanish hands and hustled into Pizarro's quarters. In the meantime, thousands of Inca soldiers, unable to get through the narrow doors leading from the plaza, pushed over a 4.5 metre (15 foot) section of the outer wall, which was 1.8 metres (6 feet) high and wide. They then raced out to the surrounding plain, followed by sixty Spanish horsemen shouting: 'After those with the liveries!' 'Spear them!' 'Do not let any escape!'

The Spanish hunted for nobles, first of all chasing down the ones on litters and gutting them with their lances, before turning on anyone in a uniform or adorned in finery. Their goal was to rob Atahualpa of his aristocracy and officer class and they were able to cause significant damage to those close to the Inca. A steward of whom Atahualpa was very fond was killed, as well as the lord of Cajamarca and 'so many commanders that [their names] go unrecorded', wrote one Spanish scribe. 'For all those who came in Atahualpa's bodyguard were great lords.'

Atahualpa's nephew Titu Cusi later said that the Spanish killed the Indians like a butcher killing cattle. Five or six thousand died that day at the hands of 168 Spanish soldiers and many more lay wounded, maimed for life, before Pizarro called for a trumpet to be sounded and the Spanish horsemen came in from the darkening plain. 'The first thing we did on arrival', wrote one conquistador, 'was to congratulate the Governor [Pizarro] on his victory'.

'*Dead men did not return*'

Francisco Pizarro's almost unbelievable victory spelled the beginning of the end for the last major Indian empire in the Americas. 'In less than two

Inca rebels are burned at the stake. Despite Spanish ferocity, the Inca fought on for forty years after the death of Atahualpa.

hours', wrote the historian Kim MacQuarrie, 'the Inca Empire had been beheaded, as neatly as one would sever the head of a llama or guinea pig'. Atahualpa was kept alive until May 1533, while the Spanish collected a huge ransom of gold and silver for him. Naturally, they did not let him go—that would have represented a problem in the volatile political situation of the time—instead sentencing him to death by burning under the pretext that he incited a huge Inca force, one that was even then heading for Cajamarca, to rebel against the Spanish.

This force turned out to be a chimera of the paranoid imagination of Francisco Pizarro, but he did not find this out until after he had ordered Atahualpa's death. As Atahualpa was led to the centre of the square and wood was placed around his feet, he was told that if he converted to Christianity, he would be garrotted instead of burned. Since burning was the worst thing you could do to an Inca—it would not allow him to enter his afterlife—Atahualpa chose Christianity and was baptised and then garrotted. He was then given a funeral mass and a Christian burial.

After the funeral, Pedro Pizarro later wrote, two of Atahualpa's sisters asked to be allowed into the quarters where he had been kept. They explained to Pedro that he had promised them that if he were not burned, he would return to them. Once inside the Inca's rooms, the women 'began to call for Atahualpa, searching very softly for him in all the corners', wrote Pizarro. 'But seeing that he did not answer, they went out making a great lamentation … I disabused them and told them that dead men did not return.'

The Inca would fight a long and bloody war against the Spanish rulers, one that would last until Tupac Amaru, the last Inca emperor, was captured and executed in Cuzco in 1572. But Pedro Pizarro was right—faced with an encounter with the new and strange, the old ways of the Inca had vanished from the face of the earth with as much finality as the dead Atahualpa.

'TO DISTURB
AND DEVASTATE
THE LAND'

Hernando de Soto and the
American Southeast, 1539–1542

There once existed, in the land that is now the southeastern United States of America, powerful native chiefdoms marked by palisaded towns—sometimes their wooden walls were three kilometres (two miles) in circumference. At the centre of these towns were built large mounds, atop which sat the temples or houses of their very powerful *caciques*, or chieftains. Farming corn was a principal occupation and patchwork fields of maize spread out around these population centres, as neatly cultivated as any one might find in Europe. The people of what is now called the Mississippian culture—since these cultures were located and spread outward from the great Mississippi River, which cleaves America in half—worshipped the sun, tattooed themselves with snakes and birds, and fielded warriors in trained cadres using deadly longbows and skull-shattering clubs as their primary weapons. They had trading networks that extended all over America, even as far as the Pacific Ocean. Their nobles took slaves and lived well. In all, there were perhaps a million Mississippians spread out across the North American states of Florida, Georgia, Tennessee, North and South Carolina, Mississippi, Arkansas, Ohio, Illinois and Wisconsin.

There is much that is still mysterious about these Indians, much that we will probably never know. For in 1539 they came face to face with another warrior culture. These men were far fewer in number—there were about six hundred of them at their strongest—but they made up for it with steel swords and armour, explosive weapons, huge charging horses and ferocious dogs, and the stealthy diseases they spread. They were Spaniards and they were, in the words of the American historian David Ewing Duncan, 'a maelstrom about to sweep over' the unknowing Mississippians. For three years and 6500 kilometres (4000 miles), these bearded men, led by Hernando de Soto—arguably, the smartest, toughest, cruellest and most ingenious of the conquistadors, including the great Hernán Cortés—careened through the American Southeast. As an almost direct result, Mississippian culture was so devastated that when, two centuries later, European settlers came to the southern part of the Americas they found only woodland Indians in small bands, and great empty spaces, and they thought they had discovered a pristine wilderness. What they had actually found, thanks to Soto, was a grave.

The great Soto

As with almost any pivotal historical figure, there is a great deal of controversy surrounding Hernando de Soto. People in the southeastern United States

think of him as a hero, the man who supposedly 'discovered' the Mississippi River, and there are numerous towns, cities, parades and festivals named after him. But many scholars of today—and even writers in his own time—call him brutal and self-serving. He was unquestionably brave and intelligent, but impulsive and careless of the lives of those around him.

Soto was born in about 1500 in the region of Extremadura, in southwest Spain, home to numerous Spanish warriors of the period. There is little known about his early years or his family, except the remark of one contemporary that he was 'a *hidalgo* and the son of *hidalgos*'—a *hidalgo* being a gentleman, although not necessarily one of great means—and that, according to the same source, he

The Indians Soto encountered in the American Southeast lived mainly by growing corn, as shown in this sixteenth century engraving.

had 'no blood of Jews, no *Conversos* [Jews converted to Catholicism], no Moors, no peasants'. Without much of an inheritance—he had an older brother to whom the family property went—Soto turned his eyes west, like many unemployed young Spaniards of the time.

At the age of fourteen, he found his way to the New World possessing 'only his sword and shield', as the Soto biographer Charles Hudson writes. He put that sword and shield to good, if bloody, use in Panama, where he fought under the infamously brutal Pedro Arias Dávila in conquering the Indians there. At a very young age, he was being called 'Captain', not because he had attained that rank but because he showed natural skills in leading men into battle. After a few years he formed a partnership with two other men in which all agreed to pool their resources and share in the profits of their ventures—a common practice for conquistadors at the time. They then took part in the grisly conquest of what is now Nicaragua, where thousands of Indians were killed by Spaniards vying with each other for the spoils of the land.

Soto came out of Nicaragua a rich man, his fortune made not so much by gold and silver, of which Nicaragua had relatively little compared to Mexico and Peru, but by capturing and enslaving local Indians and sending them off to work in the Caribbean and Spain. In 1531, bringing with him two ships full of conquistadors, he joined Francisco Pizarro on his epic conquest of the Inca, playing a pivotal role (see page 77).

Soto returned to Spain in 1536, however, disillusioned with Pizarro and his brothers, who had elbowed him out of any position of power in the newly conquered Peru. Soto was now quite wealthy. He found himself opulent quarters in Seville, married the daughter of Pedro Arias Dávila, staffed his home with servants and successfully petitioned King Charles V to be admitted into the prestigious military Order of Santiago.

But Soto was not happy. He had wealth, but he wanted power, the kind of power the Pizarros possessed in Peru.

La Florida

Casting his eyes around the New World, Soto realised that one area where great civilisation and much gold and treasure might still be found was the territory the Spanish loosely called *La Florida*, which meant not just the present, peninsular state of Florida in the extreme southeast of the United States, but all the lands bordering the Gulf of Mexico as far west as Mexico. There had been attempts to probe these mysterious and vast territories previously. Quixotically seeking the Fountain of Youth, Juan Ponce de León perished in the swamps of the present-day state of Florida around 1521. A much larger and more ambitious expedition, mounted by the one-eyed conquistador Pánfilo de Narváez in 1528, also met with ruin, with nearly six hundred men losing their lives to drowning and attacks by hostile Indians.

However, Soto was sure he could do better, and King Charles awarded him a royal contract to attempt to conquer *La Florida*. The rewards for Soto would be, at last, what he sought. Charles appointed him, effective immediately, governor of Cuba and gave him the title of marquis to all those lands he might discover in the future. And these lands seemed promising. A few months after Soto received permission for his expedition, a grizzled Spaniard named Álvar Núñez Cabeza de Vaca showed up in Spain. He was one of the few survivors of the Narváez expedition, a man who had walked across much of the American Southeast (see page 63), been enslaved by Indians, escaped and made a name for himself as a great healer. He had seen *La Florida* as no other European had, but he was also morose, difficult, tight-lipped and suspiciously (from the Spanish point of view) sympathetic to the Indians.

Naturally, however, Soto (as well as King Charles) interviewed Cabeza de Vaca about his experiences. His answers were curious—while not saying so outright, he seems to have hinted that there was the possibility of treasures, of gold and silver and other riches, in the lands where he had wandered—something that did not jibe with the incredible poverty and hardship of the tribes he had encountered. On the basis of this, Soto offered him a position on his expedition, but Cabeza de Vaca refused. It is quite possible he was angling for King Charles to name him as head of an expedition to *La Florida*, but Soto had already been awarded the franchise and Cabeza de Vaca was left behind in Spain.

Arriving in the New World

Hernando de Soto sailed for America in the spring of 1538, arriving in Cuba in June. Cuba was the stopping place for numerous Spanish voyages and there, as the new governor, Soto spent nearly a year supplying and building up his fleet for the expedition. He sent one commander out to scout the Gulf coast of Florida, seeking a suitable landing point, and the man returned with Indian captives who seemed to indicate, when showed pieces of gold, that there was plenty of the precious metal in their homeland.

On 18 May 1539 Soto set sail for *La Florida*. His fleet consisted of nine ships and about six hundred men. They were well supplied with horses (about 240 of them) as well as crossbows and harquebuses. The gentlemen of the expedition travelled quite luxuriously, with large tents, couches, trunks of clothes, barrels of wine and personal servants to prepare their food for them. Within seven days, backed by fair winds, the fleet had spotted the low-lying coast of Florida and had dropped anchor, probably in or quite near today's Tampa Bay. This was not far from where Pánfilo de Narváez had landed on his ill-fated

expedition and the local Indians—the Timucuans, an outlying and somewhat more primitive branch of the Mississippian tribes farther north and west—were horrified when they saw Soto's ships on the horizon. Narváez had treated them with signal cruelty, killing and enslaving them. They had not seen Europeans for a decade or more, but memories had not dimmed. In the very first clash between the Timucuans and Soto's men, a small band of the Indians attacked a Spanish patrol during the landing. They were driven off and five or six Indians either enslaved or killed, but from the Spanish point of view there was a disturbing note: an arrow loosed by one of the Indians had managed to go almost all the way through a horse, killing the animal. The Spaniards had never been up against bows like this.

Soto established his base camp in an abandoned Indian town called Ocita, the name of its *cacique*, or chief, and placed his large tent high atop one of the characteristic sacred mounds. From there he sent out patrols to capture Indians to act as guides to the cities of gold he hoped to find. He also sent word to the *cacique*, Ocita, telling him that he meant him no harm and that if he returned from hiding he would be well treated. But Ocita did not trust him, and for good reason—he had had his nose cut off by the Spanish under Pánfilo de Narváez some years before.

One day in early June, a heavily armed Spanish patrol came upon a group of Indians in a clearing and charged, scattering them. As one Spanish knight rode down on an Indian, preparing to lance him, he was startled to hear the man shout: *Xivilla! Xivilla!*, which sounded like 'Seville! Seville!' He reined in his horse and was then astonished to hear this man—who looked and dressed just like an Indian—shout: 'Sirs, for the love of God and of St Mary, do not kill me. I am a Christian like you and I am a native of Seville, and my name is Juan Ortiz'.

'It will cost them their lives'

Juan Ortiz was Soto's great stroke of luck. He had been a sailor aboard a small ship that had been sent to Florida by Pánfilo de Narváez's wife to search for her husband after he had disappeared. Captured by Ocita and his Timucuans, he had been nearly killed but had managed to survive among the Indians for nine years. Now here he was, the perfect guide and interpreter. On 15 July Soto broke camp at Ocita and headed north, searching for a rich city he had heard about—a town supposedly called Ocale—which had, as Soto wrote in a letter to be delivered back to Cuba, 'an abundance of gold and silver, and many pearls'.

He had received this information, he said, from 'some old [Indian] men of authority'. And they had better be telling him the truth, he warned in chilling fashion: 'May it please God [that these riches exist], for of what these Indians say I believe nothing but what I see, and must well see; although

JUAN ORTIZ AND THE FIRST POCAHONTAS

The story of Juan Ortiz is an incredible and little known New World saga. A young nobleman who accompanied Pánfilo de Narváez on his expedition to La Florida in 1528, he had returned to Cuba with one of Narváez's ships and had thus not shared the fate of the conquistador captain and his men. But he had returned to Florida the next year, hired by Narváez's widow, who was attempting to find out what had happened to her husband (who had perished in a storm in the Gulf of Mexico).

Near a Timucuan village, Ortiz and his shipmates saw 'a [sugar] cane sticking in the ground with its top split and holding a letter'. Thinking it might be a message from Narváez, Ortiz and another man went ashore to examine it, but they were captured by Timucuans. Ortiz's companion was killed immediately, but Ortiz was taken to the village, which turned out to be the home of the same Ocita who would elude Soto. Ocita's mother had been killed by Narváez's men—these same men had cut the cacique's nose off—and so he wanted to have his revenge on the Spanish. He ordered that Ortiz be laid across a grill over a smouldering fire, causing him to be literally roasted, 'raising blisters ... as large as half-oranges'. But intervention came in the unlikeliest of fashions—from the cacique's daughter. Like Pocahontas, the Indian princess who saved the life of the Englishman John Smith some decades later (see page 120), she begged her father that the young Spaniard be saved.

So Ortiz was spared, although grievously injured, and turned into a slave. Three years later, Ocita still wanted to kill Ortiz—according to one Spanish chronicler, when the proboscis-challenged chief 'went to blow his nose and could not find his nostrils, the devil possessed him to avenge himself on Juan Ortiz'. He decided secretly to execute the Spaniard but, once again, his daughter helped Ortiz to escape. Ortiz found his way to the village of a rival chief, where he was treated with great kindness until the day he met Soto's Spanish horsemen and was restored to his countrymen.

they know, and have it for a saying, that if they lie to me it will cost them their lives'.

This was the last letter Soto was to write in his own hand—he would dictate more—and it marked the beginning of his great journey through America. His long procession of men, horses and supplies headed north now, through western Florida. Within a few days they were passing through the vast Swamp of Cale, which had been the undoing of Narváez's men years before. Indians snuck up on Soto's army as it waded through deep muck or crowded single file along narrow trails and shot at them with arrows, then disappeared into the swamp, to places where horses were unable to follow. Guides they captured constantly led them astray, until Soto had five of them ripped

Many of the people Soto encountered lived in bustling towns and villages with fortified surrounds.

apart alive by dogs—a sixth then took them directly to the city of Ocale. But in fact the Indians had misled Soto—Ocale was but a small town with no gold and silver at all, although it was rich in something the Indians did value: corn. No one quite knows what happened to its inhabitants as Soto expressed his disappointment, although a twentieth century archaeological dig on what is probably the site of the town found a mass grave that included the bones of people who had obviously had their arms and heads hacked off. Dozens of other bodies, people who had died at around the same time, probably perished of European-borne disease. Such graves would mark Soto's passage through America. When they left Ocale, Soto and his army also left the swamps behind, finding themselves in rich grass and pastureland dotted with forests. Food was plentiful, as were Indians.

The pattern was usually the same—the Indians would run away on Soto's approach and Soto would try to contact their *cacique*, pretending he wanted to parlay but in reality trying to capture him and hold him for ransom or leverage over his people, as Pizarro had done in Peru. Generally speaking, the chiefs had been forewarned and would not go near the Spanish, at which point hostilities ensued. At one pitched battle fought in a clearing between two large ponds in northern Florida, Soto's horsemen captured hundreds of Indians who were chained and then 'allotted among the Christians for their service', as one Spanish chronicler put it—turned into slaves.

Being a proud Timucuan warrior one day and a slave the next was not the fate most of these Indians had in mind. The day after their capture, a spontaneous revolt began when one Indian captive rose up and punched Soto in the mouth, 'delivering a great blow that bathed [Soto's] teeth in blood', and knocked him unconscious for half an hour. The Indian then leaped upon Soto and nearly strangled him before guards killed the man.

This attack was the signal for a general uprising, which saw Indians picking up Spanish weapons such as swords and picks and fighting savagely against their tormentors.

Spurred to even sterner revenge than he had been at Ocita, Soto had two hundred Indians tied to stakes and shot to death with arrows or hacked down with halberds.

Wintering with the Apalachee

By the rainy winter months, Soto had arrived in the western panhandle region of Florida, passing into the territory of a new set of Mississippian people, the Apalachee, the Indians for whom the Appalachian Mountains are named. Soto had brought engineers with him and they built a bridge across the broad Suwannee River, despite the fact that Indians kept a rapid fire of arrows at them from the opposite bank.

As the Spanish advanced into Apalachee territory, they were facing their first truly sophisticated Mississippian kingdom. It was only sixty-five kilometres (forty miles) square, but rich in crops and game, and with large towns filled with pyramids, temples and lodge houses. According to David Ewing Duncan, the Apalachee had 'a standing army; elite classes of politicians … and a complex network of trade with other Mississippian kingdoms as far north as the Great Lakes—and, perhaps, as far south as Tenochtitlán, in Mexico'.

As the Spanish advanced farther into Apalachee territory, they were subject to carefully planned hit and run attacks, for which the natives deliberately picked areas—swamps or woods—where Spanish horses could not manoeuvre. The Apalachee used their large, deadly longbows—not unlike the medieval longbows of English archers—to fire on the Spanish. If the arrows were made of cane, as they sometimes were, they might break at the point of impact with steel armour, but if they were made of wood they could easily penetrate chain mail, dealing a fatal blow. Nevertheless, Soto forged ahead and in early October reached the Apalachee capital of Anhaica, which was located in the current Florida state capital of Tallahassee. It had, according to one Spanish chronicler, 'two hundred and fifty large and substantial houses, as well as a *cacique*'s palace built in a pyramid'.

Soto decided to spend the winter there and garrisoned his men in the Indians' homes. However, it was not long before Apalachee warriors— smeared with red ochre and bedecked with feather headdresses—mounted repeated retaliatory attacks on wood-cutting parties, introducing the Spanish to the grisly practice of scalping. Twenty Spaniards were killed in this way during Soto's five-month stay in the territory of the Apalachee. At one point, an Indian slipped past Spanish guards and set fire to a few huts in Anhaica, a fire that blazed into a conflagration and destroyed two-thirds of the town.

But not all was bad news for Soto. One of his captains had captured a talkative teenage Indian boy named Perico, who said he was a trader. Perico told the Spanish that he came from a land called Yupaha, about two weeks' march north, ruled by a woman and possessed gold and jewels 'in abundance'. Not only that, but there was another territory, even more distant, called Cofitachequi, where there was much gold and silver—Perico was even able to describe the refining process that occurred when the metals were taken from the mines.

Soto was ecstatic. At last, he was nearing what he had come to *La Florida* for. As soon as the spring came, he decided, he would march north. But before he left, he ordered one of his trusted lieutenants, Francisco Maldonado, to return to Cuba aboard one of the expedition's ships, there to describe where Soto was going and what his plans were. Maldonado was to return the following autumn, with fresh men and provisions, to rendezvous with Soto at a harbour in northern

Florida. Each year for the next three years, Maldonado would faithfully return with a small fleet, but Soto and his men never returned. They had vanished within America.

'The son of the sun'

Hernando de Soto and his men left Anhaica in March 1540 and, heavily weighed down with provisions, marched north through the uninhabited pine barrens of the present-day state of Georgia. Led by Perico, they passed through several major Mississippian towns, although they experienced only minor skirmishes. The inhabitants did not seem as threatened by the Spanish and were willing to provide them with food and guides. Still, they asked these bearded invaders understandable questions: 'Who are you? What do you want? Where are you going?'

And here, for the first time, Soto began to claim that he was a god. According to one Spanish chronicler, he said that he was 'the son of the sun and came from where it dwelt'. This is interesting, because even Pizarro and Cortés did not pretend to be immortals—unless godlike attributes were assigned to them by the Inca or Mexica. Possibly Soto, approaching what he thought was a major civilisation, felt he needed to shore up his authority. It seems to have done little good with the Indians in this territory, however. Soto gave the next chief he met a large feather from his bag of trade goods, and the man responded with what may have been elaborate sarcasm: 'You are from the heaven and this is your feather that you give me. I will eat with it; I will go forth to war with it; I will sleep with my wife with it'.

But there was nothing sarcastic about these Indians' descriptions of the fearsome warriors of the Cofitachequi—indeed, their kindness to Soto may have been because he was marching on that kingdom, which had preyed upon the Indians of Georgia for years. Soto continued on his march, and after passing through some 150 kilometres (95 miles) of uninhabited wilderness—perhaps uninhabited because no one wished to live near Cofitachequi—spied a major town on the other side of a river. Much to the Spaniards' surprise, the supposedly warlike Cofitachequi turned out to be friendly. They were dressed well in hide robes that went down to their feet, while their warriors wore breastplates and helmets made from thick 'cow's hide', which was probably buffalo skin traded by tribes farther west. The queen herself came to see the Spanish. She was borne in a litter, a woman of 'extreme perfection', according to one chronicler, dripping with fresh-water pearls 'as large as hazelnuts'.

However, the gold Perico had spoken of turned out to be copper (the Indians did not differentiate between the two) and the silver was mica. As the Spanish probed farther into the area, they found abandoned towns overgrown by the wilderness and in the ruins of these towns a few old Spanish axe blades and rosaries. These, it appeared, were all that was left of an expedition along the Atlantic coast—which was not far away—by a Spaniard some twelve years before. And the abandoned villages were probably the result of pestilence the Spanish had left behind along with their rosary beads.

Even so, Soto's men realised that they were in a fertile area, with access to the sea and a not inconsiderable supply of pearls. They asked Soto if he would consider building a colony here—'all the men were of the opinion that they should settle the land', wrote one of those present. But Soto, obsessed with the notion of finding gold, refused to stop. On 12 May, kidnapping the friendly Cofitachequi queen to ensure the continued friendly behaviour of her subjects, he travelled farther north.

The land of the Coosa

Carrying the queen with him—legends have arisen that she became Hernando de Soto's lover, but there is no proof of this—Soto headed north into the present-day state of North Carolina and the Appalachian Mountains. By the end of May, he had swung west near the current-day city of Knoxville, Tennessee, where the Cofitachequi queen made a daring escape from his custody, aided by an Indian slave of the Spaniards who probably *was* her lover. Two Spaniards also deserted but were caught and probably hanged.

Soto drove onward, now turning back south with his army, heading roughly toward the Gulf of Mexico. He entered the kingdom of the Coosa—what David Ewing Duncan calls 'the largest aboriginal empire in the Old South'—which was probably located in northern Georgia. It was a populous place filled with rich towns, proud warriors and pyramids. It took him an entire month to march through the Coosa Empire, and in true Soto fashion he left a swathe of destruction behind. Despite the fact that the *cacique* of the Coosa welcomed him with open arms and even emptied an entire town for the Spaniards, Soto kidnapped him and turned many of his people into slaves. The Spanish then continued to move to the southwest, marching at a rapid pace of over thirty kilometres (twenty miles) a day for four months. This rough journey through the land of the Coosa was to have severe effects on their empire. Although Soto finally released the *cacique* unharmed, having been taken hostage almost certainly robbed him of authority in the eyes of his people and others. And, once again, Spanish diseases spread rapidly through these Mississippian people. When another Spanish exploring party came through the area some twenty years later, they found a poor kingdom, with villages rudely constructed and temples that were falling down. By the beginning of the eighteenth century, the Coosa Empire had disappeared without a trace.

The battle of Mabila

In current-day Alabama, Hernando de Soto entered the kingdom of the Atahachi and faced his most

LET SLIP THE DOGS OF WAR

Spanish steel was one of the main reasons why the Spanish, so few in number, were able to conquer large populations of Native Americans—the protective steel of armour as well as the sharp steel blade of the sword. Another powerful weapon was the horse, which was able to run down even the fleet-footed Indians. But a third, and truly savage, weapon was the Spanish war dog.

*These dogs, descendants of the animals that had been used to herd sheep in Spain for decades, were usually either mastiffs, which were short-haired, powerfully built animals not unlike today's pit bulls, or greyhounds, fast and lean, with their ribs showing through their flanks. The latter were favoured for hunting down Indians, whom they ran to ground in the same way they cornered deer in Spain. Sometimes the Spanish brought along a type of dog called the **alano**, which seems to have been a mix of several breeds, including Irish wolfhounds. These animals were huge, fierce and, rumour had it, could attack and kill wolves.*

The Spanish had used dogs during their extermination of the Guanches, the native people of the Canary Islands, and so it was only natural that they should bring the creatures with them to the New World to corral and terrify the Indians there. One frightening thing about the animals is that they knew the difference between Spaniard and Indian and could, in fact, track down an individual Indian in a group. Shouting Tomalos!*—which means, 'Get them!'—the Spanish dog handler would unleash his animal and it would spring forward with a growl. It usually killed its victims by knocking them down, tearing open their stomachs and ripping out their intestines. Sometimes it would begin by tearing off a man's penis.*

These dogs were used in combat and also to torture Indians into giving information. The Spanish in Nicaragua turned killing into a sport, setting an Indian free with a head start and then sending the dogs after him. As soon as the animals had caught up with the poor soul, they killed and ate him.

serious challenge to date. Led by a capable and warlike *cacique* named Tascalusa, the Atahachi had an organised standing army and decided—the first of the Indian tribes to do so—to strike pre-emptively at the Spanish. After treating Soto well and inviting him to feast at their capital, they began fortifying their town of Mabila, on the Alabama River. Although Soto realised that this was happening, he dismissed it. On 8 October, he insisted on riding right into the walled town with a small group of

men, accepting the invitation of the local *cacique*. He and his men were entertained at a feast by dances performed by 'the most marvellously beautiful women', according to one of the Spaniards present. But, in secret, Tascalusa was meeting his aides in a nearby hut.

In an ironic reversal of what had happened to the Inca king Atahualpa in Peru, Atahachi warriors were hidden throughout Mabila. At a command from Tascalusa, they attacked, swarming at Soto and his small contingent with clubs, maces and bows. Cut off from the rest of the Spanish, who were bivouacked some distance away, Soto and his men fought fiercely. Five died right away, and Soto was hit by twenty arrows, which, however, did not pierce his armour.

Leaping on horses, Soto and most of his men escaped, although they were forced to leave behind a priest they had with them. They raced back to the rest of the Spanish, shouting an alarm. They then attacked the palisaded town with a fury, hacking their way into it with axes and then setting straw-roofed houses on fire. As the flames spread across the town, the Indians ran out into the nearby fields, becoming perfect targets for the Spanish on horseback, who pinioned them with lances and hacked off their limbs with swords. The battle went on for nine hours. Twenty Spaniards would ultimately die, and from one to two thousand Indians, some of them committing suicide rather than being taken alive. It was one of the bloodiest Indian battles ever fought in America and it spelled the end for this great civilisation, as well.

Marching to the Mississippi

After wintering and licking their wounds near the present-day town of Tupelo, Mississippi, Hernando de Soto and his army set off westward in the spring of 1541. Soto now had a morale problem. His men were tired, emaciated and disgruntled, having seen little gold and far too many Indian arrows. Some began to question Soto's sanity, so driven was he to find gold and glittering empires in a land where there was transparently none, although there were plenty of natural resources and rich potential farmland. This was especially the case after the autumn of 1541, when word reached the Spanish that Maldonado's fleet was at anchor a week's march away. Yet Soto, refusing to give up, turned away from the Gulf.

The battle at Mabila had staggered the Spanish—not just because of the savagery of the fighting, but because much of the Spanish equipment (guns, swords, clothes, and even the bread and wine used to celebrate Mass) had been destroyed in the fire. Ironically enough, the thing that Soto is most famous for in the United States—being the first European to sight the great Mississippi River—happened as the expedition was almost on its last legs. On 8 May, after two months' march through the country of the Chicasa Indians, who fought fiercely with the Spanish, Soto and his men came to a high bluff about fifty kilometres (thirty miles) south of the present-day city of Memphis, Tennessee, and saw that extraordinary river, incredibly wide and quite intimidating. It is not clear whether he and his men considered this a momentous occasion (the mouth of the river, where it entered the Gulf, had been seen and explored by numerous Europeans). One Spanish writer with the expedition did say that it was 'a larger river than the Danube', but most were overtaken by the practical matter of trying to cross it.

Taking about a month, Soto and his men constructed rafts and managed to float across, continuing now to travel west through Arkansas, Oklahoma and Texas and then retracing their steps in a meandering loop back to the Mississippi. The army was travelling through miserable land, through swamps and bayous filled with alligators and snakes, and through the foothills of the Ozark Mountains. They killed buffalo, which had begun to make an appearance, and found ample salt, which they craved, at natural salt springs. It was apparent that they were simply wandering in the wilderness, but Soto refused to give up. In the Ozarks, he insisted that his men sift through the

FOLLOWING PAGES Soto enters an Indian camp beside the Mississippi River. The Indians were friendly at first but soon grew tired of the Spanish presence.

rivers and creeks, panning for gold as later generations of miners would do. But by October 'winter had already come ... [with] the cold, rains and snows' he was forced to leave the mountains to find shelter for his men.

The death of Soto

At this point, even Hernando de Soto knew that the expedition was over, and it was his plan to wait for spring and then head back to the Mississippi and from there down to the Gulf, where he would send men back to Cuba or to Mexico. The winter caught them in Arkansas, their only food beans, nuts, maize and squash. The snow was so deep and the weather so fiercely cold that they did not even have to keep their slaves chained up—there was nowhere they could go. The interpreter Juan Ortiz died of disease that winter, a real blow to the Spanish, since he had been instrumental in communicating with Indian tribes.

When the weather finally broke, in April, Soto and his men travelled down the Arkansas River to the Mississippi and made camp there among Indians who were at first friendly but then began acting in a threatening manner, massing their canoes near the Spanish camp. But Soto and his men were too weak to respond aggressively. Apparently thinking that the Gulf of Mexico was much closer than it actually was, Soto sent a detachment of men on horseback down the river, hoping that they would come upon the ocean, but after eight days' march they returned with the disappointing news that it was nowhere in sight.

In the meantime, the Indians began closing in around the Spanish. Apparently to keep them at bay, Soto told the *cacique* that he was a god—'the 'son of the sun' and that the Indians needed to obey him and 'do him service'. To this, the *cacique* responded by saying that only if Soto could 'dry up the great river' would he believe him. Soto had already taken to his bed with a fever, but this answer enraged him. He wanted to cross the river and attack the Indian, but he was too weak. By May, it was apparent that he was not going to recover. He gathered his close aides about him and told them that 'he was about to give an accounting before the throne of God'. His chronicler says he seemed to accept this fate with equanimity. In any event, he slipped into a coma and died on 21 May 1542.

Because he had sworn he was a god, his men had to dispose of him secretly at night, placing his corpse inside a hollow log and rowing it out to the centre of the Mississippi, where they dumped it into the muddy waters before the Indians could discover it. Over a year later, after an arduous trek, 311 survivors of the expedition managed to stagger to Mexico, arriving after everyone thought they were dead.

Death, in fact, followed in the wake of Hernando de Soto's star-crossed expedition. Three hundred Spanish had died, as had the Spanish dreams of finding a new city of gold like those belonging to the Mexica and the Inca. Thousands of Indians had died along the course of Soto's march, and many more would die of the diseases his party left behind. It was not only men and women who would die, however, but the great early civilisations of the American Southeast, obliterated so thoroughly that, to this day, most people have never heard of them. The great sixteenth century Spanish historian Gonzalo Fernandez de Oviedo wrote that Soto's stated aim was 'neither to populate nor to conquer, but rather to disturb and devastate the land'.

If so, he had accomplished his ends.

TRAVERSING THE AMAZON

Francisco de Orellana and the unexpected river, 1541–1542

One of the greatest journeys of exploration the world has ever known was undertaken unintentionally by desperate men. The ragged band of conquistadors led by Francisco de Orellana was in search of food and safe harbour when they inadvertently entered the fast-flowing stream of the Amazon River. Some 6000 kilometres (3700 miles) later, their rough-hewn boats wallowed in the swells of the Atlantic Ocean. They had been chased by savage Indians, attacked (or so they claimed) by women warriors, and seen all manner of strange and exotic flora and fauna. But the river itself may have been the most extraordinary sight of all— flowing swiftly along, sometimes so wide its banks could be barely discerned, often so deep that no bottom could be sounded.

When Orellana finally returned to Spain with word of his wondrous voyage he expected to be backed for a second expedition to exploit this mighty waterway, the longest in the world. Instead, he was called a traitor in certain circles and shunned by the Spanish court. When at last he was given permission to return to Brazil, it was with the most parsimonious of royal support. The result would be the tragedy he had avoided on his first trip—as the Amazon historian Anthony Smith would later write: '[The expedition] started disastrously and ended that way'.

But that was in the future. In August 1542, when Francisco de Orellana smelled the ocean breeze and felt the fresh salty splatter of the waves against his body, he knew that he had undertaken a journey no European ever had.

El Dorado

Not a great deal is known about the early life of Francisco de Orellana, but initially he followed a pattern similar to that of Cortés, Pizarro and other conquistadors. He was born in 1511 in Extremadura, that breeding ground of hard-fisted, gimlet-eyed Spanish fighters, and probably arrived in the New World in 1527, when he was sixteen. It appears that Orellana was a relative of the Pizarro brothers, probably a second cousin, and so when he crossed the ocean he ended up joining Francisco Pizarro in Panama, and he was with Pizarro when he journeyed to Peru and engaged in his epic conquest of the Inca there. In fact, Orellana distinguished himself, fighting bravely in battles at Lima, Trujillo and Cuzco and losing an eye to a stone hurled by an Inca slinger.

He fought so well that, in 1538, six years after the death of Atahualpa, he was ordered by Francisco Pizarro to pacify the province of La Culata. Orellana made quick work of the Inca rebels there and even founded the city of Santiago de Guayaquil (modern-day Guayaquil, Ecuador). In 1539, Pizarro appointed him captain-general and lieutenant-governor of that city, as well as of another nearby town. Orellana was now all of twenty-eight years old and had done quite well for himself. He was far too young to retire—not something most conquistadors took easily to, in any event—and began searching around for new adventures. One presented itself when Gonzalo Pizarro, youngest of the Pizarro brothers and governor of several provinces, including La Culata, decided to mount an expedition in search of a king named El Dorado. El Dorado was supposedly a chief of a certain tribe of Indians to the east of Peru; each year, he covered himself in gold dust and then dove into a crystal-clear mountain lake. After centuries of such a ritual, the lake was now filled with molten gold.

Far-fetched? Certainly, to our ears. But Pizarro and Orellana and the other conquistadors lived in a world where, in the previous twenty years, two fabulously wealthy and almost otherworldly civilisations, those of the Mexica and the Inca, had been discovered. Who would have thought the likes of Montezuma and Atahualpa existed? So why not a lake of gold? Governor Francisco Pizarro gave his permission for such an expedition—at the very least, it would rid him of bored and restless conquistadors who stirred up no end of trouble while idle—and Francisco de Orellana had himself invited along.

'The limits of the Ancient Empire'

Gonzalo Pizarro set off from the high northern Inca city of Quito late in February 1541, in the company of 250 Spaniards and four thousand Inca captives—these latter had been kept in shackles right up until the day of the march. Accompanying the human beings were two thousand pigs (for eating) and two thousand dogs (for hunting Indians), as well as horses and llamas. All told, it was quite a procession that travelled east into unknown territory in search of the lake of gold. But Gonzalo Pizarro was hedging his bets. It was not only gold he was after, but *la canela*—cinnamon. He claimed that he had been told 'by very prominent and aged chiefs' of the existence of vast forests of cinnamon trees, an extremely valuable spice back home in Spain. And so Gonzalo wrote to the King of Spain just before setting off: 'I [have] been made to believe that from these provinces [will] be obtained great treasures whereby your Majesty would be served ...'

Francisco de Orellana wanted to obtain these great treasures as well, but he did not leave Quito with Gonzalo. He had been late raising his group of conquistadors (Francisco Pizarro's permission did not mean he provided funding—Orellana had to pay for his own soldiers). When he finally arrived in Quito from Guayaquil with a much smaller group (only twenty-five soldiers and a few Indians), the citizens of that city warned him not to follow Gonzalo—they could smell disaster. They warned him that he was heading 'to the limits of the Ancient Empire of the Incas', where there were many warlike Indians of whom even the mighty Inca had been wary.

But Orellana, true *hidalgo* that he was, ignored them and marched east with his small group of men. They followed the massive trail left behind by Gonzalo and his men. A blind man could not have missed it—the countryside was littered with dead Inca and animals and scattered equipment, and there was not an iota of food to be had. In fact, Gonzalo had made an epic march. Heading into the western foothills of the Andes, he and his party experienced a tremendous earthquake, followed by torrential rains, thunder and lightning. After that they made a dangerous crossing of this rugged mountain chain, at heights up to 3000 metres (10,000 feet). It was here that many of the Inca captives began to die

off, of exposure and malnutrition. Gonzalo finally came down into the dense jungles on the eastern slopes of the mountains and began wandering, seeking El Dorado and *la canela*. The latter he actually found, but the trees were of such poor quality that he gave up the search for cinnamon and began torturing local Indian chiefs—tearing them apart with dogs was a favoured tactic— attempting to get them to reveal the location of El Dorado.

It was at this point that Francisco de Orellana caught up with him. It had been a rough journey for him and his men, for not only was there no food along Gonzalo's path, but he had thoroughly alienated the local Indians with his rough treatment

Guests being bathed in molten gold from the lake of El Dorado. This mythical place inspired Gonzalo Pizarro to mount his expedition.

and these had taken out their frustrations on Orellana's smaller and more vulnerable group with numerous ambushes. When he finally staggered into Gonzalo's camp, he had left 'only a sword and a shield, and his companions likewise'.

But Gonzalo was quite happy to see him. He embraced him and made him his lieutenant-general, second-in-command of the expedition.

River crossroads

The conquistadors were now in a country of deep jungle. The Andes rising behind them caught and pushed back all the moisture in the air, so that it rained continually as the Spanish drove deeper into the forest—their clothes simply rotted off their backs. They were horrified by the huge snakes that slithered through the forest and were plagued by

 THE FIGHTING WOMEN

Friar Gaspar de Carvajal's descriptions of the Amazons, supposedly gleaned from actual conversations with Indians the expedition met, make for fascinating and even titillating reading—and they certainly inflamed the minds of Europeans at the time. These women, who inhabited as many as seventy villages in the interior, refused marriage but did 'consort with Indian men' when the time came to get pregnant. They did this by attacking neighbouring villages and abducting likely men. No man was allowed to enter the Amazons' villages between sunrise and sunset, but after dark, the good friar hints, anything went, and the men were kept for as long as suited their mistresses' 'caprices'.

After the women became pregnant, the men were sent back to their own country without being harmed, but if the Amazon gave birth to a male child, it was killed immediately. Female children, however, were raised 'with great solemnity and instructed ... in the art of war'. Carvajal also revealed (with more than a hint of censoriousness) that many an Indian man had travelled as many as 1400 leagues to visit these women, but that anyone 'destined to go down to the country of these women should go as a boy and return an old man'.

Aside from these revealing details, Carvajal provided numerous other details about these women— they were ruled by a leader named Conori, who ate off gold and silver plates; they travelled on animals that resembled camels but 'were as big as horses' (possibly llama); and their villages were interconnected by a series of fine roads.

What to make of all this? One of the main reasons Carvajal's narrative has been called into question is the story of the Amazons, but since it was published we have learned that numerous things about the topography and population of the Amazon basin are probably true. The most likely scenario is that there were fighting women in the Amazon at that time—as there were, in fact, in the Caribbean—and that Carvajal and the Spanish who, after all, must have been labouring to overcome a considerable language barrier, simply misunderstood the rest. However, would Carvajal have created such an elaborate society from garbled translations? We do not know, and the story will forever remain mysterious.

unrelenting heat and disease-carrying mosquitoes. Here the Inca began to die off in earnest, of various tropical diseases as well as overwork. The conquistadors captured whatever Indians they could find and forced them to act as guides, but these Indians often led the expedition astray or escaped, leaving it lost. The pigs having now all died, the Spanish were reduced to eating herbs, roots and wild fruits as they cut their way through deep vegetation, following the banks of a fast-flowing river that finally led into the Napo River, a tributary—although the Spanish did not know this—of the mighty Amazon.

Eyes watched the Spanish from the forest as they stumbled along, but these watching natives disappeared when the Spanish attempted to capture them. Those Indians unlucky enough to be caught had by now learned how savage these bearded invaders were and so repeated the same mantra—pointing down the Napo, they claimed that this mysterious golden king lived in *that* direction (anywhere but here). But at this point the Spanish, reduced to eating lizards and now dying off themselves, simply wanted to find food. Seeing Indians in their fleet canoes and realising that the rivers they increasingly encountered were the highways through this wilderness, the Spanish stopped and built a rough boat, which they called a brigantine. They put those who were the weakest aboard the ship, which was paddled down the Napo while the stronger conquistadors pushed their way through the jungles on the banks.

Soon even this halting progress became impossible. With more and more of the men sickening, Gonzalo Pizarro halted the party and held a conference on the banks of the Napo. They had heard of a great river and a wealthy country about ten days' journey away, but such were the dire straits of the expedition that Pizarro was certain that most of the men would not be able to make it that far. By now it was not gold that Pizarro was

after, simply food and shelter. Francisco de Orellana then suggested a solution—that he take a group of men down the river in the brigantine, find this wealthy land and bring back supplies to the rest of them. Pizarro thought long and hard about this, and decided to acquiesce. On 26 December 1541, Orellana left the camp with fifty-nine men and the brigantine. Pizarro and 140 men stayed behind.

The village of plenty

Orellana and his small party paddled for nine days—a distance of perhaps 1000 kilometres (620 miles)—with the swift currents becoming swifter, moving them farther and farther away from Pizarro and the stranded expedition. At one point, an underwater log stove in the bottom of the boat, but they repaired it and continued, desperate to find food, eating forest roots and gnawing on pieces of leather. In early January they heard, in the distance, the unnerving sound of heavy, incessant drumming. At first they thought that this was an auditory hallucination brought on by the delirium caused by their fevers, but as the river carried them along, they realised it was real. Orellana insisted that they put on armour and man a watch as the river coursed through unrelenting jungle. The drumming grew louder and then they rounded a bend and came upon four canoes full of Indians, who turned and paddled away as fast as they could. Orellana and his men gave chase.

In a short while they came upon a village, which was deserted but contained, blessedly, food. The men set about eating 'with so much eagerness that they thought they would never satisfy themselves'. Even so, they were wary, 'their shields on their shoulders and their swords under their arms'. Finally, the Indians, who had been watching from the jungle, returned, and here we can see the difference between the command styles of Francisco de Orellana and Gonzalo Pizarro. Instead of immediately attacking the natives, Orellana, who had troubled to learn some of the local languages, gave them gifts and asked politely for more food in return, which the Indians brought. The next day, Orellana addressed a gathering of the Indian chiefs and claimed the land for the King of Spain. No one knows how much of this the Indians understood, but they did understand that this Spaniard was not attempting to have semi-feral dogs chew them to death, and so they responded with hospitality for the bearded strangers.

Having rested for a while, Orellana and his men were faced with what was literally a life or death choice: to return to Gonzalo Pizarro and the rest of the expedition, or to push on to the huge river that the Indians assured them lay ahead.

Controversy

The dilemma was clear to everyone in the party. They had promised to return with food and supplies for their suffering comrades back upriver, but they had barely survived themselves—had paddled for days through a 'foodless country' until they came to the sound of drums and the village of plenty. To paddle back upstream through this same country would take them twice as long, since they would be moving against the swift current. They would certainly run out of any supplies they had with them, more of them would die—seven of Orellana's men had already perished on their journey downstream—and they would arrive unable to help Pizarro's men, who, no doubt, were already dying off.

The only sensible decision to make, if they wanted to survive, was to move on. Yet this was a powerful and emotional step to take, because they knew (or assumed) that they would be leaving their friends and comrades to die back there in the endless rain and pestilential jungle. Orellana, although he was pragmatic enough to realise that they needed to move on, offered to take his men back to Pizarro, but this was probably merely so that he could later say that he had offered to return. The men in any event refused. Among them was a Dominican priest, Friar Gaspar de Carvajal, who was keeping the main record of the expedition. He wrote that the men 'swore by the sign of the Cross and the four sacred Gospels' that they wanted Orellana to lead them onward. And so Orellana acquiesced.

However, Gonzalo Pizarro would not see things in quite the same light and did his best to brand Orellana a traitor for not coming back, claiming that he displayed 'the greatest cruelty that ever faithless men have shown'. This was a smear job that has lasted for hundreds of years. Ultimately, while it is only natural that Pizarro would feel Orellana's failure to return as a betrayal, moving ahead was the only responsible decision that Orellana could make, given the circumstances.

'To guide us to the sea'

Once the decision had been made, Orellana turned to practical matters. He was certain the mighty river just ahead would take them out into the Atlantic Ocean on the east coast of Brazil—in fact, he assumed it would be but a short distance before they encountered ocean waves. But the boat they were currently using would simply fall apart in the rough Atlantic swells, 'if God saw fit to guide us to the sea', as Carvajal wrote. Therefore, Orellana told the men they needed to build a bigger and better boat. This seemed a nearly impossible task, in the middle of the wilderness, for men who were not shipbuilders but, as Carvajal wrote, two men approached Orellana and said they could build a blacksmith's forge to make nails from odd bits of metal and old horseshoes. Another journal-keeper, the conquistador Antonio de Herrera, wrote that 'timber for the ship was cut and prepared with great labour, which the men endured with much willingness, and in thirty-five days she was launched, caulked with cotton, and the seams filled with pitch which was given to them by the Indians'.

On 4 April, Orellana and his men set off down the Napo. For a month, they passed through seemingly uninhabited wilderness, with the jungle coming right down to the banks. Then the river grew wider and so fast moving that they were unable to fish as they coursed along. Without realising it, they had entered the Amazon—the longest river in the world (although disputed recent measurements have the Nile beating it by a nose)—which contains one-fifth of the world's fresh water supply and runs 6000 kilometres (4000 miles) to the Atlantic Ocean. The river is so wide it is often called the 'River Sea' and contains islands the size of small countries. The first European to see the Amazon was the Spanish explorer Vicente Pinzón, who sailed into its mouth in 1500—the Amazon's estuary is some 400 kilometres (250 miles) wide—but no white person had ever traversed its entire length.

Orellana and the expedition were a fascinating sight to the Indians of the Amazon basin. Not only

 ## THE FATE OF GONZALO PIZARRO AND HIS MEN

Once he realised that Francisco de Orellana was not coming back, Gonzalo Pizarro knew that he needed to take matters into his own hands, if he were to survive. The first thing he did was to steal four or five canoes from the Indians and send men a few days upriver, hoping to find food, but they returned empty-handed. He himself began to search for Orellana and ended up finding abundant food, but (as he stated in his letter to the king) he did not try to pursue the man he now called 'the rebel'—Orellana.

Instead, he decided to return home. He probably set out with about a hundred men, having already lost forty to starvation and disease. He managed to re-cross the Napo and retrace his steps back through the jungle, but within a short space of time his food supplies ran out. The trek was a horrendous one. 'On account of constant water from above and below [from rain and swamps], we were always wet and our clothes were always rotten', wrote Pizarro. After they ate their horses, they ate their dogs. They finally emerged from the jungle and found themselves in the foothills of the Andes. After an arduous crossing of the mountains, they at last arrived back in Quito in August 1542, as Orellana was exiting the mouth of the Amazon. Two hundred and fifty Spaniards had left this high city three years before. Now eighty starving wretches in rags returned, men 'who began to eat with such will that it was necessary to stop them', lest they harm themselves.

Pizarro would blame Orellana for the failure of the expedition and would attempt to smear his reputation as best he could. But, in the meantime, he set about doing what a Pizarro did best—scheming and fighting. While he was gone, his brother Francisco, conqueror of Peru, had been assassinated by his enemies, and a new viceroy was placed over the country. Gonzalo Pizarro rose in rebellion against him and briefly controlled the country, until the Spanish monarch sent a force against him. He was defeated in battle and executed on 10 April 1548.

did the men fill the larger and newer ship they had built, but they also brought along the older one, as well as numerous dugout canoes they had stolen or traded for with the locals they encountered. In May, they were told by Indians they met that they were approaching the territory of a powerful chief named Machiparo, who held sway over some fifty thousand people. They proceeded cautiously and one morning, according to Carvajal, saw in the distance villages 'gleaming white' in the sun. All at once, the river was filled:

> *... with a great many canoes, all equipped for fighting [and] gaily-coloured. [The warriors in them] carried shields which are made of the shell-like skins of lizards and the hides of manatees and tapirs, as tall as a man, for they cover them entirely. They were coming on with a great yell, playing on many drums and wooden trumpets, threatening us as if they were going to devour us.*

Orellana knew that the time for combat was at hand. He ordered the two brigantines to be lashed together and told everyone onboard both boats to make ready with their crossbows and harquebuses. Then the men watched in grim silence as the canoes of the Indians dashed toward them, coming on 'in such an orderly fashion and with so much arrogance that it seemed as if they already had us in their hands'. When the lead canoes got close enough, Orellana gave the order to fire but, unfortunately, the gunpowder was wet and would not ignite. The battle was left to the crossbowmen, who shot their iron bolts into the enemy, knocking Indians into the water and causing the canoes to retreat momentarily. But soon they came on again, full of screaming warriors.

Running for their lives

Thus began an epic chase down the fast waters of the Amazon, with the Spanish fighting off wave after wave of canoes full of Indians, who appeared to want to board the brigantines. After some time of this, Orellana decided that he needed to land at a village, both to get supplies and to create defensive positions to fight off the harrying Indians. It was a bold decision, for after they beached the boats the party was besieged both from land and sea. It is a sign of how hungry the Spanish were that even as they were fighting they were amassing the considerable foodstuffs of one of Machiparo's villages—turtles (kept by the tribes in pens), meat, fish and biscuits made of cornmeal. Yet the fighting on land was so fierce that eighteen of the Spanish were wounded. Deciding to retreat back to the boats, Orellana carried the wounded wrapped up in blankets, so that they looked like sacks of looted corn and the enemy would not know they had hurt them.

Back on the river, the expedition headed downstream, but their relief at escape was to be short-lived. Each time they passed a village, the men would leap into their canoes and come out to fight the Spanish with arrows and blowpipes, before falling behind, and then another village would send its own canoes out. The Spanish fought continuously until they were 'thoroughly exhausted' and Orellana felt compelled to put in to shore again, this time on an uninhabited island, in order to feed and rest his soldiers. But no sooner did they light their cook fires than the Indians were attacking again, and after several skirmishes Orellana ordered the boats back in the water and the chases began all over again. Carvajal noticed that shamans had begun to appear among the Indians, 'There went about among these men and the war canoes four or five sorcerers, all daubed with whitewash and with their mouths full of ashes, which they blew into the air ... as a form of enchantment'.

The enchantment, whatever it was, nearly worked. With Indian canoes chasing them, they entered a narrow part of the river that was overlooked by high banks. Indians lined both sides of it, while the canoes closed in behind the Spanish. It was obviously going to be a tough spot to escape from, but then the expedition had a bit of luck. On shore, waving his arms and yelling, was a man who was the obvious leader of this tribe. Finding his powder at last dry, one Spanish harquebusier took careful aim, fired, and hit the man right in the chest. His warriors were so astonished at the blast and the death of their chief that they were distracted and the Spanish escaped. Finally, after two more days and nights of running fights, they found themselves free of their tormentors.

But only momentarily.

'In a country so well-peopled'

Riding down the Amazon was turning out to be akin to running a gauntlet. The area was much more heavily populated than they would have imagined—according to Carvajal, in some sections there was barely a crossbow shot's distance between villages. (Scientists for centuries have disputed Carvajal's description, thinking that the soil of the Amazon basin, beneath its triple-canopied jungle, is

Amazonian Indians, such as those encountered by Francisco de Orellano on his extraordinary voyage down the Amazon River to the ocean.

simply too poor, too deprived of nutrients and sunlight, to support such large populations. But recent studies have shown that Carvajal was probably accurate in his depiction—human beings once inhabited the Amazon jungle, especially along the rivers, in much larger numbers than they do now.)

As soon as the Spanish left the country of Machiparo they came into the land of another great chief, Omagua. At the first village they came to the warriors were lined up, ready to get into their canoes and attack, but finally Orellana had had enough. In true conquistador fashion, he decided to launch a pre-emptive strike. Landing at the village, his men charged into the Indians, slaughtering them ruthlessly and driving them away from their homes. The village was fortified with a palisade and the Spanish made good use of this to drive off attackers while they rested and ate.

It was now, according to Carvajal's diary, 16 May 1542, and the men had come, they estimated, 340 leagues (about 2000 kilometres or 1200 miles). Getting into their boats again, they wearily moved onward. The river became wider and wider and the Spanish sailed as far into midstream as possible, to avoid surprise attacks. In early June they came upon the River Negro, whose dark waters formed a visible black slash into the Amazon that could be seen for kilometres. They began to notice that they were in a more civilised countryside. Some of the villages contained 'villas' with fine plates, bowls, goblets and candelabra made of glass and a kind of porcelain. There was also a fair amount of gold and silver. From these villages ran what Carvajal called 'many roads [and] fine highways to the inland country'. Orellana ventured down one of these roads, which after a short while became 'more like a royal highway [in Spain]'. (Once again, these depictions were, until only recently, thought to be fanciful, but there is increasing evidence of sophisticated Amazonian civilisations about which we know next to nothing.)

Interestingly enough, seeing this broad highway caused the intrepid conquistador to return quickly to the boats, thinking it not 'prudent' to advance any farther. Had Orellana been stronger and had his men been in better shape, such a highway might have meant the road to a city of gold, as it had with the Inca and Mexica. But Orellana now was after not shining spires but, as Carvajal put it, 'discovery' of a different type—meaning rescue and safety. The Spanish now never spent the night ashore. 'In a country so well-peopled,' wrote Carvajal, 'it was not advisable to remain on shore during the night'.

'The excellent land of the Amazons'

Not long after they passed the River Negro, the conquistadors had the encounter that would make their trip notorious in history and give the great river they travelled its name. One morning, they landed at one village where the Indians did not try to attack them. These people told them that they were forced to pay tribute in parrot feathers to a tribe of fierce women who ruled the area. Can this have been true? It is hard to say. One wonders, really, how much of the language the Spanish understood and also whether or not it was possible that the Indians were kidding them, having perhaps heard that the Spanish, while fierce themselves, were credulous—innocents, as far as the seasoned Amazonian Indians were concerned. But as they journeyed farther downstream, the Spanish heard more and more tales of ferocious warrior women. Without yet encountering them, they began to refer to them as Amazons, after the fighting women of Greek myth who lived in what is now the Ukraine.

While no Amazons appeared as yet, the Spanish began to travel through an area terrifying in appearance. As they sped past on the current they saw, in one village, seven gibbets on which, according to Carvajal, were nailed 'many dead men's heads'. Another village appeared to be deserted, but when the Spanish approached it, five thousand warriors leaped from hiding—an obvious trap. At one point they captured an 'Indian girl of much intelligence', who told them that 'Christians like ourselves' were held captive in the interior. Carvajal speculated that these were the survivors of a shipwreck, but the party did not feel able to rescue them and they pressed forward. (No proof of Christians living in the Amazon at that time has ever been found.)

Now at last, says Carvajal, 'we came suddenly upon the excellent land and dominion of the Amazons'. Being forced to put into a village for food, Orellana attempted to trade with the Indians, but they mocked him and told the Spanish they were to be captured and taken to the Amazons. A fierce fight broke out and the Spanish were barely holding their own when suddenly about a dozen women fighters appeared, fighting 'so courageously that the Indians did not dare to turn their backs; anyone who did turn their back [the Amazons] killed with clubs right there before us'.

These fierce women, Carvajal wrote, 'are very white and tall, and have their hair very long, and braided and wound about their head, and they are very robust, and go about naked, with just their privy parts covered, doing as much fighting as ten

Detail of a 1565 map of the northern part of South America, showing the mighty Amazon River.

PIZARRO VS ORELLANA:
HISTORY'S VERDICT

On 26 December 1541, when Gonzalo Pizarro, waving and shouting encouragement, saw Francisco de Orellana and his fifty-seven men leave, he expected them back within twelve days, with life-giving supplies of food for Pizarro and his 140 ill and dying men. And when Orellana did not come back, Pizarro, enraged, plotted to exact his revenge. It was quite possibly his anger at Orellana that kept him going on his arduous trek back to civilisation. In any event, having returned to safety at roughly the same time as Orellana and his men, and having learned that his former lieutenant was alive, Pizarro sat down on 2 September 1542 and wrote a letter to the king of Spain.

In it, he laid out charges against Orellana, the main one being that as far as he was concerned, Orellana had plotted all along to leave him and his men behind and had never had any intention of returning to help them.

> Being confident that Captain Orellana would do as he said, because he was my lieutenant, I told him that I was pleased at the idea of his going for food. With the confidence that I had in him, I gave him the brigantine, the canoes, and sixty men. But, paying no heed to what he owed to the services of Your Majesty and to what it was his duty to do as he had been told by me, his captain … he went down the river …

Orellana also, said Pizarro, took all the expedition's harquebuses and crossbows with him.

There is a good deal of self-serving exaggeration here. While Carvajal and others present agree that Orellana came up with the idea of leading a party to find food, they also agree that Pizarro agreed wholeheartedly to this plan as the only feasible one. Secondly, according to Carvajal, Orellana took with him only three harquebuses and five crossbows. And why would Pizarro not have protested if Orellana—his second-in-command after all—had prepared to depart leaving him entirely without weapons?

Orellana had to make a hard choice. He did not know where he was going by heading down the Amazon—he felt certain the river would lead to the sea but did not know that it would take 6000 kilometres (4000 miles) to do so. But he knew that pushing back against a hard current to try to rescue Pizarro and his men would probably lead to death by starvation for both parties. He risked a great deal by not going back to Pizarro. As the Amazon historian Anthony Smith writes, if Pizarro or any of his party survived, Orellana would lose 'his position in Peru, his wealth there … his prestige, his everything. To fall afoul of the Pizarro family, certainly in Peru at that time, was to lose all hope of gain and probably one's life'.

Orellana, most historians now agree, made the only sensible choice. He would live with the consequences, and he did, though not for long.

Indian men'. They wielded powerful bows. In fact, the women shot so many arrows into the brigantines that they looked 'like porcupines'. Fortunately, says Carvajal, 'the Lord was pleased to give strength to our companions, who killed seven or eight' of the women, and the Spanish escaped.

This was their last encounter with the Amazons (although Carvajal would describe in great detail the customs of these women) but, in a sense, they would steal the thunder of Orellana's great journey. Although his men had begun to call the great river Orellana's River—and, in fact, it appears this way on European maps for some years after—it soon became commonly known as the Amazon.

'So great was the joy we felt'

The expedition passed out of the land of the Amazons, but continued to have to fight its way down the river. In one of many skirmishes, an arrow pierced the eye of Gaspar de Carvajal and 'went through to the other side', as he wrote. 'I have lost the eye and [even now] I am not without suffering … although Our Lord, without my deserving it, has been kind enough to grant me life so that I may mend my ways and serve him better.'

Despite this grievous injury, Carvajal 'rejoiced not a little' with the rest of the men when they suddenly felt the pulling of the tide, meaning that they were nearing the sea. On most rivers the tides do not extend far inland but, of course, the Amazon was different—they were still fairly far upstream when they felt this pull. Nonetheless, the expedition stopped to make the vessels as fit as possible for the ocean voyage they were facing, and then continued on for days. Finally, on 7 August 1542—St Louis's Day—'we passed out of the mouth of the river', as Carvajal put it, and into the ocean. They had been nine months on the Amazon. Amazingly, only

three of Orellana's men had been killed. Both brigantines then set sail north, up the coast of Brazil. Despite being separated for nine days, they reunited in Trinidad, safe at last. 'So great was the joy we felt', wrote Carvajal, 'that I shall not be able to express it'.

Leaving his men behind, Francisco de Orellana caught a ship to take him back across the Atlantic and made his report to King Charles of Spain, hoping to get royal backing for a return trip to really explore the Amazon interior. But back in Quito, Gonzalo Pizarro—having survived an arduous trip of his own—was writing a letter accusing Orellana of high treason. There were many who felt Orellana had betrayed Pizarro by leaving him there to die, while others believed he took the only course of action open to him. The result was that Charles did sponsor Orellana for another expedition to Brazil, but in half-hearted fashion. His ships were poor, his sailors lacked experience, and his supplies were deficient. By the time he arrived at the mouth of the Amazon around Christmas 1545, he had lost some ninety sailors to sickness.

Even so, Orellana headed upriver for 100 leagues. Now the scenario repeated itself: his men began to starve and die—fifty-seven more died during his three months' sailing up the great river— and Orellana went off with a small party to find food for them. There ensued months of grievous wanderings as the party was whittled down by disease, starvation and hostile Indians. A few men managed to patch together boats and sail them back to Trinidad, much as Orellana had three years earlier. Francisco de Orellana was not with them, however. He had died of disease deep in the jungle, having succumbed, finally, to the irresistible but deadly pull of the Amazon.

PART 3

FRONTIER ENCOUNTERS IN AMERICA

Pocahontas, the Indian maiden who saved the life of John Smith. In later years she joined the English colonists, marrying one of them and travelling to London.

Ætatis suæ 21. Aº. 1616.

...oaks als Rebecka daughter to the mighty Prince
...hatan Emperour of Attanoughkomouck als Virginia
...verted and baptized in the Christian faith, and

FIRST ARRIVALS IN VIRGINIA

The English in Jamestown, 1606–1609

By the 1570s, the English were growing worried. Despite the efforts of such explorers as John Cabot, who discovered the North American continent five years after Columbus sailed—and, of course, 500 years after the Norse—they did not have a real stake in the New World. Their sworn enemies, the Spanish, were growing rich off their discoveries in the Caribbean, South America and Mexico, had established a foothold in Florida and were slowly moving north. While the French had not yet organised a real effort to control what would become Canada, their trappers and fishermen were an increasing presence along the St Lawrence River and off the coast of Newfoundland.

There had been a few English expeditions to the American mainland during the sixteenth century, expeditions undertaken by now mainly forgotten men like Richard Hore and Sir Humphrey Gilbert, and although these had not met with much success,

they had whetted English appetite for more exploration in the area that would come to be called Virginia after England's Virgin Queen, Elizabeth I. Virginia, as the English envisioned it, originally extended along America's Atlantic coast from Canada south to the present-day state of South Carolina. Of course, France and Spain scoffed at such a massive claim and they were right—had the English defeated any savage nation there, won any vast territory through their blood, sweat and tears?

By 1584 Elizabeth I knew it was time to take action, and thus she granted her favourite courtier, Sir Walter Raleigh, a patent to become 'Lord and Governor of Virginia'. In the spring of that year, Raleigh sent out a scouting expedition consisting of two ships captained by Philip Amadas and Arthur Barlowe, both colleagues of his. It was their job to sail their little barques across the Atlantic to the Caribbean—the prevailing winds made this a faster route than going directly across the ocean—and then head up the American coastline seeking likely spots to plant the first English colony in the New World.

'You have nice clothes'

The two ships sailed to the coastline of what is now North Carolina and discovered the Outer Banks, a 300-kilometre (185-mile) long string of sand dunes and barrier islands that conceal a huge, island-dotted sound, beyond which is the mainland coast. The area within the Outer Banks would be a perfect place to begin a small and vulnerable colony, Barlowe thought, hidden from the eyes of probing Spanish men-of-war. Entering what is now Pamlico Sound, the ships landed on the island

of Hatarask, taking possession of it 'in the right of the Queene's most excellent majestie'. Then they noisily explored the game-rich landscape, firing off their guns to flush birds from the trees.

After several days on the island, the rather oblivious English began to realise they were being watched. Strange noises emanated from the underbrush. Figures flitted back and forth in the shadows. At last a few Indians—these were Algonquin, woodland Indians who inhabited much of the eastern seaboard of America at the time—approached in a small canoe. Things did not go so well. 'As soone as they saw us, [the Indians] began to make a great and horrible crye, as people which never before had scene men appareled like us, and camme away makinge out crys like wild-beasts

A weroance, or chieftain, of the Algonquin, the Indian people who inhabited the area of Virginia at the time of the first English settlement.

THE MYSTERY OF
ROANOKE ISLAND

One of the reasons John Smith and his men spent so much time tracking through the back country around Jamestown—aside from seeking food and a water passage to the Pacific—was to find survivors from Walter Raleigh's colony at Roanoke.

Over a hundred men and women had been left behind on the island in 1587 when John White, Walter Raleigh's friend who had landed them there, sailed back to England. He promised to return that spring of 1588 with supplies and more colonists. In the meantime, a signal was arranged—if they left Roanoke, they were to carve their destination on a tree. If they were in trouble—under attack by the Indians or the Spanish—they were to carve a cross next to the destination.

Unfortunately, the outbreak of the Anglo-Spanish War in 1588 prevented White returning to Roanoke Island until 1590. When he and his men landed, they walked about the island blowing a trumpet, but got no reply at all—the entire island, once inhabited by numerous tribes, was completely empty. However, in the forest, he found the letters 'CRO' and 'CROATOAN' carved into two trees—these were sure to stand for Croatoan Island, which was nearby. There were no crosses, so this meant that the colonists had left of their own accord.

White spent the night on the island and then decided to go to Croatoan Island the next day, but a powerful storm arose, one so fierce that it blew his small ship as far across the Atlantic as the Azores, making return impossible. When an English ship finally arrived to search Croatoan Island, it was empty, and thus the mystery of what quickly became known as 'the lost colony' grew. Historians have put forth several theories—that the colonists decided to sail back across the Atlantic in their small pinnace (almost suicidal) or that they were massacred by the Spanish or Indians. This latter possibility might seem likely, but White found absolutely no sign of carnage on Roanoke and the settlers, being heavily armed, would not have allowed themselves to be taken away without a fight.

Another possibility, which has gained credence in recent years, is that the settlers were assimilated into an Indian tribe. As this story goes, they did indeed move to Croatoan Island, where a split in the company occurred. The smaller group stayed with the Croatoan Indians, which points to the prevalence of grey eyes among their people, as well as surnames that belonged to the Roanoke colonists, as proof of this. The larger group moved with an Indian tribe to the Chesapeake Bay area, where eventually they were murdered by Chief Powhatan to keep them from linking up with the Jamestown settlers. Supposedly, Powhatan confessed this to John Smith, although many historians do not believe this part of John Smith's Jamestown account.

In any event, without definitive proof, the mystery of the lost colony will remain a mystery.

or men out of their wyts', wrote one member of the expedition.

However, the English managed to calm these Indians down by offering them 'glasses, knives, babies [dolls] and other trifles'. The next day the brother of the Indian king approached, with a party of forty others, and the two groups examined each other curiously. Barlowe described these men as a 'very handsome and goodly people', but their appearance was, from the English point of view, quite curious. The leader's skin was dyed a 'colour yellowish' and his head was shaved on both sides with only a centre ridge atop his skull. He wore only a tiny loincloth.

The Indians for their part were just as impressed by the English. They kept exclaiming *Wingandacoa!* which Barlowe assumed was the name of the country they lived in and thus put it in his official report to the queen. It turned out the Indians were just repeating the compliment 'You have nice clothes!' After a bout of trading with their hosts, in which the English got by far the better of the deal, from their point of view—the Indians were willing to trade twenty animal skins for a single knife or tin bowl—they were invited to dine with the Algonquin. Barlowe and the other men were quite impressed by the Indian women, particularly the wife of Granganimeo, the king's brother. Unlike the rest of the women, she did not leave her breasts bare, but 'was well-favoured, of meane stature, and very bashfull'. She and the other women of the village insisted on stripping off the stinking clothes of the English and washing the men from head to toe, which naturally met with their approval.

The first colony

Exploring the area, the English decided that the best place for a colony, among the hundreds of islands that abounded in the sound behind the Outer Banks, was Roanoke Island, a fertile, heavily wooded strip of land. Thirteen kilometres (eight miles) long,

it abounded with game and had numerous sources of fresh water. After five weeks, Barlowe and Amadas sailed back to England and reported to Sir Walter Raleigh that they had found the site for the first English colony in the New World.

In 1585 a group of colonists landed on Roanoke, all men, with the intention of building a fort and preparing the way for settlers. Unfortunately, in a pattern that would become typical of them in their dealings with the inhabitants of North America, the English did not consider for a moment that the land they were settling had belonged to the Algonquin for generations. Roanoke Island itself was already heavily settled by the Indians and its resources were stretched to the maximum. At first the Indians were willing to help the English, but soon friction arose, resulting in the sacking of an Indian village and the execution by burning of its *weroance*, or chieftain. In 1587 more colonists arrived, including women, but tensions with the Indians, as well as scarce resources, made it difficult for them to survive on any more than a subsistence level—and they were in constant fear of Algonquin attack. Because of war with the Spanish, a relief force was unable to return to supply this group until 1590, at which point—in one of the most famous disappearing acts in American history—it was discovered that everyone had simply vanished.

This put a damper on British hopes of colonisation, but not for long. The defeat of the Spanish in the Anglo-Spanish War of 1585–1604, particularly the destruction of the Spanish Armada in 1588, gave the English a huge morale boost and encouraged them to expand into North America. In 1606, three years after the death of Queen Elizabeth I, the Virginia Company was formed 'to establish a colony of sundrie of our people'. One group of settlers would eventually be sent north, to what is present-day New England, but the first group was to go to America at a more southerly latitude and colonise Virginia.

'The soil was good and fruitful'

In the December of 1606, about a hundred 'gentlemen, artisans, and laborers' sailed to America aboard three ships, which took four and a half months to cross the stormy Atlantic. On board were men who would figure prominently in the future of the English in America: George Percy, son of an earl, would become a president of the colony, as would Edward-Maria Wingfield, another high-ranking passenger.

Also along was a soldier and commoner named John Smith. Smith, who would become the most famous by far of the men who sailed to America on that first expedition, was short, even by the standards of the day: probably no more than 1.6 metres (5 feet 4 inches). He had bright red hair and a shaggy beard, which gave him the appearance of a hirsute elf or leprechaun. Yet he was a person one needed to take very seriously. The most experienced soldier aboard, Smith had fought all over the world—with the Dutch against the Spanish, and with the Austrians against the Turks. The last captured and enslaved him, but the redoubtable Smith escaped and made his way back to England in time to join the Virginia Company expedition.

In his mid-twenties at the time, Smith had a knack for making powerful friends and enemies in equal number. His friends would include mariner Henry Hudson (see page 134) and high-ups in the Virginia Company, but his enemies numbered both Percy and Wingfield.

During this first Atlantic crossing, Smith, no shrinking violet, made his dissatisfaction about how the expedition was being run so far—everything from the ocean route being taken to how rations were divided on shipboard—amply evident. He was so annoying (probably in part because he was usually right) that Wingfield had him arrested on trumped-up charges of fomenting a mutiny and thus John Smith arrived in the New World under heavy guard.

On 14 May 1607 the expedition landed on Jamestown Island, in the James River—named, like the settlement, after King James—100 kilometres (60 miles) from the mouth of Chesapeake Bay. The Virginia Company had ordered the men to settle at least 160 kilometres (100 miles) from the ocean, both for protection against the Spanish and in order to better explore the interior of the country, for England, like other European powers in the New World, still hoped to find a water route through the American continent to China. Jamestown Island was not quite that far west, but it seemed the perfect place. It was actually a peninsula that became an island at high tide but was connected to the mainland only by a narrow, easily defensible strip of land. The water was so deep that ships could tie up to trees right on its shores. And, in the height of the Virginia spring, it was beautiful to these weary voyagers. 'The soil was good and fruitful', George Percy wrote, 'with excellent good timber. There are also great store of vines in bigness of a man's thigh, running up to the tops of trees, in great abundance ...'

When the ships had neared land, the leaders had opened a sealed box, which contained orders from the Virginia Company as to who among the passengers would be the officials in a council that would help govern the new colony. Smith's name was among this august company but Wingfield, who had been appointed president, refused to seat him.

Jamestown

At least, however, Smith was removed from chains to help begin the settlement that would first be known as James Fort and then Jamestown. Literally the day after landing, as Smith would later write, 'now falleth every man to work ... cut down trees ... pitch tents ... some make gardens, some nets'. However, Smith added critically, there were at first no fortifications 'but the boughs of trees cast together in the form of a half moon'.

This was to become an important issue in the colonists' first encounters with the Indians. Within a few days, two Indians from a local Algonquin tribe known as the Paspahegh came to the makeshift English settlement and told the English that their *weroance*, or chief, would be arriving in a few days with a deer as a gift. In fact, four days later, the chief arrived, not with fresh venison, but with '100 salvages armed'. This was a way to let the English know that they were at the mercy of the Indians in this strange land, yet at first the Indian chief seemed conciliatory, telling Wingfield through signs that 'he would give us as much land as we would desire'. It is hard to know how the English ascertained this, given the language barrier, but all seemed well until one of the Indians tried to snatch a prized metal axe from the belt of an English soldier. A scuffle ensued and the Indians left in a huff.

A short while later they returned, finally bringing with them the fresh venison that had been promised and, in apparent innocent friendship, proposed they stay the night within the English 'fort'. This the English were too wise to allow them to do and the Indians left, once again unhappy. On 27 May two hundred of them crept out of the woods and launched a furious assault on the colony. 'They came up allmost into the fort, shott through the tenttes', wrote Smith. Seventeen Englishmen were injured, one of them fatally, and a serving boy aboard one of the vessels also died. The English killed at least one of the Indians. Wingfield was nearly killed himself—an arrow went right through his beard.

After a battle that lasted an hour, the English trained their ships' cannon on their assailants and fired, in the process knocking down a huge tree limb and frightening away the Indians. But now the English realised that this new world was not going to be theirs for the plucking. Working at a furious pace, the colonists built a triangular fort whose walls were made of palisades—giant logs weighing

perhaps 400 kilograms (880 pounds) apiece—set upright next to each other in the ground. It took them only twenty days, but each day the workers were harried by Indians. Colonist Gabriel Archer kept a diary of the attacks:

> *May 28: Thursday we labored, pallozadoing our fort.*

> *May 29: Friday the salvages gave on again, but with more feare, not daring approche scarce within musket shotte. They hurt not any of us, but finding one of our dogges they killed him . . .*

> *May 30: Saturday we were quyet. Sunday they came lurking in the thickets and long grasse; and a gentleman one Eustace Clovell unarmed straggling without the fort, [they] shotte six arrows into him, wherwith he came runinge into the fort, crying Amre, Arme, thes stycking still. He lyved eight days, and dyed.*

In some instances of European contact, native weapons were no match for European guns, but this was not the case at this point in Virginia, where the Indians unleashed arrowheads made of bone or stone that were highly accurate at forty metres (130 feet)—Algonquin warriors could bring down a bird in flight—and could be fired faster than the clumsy harquebuses of the English. Outnumbered, and in some sense outgunned, the English were facing a formidable enemy.

The prophecy

The Jamestown colonists were not experiencing the random attacks of an enraged but minor tribe of Indians. Unbeknown to them, they had stumbled into a massive and highly organised Indian nation run by a single leader: the great Chief Powhatan. Powhatan, whose people called him Wahunsenacah, was a vigorous man in his late sixties whose empire ranged from Virginia all the way down to North Carolina. He was the son of a chief who had inherited the rule of six tribes from his father but, because he was ambitious, had ended up conquering twenty-two others. This was partially because his empire—like those of the Mongols or Shaka Zulu in Africa—was a martial one. Beginning at six years of age, boys were trained in the use of the bow and arrow, and their mothers would not give them food each morning until they finished their archery practice.

Because of Powhatan's broad empire and relative longevity, he was aware of the white men long before these English people came to settle in James Fort. He knew of Sir Walter Raleigh's abortive attempt at colonisation at Roanoke and also remembered an even earlier moment, when the Spanish landed at Chesapeake Bay and stole an Indian boy to take back to Spain with them.

Powhatan had no doubt that he could handle this small group of white men on their island, but something else disturbed him. Before the arrival of the English, one of his priests had issued a dire prophecy that 'from the Chesapeake Bay, a nation should arise which would dissolve and give end to his empier'. Powhatan had immediately ordered the extermination of a tribe of Indians living in Chesapeake Bay and thought no more of the matter. But now, with the arrival of these people, he began to wonder if the prophecy did not actually relate to them, instead.

For the time being, he decided that an attitude of watchful waiting would be best. It might be that the Indians would have to do little against the Europeans, after all. For one thing, on 22 June two of the three ships that had brought the colonists to James Fort had departed, as was planned, on their way back to England to make a report (a glowing one, despite circumstances to the contrary) to higher-ups at the

John Smith's map of Virginia, showing Chesapeake Bay, with the James River and Jamestown on the left.

Nova **VIRGINIÆ** TABVLA

Maſſawomeck

Maſſawomecks.

MANNAHOACKS.

Notar. explicatio.
⊞ *Domus Regum*
○ *Ordinariæ Domus*
✠ *Lucubrationes Anglorum*

HONI SOIT QVI MAL Y PENSE

Habitus fœminarum in Provincia Sasque ſahanougs.

Cheſapeack Bay.

SASQVESAHA·
NOVGH.

FINIFIMA

TOCKWOGHS.

KVSKARAWAOKS.

ATQVANAC

HVKES.

Chickahokin

Accocke

Virginia Company and to gather more supplies and colonists. For another, Powhatan's spies told him, that summer of 1607, that the white men were beginning to die off, one by one.

The English were subject to a number of pressures apart from being shot at every time they went outside the fort to answer the call of nature (Gabriel Archer records a couple of instances when colonists were turned into pincushions by Indian arrows while squatting over holes they had dug in the underbrush). Since they were unable to do any serious hunting or planting, their rations were running low, and they were allowed to eat from a communal kettle each day only 'a halfe pinte of wheat and as much barly boyled with water … and this having fried some 26 weeks in the ship's hold, contained as many wormes as graines'.

Many of the gentlemen along on the trip could not stomach such fare; with the daily dose of hard work thrown in, they grew weaker and weaker. There was also little fresh water. When they had settled at Jamestown, the river flowing by had been mainly fresh, but it became salty and brackish as the summer went on. By August, men were dying literally every day, until there were only about forty of the original colonists left. Most historians believe that the cause of the deaths was manifold—typhus, dysentery, starvation. The only bright spot for Jamestown's future was that John Smith had finally been awarded his rightful place on the council. People were beginning to realise that they were at war—with the Indians, with the elements—and that a strong soldier was needed.

'The fury of the salvages'

It was perhaps only natural in this atmosphere that men would begin to look for scapegoats to blame the colony's misfortune on, and President Edward-Maria Wingfield—an arrogant and egotistical fellow—came under fire. Smith, among others, accused him of hoarding food for his own private consumption, something he was probably not guilty of, although he did admit to roasting a squirrel, which he kept mainly for himself. His chief crime was that he was not, in fact, a true war leader—he did not know how to rally his people in adversity, had even neglected to cut down the tall grass around the fort, an elementary precaution to keep the Indians from using it for cover.

Wingfield was put under guard to await trial for his supposed crimes and a new president, John Ratcliffe, was elected. In the meantime, the surviving colonists, many of whom spent most of their time digging graves for their dead comrades, were merely waiting for 'the fury of the salvages' to fall upon them at any moment and annihilate them. But this did not happen. The reason is debatable. The Jamestown historian David A. Price calls the decision not to mount an all-out attack on the English 'a failure of leadership' on the part of Chief Powhatan. The chief may not have known quite how weak the English were but, given his ruthlessness with other Indian tribes, it is curious he let them stay alive— curious, and a fatal error.

In September, the English made an inventory of the supplies left in their storehouse and realised that they had only enough left for another two weeks. Food must be found or they would all starve to death. The colony's chief merchant, or supply officer, had died of disease, and so it was agreed that John Smith would be appointed in his stead. Smith took charge instantly and his commanding presence had a galvanising effect on the colony, many of whose members, especially the gentlemen among them, were refusing to work. As the autumn progressed, Smith led small groups of men on trading missions deeper into the country. Instinctively understanding the way the Indians thought, he acted as if he were not hard up for food and dispensed gifts generously—for he knew that Indians despised people who seemed poor and unable to care for themselves.

Playing the wealthy benefactor had the effect of opening up the floodgates of trade and Smith began to return to Jamestown with bushels of corn, fish, oysters, bread and venison. And now that autumn had arrived the broad Jamestown River was 'covered with swans, geese, ducks, and cranes'. With enough food being brought in, the colonists could turn to other concerns. Some of them began to criticise John Smith because he had not performed what was, after all, a chief mission of the Virginia Company trading officer—to head west looking for a water route to the Pacific Ocean. Thus, with such criticisms stinging his ears, Smith betook himself, on 9 December 1607, into the wilderness on a journey that would result in one of the most famous—and most debated—European–Indian encounters in history.

'My armes I cast from me'

Smith and nine men headed their small boat, or shallop, up the Chickahominy River, a tributary of the James, passing richly cultivated fields and towns teeming with people. They went at least sixty-five kilometres (forty miles), to a point where the river was only about two metres (six or seven feet) deep and where Smith began to think about turning around, lest he damage their precious boat. But, thinking of the 'malicious tungs' that would be wagging if he did not go farther in his journey, he stopped at a native village and engaged a guide and a canoe. Taking with him two colonists, he left the other seven behind with strict orders to remain on board the shallop and out in the river at all times. For while the Indians had seemed cooperative, Smith did not trust them.

He was right. When he disappeared around a bend in the river, a group of nearly naked Indian maidens appeared on the shore opposite the shallop and made signs to the men, indicating that they were interested in having them come ashore for a chat. These Jamestown colonists had lived without women for quite some time, and so it did not take much urging for them to row the shallop closer and leap onto the beach to engage the women in flirtatious conversation. Of course, it was a trap. Armed Indian warriors leaped out of hiding and attempted to capture the English, who raced back to the boat and headed back downriver.

All of them, that is, but an unfortunate gentleman named George Cassen, who was taken hostage, stripped, bound and then had his fingers cut off, joint by joint, with dull mussel shells. After this was accomplished, the skin was stripped from his face in the same way, he was disembowelled and his guts tossed into a fire in front of his eyes. Finally, he was tied to a stake and burned to death.

A similar fate was planned for Smith and his fellows. The Indians shadowed them upriver and, while Smith was out hunting with the guide, attacked the two Englishmen he had left behind and riddled them with arrows. The Indians then pursued and surrounded Smith, who, thinking quickly, took his guide captive and, his arm around the man's neck, fired off his pistol at the Indians as they hollered and shot arrows at him. His guide was yelling at the top of his lungs, telling his fellow warriors that Smith was the white men's leader, and thus should at all costs be taken alive.

Smith finally realised his position was hopeless. 'My armes I caste from me, til which none durst approch me', he wrote. He was then taken captive.

'A thunderous shout'

It turned out that the leader of the warriors who had captured Smith was a half-brother of Powhatan. He was intrigued and puzzled by this fierce, red-haired Englishman, whose thick winter clothing sprouted numerous arrows that had stuck but not penetrated. Smith's brave stand marked him as a warrior; what he did next probably helped save his life. He took out a compass and showed how the needle pointed in only one direction, no matter how many times they turned it. He then, he later wrote, gave the Indians a short lecture on 'the roundnesse of the earthe; and skies, the spheare of the sunne, moone and starres'. This incredibly self-possessed monologue on the nature of the universe bought Smith time—the Indians simply could not figure out what to do with him.

Powhatan's half-brother kept Smith captive for a few days in a hunting camp. On a few occasions he tied Smith to a tree and made as if to execute him, but then apparently changed his mind. Deciding that only Powhatan could make such a decision, he had Smith escorted through a bitterly cold Virginia winter on a week-long wilderness journey. By now it was shortly after Christmas, 1607. At one village, Smith was taken to a longhouse, where men he realised were high priests—including one wearing a Medusa-like hat made of stuffed snakes—performed rituals over him. After three days Smith was taken to Chief Powhatan's capital town of Werowocomoco, where no European had ever been. Outside Powhatan's palatial longhouse, two hundred 'grim courtiers', their heads painted bright red, looked at Smith as if 'he had beene a monster'.

Smith was finally taken inside and brought in front of the great chief, a well-built, though somewhat elderly, man wearing a raccoon robe and sitting on a low bed, surrounded by women whom Smith (with his experience as a Turkish captive) assumed to be his harem—and, in fact, the chief did have about a hundred wives. As Smith was led closer, everyone present gave a 'thunderous shout'. Powhatan, however, was calm, made sure that Smith was fed from a platter filled with 'various sundries', and then began to question him closely. He wanted to know, basically, what Smith and the English were doing in his country. Smith lied, telling the chief that after a fight with the Spanish, the English had been driven ashore with one of their ships disabled and had then sent the other two back to England for material to repair it.

He then told Powhatan that he had come this far inland because he was searching for an ocean on the other side of the country, a statement that was, as far as it went, true. Powhatan began to speak to his counsellors and priests, making a decision concerning his captive's fate. Should he execute Smith, as the leader of the people from Chesapeake Bay who may have been the ones the dire prophecy concerned? Or should he keep him and his booming new weapons around in order to make him fight against Powhatan's enemies?

Ultimately, the chief decided that it was safer to have Smith killed. He ordered two huge flat stones brought before him and placed by his feet, and then he summoned forth an executioner with a huge club—he would do Smith the favour of killing him instantly, rather than torturing him. Smith was led forward and forced to kneel, his head on the stones, and as the executioner raised his club, the English captain said his prayers. Probably greatly to his surprise, Smith then received divine intervention.

Pocahontas

Just as the club was about to come smashing down on Smith's head, the chief's favourite daughter leaped forward and threw herself over Smith, refusing to allow the executioner to proceed. Her name was Matoaoka, but her nickname—for her wild and mischievous ways—was Pocahontas, meaning 'little wanton'. Smith described her as quite lovely, a child 'of tenne years old [she was probably twelve], which not only for feature, countenance, and proportion much exceedeth any of the rest of his [Powhatan's] people, but for wit and spirit the only nonpareil in the country'.

Numerous American and English artists have captured this moment, with Pocahontas draped suggestively over Smith while looking pleadingly up at her father, but, whatever was going on there, it was not romance that inspired the young girl. If Smith's account is to be taken at face value—and after a period in which it was debunked most historians now accept that it happened as he said it did—it is possible Pocahontas felt what she perceived to be the unfairness of the situation. Possibly she wanted to demonstrate her power over Powhatan, for by all accounts she was quite spoiled. Given this interpretation, Powhatan was now faced with a dilemma. He did not want to argue with his daughter openly in front of the assembled multitudes—like many another man with a beautiful daughter, he had probably learned that he would lose such an argument and also lose face before his people. So he took the only course open to him. Declaring that Pocahontas's intervention had been a sign from the gods, he told Smith he could live. He then adopted Smith into his

tribe, named him a *weroance*, and sent him back to Jamestown with orders to deliver back to Powhatan two guns and a grindstone.

However, there is another point of view shared by numerous historians—that it was all an act, staged by the Indians. This point of view postulates that Smith did not understand that he was experiencing an adoption ceremony or ritual, which made him a vassal of Powhatan (in fact, made the entire English colony at Jamestown a servant nation of the Indian chief) and that there was never any intention of killing him. The only difficulty with this theory, as David A. Price points out, is that Smith remained in close contact with the Indians, including Pocahontas, for some time afterward and yet never appears to have ascertained the truth of the matter. Since

Pocahontas intercedes to prevent her father, Powhatan, killing John Smith, a pivotal moment in the history of English settlement in Virginia.

being rescued by a twelve-year-old is not exactly the light any brave soldier wants to put himself in, had Smith found out it was all staged he would certainly have written something to that effect.

The survival of the colony

By early January 1608, Smith was back at Jamestown. He had tricked the Indians who accompanied him out of giving them guns by offering to hand them two cannon, which weighed so much that they were naturally unable to budge them. But he did send numerous gifts to Powhatan, beginning a period in which a game of cat and mouse was played between the white men and the Indians. More supplies and colonists arrived in early 1608 and Smith, although he had probably saved the colony,

 THE LEGEND OF POCAHONTAS

Pocahontas has been celebrated in song, story, poetry and Disney cartoon, but most of these romantic fables bear little relation to reality. In some ways, however, her real life was even more incredible than the far-fetched stories told about her.

After saving John Smith's life and spending time learning English at the Jamestown colony, Pocahontas became one of the first Indians genuinely torn between two worlds—her family and ancestral way of life and the new and seemingly more glamorous world of the English. Her innocent visits to John Smith ended when he left the colony to return to England (she was told, cruelly, that he was dead) and around 1610 she married an Indian warrior. However, her relations with the English were far from over. Because hostilities with Powhatan continued, an Englishman named Samuel Argall—probably in his own way as good and aggressive a soldier as Smith—decided to kidnap Pocahontas and hold her until her father released some English prisoners he had detained.

Powhatan eventually agreed to a partial return of prisoners, but Pocahontas stayed with the English—according to Argall, because she wanted to. She was taken to another English settlement at Henrico in 1613 and there schooled in Christianity. She also met a tobacco planter named John Rolfe and seems to have genuinely fallen in love with him—and he with her, a struggle for a respectable English merchant. In any event, she was reunited with her father, who gave her his blessing, and she then married Rolfe on 4 April 1614, after being baptised and given the name Rebecca.

When a Virginia Company ship headed back to England in 1616, Rolfe, Pocahontas and their young son, Thomas, were on it. Pocahontas was dressed in English clothes, presented to the court of King James I and even got a chance to see her old friend John Smith again. After seven months in London, Pocahontas and her husband and child boarded a ship, heading back to America, but the vessel had only got as far as Gravesend, on the English coast, when Pocahontas grew ill and had to be taken off. With her distraught husband at her side, she died, possibly of tuberculosis, at the age of twenty-two. She is buried in Gravesend, never having made it home, but will always be seen as a link between two peoples.

remained a controversial figure, since he had begun to insist that all men, including gentlemen, work or they would not receive any food at all. On a lighter note, one visitor to the fort at Jamestown that year was young Pocahontas, who had taken such a liking to the English that she now spent a good deal of time with John Smith, whom she called 'father' and who had an avuncular relationship with her. When the two were not exchanging stories, Pocahontas liked to play with a few of the English children who had arrived with the second shipload of colonists, doing cartwheels (Pocahontas completely naked) on the hard-packed dirt of the fort.

Pocahontas would be an important factor in Jamestown's survival, eventually marrying the tobacco merchant John Rolfe and moving to England in 1616. Smith himself garnered enemies, as usual, because of his brusque manner and because he continually claimed that the gentlemen among the colonists were not doing their share—that these privileged men from England were 'ten times more fit to spoil a commonwealth then either to begin one or but help maintain one'. In the summer of 1609, more ships arrived bearing colonists, and among this group were numerous gentlemen who were literally out to murder Smith. One day that autumn, while out on the river in search of more food for the colony, someone—at least, as Smith tells it—set fire to the powder bag he carried, causing it to explode and cause him serious injuries.

Smith then decided it was time to head back for England, which he did in October 1609, never to return to Virginia, though he later headed a voyage to Massachusetts Bay and was responsible for naming the northeastern portion of the present-day United States New England. After his departure from Virginia, the colony nearly perished in a winter that was dubbed 'the starving time'—only sixty settlers out of 214 emerged alive in the spring. But gradually the colony got stronger, fighting off disease, starvation and Indian attack, to become the first real English foothold in the New World. As was typical of English colonisation, this was a mixed blessing. Powhatan's people were gradually decimated and, in 1619, the first of hundreds of thousands of African slaves were brought to the colony. But, the same year, the first real representative assembly in North America met in Jamestown Church on 30 July, a harbinger of the American democracy that would grow 150 years later.

SAVAGE MEETINGS
IN AN UNFORGIVING
WILDERNESS

Henry Hudson, 1609–1611

On a frigid June day in 1611, in a salty bay still filled with ice and surrounded by frozen wilderness, one of the great explorers of the Age of Exploration was forcibly placed in a small boat, along with his son and seven other sickly men. They were given a little powder and shot, and some rope, and a small amount of food, and then the line tying them to the larger ship they had come from—the *Discovery*—was severed.

The explorer's name was Henry Hudson and he had just been abandoned by his mutinous crew. This was not like being cut loose in the balmy seas of the South Pacific. He was in the large saltwater gulf that Hudson had thought would carry him to the Northwest Passage he sought and that would soon be named after him: Hudson Bay. But there was nowhere for his small boat to go and little sustenance, and he and his young son and the other men aboard would surely die of hunger or exposure,

which was, in fact, the intention of the mutineers. Aboard the *Discovery*, they quickly set sail and fled, one later wrote, 'as if from an enemy'. Hudson set his small boat's sail and chased them for a time, but the larger vessel quickly outdistanced him and the last the mutineers—or anyone—saw of Henry Hudson was his bearded, impassive figure staring after them with gaunt eyes as his little ship fell farther and farther behind.

Northeast Passage

Henry Hudson springs full-blown into history in 1607 and then disappears (literally) four years later, having made four voyages of exploration that opened up the famous river, strait and bay named after him. We know almost nothing about his life before this. He was born in London in about 1570 and probably began going to sea relatively young, as a cabin boy, and then worked his way up to master.

Along the way he married a woman named Katherine—we do not have her maiden name—who bore him three sons: Richard, John and Oliver. Hudson became sought after as a captain and navigator; it was probably the latter skill, in particular, that attracted the attention of the English Muscovy Company. In the early seventeenth century, the big merchant companies, particularly the Dutch and English ones, sought a northern passage to Asia that would preclude their vessels having to sail southern waters, either through the Strait of Magellan or around the Cape of Good Hope. This was partly because of the distances involved and partly because they wanted to avoid the hostile and proprietary navies of Spain and Portugal, which patrolled the New World and the routes to the Spice Islands.

The English Muscovy Company, more colloquially known as the Russia Company, traded with Russia and so sought a Northeast Passage that would lead to Russia's northern ports and also down the Pacific Ocean to China. They signed up Henry Hudson to make the search for such a passage, giving him a small crew and a vessel, the *Hopewell,* and sending him off in May 1607. Hudson subscribed to the theory that the three months of constant summer daylight around the northern waters of Russia would melt the ice and allow a free water passage, but he was sorely mistaken. On this first voyage he sailed north between Greenland and Spitzbergen and actually came within ten degrees of the North Pole—closer than anyone had ever been—before turning east, but massive pack ice forced him back.

It was a valiant effort and the Russia Company signed him up again to repeat the voyage in 1609, but this time he got little farther. He was, in fact, attempting the impossible—there exists a Northeast Passage, but for ships of Hudson's day it would not have been navigable. Still, he persisted in trying to convince the Russia Company to hire him again for yet a third voyage. When they declined, he offered his services to the Vereenigde Oostindische Compagnie (VOC), the Dutch East India Company.

The Half Moon

After some trepidation—Hudson's star had become tarnished because of his two unsuccessful previous voyages—the VOC hired Hudson to make another attempt to press through to the Northeast Passage. However, he had apparently told the officers of the VOC that it was his real belief that a way through to Asia was to be found in the northwest, across North America. He based this in good part on letters from his friend John Smith, the English explorer who had helped settle Virginia Colony, who told him that he thought there existed, somewhere north of Virginia, a strait that led to Asia.

The VOC officials refused to allow Hudson to explore west and he agreed to this proscription, but one wonders if it was in the back of his mind when he set sail from Amsterdam on his third voyage, on 6 May 1609. He was aboard a tiny vessel—described in his VOC contract as a 'yacht'—called the *Half Moon* and had with him a crew of eighteen, including, significantly, a fifty-year-old mariner from London whose name was Robert Juet. Juet, a surly malcontent, was to figure prominently in Hudson's life and in history, too, for Hudson's log of his famous third voyage has mainly disappeared and it is only Juet's accounts that we have.

From Amsterdam, the *Half Moon* sailed up the west coast of Norway, rounded what is called the North Cape, and then headed east into the Barents Sea. Hudson soon found himself at Novaya Zemlya, an island group that juts out from the northern coast of Russia into the Arctic Ocean. In these treacherous seas he faced pack ice, violent winds, blinding snow and frigid temperatures, something the Dutch among his mixed English–Dutch crew were unfamiliar with, having spent most of their sailing time in the sunnier climes of the Dutch East

Indies. Still Hudson persisted until, in mid-May, he realised he had a mutiny on his hands. His men refused to sail the ship a league farther and demanded that he turn around. Normally speaking, no self-respecting ship's master would give in to such demands—on the high seas, a ship's captain was a godlike figure in his own vessel—but it appears Hudson was prepared for the mutiny, and may even have welcomed it.

According to an account Hudson gave to Emanuel von Meteren, the Dutch lawyer who had helped connect Hudson with the VOC, Hudson brought out charts to show to his mutinous crew that they should go to the American coast, 'to the latitude of about 40 degrees'. It was there, Hudson said, that 'his friend Captain Smith … informed him that there was a sea leading into the western ocean to the north of the southern English colony [Virginia]'.

 ## SEEKING A NORTHERN PASSAGE

There were numerous attempts on the part of explorers, mainly those working on behalf of England and Scotland, to find a northern passage to Asia. In 1497 John Cabot—a Genoese explorer sailing in the employ of the English—set out on a northern voyage to try to find Cathay (China) and ended up in Maine. He tried again in 1498 and simply disappeared. In the late sixteenth century, a Dutchman named Willem Barents three times attempted the same route Henry Hudson would later follow, north of Russia (the Barents Sea carries his name) and through the treacherous archipelago of Novaya Zemlya. In 1596 he was marooned on those islands, but he and most of his men managed to survive the frozen Arctic winter in a makeshift shelter.

Another prominent searcher for a northern passage—this time the Northwest Passage—was Martin Frobisher, who led an expedition west from England in 1576. Frobisher sailed into a large bay off Baffin Island and proclaimed it 'Frobisher's streytes, like as Magellan at the southwest end of the world'. But, in fact, it was only a bay. Frobisher then spent two voyages mining what he thought was gold from this area of northern Canada, but it turned out to be worthless ore.

In 1845 Sir John Franklin sailed from England on a well-equipped expedition to the Canadian Arctic, confident he, at last, would find the passage, but he and his entire expedition disappeared, poisoned by food into which lead had leeched from improperly sealed tin cans. The evidence suggests that the last crewmembers alive resorted to cannibalism.

The first man to finally sail the Northwest Passage was the Norwegian explorer Roald Amundsen. In 1906 he completed a three-year voyage over the top of the world, from the Atlantic to the Pacific, in a converted herring boat. However, some of the waterways in the route he took were extremely shallow, making the route impracticable for any real commercial use.

The Northeast Passage was navigated in the late nineteenth century by a Swede named Nils Nordenskjöld, but it is so ice-clogged that it is of relatively little use to Russia, commercially.

This was met with general agreement and Hudson turned his ship around and headed back west through the Barents Sea. He was breaking his instructions from the VOC not to explore for a Northwest Passage, which is presumably why he did not bring the *Half Moon* to Amsterdam for refitting but instead chose to sail all the way to North America. Fighting off stormy seas—the ship lost its foremast and sail in one North Atlantic gale—the *Half Moon* arrived off the coast of Newfoundland on 3 July, spotting what Robert Juet called 'a great fleet of Frenchmen' fishing off the Outer Banks. They sailed past these vessels without trying to make contact and finally came within sight of the coast of Cape Sable, Nova Scotia, on 13 July.

Murderers

Mist shrouded the Nova Scotia shore as the *Half Moon* tried to beat its way closer, so Hudson had to hold off, lest he break up on the rocks that lined the coast. Finally, about ten o'clock in the morning, two canoes carrying 'six of the savages of the country', as Juet put it, paddled out and the Indians were brought on board. They claimed to be very happy to see the *Half Moon*. They had a meal with Hudson and his crew and told them that 'there were gold, silver and copper mines hard by us, and that the Frenchmen do trade with them', something Juet found easy to believe as one or two of the Indians had a smattering of that language.

After stopping in 'a very good harbour' and cutting themselves a new foremast, the *Half Moon* and its crew were on their way again. They next stopped near the mouth of the St George's River in what is now the state of Maine, and here begins the puzzling saga of Hudson and the *Half Moon* when it comes to their contact with native people. Juet writes of a fairly peaceful scene—the crew of the *Half Moon* finding fresh water, plucking thirty-one lobsters from the sea for a fine dinner and allowing the local 'country people' (that is, the Indians) on

Henry Hudson, the first European to sail up the Hudson River, where he encountered the Lenni Lenape Indians.

board to trade. But then he says: 'The people coming aboard showed us great friendship, but we could not trust them'.

Why? Juet goes on to write that in the morning two more boatloads of Indians came to trade, people who 'offered us no wrong, seeing as how we stood upon our guard'. These Indians had come in French-built shallops, so it is possible that Juet thought they might attack the English (although at the time there existed no official state of hostilities between France and England). Yet the Indians somehow frightened Juet and, presumably, Hudson, for on 25 July, two days after their initial landing at St George's River, Juet writes:

*We manned our boat and scout [smaller boat]
with 12 men and muskets and two stone pieces or*

*murderers [a murderer being a small, short range
cannon] and drove the savages from their houses
and took the spoil of them as they would have done
to us. Then we set sail and came down to the
harbor's mouth and rode there all night.*

Why attack and rob these Indians? There is no
mention of an Indian assault, no mention of any
Indians stealing from the *Half Moon*, no mention of
any inciting incident at all. The grimly paranoid
tone of Juet's notes is frightening, almost as if
insanity lurks. Yet it would seem likely that Hudson
countenanced such an attack. Whatever happened,
compared with the far kindlier treatment the
Indians were getting at exactly that moment at the
hands of Samuel de Champlain (see page 148), this
incident certainly put the English and Dutch in a
bad light.

'A great stream'

The *Half Moon* continued down the coast, having
cautionary encounters with the local Indians. Near
what is now Cape Cod, Massachusetts, 'the voices
of men' were heard shouting from the shore: 'We
sent our boat on shore thinking they had been some
Christians left on the land, but we found them
to be savages', Juet writes, apparently unable to
understand why anyone who was not a 'Christian'
would call out to them. When the Indians came on
board the ship, they were quite friendly, pointing
out a nearby river where the Europeans could fish.
Juet's description of them smacks of envy: 'The
people have green tobacco and pipes, the bowls of
which are made of earth and pipes of red copper.
The land is very sweet.'

By 17 August, the ship had sailed far enough
down the coast to reach Chesapeake Bay, where
Captain John Smith had helped found Jamestown
in 1607. Although they were near 'the entrance to
the King's River, where our Englishmen are', Juet
wrote, Hudson chose not to land there, perhaps

because they were sailing under a Dutch flag.
After being blown as far south as Cape Hatteras,
North Carolina, in a violent storm that arose, the
Half Moon began to beat its way back north again,
now closer to shore, searching for the strait to the
Pacific that Smith said he thought existed. Hudson
reached the mouth of the Delaware River, which
had not yet been explored by any European, but
shoals prevented him entering the waterway and
so he continued north.

On 2 September, Juet wrote in his journal:

*We saw a great fire but could not see the land.
From the land which we had first sight of,
until we came to a great lake of water, as we
could judge it to be, being drowned land which
made it rise like islands.
We had a great stream out of the bay.*

What Juet was describing was the very mouth of the
enormous bay that is now New York Harbor. 'The
great stream out of the bay' was, in fact, what would
come to be called the Hudson River.

'Ever-flowing waters'

This great bay had, in fact, been discovered over
three quarters of a century before, by Giovanni da
Verrazano, an Italian explorer in the employ of the
French, but he had only spent a short amount of
time there and soon his discovery was forgotten.
Since that time, no European had visited the bay or
entered the mighty river, which was called
Mahicanituk by the local Lenape Indians, meaning
'ever-flowing waters'.

Even far out to sea, the current of the Hudson
River was strong, and Henry Hudson was hopeful
that this, at last, was the broad river that would
provide passage to the Pacific Ocean. The *Half Moon*
sailed New York Harbor for several days, with the
crew taking depth soundings and marvelling at
the incredible profusion of fish—in one afternoon

GIOVANNI DA VERRAZANO:
THE FORGOTTEN MAN

Between the New York borough of Staten Island and the island of Manhattan, across a turbulent body of water known as the Narrows, stands one of the most beautiful bridges in the world. With two decks, weighing nearly 1.3 million tonnes, it spans 1405 metres (4620 feet) and is the longest suspension bridge in either North or South America. The bridge, completed in 1964, is known as the Verrazano-Narrows Bridge, after the first European who sailed into New York waters—and then was forgotten: Giovanni da Verrazano.

Verrazano was born in Italy about 1485 and became an expert Mediterranean sailor. He was hired by King Francis I of France in 1523 to explore the coast of North America to find a passage through to the Pacific. Taking fifty men with him, Verrazano traversed the Atlantic, landed in Florida and headed north up the American coastline, getting as far as Newfoundland before returning to France. But during this voyage he spotted what he thought was a large lake, although it turned out to be the Hudson River. He stayed for only a few hours in the vicinity but recorded his impression of the native peoples:

> The people are ... clad with feather of fowls of diverse colours. They came towards us very
> cheerfully, making great shouts of admiration, showing us where we might come
> to land most safely with our boat. We entered up the said river into the land about
> half a league, where it made a most pleasant lake [the Upper New York Harbor] about
> 3 leagues in compass ...

However, a heavy wind suddenly arose and, reluctantly, Verrazano was forced to make his way back to his ship. Had he gone a little farther, he would have found the 'pleasant lake' to have been a mighty river: the Hudson. But he did not, and so his short afternoon in New York was forgotten until his reputation was revived in the twentieth century, especially by New Yorkers of Italian descent, and the mighty bridge was named after him.

they caught 'ten great mullets, of a foot and a half long apiece, and a ray as great as four men could hale into the ship'. They landed in what is now the New York borough of Staten Island and were met by Indians who were, according to Juet, very polite: 'They go in deer skins loose, well dressed. They have yellow copper … they have a great store of maize or Indian wheat, whereof they make good bread. The country is full of great and tall oaks'.

Yet, once again … the note of fear, suspicion, paranoia on the part of Juet. The Indians visited the ship and all went well, but 'at night they went on land again, so we rode very quiet, but durst not trust them'. And perhaps he was right. On the morning of 6 September, Henry Hudson sent a seaman named John Colman along with four other men to explore another river that entered the ocean about twenty-two kilometres (fourteen miles) away. The men did this, finding nothing remarkable, but when they were returning that night they encountered two canoes filled with Indians, who fired arrows at them for no apparent reason. Two sailors were slightly wounded and John Colman's throat was pierced by an arrow and he died there in the boat.

As evening came on and it began to rain, the sailors escaped their assailants but in the darkness could not find the *Half Moon*, and thus were forced to spend a terrifying night rowing about the harbour, since the current was too strong for their small anchor to gain any purchase on the bottom. The next morning they returned to the *Half Moon* and related what had happened. Hudson ordered that Colman be buried and that waist-high boards be placed around the ship's gunwales to protect against attack—but, interestingly enough, allowed on board yet another group of Indians who wanted to trade.

These Indians, said Juet, 'offered no violence', but the next day two canoes approached the *Half Moon*, filled with Indian men with bows and arrows.

Could these have been the Indians who attacked Colman and his men? It is hard to say. The wary Europeans only allowed several on board and then promptly kidnapped them, although one leaped overboard and swam away. Having decided that enough was enough, Hudson weighed anchor and sailed into the upper bay of New York Harbor and then into the Hudson River, anchoring for the night off a hilly, thickly wooded island the Lenapes called 'Manna-hata'.

In search of the passage

The next morning, the *Half Moon* travelled up the river that would one day bear Hudson's name. The Hudson River is really a huge estuary, with the water salty as far as 100 kilometres (60 miles) inland and tides extending for half its 510-kilometre (315-mile) length up into northern New York State. At first Hudson and the crew of the *Half Moon* were extremely excited. A few miles north of Manna-hata, around the area that became known as the Tappan Zee, the river widens to five kilometres (three miles) across and it must have begun to seem to Hudson—who had no idea of the 5000-kilometre (3000-mile) width of the American continent—like the broad strait that would take him to Asia.

As morose as ever, Juet reported more canoes approaching the ship: 'This morning there came … eight and twenty canoes full of men, women, and children to betray us, but we saw their intent, and suffered none of them to come aboard'. It would have been highly unusual for Indians to put their women and children in harm's way during an assault. It is also more than possible that these Indians had traded with the French and assumed that these Europeans wanted to trade as well. But Juet darkly saw danger everywhere, despite the glory of the scene: the high cliffs, or Palisades, on the western side of the river, the brilliantly coloured autumn foliage of the forests falling away endlessly to the east. The sun remained out; the weather was warm. Much to Juet's chagrin, on the morning of 15 September, 'our two [kidnapped] savages got out of a porthole and swam away. After we were under sail they called to us in scorn'.

At around the same time, however, the river literally took a disturbing turn. The Hudson makes a sharp 'S' at the promontory where the United States Military Academy at West Point currently sits and then becomes much narrower and shallower. After this, it broadens out again, but in the next few days, as Hudson sailed on at an average of thirty kilometres (twenty miles) a day, he could see that this waterway was almost certainly not a strait that was leading anywhere. The water was becoming more and more shallow and filled with silt and sandbars; it was apparent to him, with his vast experience, that he was reaching the headwaters of a river.

About sixty kilometres (forty miles) south of the present-day New York State capital city of Albany, Hudson stopped and allowed himself to have dinner with Indians who had sailed forth in their canoes—he tells the story in one of the few excerpts from his journal to survive:

> I sailed to the shore in one of their canoes, with an old man, who was the chief of a tribe consisting of 40 men and 17 women ... Two men were also despatched at once with bows and arrows in quest of game, who soon after brought in a pair of pigeons, which they had shot. They likewise killed a fat dog and skinned it in great haste with shells which they had got out of the water ...
>
> The natives are very good people, for when they saw that I would not remain with them [for the night], they supposed that I was afraid of their bows, and taking the arrows, they broke them in pieces and threw them in the fire.

Hudson's journal has a far more reasonable tone than that of Robert Juet's, leading one to wonder on what level Hudson was in control of the ship—who was in charge, really, during their skirmishes with the 'savages'?

'We saw no people to trouble us'

After a few more days on the river, the *Half Moon* arrived near the present-day city of Albany. The river had definitely narrowed but, just to make sure, Hudson sent five men up the river in the ship's boat, to take soundings. The men returned that night, 'in a shower of rain', Juet writes, to say that the river 'was at an end for shipping to go in ... For they had gone eight or nine leagues [roughly fifty kilometres or thirty miles] and found but seven foot [two metres] water and inconstant soundings'.

It was time to turn back. While the ship's boat had been away, many Indians had visited the *Half Moon* and, according to Juet, Hudson decided to find out 'whether they had any treachery in them. So they took them down into the cabin and gave them [so] much wine and Aqua Vitae that they were all merry'. This little trick, however, failed to bring out any grand plot on the part of the Indians—in fact, it just put them peacefully to sleep.

At midday on 23 September, Hudson headed the *Half Moon* south down the Hudson. All the way back, they were visited by Indians wanting to trade with them. These encounters occurred peacefully, until the ship had nearly reached Tappan Zee, at which point an Indian in a canoe pulled up to the *Half Moon*'s stern, climbed the rudder and through a stern porthole, and stole a pillow and two shirts that happened to belong to Juet. The ship's first mate shot and killed the man. Then Juet and other sailors got into the ship's boat and went to recover Juet's belongings from the canoe, at which point a swimming Indian put his hand on the gunwale of the boat, as if to overturn it. According to Juet, at

FOLLOWING PAGES Hudson traded with many local Indians but his suspicions of them often led to violence.

this point 'our cook took a sword and cut off one of [the Indian's] hands and he was drowned'.

The final blaze of violence was to occur above the island of Manna-hata, site of the future city of New York. According to Juet, 'one of the Indians who swam away from them' (that is, one of their former captives) led an attack against the *Half Moon*:

> *Two canoes full of men, with their bows and arrows shot at us after our stern. In recompense thereof we discharged six muskets and killed two or three of them. Then above a hundred came to a point of land to shoot at us.*
>
> *There I shot a Falcon [a small cannon] and killed two of them whereupon the rest fled into the woods. Yet they manned off another canoe with nine or ten men which came to meet us. So I shot at it also a Falcon, and shot it through, and killed one of them. Then our men with their muskets killed three or four more.*
>
> *So they went on their way and [after a while] we anchored in a bay clear of all danger of them on the other side of the river. We saw a very good piece of ground and hard by it there was a cliff that looked of the color of a white-green, as though it were either copper or silver mine ... It is on that side of the river that is called Manna-hata.*
>
> *We saw no people to trouble us.*

A few days later, the *Half Moon* entered New York Harbor again, and then found itself in the vast ocean. And Juet wrote: 'By the seventh day of November, being Saturday, by the grace of God we safely arrived in the range of Dartmouth, in Devonshire'.

Fourth and fatal voyage

Although Hudson had begun his voyage contracted to the VOC, he ended it in England, for when he landed there, that November of 1609, the English government confiscated his ship and his papers and forbade him to leave the country. It appears that Hudson was able to send his Dutch employers a report on his activities—and quite a valuable one, too, for although he had failed to find a Northwest Passage (let alone a Northeast one, as he was charted to do) he had found fertile new land in America, all the time sailing under the flag of the Dutch. Within two years, the Dutch would have a settlement on the island of Manna-hata.

The English now regretted that they had not sent Hudson west themselves and soon set out to rectify that error. A group of private investors formed a company to finance Hudson's fourth voyage of discovery. His orders were to head for the poorly understood waterways of the Canadian Arctic, in order to discover 'if any passage might be found to the other ocean called the South Sea [the Pacific]'.

On 17 April 1610, Hudson set off in the ship *Discovery*, this time accompanied by his son John, perhaps ten years old, who was serving as ship's boy. Robert Juet was with him again, as first mate, as well as a passenger (perhaps hired by Hudson's employers, his status is not entirely clear) named Abacuk Prickett, who later published an account of the journey. Although fragments of Hudson's log for this fourth voyage do exist, it is mainly Prickett's story that historians have relied on.

Apparently, the voyage was fraught with tension from the beginning. Hudson fired one crewman before the ship had reached Gravesend—still on the Thames River, in other words—and hired another, Henry Greene, a young reprobate of 'lewd life and conversation', according to Prickett. Hudson may have seen Greene as a reclamation project. However, it is disturbing that this great explorer seems not to have been a great appraiser of human beings, for both Juet and Greene were to cause great trouble on this, Hudson's last, adventure.

The *Discovery* barely reached Iceland when trouble began. Greene picked a fight with the ship's surgeon and instead of disciplining the young man, Hudson blamed the whole thing on the surgeon's sarcastic tongue, causing 'all the ship's company to fall into a rage'. Juet—as easily incensed as ever—walked about the boat muttering that the expedition would end 'in manslaughter, and prove bloody to some'. Juet also began telling people that Greene had been hired by Hudson to spy on the crew, something so palpably untrue that Hudson nearly set Juet ashore in Greenland, but then reconsidered.

Finally, battling icebergs and gales, the *Discovery* found its way to the mouth of Hudson Strait, where the awestruck Prickett described their tiny ship manoeuvring between huge icebergs: 'In this our going between the ice we saw one of the great islands of ice overturn, which was a good warning to us not to come nigh them, nor within their reach … Some of our men this day fell sick. I will not say it was for fear …'

But Prickett leaves the impression that the crew was terrified, with the exception of Henry Hudson, who boldly moved his ship farther down the strait, a 720-kilometre (450-mile) long channel that runs between Baffin Island and the Canadian mainland.

'A sea to the westward'

The *Discovery* passed through land that appeared as if it belonged on the dark side of the moon, especially to those crewmen who had explored the verdant Hudson with their ship's captain. Here were forbidding rocky shores, and the only vegetation was weeds and so-called 'scurvy grass', which at least contained anti-scorbutic properties. Hudson began to give islands they encountered names— optimistic names like 'Hold with Hope'—but the crew muttered so much that he at last allowed them to vote to see whether the voyage should be continued. A slim majority said yes, and onward

 THE LENNI LENAPE

The Indians Henry Hudson met in what is now New York were the Lenni Lenape, who later became known to the Europeans as the Delaware. They lived in the lower Hudson Valley, New York, New Jersey and parts of Pennsylvania and Delaware.

The Lenni Lenape were a mobile hunter–gatherer group who moved from location to location seasonally, depending on what game, fish or berries might be found there, although they also practised agriculture (mainly Indian corn or wheat) on a very large scale. Thus the Indians Hudson met that early autumn were probably in the area hunting or fishing; earlier in the year, they might have been in southern New Jersey, digging for shellfish. They were not a particularly violent or warlike tribe, like their Iroquois neighbours farther to the north, and they adapted European ways fairly easily after the Dutch occupied the territory around New York in the early seventeenth century—particularly when it came to using metal tools for agriculture. Unfortunately, their dependence on European goods came at a high price, since they over–trapped their fur sources to provide furs for the Dutch to pay for these goods. The Dutch and other Europeans then moved on to other tribes to get their furs and the Lenni Lenape, wracked by European disease and with European settlers taking over their land, fell into decline.

they went until, in early August, they reached a vast open sea. Hudson's last existing journal entry reads: 'Then I observed and found the ship at noon in 61°20' [latitude] and as sea to the westward'.

The sea was, in fact, the great gulf of water that would be called Hudson Bay. Hudson, for the moment, dared to think he had reached the northern Pacific Ocean. Jubilant, he headed south. Jubilant, he did something that he had been probably thinking of doing for some time: he fired Robert Juet, who had been stirring unrest among the crew or, rather, replaced him as first mate with a man named Robert Bylot.

Unfortunately, things did not thereafter go as Hudson wished them to. He sailed south, but by early September reached the confines of James Bay, in the southeastern part of Hudson Bay. Unable to believe that he was not in the Pacific, he began to tack north and south, east and west, repeatedly, 'in a Labyrinth without end', as Prickett wrote. The early northern winter began to set in and 'the nights were long and cold, and the earth was covered with snow'.

Still Hudson sailed on, crossing and re-crossing his own path, and some of the men began to suspect he had gone mad. At last, on 1 November, he brought the ship into James Bay and announced his plans to spend the winter in this desolate spot. They built a crude shelter, but there was very little food and the men began to slowly starve, despite the fact that they were able at first to shoot wild fowl and catch fish. The gunner, John Williams, died within a few weeks, perhaps of scurvy. One lonely trapper of the Cree Indian nation came to them over the winter and Hudson treated him well, but he did not provide them with much food and the men were reduced to eating frogs. With the arrival of spring, birds returned from the south and it was this that saved the crew. With enough rations amassed for two weeks, the *Discovery* set sail in early June, sailing gingerly between the broken ice of James Bay.

Mutiny and death

As the *Discovery* headed north, Hudson replaced first mate Robert Bylot, with whom he had feuded, with an illiterate and unqualified sailor named John King. This caused a number of the men to mutter that Hudson was going to continue his search for a Northwest Passage, instead of heading home for England. Hudson, for his part, suspected the men of hoarding food and ordered searches of their belongings, something the men hated. The tensions of months now finally exploded into open mutiny, with Robert Juet muttering that 'he would rather be hanged at home than starved abroad'. Led by Juet and Hudson's former friend Henry Greene, the mutineers stormed Hudson's cabin on the morning of 22 June 1611, dragged the protesting master out and put him in the ship's boat along with his son and seven other sailors, most of them sickly. Prickett writes that they gave Hudson supplies, but this may have been written with an eye toward the court of inquiry that was sure to follow. In any event, the intent was certainly to abandon Hudson in an inhospitable wilderness, which was tantamount to killing him. And it did—no one ever saw Hudson, his son or those seven other sailors again.

The *Discovery*, after an arduous voyage, arrived back in England. Conveniently, Hudson's journal had disappeared by that time, probably destroyed by the mutineers. With equal convenience, Robert Juet died a few days before the vessel raised England. One would think, given the fate of other mutineers in British history, that the crew of the *Discovery* would be severely punished but, curiously, this was not the case. Several of the survivors were immediately sent back to Hudson Bay—on the self-same *Discovery*—in order to chart fur-trading routes. They were considered too valuable to hang. Finally, in 1618, seven years after the fact, four of the crew, including Prickett, were tried but acquitted of the crime.

This was partly because Prickett had been successfully able to place most of the blame for the mutiny on Juet and Henry Greene. Greene's fate is quite interesting. As the *Discovery* reached the northeastern tip of Hudson Bay after abandoning Hudson, they stopped and sent a party of men ashore to bargain with Indians they saw—possibly Cree or even Inuit. Something went wrong, somehow, and the Indians attacked them, badly wounding Prickett and killing Henry Greene, along with three others. The survivors barely made it back to the ship. Even without Henry Hudson, it seems to have been the fate of his men to have bloody encounters with native peoples.

Mutineers lead Hudson and his son to the ship's boat, in which they were set adrift with seven sailors to perish in the icy waters of Hudson Bay.

NORTH AMERICAN ENCOUNTERS

Samuel de Champlain,
1609–1616

Very early on a warm summer morning in 1609, two groups of North American Indians faced each other across a grassy meadow near the shores of a huge lake whose waves sparkled in the light of the rising sun. The first group of about sixty Indians comprised Huron, Algonquin and Montagnais, all natives of what is now Canada. The other and much larger group, numbering about two hundred, were Mohawks, the most feared of the tribes that constituted the Iroquois Confederacy of Five Nations. The ground on which they stood now forms the borderline between the American states of New York and Vermont.

The Mohawks, in their wooden armour, which was impervious to arrowheads, were confident, shouting scathing insults at their opponents. This was their territory and they outnumbered the Canadian Indians by more than two to one. They moved forward quickly, forming a semi-circle that threatened to envelop their smaller foe. With a brisk whisking sound, arrows were pulled from quivers and strung onto bowstrings. The Mohawks were only waiting for a command from one of their chiefs when something bizarre occurred. The ranks of the Canadian Indians parted and there strode forth an unusual being. The Mohawk were not at first sure whether this creature was human. He was dressed in gleaming armour that was not made out of wood, but of what appeared to be some harder, shinier substance. He wore a helmet with a huge white plume. And he carried a wooden stick embedded with metal—not a club, but something else.

The Indians stared in astonishment as the being, who was indeed human and whose name was Samuel de Champlain, raised his stick and pointed it at them. What was about to happen in the next few seconds would change the course of North American history.

The 'Father of New France'

Samuel de Champlain is generally called the 'Father of New France' the territory that now forms the eastern half of Canada—but even in Canada today, few people have any real idea of who he was. This is partly because Champlain did not reveal much of himself—we have almost no idea of his personal life, nor what he looked like—but also partly because there have grown up so many misconceptions about him. He has been seen at different times through history as a romantic hero, as a hard-nosed merchant-explorer and as a Machiavellian schemer whose main goal was to keep the English from the spoils of North America.

In some ways, Champlain was all those things. But when it came to his contacts with the native peoples of North America he was the most even-handed European they could ever have hoped to meet. Unlike other white men, he had a vision of the French and Indians living side-by-side, separate but equal, in a great North American empire linked by bonds of trade and fellowship. Of course, it was not to be, but during Champlain's tenure as the most powerful Frenchman in America—a tenure that lasted a good thirty years—there were tantalising glimpses of what might have been.

No one is quite sure when Champlain was born. The best guess is around 1570. The place was Brouage, a seaport town on the west coast of France, south of Brittany. We know very little about his early life. Brouage was a Huguenot town and Champlain was probably raised as one, but by the time he was in his early twenties he had become a Roman Catholic and he was to remain a devout one for the rest of his life. Probably by his late teens he had become a soldier, and he would distinguish himself in the service of King Henry IV, fighting against the Spanish. When the war against Spain ended in 1598—and when, during the same year, the religious strife between Catholics and Protestants within France was temporarily settled by the Edict of Nantes—the king turned his eyes to the New World.

While Spain had long settled the southern part of the American continent, it was taking longer for European countries to establish a presence in North America. The climate was less hospitable, the landscape more impenetrable, the tribes numerous and warlike and the chance of finding gold almost nil, although many Europeans did believe that there might exist a Northwest Passage to the Orient. John Cabot had visited Newfoundland from 1497 and French, Portuguese and English fishermen began a lucrative industry, bringing in record hauls of cod as well as trading with the natives who came to their temporary summer camps on the beach.

The first attempt at a European settlement in the area had been made by the French mariner Jacques Cartier, from 1534 to 1541. Cartier sailed up the St Lawrence River as far as present-day Quebec, where he twice tried and failed to found a colony, his attentions consumed by a foolish quest for the so-called Kingdom of Saguenay, a mythical land—far beyond the Great Lakes—filled with gold and diamonds.

While Cartier's settlements failed he did leave behind something permanent—a hatred in the hearts of the Indian peoples he met, since he made it his practice to kidnap their children and take them back to France with him. In any event, since Cartier's time, while fishermen visited and traders traded, no real attempt had been made to colonise Canada. Samuel de Champlain would change all that.

'The mere account of it'

By 1600, Samuel de Champlain had become an experienced sailor, making at least six trans-Atlantic voyages to the West Indies (in all, during his lifetime, Champlain would cross the Atlantic some fifty times safely, a record during a period when such journeys were fraught with peril). He was becoming well known. He was an intuitive and uncannily smart sailor, a mapmaker of extreme precision and accuracy, and a writer whose book *A Treatise on Seamanship* can still be read profitably today.

And he was something else—a spy for King Henry IV. Attempting to keep an eye on the Spanish, ministers of the king sent Champlain to New Spain—Mexico—around 1599, disguised as a merchant. It is unlikely that Champlain's sojourn there provided much real information for the king, but it did provide something quite valuable to Samuel de Champlain. For he saw the brutal way the Spanish treated the Indians there—one of Champlain's drawings graphically captures an Indian beaten for not attending Mass. He was appalled and later wrote: 'The King of Spain ... at the commencement of his conquests, established the inquisition among them [the Indians] and enslaved them or put them to death in such great numbers that the mere account of it arouses great compassion for them'.

Actually, the account of it probably aroused compassion in relatively few Europeans, but it did in Champlain, who was naturally a fair-minded person who hated cruelty, especially to those in a weak or subservient state. His experience in New Spain merely reinforced these feelings and would have an important impact on the future of New France.

In 1603 Champlain sailed for New France with instructions from the king to develop the fur trade between the French and the Micmac, or Montagnais, Indians. Between 1604 and 1606, he made several voyages to the country with fur-trading groups chartered by the king to form monopolies. Champlain, in his own ship, sailed down the North American coastline as far as Cape Cod, in present-day Massachusetts. Unlike many other explorers, he preferred to do his exploring close to shore, so that he could carefully chart every bay and inlet, every stream, every rocky promontory. It was what made his maps so astonishingly accurate.

Champlain also studied the Indians. Unlike Cartier, he was not looking for some mythical kingdom of diamonds and thus was able to see treasure right in front of him—the furs the Indians traded, many of which did not come from near the seacoast. When he attempted to get the Indians to take him farther into the interior, to show him their trade routes, they baulked, and thus he decided to probe deeper into the continent on his own.

Kebec

In the summer of 1608, Champlain returned to Canada with a ship and thirty men and sailed up the St Lawrence River to a place the Montagnais Indians called *Kebec*, which meant 'a narrowing of the waters'. The place where Champlain was to found the city now called Quebec was a high, rocky point of land that completely commanded the all-important waterway. On 3 July, he began building a strong, three-storey 'habitation', a walled, fortified house that contained a central courtyard and storehouse. Knowing how brutal the winters could be, Champlain had his men lay in as much game and salted fish as they could, but even so disease—dysentery and scurvy—set in. By the spring of 1609 only eight Frenchmen survived out of twenty-eight.

But the plight of the Montagnais had been far worse. Because the winter, while brutally cold, had been relatively snowless, they were not able to do their usual snowshoe hunting of big game like moose and, therefore, began to starve. Ultimately, a band of them crossed ice flows on the St Lawrence to Quebec and Champlain helped them with food as much as he was able, horrified that they even ate the rotting carcass of a dead dog left in the fort. It was the beginning of a long friendship with these and other Indians, particularly the Algonquin and the Huron, much farther to the west near the Great Lakes. When he finally gained the Indians' trust after that terrible winter he heard about the rich

ENCOUNTER WITH AN
INDIAN MAIDEN

A great deal about Samuel de Champlain remains a mystery, including his personal life. He did not marry until he was forty, and then it was to a twelve-year-old French girl (the marriage contract stipulated that the union would not be consummated until the girl was fourteen). The marriage lasted until Champlain's death, but there are signs that it was an unhappy one.

Champlain reported on, but did not seem overly shocked by, the sexual practices of the Huron Indians, whom he wintered among after his unsuccessful attack on the Iroquois fort in New York in 1615. It was the custom of young Iroquois women to sleep with as many as twenty men before finding the partner they wanted to settle down with for the rest of their lives. Nights, in Huron villages, were alive with young men and women seeking each other out for sexual coupling. Champlain apparently did not realise this on one night when, driven crazy by fleas —'which were in great number and a torment to us'— inside the lodge he was sleeping in, he stepped outside and walked alone through the village. As he did so, 'a shameless girl approached me with effrontery, offering to keep me company, for which I thanked her, sending her away with gentle remonstrances'.

He then found another hut to sleep in, presumably one with fewer fleas. While his behaviour was considered odd among the Huron, his refusal to bed the young maiden who approached him actually helped increase his standing, for it appeared to the Indians that he was acting like a holy man.

fur-trading land called Huronia, the land of the Huron around the shores of present-day Georgian Bay in Canada. He also came to understand that an epic network of waterways, beginning with the St Lawrence, could serve as the highways to bring furs out of the interior of the continent.

The problem, however, was the Iroquois. The name 'Iroquois' derives from a Huron insult meaning 'black snake' and refers to an alliance of five eastern woodlands Indian nations: the Seneca, Mohawk, Oneida, Onondaga and Cayuga, whose territory stretched from Ohio as far east as Pennsylvania's Susquehanna River. These bands were linked together by a remarkable political system, an early form of American democracy. But

they were also aggressive, warlike and extremely brutal, even in a world where brutality was commonplace. The Mohawk tribe of the Iroquois were now expanding north and west and interfering with Huron trading routes from the Great Lakes region to Quebec.

Champlain decided that he would put a stop to this. Travelling fifty kilometres (thirty miles) upriver in his small sailboat, or shallop, he made a rendezvous with two Indian chiefs of the Huron and Algonquin nations. The chiefs came out to Champlain's shallop while hundreds of their followers watched from shore in silence. Some of these men had never seen a white man before. Champlain told the chiefs that he wanted to help

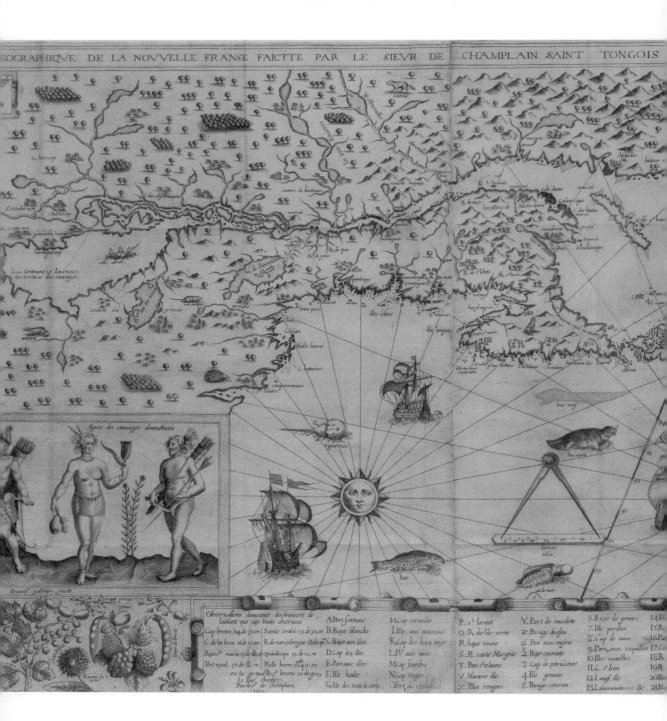

them in fighting the Iroquois. He would bring his men with their harquebuses—which the Iroquois had never seen—and kill as many of them as he could. In return, the Huron would guide Champlain into the interior.

The chiefs sat on Champlain's boat for a moment, smoking their pipes in silence. Suddenly, they stood up and shouted to the warriors on the shore that Champlain was going to help them defeat their bloody enemies, the black snakes—the Iroquois. From the warriors on the shore arose a great cry.

'No Christians but ourselves'

On 28 June 1609, Champlain, twelve Frenchmen armed with harquebuses, and four hundred Huron, Algonquin and Montagnais warriors set out up the St Lawrence in the French shallop and one hundred canoes, an incredibly colourful flotilla. The Indians' canoes, made of birch bark, were decorated with images of dead enemies or stained vivid reds and blues with berries. The Indians themselves were a proud lot, especially the Huron, whom Champlain favoured above all the Indian nations—they were well built, smart and generous, although often cruel, obscene and sometimes devious. They carried clubs, tomahawks, arrows and shields. The small fleet travelled from the St Lawrence to the Lake of St Peter and finally to the river Champlain called the River of the Iroquois, because it pointed like an arrow straight into the heart of Iroquois country (today it is known as the Richelieu River).

Champlain was aware that he was making history. 'No Christians but ourselves had ever penetrated this place', he later wrote. However, there were a few immediate setbacks. As they progressed deeper and deeper into Iroquois country, many of the Canadian Indians began to think twice

Map by Samuel de Champlain, showing the known areas of Canada and North America in 1612.

about taking on the fearsome Mohawks and made up excuses to slip away, so that the four hundred warriors dwindled to sixty. The Indians had told him that the river was deep enough for the French ship, but about sixty kilometres (forty miles) into their journey they came upon a set of rapids that the shallop could not traverse. The Indians could carry their far lighter canoes around the white water, but many of the Frenchmen with Champlain baulked at going forward in Indian canoes, so finally he sent them back to Quebec, taking only two trusted soldiers with him.

Continuing on, Champlain was impressed by the Hurons' cleverness. Each night before going to sleep, they built nearly impenetrable forts by felling trees—each of these 'forest forts' could be completed in less than two hours. On 14 July they reached the point where the River of the Iroquois flowed into a massive lake some 200 kilometres (125 miles) long, which today is Lake Champlain. The Adirondack Mountains rose to the east and game and fish were plentiful. Now, the Indians explained, they were deep in Mohawk country. They began to move with far more stealth, remaining hidden in the woods until the full moon passed, and then travelling only at night over the dark water, heading south.

'A lake near a mountain'

During the day they slept, ate cold food without fires and set a strong lookout. One morning during this period, Champlain fell asleep and had a dream. 'I dreamed that in a lake near a mountain', he told the Canadian Indians when he awoke, 'our enemies, the Iroquois [were] drowning before our eyes'.

The Indians were overjoyed when they heard this, for they believed firmly in the power of dreams to foretell. Not only that, but the spot Champlain was describing was actually just a short distance ahead. That evening—29 July—they were paddling their canoes across the dark lake when Champlain saw a high promontory projecting into the lake.

Amazingly, this seemed to be the place of his dream, the mountain over the lake. It was actually a point where two lakes met, where Lake Champlain flowed into what would be called Lake George. The Indians called the place *tekontaro:ken*, but the Europeans pronounced it Ticonderoga. A fort would much later be built on this spot, which would prove pivotal in American history.

Champlain and his Indians glided along through the night—Champlain was always amazed at the way the Indians moved so soundlessly through the water in their canoes—rounded the promontory and, looking over to the western shore of the lake, saw dark shapes in the water, also gliding along. The Huron recognised them instantly as Mohawk elm-tree canoes, which were heavier and thicker than the Canadian Indians' birch-bark vessels. It was a war party of perhaps two hundred Mohawk moving through the night. Perhaps they had wind of the Canadian Indians' presence or perhaps they were on their way to make a raid of their own, but they shouted when they saw the Huron and Algonquin and the Canadians did the same.

Much to Champlain's surprise, however, a parlay occurred between the adversaries right there on the dark water. The Huron sent two canoes over to the Iroquois 'to learn from their enemies whether they wished to fight'. The Iroquois replied very strongly that they did, but that 'for the moment nothing could be seen and it was necessary to wait until daylight in order to distinguish one another'.

And so it was agreed. The Iroquois turned to shore and instantly set about making a forest fortress of the type that the Huron created so admirably, while the Huron remained in their canoes on the water 'within a bowshot' of the Iroquois, shouting scatological insults at their enemy and 'telling them that [in the morning] they would see feats of weaponry that they had never known before'.

In fact, they were not lying, for Champlain was about to introduce the Mohawks to their first gunfire, via the harquebus. The harquebus was a matchlock weapon, that is, a pan filled with powder held a fuse (or match) in a lock near the breech of the gun. When the fuse was lit, the powder ignited and the gun fired. But Champlain and his men carried a more advanced version of the harquebus known as the *arquebus à rouet,* which used a rotating steel wheel to provide ignition for the powder and thus the gunner did not have to give his position away through a flaming match. This was very important, for Champlain and his men were being used as a highly secret weapon. As soon as light began to dawn on the lake, Champlain wrote, 'My companions and I were … kept carefully out of sight, lying flat in the canoes'. The Canadian Indians now paddled quickly to a secluded spot out of sight of the Iroquois fort and pulled their canoes ashore. Then, with Champlain and his men following slightly behind, the Indians moved like shadows through the forest on the shore.

The fight

The Canadian Indians sent out scouts to approach the Mohawk fortress: Montagnais archers who were

 CHAMPLAIN'S ASTROLABE

An astrolabe is an old-fashioned but highly functional instrument for figuring out one's latitude on Earth by taking a sighting on the noon sun or the pole star. Samuel de Champlain, expert navigator and explorer, had many of these instruments, including a small, artfully crafted one that he took with him on his explorations of Canada, in order to fix his position as best he could.

Unfortunately, while Champlain was portaging around rapids in the Ottawa River in 1613, he dropped his astrolabe in a tangle of fallen timber and did not realise it until later. There it lay until 1867 when a Canadian farm boy named Edward Lee was hired, along with his father, to clear the land on a farm belonging to a man named Charles Overman. Young Lee was using a team of oxen to tear down trees; when the mud at the water's edge was disturbed by a dragging log, the astrolabe appeared. Charles Overman showed up and offered the boy ten dollars for the compass (Lee apparently never received the money) and then sold it himself to his boss at the freight company for which he worked.

No one thought that this was Champlain's astrolabe until a few years later, when a translation of Champlain's Journals was published. Historians in Canada noticed two things—one, Champlain's description of having lost his astrolabe in the same area as the Overman farm, and, two, the fact that directly after the loss of the instrument his usually accurate latitude readings were greatly in error, indicating that he was estimating. Although there are nay-sayers who do not accept the coincidence that the same astrolabe would turn up 254 years later, the astrolabe in question is an early seventeenth century instrument and it would seem to be quite a coincidence for another explorer to have dropped it in this very remote part of Canada. In any event, it now resides in the Canadian Museum of Civilization, on the banks of the Ottawa River.

renowned for their accurate aim. As they got nearer, a Mohawk sentinel crept out from behind the wooden barricades and a Montagnais arrow caught him in the throat. His dying gurgle brought shouts from the Iroquois inside. They came rushing out just as the sixty Canadian Indians poured into the clearing outside the fort, with the woods on one side and the great, shining lake on the other.

Champlain and his two men remained carefully hidden behind the Huron, Algonquin and Montagnais, but he was able to peer through their ranks and he watched as the Iroquois approached. They did not give the picture we have of woodlands Indians, attired only in loincloths, hiding and firing with stealth from behind trees. Many of them wore armour made of slats of wood

woven together with cotton thread or animal sinew, carried wooden shields covered with cotton thread, and wore wooden helmets with plumes. Champlain wrote that the Iroquois 'advanced slowly to meet us with a gravity and assurance I greatly admired'. They were in tight order and close ranks, like a European infantry formation. As the two groups closed in on each other, Champlain sent his two gunners to creep stealthily into the woods, with orders to fire on the Iroquois only after Champlain himself did so.

The enemies were now about fifty metres (165 feet) away from each other. Some of the Huron warriors whispered to Champlain that he needed to kill the three chiefs of the Iroquois, who were distinguishable by the large plumes they wore on

Champlain fires his harquebus to help the Huron and their allies defeat the Mohawks near Lake Champlain in July 1609.

their helmets—not unlike the plume that Champlain himself was wearing, which was made of feathers and called a 'panache'. Now, suddenly, the Huron, Montagnais and Algonquin 'began to call to me with loud cries', Champlain later wrote. On this signal, the Canadian Indians parted in front of him, and Champlain was at last exposed to the Iroquois. Their surprise could not have been greater if he had dropped from the sky, which, as far as they knew, he had. In his glittering armour of an unknown substance, with his white face and his beard, he did indeed seem like someone from another dimension. The Iroquois simply stared at him. Champlain strode forward another twenty metres (sixty-five feet) until he was only thirty metres from the Indians. Then one of the Mohawk chiefs raised his bow and aimed at Champlain.

Champlain, in return, put his harquebus to his cheek and fired. The huge explosion and column of smoke shocked the Iroquois, but what was even more shocking was that two of their chiefs suddenly fell dead to the ground, and another was badly injured. Champlain had loaded his gun with four bullets, a dangerous practice that could sometimes make the weapon explode in the shooter's face (this had, in fact, happened before to Champlain) but that was now highly effective. 'The Indians', Champlain wrote, 'were much astonished that two men had been killed so quickly … this greatly frightened them'. The Canadian Indians, seeing that the Iroquois chiefs were dead, gave a great shout and began unloosing their arrows. The Iroquois valiantly followed suit, but then, as Champlain reloaded his gun, his two companions fired their own weapons from the forest, killing another chief. The surprise of this was simply too much for the Iroquois, who turned around and ran as fast as they could, 'abandoning the field and their fort, fleeing into the depth of the forest. I pursued them and laid low still more of them'. So did Champlain's Indian allies, who ran screaming into the woods, only too

happy to take their revenge on the Iroquois who had so persecuted them.

The Huron, Montagnais and Algonquin took about ten prisoners. Altogether, perhaps fifty Iroquois were killed, twenty-five per cent of their total force—which were very high casualty numbers for woodland combat. The French were not at all hurt and their Indian allies suffered only superficial arrow wounds.

'A very sad song'

The victorious Canadian Indians, yelling triumphantly, soon returned from the forest with their prisoners. They looted the Iroquois fort, taking with them bushels of corn and any of the wooden armour that the Mohawks had dropped, and had a ritual feast 'with singing and dancing to propitiate the spirits of the living and the dead', Champlain wrote. But within a few hours his Indian allies realised that they had better soon be on their way— they were still deep in Iroquois territory and outnumbered, and at any moment their enemy might return with reinforcements. Therefore, they got into their canoes and headed north, back up the lake toward the River of the Iroquois. Night came and they made camp some twenty-five kilometres (sixteen miles) or so from the battlefield and began a ritual that deeply disturbed Champlain.

The Canadian Indians stood in front of the bound captives and taunted them. They reminded them of all the tortures that the Mohawks subjected Huron captives to and told them that they would soon be suffering the same awful fate. They picked out one of the prisoners and told him to begin singing his death song, the personal song that each Indian would chant if he knew his end was near. It was, Champlain related, 'a very sad song'. The victim was then taken to a large fire that was built for the purpose and the torture began. His tormentors burned him a little at a time with burning brands, throwing water on his back to

'ROSES AMONG THORNS'

Although religious conversion was not one of Champlain's chief goals for the North American Indians, he was a devout Catholic and worked closely with the Jesuit missionaries who risked their lives to convert the Huron and Iroquois at this early stage of French occupation of Canada.

One such Jesuit, Father Paul La Jeune, who worked closely with Champlain and lived among the Huron, had practical advice for young Jesuit missionaries thinking of coming to New France. Whatever you do, do not keep the Indians waiting at the beginning of a canoe trip. Always bring flints in a tinderbox to help them start fires or light their pipes 'for these little services win their hearts'. Pretend to like the food even if it is barely cooked and full of dirt, because you will not get anything different. Inside the canoe, take off your shoes and tuck your cassock up—Indians hate water and sand tracked into their canoes—and do not wear your broad-brimmed hat, which creates wind resistance and irritates the rear paddler by cutting off his view. Do not try to talk to the Indians while they are paddling—'silence is then a good companion'. Be sure not to start anything that you cannot finish, such as paddling, and also be sure to carry some of the supplies when portaging—the Indians are contemptuous of anyone who does not carry his own weight.

Finally, do not try to 'civilise' the Indians. In other words, let go of the fact that they are obscene in manner, promiscuous and dirty. Focus instead on their souls, and you 'will find roses among thorns, the sweet with the bitter, all in nothing'.

alleviate his suffering slightly before starting in again with renewed energy. They pulled out his fingernails. They burned the tip of his penis and his fingers. They carefully scalped him and then poured hot gum or pine resin into the open wound on his head.

Then, Champlain wrote, they:

> *... pierced his arms near the wrists and with sticks tried to pull out the sinews by brute force. When they could not get them out, they cut them off. The poor wretch uttered strange cries and I felt pity to see him treated in this way. Still, he bore it so firmly that sometimes one would have said that he felt scarcely any pain.*

Unable to watch any more of this treatment meted out, Champlain offered to shoot the man to put him out of his misery. At first, the Indians said no, but when they saw that it displeased him, they acquiesced and Champlain shot the man from behind 'without his perceiving anything, causing him to escape all the tortures he would have suffered'. But even after the Mohawk was dead, the Indians continued to mutilate his body, cutting out his heart and forcing the other Mohawk prisoners to eat it. While Champlain understood that Indians had been torturing their captives literally for centuries before he came on the scene, he once again had an instinctive hatred of harming the helpless. This was not the only time he sought to intervene when prisoners were being tortured, for he was not afraid to let his allies know that he did not approve of this practice.

'A large sea'

Champlain returned triumphantly to Quebec that August, having accomplished numerous goals with a single battle. He had badly frightened the Iroquois, providing a warning that they needed to leave the fur-trading routes to the west alone, had become a legendary figure to the Huron, Algonquin and Montagnais, and had secured a promise that he would be taken into the western territories—especially 'to the place where there was such a large sea, that they could not see the end of it'.

Champlain thought that this might be Hudson Bay, the vast, saltwater gulf in northern Canada where Henry Hudson (see page 134) met his end. It was not until 1615 that he was able to get to this large sea, pioneering the route that ultimately all French fur traders would take into the west, up the St Lawrence River and the Ottawa River to Lake Nipissing, and then down what came to be called the French River to the 'large sea'. Except that this body of water was not Hudson Bay, much farther to the north, but Lake Huron, a freshwater ocean seemingly without end.

Champlain travelled through Huronia, visiting his Huron allies, seeing their thousands of hectares of cultivated corn and their palisaded towns, eating the rich blueberries and raspberries that grew wild in great profusion, and marvelling at the 2.75-metre (nine-foot) long sturgeon that swam in the lake. 'The countryside is so fine and fertile', he wrote, 'that it is a pleasure to travel through it'.

This was Champlain's ultimate vision of New France, a vision that was not shared by other European conquerors. He loved the Huron people and their customs and wanted them to live as they were, not supplanted by the French but in tandem with them, trading in peace, with Quebec as the great centre of the fur trade and Huronia the place from whence the furs flowed.

In aid of this, he even accompanied the Hurons on another excursion against the Iroquois, this time against the Onondaga nation, whose capital was a heavily fortified town in what is now central New York State. But, plagued by a series of mishaps, the Huron, along with a badly wounded Champlain, were forced to withdraw. Even so, they were able to inflict serious casualties on the Iroquois during a bloody battle and to keep them, for the near future in any event, away from Huron trading routes. And, despite the loss, the fact that Champlain had tried mightily to help the Canadian Indians (and been injured in the process) only helped to raise his stock among native peoples.

The New York raid was Samuel de Champlain's last great adventure in New France, although he would live on for another twenty years, building up his great capital city of Quebec—which the French held for well over a century before it fell to the English in 1759—and keeping the fur trade lucrative for all parties. Champlain was a humanist who used what the historian David Hackett Fischer calls 'limited force' to attempt to achieve his goals. Fischer goes on to write:

> *Many stories have been told about first encounters between American Indians and Europeans. Few of them are about harmony and peace ... [But] Frenchmen did not try to conquer the Indians and compel them to work, as in New Spain. They did not abuse them, as in Virginia, or drive them away, as in New England. In the region they began to call Canada ... small colonies of Frenchmen and large Indian nations lived together in a spirit of* amitié *and* concorde.

And this spirit, unique in the American experience of the time, came directly from the exploits of Samuel de Champlain.

SINGLE-MINDED PURSUIT OF A DREAM

La Salle and the great Mississippi River, 1669–1683

During the fierce winter of 1668–69, René-Robert Cavelier, Sieur de la Salle, often sat in front of a blazing fire entertaining guests. Gale-force winds might howl outside, through the tiny settlement of Montreal, Canada, but inside things were comfortable enough, although, had he seen La Salle's guests, Samuel de Champlain, dead some thirty years, would have rolled over in his grave. The men who smoked and laughed by the fire with La Salle were Iroquois Indians of the Seneca tribe, some of the same Indians who had so bedevilled the Huron who had come to Champlain for protection.

These Seneca had arrived in Montreal late that autumn to trade furs but had then stayed on, all through the bitter Canadian winter, mainly because of the presence of La Salle, the one Frenchman who, even better than Champlain, understood Indians. He spoke seven or eight Indian languages—Champlain was forced to rely on interpreters—and knew how to listen. That winter, he listened very carefully.

These visiting Seneca spent most nights gathered in La Salle's home. They wore breechcloths and leggings made out of deer skin and leather caps with a single feather stuck in the top, and they kept their hair short, although not in the traditional scalp lock or crest down the centre of the head known as the Mohawk, which they saved for times of war. Sitting around La Salle's fire, with bearskins thrown over their shoulders, they told La Salle about a massive river that began three days' journey north of their territory (which was in present-day western New York State) and flowed into a vast sea. The river was so long, the Indians told La Salle, that a man in a canoe would take six or eight months to float down it to the ocean.

The Indians called this river the Ohio—meaning 'beautiful river'—and said that its banks were alive with game, including wild cattle, by which they meant buffalo, and that Indian tribes too numerous to count resided along its mighty flow.

When the Indians left for the evening, La Salle would write down what they had told him and he would begin to dream. It was his dream that this great river flowed into what he knew as the 'Vermillion Sea', the Gulf of California. If this were the case, then he had found a way across the American continent to the Pacific Ocean, a way that would be worth more in trade than all the gold and silver the Spanish hauled out of gold mines in Mexico.

And that, La Salle decided during the long and dark winter nights, was a dream worth pursuing.

A place of opportunity

Born to a wealthy and politically connected family in Rouen, France, in 1643, René-Robert Cavelier, Sieur de la Salle (this last referred to the name of the Cavelier estate near Rouen), grew up in wealth and privilege but was an ascetic young man, a fact that makes his transformation into one of North America's greatest explorers even more astounding. He entered the Jesuit order—the most powerful Catholic religious order in France at the time—with the intention of becoming a priest, but although he was brilliant at his studies, he was also, according to his teachers, stubborn and intractable. While he ended up taking his vows as a Jesuit, he soon renounced them, but this left him with the little problem of what he was going to do with his life. Taking vows in a religious order, even if they were renounced, disqualified a person under French law from inheriting from his family. La Salle thus sailed to New France, where his brother Jean was a Sulpician monk in the new settlement of Montreal (the Sulpician and Recollect friars, both groups part of the Franciscan religious order, would ally themselves with La Salle for his entire life, much to the jealous dismay of the Jesuits).

La Salle arrived in Montreal in 1666 and immediately began seeking his fortune. Montreal was originally established by Champlain in 1611 as a trading post on the St Lawrence River, but the city itself was founded by Sulpician friars, who were only too happy to sell the ambitious young La Salle a large tract of land located along the river some fifteen kilometres (nine miles) southwest of Montreal. For the next three years, La Salle set to work clearing the land, building houses and forts, and attracting settlers to live there, to work farms or hunt in the surrounding wilderness.

New France at this time was undergoing a sea change. Champlain had founded the colony, but after his death in 1635 little had been done to improve it—as late as 1660 there were only twenty-five settlers in Quebec in any given year, and these had to fight to survive Indian attacks and harsh winters. But now the glorious Sun King, Louis XIV, had finally recognised the importance of a North American empire to rival the one the British were establishing farther south, and he was offering inducements (including women) to get settlers to brave the dangers of the New World. There was a sense that the mainly uncharted wilderness beyond the fragile settlements was a place of opportunity, for those strong enough to grasp it.

In search of the 'Beautiful River'

In the spring of 1669, after his conversations with the visiting Iroquois, La Salle was determined to find the river they had talked about. He was so obsessed with a passage across America to Asia that scoffers named his little settlement *La Chine*, meaning 'China'—a name for the area that persists to this day—but no amount of ridicule was going to deter La Salle. On 6 July he headed up the St Lawrence River with nine canoes, which carried an assortment of backwoodsmen, Iroquois guides and Sulpician friars, whose goal was to find Indian tribes that had not yet been converted by the Jesuits.

DAUGHTERS OF THE KING

When King Louis XIV and his ministers decided something had to change in their New France policy—that the land needed to be settled, built up, protected, further explored—they sought an inducement to draw men out to this wilderness peopled with savages. The government of France simply did not have the money to pay huge sums to would-be settlers, so one minister of the king, Jean-Baptiste Colbert, came up with a program featuring a bribe of another sort: women.

The program was called filles du roi*, which means 'daughters of the king'. From about 1663 to 1673, women willing to go to New France were actively sought by French 'royal agents', who went from town to town looking for likely candidates. Some women from so-called 'good families' were sought so that they might be married to officers and gentlemen. However, more were deliberately chosen from working-class families in provinces like Normandy—young girls used to backbreaking labour, who were obedient and 'full of virtue' (that is, virgins). Once they (or their parents) signed a contract, the women were taken to convents where they were watched over by vigilant nuns before being shipped overseas.*

In a decade, about six hundred 'daughters of the king' made their way to the New World. It was a dangerous journey. Sixty died in shipwrecks; one was captured by Indians on her way to Quebec and disappeared into the North American wilderness, never to be seen again. Of those who survived, many did marry (with dowries of 50 livres*, or pounds, provided by the king) and raise families, although there were numerous women who, for one reason or another (including being 'ill-used', or raped, on the voyage over) could not find husbands and were reduced to a state of public begging. This was something that New France officials hushed up so as not to jeopardise the king's program, which in the end was a fairly successful one—millions of people of French–Canadian descent, in both Canada and America, can trace their lineage to the* filles du roi*.*

Like so many explorers at the time, La Salle had no idea of the size of the North American continent or what he was really looking for. The 'Beautiful River' the Seneca were referring to, given where they told La Salle it was located, was probably the Ohio River itself, which flows into the Mississippi (although, confusingly, the Iroquois referred to the Mississippi as the 'Ohio' as well). By 2 August the expedition had reached the easternmost of the Great Lakes, Lake Ontario, which appeared to La Salle 'like a great sea with no land beyond it'. They

paddled along the southern shore of the lake until they reached the home of their Seneca guides, a place where most of the Indians had seen few white men. While there was currently a peace treaty with the Iroquois, La Salle knew the Indians enough to be wary of them and thus, while he gave the Seneca trade goods and they feasted him in return, he wanted to be off as soon as possible.

But he needed a guide for this journey farther west and the Indians kept putting off the moment when they were going to provide him with one; this began to concern him. The Iroquois also began to drink some brandy they had received from Dutch traders in the Hudson Valley, after which they would threaten the French mockingly with the very knives the French had given them as gifts. The final straw was when a Shawnee prisoner was brought into the centre of camp and tortured to death in front of the French; the poor man was then dismembered and eaten, with the Iroquois trying to get the French to have a bite or two.

This behaviour seemed so blatantly hostile that La Salle decided to move the expedition along on his own. Guideless, they departed the Seneca village in early September and made their way farther along the southern shore of Lake Ontario. When they got to the western part of the lake, they heard a great roaring sound that was actually the sound of the Niagara River where it pours over Niagara Falls, a huge, 60-metre (200-foot) high waterfall the Seneca had told La Salle about.

The falls were fifty kilometres (thirty miles) away, yet their booming noise could be heard on the lake, which impressed La Salle, but not enough to make him deviate from his route to become the first European to see them—that would be Father Louis Hennepin, some years later.

When La Salle's expedition reached the far western end of Lake Ontario, they met a French trapper, Louis Jolliet, who had great familiarity with the region and told La Salle that the way to reach the fabled Mississippi was not to head straight west but to follow the Great Lakes route—Lake Erie to Lake Huron and down around Lake Michigan's coastline to Green Bay or points farther south. La Salle refused to believe he would have to travel that far north to go west, so here, in late September, his group split up. The Sulpicians decided to head north to try to convert the Indians in the Upper Great Lakes, while La Salle moved west with a small group of men and a Shawnee guide he had picked up along the way.

'Empty dreams and empty pockets'

Guided by the Shawnee, La Salle led his canoes along the southern shore of Lake Erie, seeking a water route to the Ohio River. The expedition got lost numerous times in trackless wilderness. Finally, his men abandoned him, slipping away one night and leaving La Salle completely alone. This would have daunted a lesser explorer, but not La Salle, who had an incredible capacity to endure hardship. He went on, alone with his guide, canoeing along the shores of Lake Erie until he found a route to the Allegheny River, which in turn led him to the Ohio. He then headed down the Ohio. The Indians he met had, for the most part, not seen white men, and his encounters with them were part of what made him different from most Europeans. Like

An Iroquois warrior scalps his enemy. The Iroquois intimidated La Salle by torturing and eating a prisoner in front of him.

Champlain before him, he treated the Indians with respect (although he did not idealise them), and they returned it by providing him with food to supplement the game he caught hunting.

Thus, La Salle travelled along through the wilderness, all the way down the Ohio River to a point, near the present-day city of Louisville, where fierce rapids impeded his progress. Here he decided to return home. Although some historians have claimed that he reached the Mississippi on this solo expedition, it does not appear that he did so, but he became the first to explore the land south of the Great Lakes. At the time, this was small consolation for La Salle. As the historian Donald S. Johnson writes, he returned to *La Chine* 'with empty dreams and empty pockets' late in 1670 and was forced to head out again into the wilderness as a trapper to replenish his depleted coffers.

He had not given up on his dream, but he was soon to receive disappointing news, for in 1673 the same Louis Jolliet he had met along the shores of Lake Ontario—who had advised him to find a Great Lakes route to the Mississippi—had found the great river and travelled down it with the Jesuit Father Jacques Marquette. While they had not gone all the way down to the river's mouth—and while the information they provided actually helped La Salle's own plans—he could feel his opportunity slipping away. He needed to have funding for his great expedition to the Mississippi and began to lobby for it. Making a powerful friend in Count Frontenac, New France's new governor-general, La Salle had himself appointed governor of Fort Frontenac, a new fort and trading post that had been placed in the wilderness at the juncture of the St Lawrence River and Lake Ontario. The furs that flowed into this fort from the west, brought by Iroquois Indians, proved so profitable that La Salle felt he now had a case to make for a government-funded expedition down the Mississippi. And he decided to make the case to the Sun King himself.

'We have received with favour'

Returning to France in 1677, La Salle—his skin tanned by years in the wilderness, his long black hair flowing down his back—laid it on thick for the French court. The area west of New France and south of the Great Lakes, he wrote in a petition submitted to a minister of the king, was 'Nearly all so beautiful and so fertile; so free from forests, and so abounding in meadows, brooks and rivers; so abounding in fish, game and venison, that one can find there in plenty and with little trouble, all that is needful for the support of flourishing colonies'. There are even 'native wild cattle', La Salle wrote, obviously referring to buffalo, 'which, instead of hair, have a fine wool that may answer for making cloth and hats'.

On 12 May 1678, La Salle received a reply from the king, which read, in part: 'We have received with favour the very humble petition made us in your name, to permit you to labour at the discovery of the western parts of New France'. The king then conferred on La Salle a five-year monopoly to explore and trade in the Mississippi Valley. It was all La Salle could have hoped for and he headed back for New France in great excitement, despite the fact that the king was not going to actually back the enterprise financially—La Salle would have to raise the money himself, which he did by dint of some wealthy backers.

Once in New France, La Salle began to gather men and supplies for the expedition at Fort Frontenac. He hired as second-in-command an Italian named Henri de Tonty, one of the most colourful characters on the frontier at the time. A Sicilian of good family who affected aristocratic airs, he was a tough-as-nails soldier who had lost his right hand in a grenade explosion fighting in Sicily and thus wore a gloved iron hand in its place.

La Salle also decided that his expedition was going to be too big for canoes, so he commissioned the building of a sailing vessel, the *Griffin*, a 45-tonne barque (a three-masted, square-rigged ship), on the western shores of Lake Ontario, near the mouth of the Niagara River and the roaring of the mighty falls upstream. The builders had to be careful—the Iroquois understood instinctively that such a large vessel represented a quantum leap in the capacities of the French to plunder further the lands to the west—which the Iroquois themselves were beginning to spread into—of the bounty of furs so important to both the whites and the Native Americans.

It appears that the Indians may have twice tried to sabotage the ship during its building.

 ## THE JESUIT EXPLORER

While the scheming and intriguing of the Jesuits in New France often gave them a bad name, Father Jacques Marquette was the kind of man who represented the Jesuit order at its best. Marquette, born in France in 1637, came to Quebec in 1666 possessed of a missionary zeal to convert the savages. By 1668 he had found his way to the remote Jesuit mission at Sioux Sainte-Marie, between Lake Michigan and Lake Huron, where he laboured baptising the local Huron, but also members of the Illinois tribe, who came from farther west and south.

It was the Illinois who told him of a great river that they called the Mississippi, which ran into a great ocean. They even invited him farther south in order to visit them and see it for himself. In 1673 Marquette received permission to try to locate the river and see if it ran into the Gulf of Mexico or the Pacific Ocean. With him was fur trader and adventurer Louis Jolliet, who had been trained as a Jesuit in France but left the order to come to the New World to make his fortune. The two men were quite experienced in the wilderness, with Marquette speaking numerous Indian languages, and they set out in two canoes with five other men. In fairly short order, they found their way up the Fox River and then down the Wisconsin River, and entered the Mississippi in June 1673. They were apparently the first Europeans to view the Mississippi this far north and possibly the first to view it at all since Hernando de Soto (see page 91).

In any event, they sailed without problems down the Mississippi, charting their course until they came to the point where the mighty Missouri River comes crashing into the Mississippi. 'Floating islands of debris' swirled around their canoes in the rushing current; whole trees shot straight by them. They survived this experience and continued for another 500 kilometres (300 miles) until, running out of supplies and ammunition, they turned back. They were now certain, because of its southerly direction, that the Mississippi flowed into the Gulf of Mexico, although Marquette thought that the Missouri might flow into the Gulf of California.

In any event, although they did not reach the mouth of the river, Marquette and Jolliet certainly made things a good deal easier for the Sieur de la Salle.

THE FATE OF THE *GRIFFIN*

As the first sailing ship ever to ply the Great Lakes, the fate of La Salle's Griffin holds special interest—and has become a special mystery—for historians and La Salle buffs alike.

The vessel was last seen leaving the mouth of Green Bay, the long, narrow bay in the northwestern part of Lake Michigan, heading north, just as the autumn gales of 1679 began to blow. La Salle had sent the Griffin back to Fort Niagara with a hold full of furs. It was to return as soon as possible to rendezvous with him on the southern shore of Lake Michigan, but it never materialised, a grievous loss for La Salle.

There are numerous opinions as to what happened to it. The nineteenth century historian Francis Parkman enumerated some of them. One of the main theories was that the Iroquois, realising just what an advance in technology the Griffin represented, decided that they needed to 'disgust the French with this mode of navigating' and thus lured the ship to shore and burned it, killing the crew. La Salle believed that the ship, which carried a valuable cargo of furs, was scuttled by the crew themselves, who attempted to barter the furs with the Indians and were killed or captured. La Salle heard rumours of a white man held as a captive among the Sioux Indians and grew convinced that he was the pilot of the boat. There were even stories that the Jesuits, from dislike of La Salle and his Sulpician followers, had the ship destroyed.

However, the most likely explanation is the least mysterious—that the Griffin went down in one of the fierce storms that plague the Great Lakes in autumn and that have claimed as their victims modern vessels far larger than the Griffin. This explanation is supported by the testimony of Father Hennepin, who claimed that Indians had told him they had seen the crew of the boat resting in a harbour in the northern part of Lake Michigan and had warned them that a storm was rising and that, when they sailed, they should stick close to land. But, as Hennepin puts it, the pilot said, 'he would steer as he pleased without hearing to the advice of the savages who, generally speaking, have more sense than the Europeans think at first'.

The Indians then said they watched the ship sail off into a storm—and saw it quite simply disappear, probably hit by a huge wave.

However, by August 1679 the *Griffin* was finally ready. It was towed up the Niagara to Lake Erie and launched with great ceremony, which included a three-gun salute and a priestly blessing. La Salle was aboard, but just barely—rumours had been spread by his enemies in Montreal and Quebec that his expedition was in bad shape, and many creditors tried to recall their loans. Promising that he would send back furs to them to pay his debts, La Salle set off on the adventure of his lifetime.

Fort Heartbreak

Becoming the first sailing vessel ever to ply the Great Lakes, the *Griffin* headed across Lake Erie, through the Detroit River and Lake St Clair, and into Lake Huron. Sailing north along the lake's stormy shores, the ship arrived at Fort Michimilimackinac at the juncture where Lake Huron meets Lake Michigan. This important, though squalid, trading post was run by Jesuits, who, La Salle discovered to his horror, were out to do him serious damage. Jealous of the royal patent La Salle had received, the Jesuits were stirring up trouble among the Indian tribes farther to the south, in the Illinois Valley, which La Salle would have to traverse to reach the Mississippi. Not only that, but La Salle had sent men ahead to Fort Michimilimackinac to trade for furs and help prepare for his voyage—these men, it turned out, had squandered his money and goods and had now fled into the wilderness. Sending Tonty after them, La Salle sailed aboard the *Griffin* to the head of Green Bay, on the western side of Lake Michigan. There other men of La Salle's had indeed traded for furs, which La Salle decided to send back to Niagara aboard the *Griffin* in order to try to assuage his creditors.

La Salle himself then took canoes and paddled with his men and supplies to the southern shore of Lake Michigan, where he waited for Tonty to arrive, for from this agreed-on rendezvous point they would launch their descent of the Mississippi

as soon as the *Griffin* rejoined them. Tonty finally joined La Salle in mid-November but, though the expedition waited and waited, there was no sign of the *Griffin*. Deciding he must push on, La Salle led his men through the wintry Midwestern plains south to the land of the Illinois, which they reached in January 1680. At first these Indians welcomed them graciously, but then an agent of the Jesuits reached them from Fort Michimilimackinac and told them that La Salle was secretly in league with their age-old enemies, the Iroquois. The persuasive La Salle denied this and managed to calm the Indians down. Even so, six of his party, afraid of being massacred, deserted, and to calm the rest down La Salle was forced to build a small fort apart from the Indians. He named it Fort Crèvecoeur, or Fort Heartbreak.

This expedition, which was intended to bring La Salle fame and glory, was ending up in bitter disappointment for the French explorer. Chief among his worries was that the *Griffin* was long overdue to return with badly needed supplies. Unable to figure out what had happened to the ship and unable to wait any longer, the extraordinary La Salle set off with a few men on what the historian Francis Parkman called 'the hardest journey ever made by a Frenchman in America'. On 2 March, leaving Tonty in charge of the fort, La Salle took several men and headed back overland to Niagara to discover the fate of his ship.

The journey covered 1600 kilometres (1000 miles) and took them sixty-five days. It was, as Parkman wrote, 'the worst of all seasons' to undertake such a trip, since the sun warmed the snow into a morass of semi-frozen muck at noon, then froze it again at night. The small party traversed the previously unexplored wilds of southern Michigan, pushing through forests so dense that, as La Salle later wrote, 'our faces were so covered with blood that we hardly knew each other'. At one point, they had to outrun a war party of marauding

Indians and spent three days hiding in trackless swamps. When they finally reached Niagara, only La Salle and one other man could walk. Two men died of pneumonia shortly after the arduous trek ended.

The Mississippi, at last

La Salle was nothing if not resilient. By July 1680, he was off again with a new group of men to return to Fort Heartbreak and begin his exploration anew. However, on his way there he discovered that Tonty's men had mutinied and that rampaging Iroquois had destroyed the nearby village of the Illinois—La Salle arrived there on 1 December and found, according to Parkman, 'nothing but signs of fire and the rage of the Iroquois. There remained standing only some charred stakes, showing what had been the extent of the village. Upon most of these stakes the heads of the dead had been affixed to be devoured by the crows'.

Searching desperately for Tonty, La Salle explored farther out into the prairie and found 'the heads and entire bodies of women and children, empaled and roasted and then set up in a field'. There was no sign of Tonty or any survivors of any type. La Salle was forced to winter nearby. However, in June 1681, he received some good news—Tonty, having had a narrow escape from the Iroquois, was safe in Fort Michimilimackinac. The two of them returned to Fort Frontenac, raised an entirely new expedition and in February 1682 at last canoed down the Illinois River and into the great Mississippi. With them, in a flotilla of canoes, were twenty Frenchmen and an equal number of Indians.

Canoeing the Mississippi was an experience La Salle would never forget. It was a dangerous river, especially as spring came on, filled with fast-moving floating objects—ice floes, trees, dead animals. Yet it was a place of great beauty, its wooded banks teeming with animals, low forested hills rising in the distance, other great rivers—the Ohio, the Arkansas, the Missouri—pouring into it, as if all the waters in the world were joined in this one broad stream. Although La Salle took the precaution of camping on islands whenever possible to ward off Indian attack, the French had little trouble with the native peoples they met along the way—the Chickasaw Arkansas, Tensas, Nachez, Coroas and Oumas—with the exception of two incidents. At one point, near the present-day city of Memphis, Tennessee, an expedition member went missing while hunting, but La Salle presented gifts to a nearby tribe of Chickasaw and, while the Indians never admitted taking the man, he soon came floating down the river on a log, nearly starved to death but alive, having been released by his captors. Farther south, they met Choctaw Indians who fired barbed arrows at them from the bank, an invitation to battle that La Salle wisely ignored, keeping his flotilla moving along.

The priests accompanying La Salle's expedition erected crosses wherever they went and held ritual Masses for the Indians. The Indians could not possibly have understood much of what was going on but, according to one priest, 'they showed that they relished what I said, by raising their eyes to heaven and kneeling as if to adore'.

Finally, there were signs they were reaching the ocean—the water had a brackish taste and the shores slowly widened out, going from swamp to sand. At last, on 6 April 1682, they reached the Gulf of Mexico. On a small hillock near the shore, La Salle erected a column with the words: 'Here Reigns Louis the Great, King of France Navarre'. He then made a speech claiming the entire territory for the king.

It was a momentous occasion in the history of New France, and in the life of La Salle—for both the dreams of the country for a territory to rival that of Spain and England, and the dreams of one man for glory were finally fulfilled.

'One of the greatest men of his age'

Following the Mississippi to the Gulf was one thing, but creating a territory there was quite another. With but a short time left on his patent, La Salle headed back up the river and arrived in Quebec by November 1683. But his patron Frontenac had been recalled to France and those in power were unfriendly to La Salle, causing him to take the first ship he could get to France to persuade the king that a colony at the mouth of the Mississippi would be a great boon to France.

In January 1685, La Salle, in command of a fleet of four ships, sailed across the Atlantic and into the Gulf of Mexico, completely bypassing Canada and his enemies there. Unfortunately, taking this unfamiliar route, he was unable to find the mouth of the Mississippi and sailed past it into Texas, into the same bleak regions where Cabeza de Vaca had wandered (see page 63). He finally landed and established a fort, but by the following year two-thirds of his settlers had died of sickness or bites from the many poisonous snakes that inhabited the region.

Desperate, La Salle set off with twenty men to try to find the Mississippi, intending to ascend it and head back to Canada for help, but on 18 March 1687 his men turned on him and murdered him with a single shot to the head. They then stripped him and left his naked body to be eaten by crows. 'Such was the end', said Henri de Tonty, 'of one of the greatest men of his age'.

La Salle takes possession of Louisiana for the King of France on 6 April 1682, at the end of his epic journey down the Mississippi River.

PART 4

THE GREAT
SOUTHERN
OCEAN

Captain Cook receives a friendly
greeting in Tahiti on his second
voyage in 1773.

ENCOUNTERING THE WORLD

Ferdinand Magellan circumnavigates the globe, 1519–1521

Even in Magellan's time, they knew how important his voyage around the world had been. Writing only twenty years after the great sailor's death in the Philippines, the Spanish historian Gonzalo Fernandez de Oviedo effused: 'The track that [Magellan] followed is the most wonderful thing and the greatest novelty that has ever been seen since God created the first man and ordered the world unto our own day'.

Praise of this nature was not accorded even Columbus, and with good reason: Columbus sought the Indies—the Spice Islands—just as Magellan did, and merely blundered into the Americas. But Ferdinand Magellan, driven by passion, courage and anger, knew that the Pacific Ocean existed and knew that the Spice Islands lay on the other side of it. His dogged determination to find a way through ended up with him proving that a man could take a ship and sail around the planet Earth.

As Oviedo further wrote: 'Nothing more notable in navigation [has] ever been heard or described since the voyage of the patriarch Noah'. And nothing more extraordinary would be done in terms of opening up human horizons until man landed on the moon.

Adventure and betrayal

Ferdinand Magellan is hugely important in human history, yet we know relatively little about his early life. He was born, probably in 1480, in northern Portugal. His family were minor nobility fallen on hard times, although his father still had the connections to send twelve-year-old Ferdinand off to Lisbon, to serve as a page to the Portuguese Queen Leonor, wife of King John II. He seems to have received military training at court, not unusual for a young man of his relatively impoverished station—the other options would have been for him to become a colonial officer, a clerk or a priest—and launched his life of adventure in 1505 when he sailed with a Portuguese expedition to India. He spent the next seven years fighting in the service of king and country as Portugal sought to colonise India, present-day Malaysia and the Moluccas—the Spice Islands themselves. These places were essential to Portugal if it were to compete for world hegemony against Spain, which had a stranglehold on the riches of the New World Columbus had discovered.

Magellan proved himself to be a courageous and loyal officer. He fought at Cochin, India, in 1510, participated in the attack on Goa the same year, and took part in the fall of Malacca, in modern Malaysia, in 1511. After briefly returning to Portugal, he again left in the service of his country, fighting the Muslims in Morocco in 1512. It was here that he received a lance wound that partially severed the tendons at the back of his right knee and left him so lame that many people meeting him for the first time mistakenly thought he had a club foot. This injury changed Magellan's life in other ways, too. When he returned to Portugal, he asked for an annuity because of his injury, but he was turned down by King Manuel I, with the suggestion that his wound was not as disabling as he made it out to be. (In other versions of this story, Magellan was also accused of illegal trading with the Muslims in Morocco and refused further service by King Manuel, even though he was acquitted.)

Enraged by such treatment on the part of the country for which he had fought so long, Magellan turned his eyes to Spain.

Setting off for the South Sea

Rage is often underrated as the mother of invention, and when Ferdinand Magellan arrived in Seville in October 1517 he had a plan to present to Charles V, King of Spain, Holy Roman Emperor and grandson of Ferdinand and Isabella. Magellan knew that Pope

Leo X, acting as arbiter, had agreed that the eastern route to the Spice Islands—around the tip of Africa at the Cape of Good Hope—belonged to the Portuguese. If Spain, which, after all, was benefiting from the riches of the Americas, wanted to reach the Indies, Spanish mariners would have to sail west to do so.

This was exactly what Magellan proposed to Charles—a way to compete with Portugal in its own backyard. The ocean called the 'South Sea' had been discovered when Vasco Nùñez de Balboa crossed Panama, and it was Magellan's notion that he could find a western route to it. Along with his friend, the astronomer Rui Faleiro, Magellan poured over maps and charts of the Americas. He knew that the continent had been explored by John Cabot to the north and that Amerigo Vespucci had charted it as far south as Brazil. Magellan was certain, he told

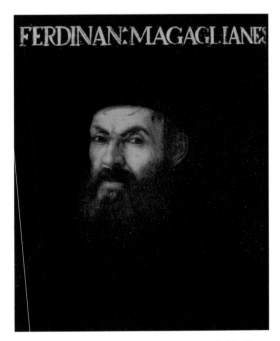

Ferdinand Magellan, the visionary captain who reached the East Indies by sailing westward across the Pacific.

the king, that with the right backing he could travel even farther south and find a way to the South Sea.

King Charles was bright and ambitious, although only eighteen years old, and he saw the merit in Magellan's scheme. He thus had a contract drawn up agreeing to provide the Portuguese navigator (although by this time Magellan had assumed Spanish citizenship) with a fleet of five ships, along with the money to hire five crews. Magellan was awarded the military title 'captain-general' and would become governor of any islands he discovered. In return, the king would receive four-fifths of the proceeds of the voyage.

Magellan was ecstatic, even though more pitfalls lay ahead. The ships—his flagship, the *Trinidad*, the *Victoria*, the *Concepción*, the *San Antonio* and the

ANTONIO PIGAFETTA'S GRAND JOURNAL

Had Ferdinand Magellan circumnavigated the world and Antonio Pigafetta not been there, we would know very little about this epic voyage. Had Magellan lived, Pigafetta's testimony would be less valuable, but in the absence of the great captain-general's own words, Pigafetta's journal is the only complete picture we have of the unknown lands and people and the drama of the world's first circumnavigation.

Pigafetta was born around 1491 in the town of Vicenza, which was controlled by the city-state of Venice. We do not know a great deal about his upbringing, except that he appears to have been a member of minor nobility and probably joined the fighting Order of the Knights of St John of Jerusalem, who were based on the island of Rhodes, in the Mediterranean. He probably joined these Christian knights fighting against the Muslim Turks, perhaps seeing service as a soldier aboard Mediterranean galleys. In 1520 he gained permission from both the Grand Master of the Knights of St John and Charles V to set sail with Magellan. Pigafetta is listed on the muster rolls, which give each crew member's name and duty, as a soldier, but also as simply a passenger, which has led to some speculation that he may have been a spy in the employ of Venice as it was unusual then for someone to travel simply for pleasure.

Whether he was a spy or not, he certainly became extremely loyal to Magellan, fighting at his side on the beach on the island of Mactan where Magellan fell, and receiving a poison arrow wound that caused his head to swell for days. After becoming one of the very few survivors of the expedition, Pigafetta wrote up his notes in journal form (including glossaries of indigenous languages) and presented them to Charles V, among others. Versions of the book were published in France and Italy, and thus Europe learned about the fate of Magellan.

As for the fate of Antonio Pigafetta, no one is quite certain, but he seems to have rejoined the Knights of St John and died on Malta in 1534.

Santiago—were old, small and poorly armed, a fact remarked upon by a spy for King Manuel of Portugal, who was keeping a jealous eye on Magellan's doings: 'I assure your Highness that I should be ill-inclined to sail in them [even] for the Canaries'.

Also, Magellan was forced to sail with three Spanish captains in his fleet, because the Spanish were worried that too many Portuguese were on the expedition. But, finally, all was in readiness. Accompanied by his slave Enrique, who would prove invaluable as an interpreter, Magellan boarded the *Trinidad* and his little fleet set sail on 20 September 1519.

'The great and awful things'

Along with his 250 officers, crew and soldiers, Magellan had along with him a passenger, one Antonio Pigafetta of Venice. Pigafetta was probably in his late twenties, a man of noble birth and some means. There is some mystery as to what he was doing with Magellan. Some sources indicate that he was the kind of adventuring gentleman who would become familiar on journeys of exploration in later centuries—a tourist out for extreme thrills. But there has also been the suggestion that he was a spy for Venice, the city-state most hurt by the Portuguese—and now, potentially, Spanish— inroads into the lucrative eastern spice trade. Whatever his motives, Pigafetta would provide the only complete record we have of Magellan's epic journey—of 'the very great and awful things of the Ocean', as he put it—and he also came, during the course of the trip, to admire the captain-general immensely.

The first part of the trip was familiar. Magellan set sail south for the Canary Islands and Cape Verde, and then headed west across the Atlantic, from the bulge of Africa to the bulge of Brazil. But the trip from its very beginning was not without incident. The weather was troublesome. At first, the vessels were often becalmed, at which point they were, according to Pigafetta, surrounded 'by great fish called *tiburoni* [sharks] … which have terrible teeth and eat men when they find them alive or dead in the sea'. Then there arose storms that were so violent the tops of the masts tipped to touch the tops of the waves and lightning was so fierce that St Elmo's fire—static electricity that often gathers at mast-tops during storms—was seen for hours in the rigging.

But the weather was not the most serious problem: that was Magellan's relationship with the Spanish captains and crewmembers. Magellan was a hard taskmaster and insisted that his fleet follow him closely and take no actions without his approval. Even at night, they had to watch the rear of the *Trinidad* for a series of torches that would give them direction—one torch to change tack, two to reduce speed and so on. The proud Spanish captains of three of the ships thought their competency was being called into question. One of them, Captain Juan de Cartagena of the *San Antonio*, refused a direct order from Magellan, causing Magellan to relieve him of his command and put him in irons.

By the time the fleet reached Brazil, after a crossing of seventy days, discontent ran rampant through the expedition.

Painting with fire

Because of Pigafetta's journal, we have an unusually detailed picture of Magellan's encounter with the inhabitants of Brazil—it was known as 'the land of Verzin', after *verzino*, the Italian name for the brazil wood trees that grew there in abundance. Pigafetta wrote, correctly, that the country is 'very vast and larger than Spain, Portugal, France and Italy combined'. He was not quite so accurate about other things. The people who thronged in dugout canoes to meet Magellan's ships reach an age of '125 to 140 years', the Italian gentleman wrote, mainly because they live their lives 'according to the laws of nature', even though they also are cannibals. But Pigafetta did observe that the people slept in great longhouses and 'paint their whole body and the face in a wonderful manner with fire', meaning tattoos. He also sniffed that the Indians 'dress up in parrot feathers with a huge wheel [of feathers] on their backsides, in such a fashion that it looks ridiculous'.

Magellan and his fleet sailed 3000 kilometres (2000 miles) down the Brazilian coastline and spent some time refitting in the protected harbour of present-day Rio de Janeiro. There, Pigafetta and the other crewmembers traded with the Brazilian tribes quite satisfactorily: 'For a king of playing cards', wrote the Italian traveller, 'the Indians gave me five fowles, and even thought they cheated me'. Soon enough, however, Magellan pushed the fleet farther south, looking restlessly for a passageway that would lead west. By January 1520 they had reached latitude 35 degrees south, farther than any European had gone. Still they continued in search of a western passageway, even as the weather turned colder. South of today's Montevideo, the fleet met its first penguins. Pigafetta reported that they were present in such great numbers that 'in one hour they were able to fill their five ships with geese [penguins], and they are completely black and unable to fly and they live on fish, and are so fat it is necessary to peel them'.

Winter—and mutiny

By this time it was the end of March and the southern winter was about to begin. Magellan took his fleet to a small, desolate harbour at a place he called Port St Julian, in what is now southern Argentina. He gathered the officers and men together and told them that they would winter there for five months and that they would have to exist on half-rations during that time. This enraged many of the men, especially the Spanish captains, who on the night of 1 April staged a violent mutiny. They took over the *San Antonio* and killed its captain, a Portuguese

man who was a friend of Magellan's, and then put Juan de Cartagena (clapped in irons previously by Magellan) in charge of the vessel. When Magellan awoke, he found he was in command only of the *Trinidad* and the *Santiago*, which was captained by João Serrão, a friend of his brother.

Magellan, with typical stubborn courage and audacity, fought back. He sent five crewmen in a longboat with a letter to one of the rebellious captains, agreeing to a parlay. As the man opened the missive, one of Magellan's crewmen stabbed him to death. Sailors loyal to Magellan quickly captured the other ships. The ringleader of the mutineers was executed and his body drawn and quartered, while Cartagena was marooned on this wild and remote shore when the fleet finally set sail in the spring. He was never seen again.

Magellan sentenced forty other mutineers to death but then pardoned them, earning their gratitude, although there still remained malcontents. As winter wore on, Magellan explored this wide, flat, freezing area, which he named Patagonia because the Telhuelche Indians who lived there had such big feet and wore huge shoes made out of thick skin and stuffed with straw (*patagon* in Portuguese means a huge, clumsy foot). In fact, these Indians fascinated Pigafetta and the rest of the Europeans. In their first encounter with one, they saw 'a man as large as a giant … dancing and singing and putting dust on his head'. Magellan ordered that the man be brought to him and when he came near, the Patagonian 'was struck with great wonder, and he made a sign with his upraised finger, believing that [the Europeans] came from the sky'. This giant was supposedly so tall that the Europeans did not even reach his waist. According to Pigafetta, this altogether extraordinary figure had 'a large face, encircled with yellow paint and two hearts painted on his two cheeks, [and] his hair dyed white'.

The Europeans were fascinated by Patagonian customs—'when these people feel sick to their stomachs', Pigafetta wrote, and one can hear the Italian gentleman grimace, 'they thrust an arrow into their throats to the depth of two palms and more and vomit up a green-coloured substance mixed with blood'. Not contenting themselves with staring, the sailors tried to capture a few of these giants and ultimately trapped two, 'who began to blow and foam at the mouth like bulls'. Cramped in the hold of one of the ships, both men were to die within the year. As a last adventure of this terrible winter, Magellan sent his friend João Serrão, commanding the *Santiago*, southward, but a storm wrecked the ship 100 kilometres (70 miles) away. Serrão and all his crew but one made it safely to shore, but his trek back to Magellan's camp is one of the unsung epics of endurance in history.

 ## THE ADVENTURES OF JOÃO SERRÁO

The fascinating—and ultimately sad—fate of João Serrão makes for engrossing reading. Serrão was a friend of one of Ferdinand Magellan's brothers and thus came along on the voyage as someone the great navigator could trust implicitly. It turned out Magellan desperately needed friends when, deep in the South Atlantic, the Spanish captains of the fleet rebelled against him. Serrão helped Magellan fight them off and was rewarded when a grateful Magellan made him captain of the Santiago. *During the months when the fleet was wintering in harbour in Patagonia, Magellan sent Serrão in the* Santiago *on an exploratory probe farther south. But on 22 May, the* Santiago *was driven ashore during a storm and wrecked.*

Serrão managed to save all but one of his crew, but was then forced to make an arduous trek back overland to Magellan's camp, some 100 kilometres (70 miles) up the windswept coastline. There was no food in the Patagonian wilds and for four days Serrão and his men trekked desperately through uncharted wilderness, before coming upon a river that provided them with fish. Exposed to the elements, the crew built a tiny raft, which they used to send two men across the river. These two men then walked for a further eleven days, until they reached Magellan, who sent a relief party back to save Serrão.

Unfortunately, Serrão, one of the bravest and most admired men among the crew, met a terrible death. After Magellan died, Serrão and another man, Duarte Barbosa, were voted co-captains of the expedition, but Serrão was captured by Philippine islanders who had been incited by Enrique, Magellan's former slave. The last the crew of the expedition saw of him, he was bound on the shore, weeping and begging for them to return to save him. They were all too frightened to do so, especially navigator João Lopez Carvalho, Serrão's close friend, who would not put in to shore. According to Pigafetta, Serrão then cried out that he 'prayed God that at the day of judgment He would demand the soul of his friend Carvalho'.

The expedition departed and Serrão was never seen alive again. Carvalho was to die a few months later of illness.

The Pacific Sea

On 18 October, in the southern spring, Magellan set sail south with his fleet, now reduced to four ships. Within three days' sailing time, they came upon a cape that Magellan named the Cape of Eleven Thousand Virgins. Beyond the cape was an inlet and at the end of the inlet there was what Pigafetta called 'a very hidden strait', extremely narrow, with high mountains on either side of it. The fleet anchored there, finding that the water was so deep that their anchors would not reach the bottom and they were forced to tie up to the land. The next morning, Magellan told his captains that he had seen this strait marked on a secret map in the archives of the King of Portugal and that this strait led to the Southern Ocean. Although this was a lie, even Pigafetta reported it as the truth. It gave Magellan's officers the courage to proceed down this narrow, windy corridor, with mountains looming over it, that everyone but Magellan assumed was a river.

The *Concepción* and the *San Antonio* went ahead to reconnoitre. They were gone for so long that Magellan and the others aboard the *Trinidad* and *Victoria* thought them lost, but suddenly they heard a great commotion of guns—the two vessels had returned and were firing off signal cannon.

It turned out the strait had opened up into a bay, and then proceeded into a larger bay, at which point the two ships had returned to report to Magellan that, just possibly, there was a way through here. All four vessels now proceeded, with Magellan leading the way, carefully moving between islands, through narrow channels, taking soundings in order to avoid running aground. They came to a point where the channel divided, with one strait leading to the southwest, while another turned southeast. Magellan took the southwest route with the *Trinidad* and *Victoria*, leaving the *San Antonio* and the *Concepción* to explore the southeast. After sailing for a short time, Magellan anchored and sent a ship's boat ahead to explore. The boat was gone for three days and came back with the momentous news that they had found 'a great and wide sea'.

Magellan was so moved that he wept. But then came bad news: the *Concepción* returned from its search to the southeast, but the *San Antonio*—the expedition's largest and most well-supplied vessel— did not. After searching fruitlessly for the ship, it became apparent that it had probably turned around and headed back to Spain, deserting Magellan (as, in fact, was the case).

But Magellan would not be stopped. 'On Wednesday the twenty-eighth of November, 1520', wrote Pigafetta proudly, 'we issued forth from the said strait and entered the Pacific Sea'.

A mouse for a ducat

The ocean they entered had heretofore been called the South Sea, but Magellan was so impressed with its long, calm, rolling swells that he renamed it the Pacific. The first thing he did was turn his vessels northward and sail up the west coast of South America, always keeping land in sight in the far distance. According to a pilot on the *Trinidad*, they kept their northern course for twenty-three straight days. Pigafetta wondered at the sights of the ocean, particularly the flying fish, called *colondrins*, from the Spanish word for a swallow. When predatory albacores or bonitos encountered the *colondrins*, Pigafetta wrote, 'the flying fish immediately leap out of the water and fly as far as a bowshot without wetting their wings. But the other fish dart under the shadows of the flying fish, and no sooner do they fall into the water, than they are immediately seized and eaten'.

By 22 December, the fleet had made 2500 kilometres (1600 miles) up the coast of South America and was now opposite Chile. With the climate warming and the sailing easy, Magellan turned due west and now headed straight out into the Pacific, coursing over uncharted waters.

He had, however, made a serious mistake. Drastically underestimating the size of the Pacific—he thought it was 3000 kilometres (2000 miles) across, rather than 20,000 kilometres (13,000)—he had not stopped at any harbour along the coast of South America to find fresh water and food. At first, this mistake was not apparent and the men on Magellan's ships found their swift passage exhilarating. 'We made each day fifty or sixty leagues or more', wrote Pigafetta, borne along by a strong wind and by a current, the South Equatorial Drift, which coursed due west. But all became alarmed when they had travelled for 5000 kilometres (3000 miles) without sighting any land at all, let alone the Spice Islands.

By mid-January, the crews were suffering terribly. Pigafetta records the misery:

> They ate biscuits, and when there were no more [biscuits], they ate the crumbs, which were full of maggots and smelled strongly of mouse urine. They drank yellow water, already several days putrid ... A mouse would bring half a ducat or a ducat. The gums of some of the men swelled over their upper and lower teeth, so that they could not eat, and so died. And nineteen men died from their sickness ...

The Island of Thieves

Magellan's error in not reprovisioning his ships was compounded by his bad luck. Had he continued sailing west, he would have come to Tahiti, a land of plenty. But instead, faced with the suffering of his crew, he turned to the northwest, heading more directly to the Equator, since he knew the Spice Islands lay along that latitude. He was still far from the Moluccas but, even so, would have found his way to the Marquesas Islands had his crew not spotted a huge, stacked cumulus cloud, a sign of land, and steered again southwest, only to find the tiny island of Pukapuka, where swift currents and deep water kept the fleet from landing.

Sailing on, with men dying daily, Magellan finally made landfall at another island, which was probably Caroline Island, a place where the harbour swarmed with sharks, which the hungry men fished for, despite risking loss of life or limb to one of the snapping *tiburoni*. At last, on 6 March, with many of the men now too weak to handle the sails, Magellan came upon two islands belonging to the Marianas chain. He anchored near the biggest one, probably Guam, hoping to rest his crew and bring fresh supplies aboard. But his encounter with the tribes of Guam was a startling and violent one. Immediately after the little fleet anchored, the islanders—whose lack of experience with Europeans did not make them the slightest bit shy—swarmed all over Magellan's ships, stealing whatever was not tied down, 'to such an extent that our men could not protect their belongings', Pigafetta wrote. Magellan, normally even-handed, lost his temper when the islanders, in their fast-moving skiffs with triangular sails, stole one of the ship's boats tied directly under the poop deck of the *Trinidad*. He sent ashore a force of forty armed men, who killed at least seven of the islanders with crossbows. Having no experience with European weapons, the reaction of the wounded natives was startling. Pigafetta wrote that 'whenever we wounded any of these people with a shaft that entered their body, they looked at it and then marvellously drew it out, and so died forthwith'.

Having set fire to forty huts, the shore party made their way back to the ships. So hungry were the weakened men on board, according to Pigafetta, that they begged the landing party for the entrails of those they had killed, so that they might have fresh meat.

FOLLOWING PAGES Map showing European knowledge of the Pacific at the end of the sixteenth century.

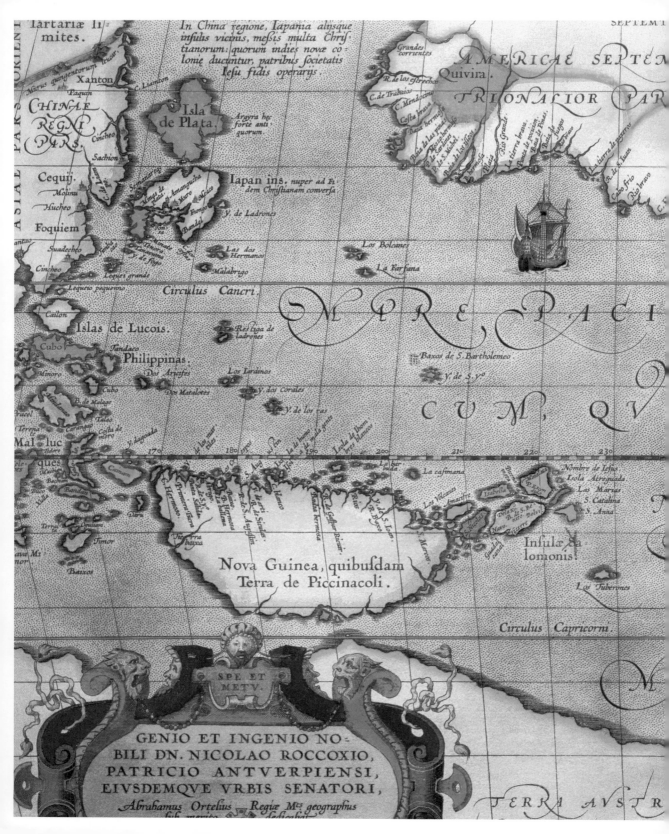

Tartariæ li-
mites.

In China regione, Iapania aliqsque
insulis vicinis, messis multa Chri-
stianorum: quorum indies novæ co-
loniæ ducuntur, patribus societatis
Iesu fidis operarijs.

SEPTEM

Grandes
corrientes

AMERICAE SEPTEM
TRIONALIOR PAR

Quivira.

CHINAE
REGNI
PARS.

Xanton
Paquin
C. Lianton

Isla
de Plata.

Argyra hæc
forte anti-
quorum.

R. de los estrechos
C. de Trabaias
C. Mendocino
Costa brava
Baia hermosa

Cinchco
Sachion

Cequij.

Molinu

Hucheo

Foquiem

Iapan ins. nuper ad Fi-
dem Christianam conversa

Y. de Ladrones

Cincheo
Cinchco

Suadecheo

Las dos
Hermanos

Malabrigo

Los Bolcanes

La Farfana

Cubo
Mal luc
ques

Circulus Cancri.

MARE PACI

Islas de Lucois.

Res-tiga de
ladrones

Baxos de S. Bartholemeo

Y. de Syo

CUM QV

Cubo

Philippinas.

Dos Arecifes

Los Iardinos

Minoro

Cubo
Don Matalotes

Y. dos Corales

Y. de los vas

17°   180°   190°   200°   210°   220°   230°

La casmana

Nombre de Iesus
Isola Atrequada

Los Volcanes

Las Marias
S. Catalina
S. Anna

Insulæ Sa-
lomonis!

Nova Guinea, quibusdam
Terra de Piccinacoli.

Los Tuberones

Circulus Capricorni.

SPE ET
METV.

GENIO ET INGENIO NO-
BILI DN. NICOLAO ROCCOXIO,
PATRICIO ANTVERPIENSI,
EIVSDEMQVE VRBIS SENATORI,

Abrahamus Ortelius   Regiæ Mtis geographus

TERRA AVSTR

MARIS PACIFICI,

(quod vulgò Mar del Zur)
cum regionibus circumiacentibus, insulísque in eodem
passim sparsis, novissima descriptio.

MARIS ATLANTICI,

SIVE MAR DEL NORT

PARS.

Bermuda

Florida

Cuba

Spagnola

Noua Hispania.

Messico.

Lamaica

S. Ioan

La Trinidad

Cali-formia

Mar Ver-mejo

Cartagena

Caribana.

Y. de Cocos

Malpelle

Quito.

VVLGO

Circulus Aequinoctialis.

AMERICAE

MERIDIONA

LIOR PARS.

Peru.

Charcas.

Chili.

Patagones.

Prima ego velivolis ambivi cursibus Orbem,
Magellane novo te duce ducta freto.
Ambivi, meritoq; vocor VICTORIA: sunt mi
Vela, alæ; precium, gloria, pugna, mare.

DEL

ZVR.

Archipe

'Rational people'

Leaving this horrific scene behind, Magellan sailed on for another week before sighting Samar, an island in the Philippines. At first, it seemed as if they had arrived in paradise. Resting on the beach near two fresh streams—the water tasting as fine as the finest wine to men who had been drinking ship's water from which they had had to strain the algae with their teeth—and eating fresh fruit and coconuts, the crew began to recover. Magellan himself, according to Pigafetta, walked among the men giving them coconut milk to drink.

Samar was uninhabited, but within a few days of their landing, the Europeans were visited by a delegation of islanders from a nearby island. Much to the relief of Magellan and his crew, these were 'rational people', unlike the thieves on Guam. After Magellan gave them gifts of mirrors, combs and bells, they returned the favour with fish, palm wine and figs. They left, but promised to return in four days with more food, and this they did, coming back laden with supplies for the hungry men, and this time bringing their chief and other dignitaries. These men wore gold jewellery, but Magellan, unlike Columbus and his men, did not press them for its source. Instead, proceeding with great diplomacy, he insisted on exchanging gifts and treating those he met as equals. His slave Enrique, originally Malaysian, understood the Tagalog language of the islanders and helped translate.

After eight days of rest, Magellan now sailed his ships farther into the Surigao Strait, exploring the islands. On 28 March, Holy Thursday, Magellan anchored off the island of Limasawa and decided to observe Easter there. He put on a glorious show, celebrating a Mass, shooting off cannon (which, as usual, overawed the islanders watching) and having his men display their fencing ability. After this, he erected a cross, telling the islanders that any Spanish ships that happened by in the future would see this sign and would therefore leave them in peace, except to trade with them.

'Our mirror, our light, our comfort'

For the next month, Magellan and his three ships coursed through the Philippines, with Magellan making contact with the island peoples and their 'rajahs', or chiefs. With his fine but at times prurient eye for detail, Pigafetta continued to observe the people they encountered. They all went about naked, except 'for a bit of cloth over their shameful parts'. The men 'have their members pierced from one side to the other, with a golden spike as thick as a goose quill ... Some have a pointed star above the glands of the member, also of gold'.

Unfortunately, this idyll would soon end. Near the end of April, arriving at the island of Cebu, Magellan befriended a chief named Zula, who begged Magellan to do battle against his rival on a nearby island, a rajah named Lapulapu. Here Magellan had trapped himself, for his displays of Spanish power—the cannon, the swords, the armour—would be seen as mere braggadocio if he would not help those who had become his allies.

So, on the morning of 27 April, Magellan anchored off the island of Mactan, Lapulapu's home. Perhaps 1500 angry islanders could be seen milling about on the shore, carrying wooden spears whose tips had been sharpened and hardened in fire. Because the water was extremely shallow for up to 800 metres (2600 feet) offshore, Magellan's three ships were unable to approach the beach and, therefore, their cannon—the outnumbered Europeans' trump card—would be useless in the fight.

Nothing daunted, Magellan put on his armour and prepared to lead a party of some sixty men to the shore. Pigafetta and others implored him not to join the soldiers—'for a long time', Pigafetta relates, 'we begged him not to go there, but like a good captain, he did not want to abandon his allies'.

THE TALE OF THE *TRINIDAD*

While the Victoria is famous as the first vessel to have circumnavigated the globe, and under terrible circumstances, the fate of the Trinidad, the other of Magellan's last remaining ships, is just as startling. After the ship was forced to put back into harbour at the Moluccas, the crew spent three months repairing the leaky vessel. During this time, their extremely competent pilot, João Lopez Carvalho, died of disease. Therefore, when the crew and its captain, Gonzalo de Espinosa, sailed in March, they were without an experienced navigator.

Because the prevailing winds had shifted, Espinosa made the decision to take the ship west across the Pacific, to Panama, rather than east around the Cape of Good Hope. In Panama, the cargo of cloves could be offloaded to Spanish forces for a journey across the isthmus. This was an unrealistic plan, to say the least. When they set sail, they were buffeted by unfavourable winds, which blew them north for fifteen straight weeks, while the crew began to die, one by one. Soon they found themselves off the coast of Japan, and freezing in the unexpectedly cold weather. As if that was not enough, the Trinidad was hit by a storm that tore away the mainmast and the foredeck. Finally, after three and a half months, Espinosa brought the ship back to the Moluccas with only nineteen men alive. Sailing into harbour, they found a Portuguese fleet waiting there and they were immediately taken into custody.

The Portuguese shuttled the Trinidad's crew from one island prison to another; the men were starved and beaten, until only Espinosa and one other man were left alive, three years after they were captured. The Portuguese at last released them and these two wretches found their way home. In a final irony, Espinosa was denied his back wages as a captain because the Spanish government said he had been in a Portuguese prison—and thus had not been earning them.

Magellan and his men, Pigafetta with them, were forced to wade for hundreds of metres to the shore in full armour. When they got close to shore, they were immediately assailed by islanders throwing wooden lances, shooting darts from blowpipes and throwing rocks and chunks of coral. The situation quickly deteriorated. Magellan sent a squad to burn the huts of the islanders, thinking this might intimidate them, as it had the people of Guam, but it merely enraged the warriors further, and they pressed in on the Europeans from all sides. Magellan ordered his men to withdraw slowly, but instead they took panic and fled back through the shallows, leaving Magellan to fight on accompanied by Pigafetta and only six or eight others.

The enemy, Pigafetta wrote, 'recognised the Captain [Magellan] and so many assailed him that twice they knocked the sallet [helmet] off his head. And he, like a good knight, continued to stand firm with a few others and for more than an hour refused to retreat'. But then the end came swiftly: 'An Indian threw his bamboo spear into [Magellan's] face and he immediately killed him with his own spear, but it remained in [the Indian's] body'. Magellan tried to draw his sword, but a wound in his right arm made this difficult. Seeing this, one of the islanders 'with a large javelin thrust it into [Magellan's] left leg, whereby he fell face downward. On this, all at once rushed upon him … and slew our mirror, our light, our comfort and our true guide'.

A miraculous circumnavigation

In shock, Pigafetta and the surviving Europeans fought their way back to the ships. They sought to parlay with the Mactan islanders to get Magellan's

body back, but they refused, saying that 'they wanted to keep him so that they would not forget him', a tribute to Magellan's courage. There was nothing to do but keep sailing, but the journey back to Spain would be a long, arduous and treacherous one. Soon after Magellan died, his slave Enrique asked for his freedom, claiming that Magellan had promised this to him. He was denied by Duarte Barbosa, one of the new captains—the other was João Serráo—and, therefore, slipped ashore at one island and plotted with the islanders against the Spanish. One night at a feast, the

Magellan is killed by Lapulapu and his warriors on the island of Mactan, in the Philippines. His death was to cost the Spanish dearly.

Spanish were attacked and many were massacred, including Serráo.

After wandering for a month through the Philippines, the decision was made to scuttle the *Concepción*, since there were no longer enough men to crew it—there were now only 130 left out of the 250 who had originally left Spain. Everyone was transferred to the *Trinidad* and the *Victoria* and the ships set sail for the Spice Islands, finally arriving at these much-dreamed-of isles in December. Wary of the Portuguese, the two ships quickly loaded up with cargoes of cloves and set sail on 18 December, but the *Trinidad* began taking on water and was forced to turn back to harbour for repairs, and thence to set forth on its own incredible odyssey. The *Victoria* steered past Timor and out into the Indian Ocean, from whence it rounded the Cape of Good Hope, reaching the South Atlantic on 19 May 1522. But, faced with rough weather, their journey was so slow that more and more men began to die of starvation and scurvy.

'We sailed northwest for two months,' Pigafetta wrote, 'and in that short space of time twenty-one men died'. With his eye for the curious and macabre, Pigafetta also noted that 'when they throw the Christian bodies into the sea, they sink to the bottom face up, and the Indians [Moluccans who had been hired at the Spice Islands to help crew the vessel] sink face down'.

Desperately, the *Victoria* put in at the Portuguese-held Cape Verde Islands to find food, but the Portuguese captured three men who had been sent ashore to bargain, and so the rest set sail immediately. Finally, on Sunday, 8 September 1522, the *Victoria* dropped anchor in the port of Seville, Spain. The ship's guns blasted out. Eighteen men out of Magellan's original 250 had arrived back. Starving, they tottered off the ship and 'gave thanks to God, in our shirts, barefooted, and with torches in our hands'.

Magellan had not made the entire journey, but without him none of these men would have either. And his opening up of the Pacific—and its peoples—to European influence would forever alter the course of history. Although Spain would never profit from the spice trade the way the Portuguese would, the Philippines, already indelibly marked by Magellan's presence, would become a rich possession for the Spanish crown for nearly four hundred years.

'LET NOTHING PASS YOU UNOBSERVED'

The Dutch discover Australia, 1623–1642

After Magellan's voyage, further attempts were made to explore the Pacific, for he had obviously only sailed over a small portion of a body of water that covers an area greater than all the landmasses of the world—seen from outer space, the Pacific Ocean shows itself to be the defining geographical feature of the entire globe. Magellan had sought trade routes, and so did those who followed him, but they also pursued the myth of *terra australis incognita*, the Unknown Southland, a continent supposedly lying in the south of the Pacific to 'balance' the continents in the northern hemisphere. There were a lot of rumours in those heady post-Magellan days of the late sixteenth and early seventeenth centuries—stories of Marco Polo's exotic land of Locach (or Beach, or Veach), a place of incalculable wealth, either a large island or a continent, lying to the south of Java. There were also islands of gold out there in the Pacific—tales

were spun in whispers all over the Portuguese and Spanish courts about isolated paradises whose glitter was so bright they shone like stars across the dark expanse of the ocean.

And so voyagers set forth. Many of them are now unknown or forgotten, but even so they provided a body of knowledge that they passed on to other mariners of the time, so much so that most historians believe that the early navigators of those years probably sailed with more information than we thought they possessed—perhaps even Magellan had some marginal idea of where he was going because of a chart passed down (and now lost) from an adventurer whose name we will never know.

In any event, in 1567 the Spaniard Mendaña de Neira sailed from Callao, Peru, to try to find an island of gold he had heard about from the conquered Incas—one supposedly discovered by the Incan seafarer Paullu Tupac Yupanqui, who had sailed across the Pacific for nine months and found untold wealth in a far-off land. With Mendaña went the extremely able sea captain Sarmiento de Gamboa. After sailing thousands of kilometres they came upon and named four of the Solomon Islands—Guadalcanal, Malaita, San Cristobal and Santa Isabel. Mendaña tried to found a settlement on San Cristobal, but the Melanesian islanders fought him fiercely and he departed. Almost thirty years later he sought to return, this time with four ships and numerous women—for he really wanted to start a colony—but, lo and behold, he was unable to find the Solomons again (they were not rediscovered until James Cook came upon them in the late eighteenth century) and died of disease during the voyage.

'A full and particular report'

However, Mendaña's chief navigator on this journey, Fernández de Quirós—a visionary who may have been mad—returned in 1605 to search, not for the islands of gold, but for *terra australis incognita*. He found the island group we know as the New Hebrides and rapturously named one isle Austrialia del Espiritu Santu. In an ecstasy of religious mania, he founded a city known as New Jerusalem and created a new chivalrous order, the Knights of the Holy Ghost. This was too much for Luis Vaez de Torres, his navigator, who left and sailed 650 kilometres (400 miles) to the southwest, continuing to look for the Unknown Southland. Torres went around the southern coast of New Guinea and entered the strait, between Australia and New Guinea, that would bear his name. If he saw Australia's northern shores, he did not note them—he may have thought of them as simply an extension of New Guinea, since the entrance to Torres Strait from the east is shallow and reef-filled.

Torres Strait proved to be an easier route to the Philippines, which is what the Spanish used it for (keeping it a secret for the next 150 years). It would take the Dutch, coming from a completely different direction, to make contact with the inhabitants of the real (and not mythical) Australia. Most of these Dutch were working for the newly formed Dutch East India Company (the Vereenigde Oostindische Compagnie, or VOC), that august, quasi-governmental trading organisation of wealthy Dutch merchants who sought to corner the market on the lucrative East Indies spice trade.

It was not just trade, however. The VOC council instructed their merchants to 'let nothing pass you unobserved and whatever you find bring us a full and particular report of it, by which you will do the States of the United Netherlands a service and lay up special honour for yourself'.

The first European to sight Australia—or report sighting it—was Wilhelm Janszoon, aboard the VOC vessel *Duyfken* in 1605. Janszoon journeyed along the southern coast of New Guinea and then turned south into the Gulf of Carpentaria, then headed along the west side of the Cape York Peninsula as far as Cape Turnagain. It appears that he thought he was in a part of New Guinea that had previously been unexplored, though, and did not realise he had reached a southern continent. Every time Janszoon tried to land along these shores, he was opposed by naked Aboriginals ('blacks' or 'savages', as he put it), who kept him from safely taking on water or food. The coastline itself was dull and featureless and Janszoon returned home thinking that he had not found very much of anything at all.

'Get hold of some adults'

Janszoon's journals are lost to us, so we do not have the exact particulars of his first encounters, but they were obviously available to Jan Carstensz (or Carstenszoon) when he made his own voyage in 1623, tracing much of Janszoon's route. Aboard the *Pera*, sailing in tandem with its sister ship, the *Aernem*, Carstensz explored the northern coast of Australia, sighting the western side of Cape York Peninsula on 12 April. Three days later, Carstensz went ashore, thus providing the first detailed description we have of the Aboriginal people of Australia and of the country generally.

It should be noted here that Carstensz was not merely exploring, but actively seeking something—human beings. His instructions from the VOC read in part: 'In places where you meet with people, you will, by dexterity or otherwise, get hold of some adults, or still better, young lads or girls, to the end that they should be brought here, and later, when opportunity offers, be broken in at the said quarters'. Some historians take this to mean that the Aboriginals Carstensz would capture should be trained to act as interpreters, but this is the kindliest way of looking at it. In essence, Carstensz was a slave hunter.

Going ashore around Cape York Peninsula, Carstensz and his men saw 'great volumes of smoke' from Aboriginal bushfires billowing up inland. Gradually, the inhabitants of the land crept closer, watching the Dutch from the trees, and Carstensz ordered 'some pieces of iron and strings of bead be tied to a stick' in order to entice them out of cover, but this did not work and at night the Dutch returned to their vessels. A few days later, other men from the *Pera* went ashore in two pinnaces. Carstensz relates what happened.

As soon as [they] had landed, a large number of blacks, some of them armed and others unarmed, had made up to them. These blacks showed no fear and were so bold as to touch the muskets of our men and to try to take the same off their shoulders ... Our men accordingly diverted their attention by showing them iron and beads, and espying vantage, seized one of the blacks by a string which he wore around his neck and carried him off to the pinnace. The blacks who remained on the beach set up dreadful howls ...

Carstensz went on to describe the Aboriginals, having no doubt had a close look at the one his men brought to the ship.

These natives are coal-black, with lean bodies and stark-naked, having twisted baskets or nets round their heads. In hair and figure, they are like the blacks of the Coromandel [India] coast, but they seem to be less cunning, bold and evil-natured than the blacks at the western extremity of Nova Guinea.

'Divers human bones'

We do not know a great deal about Jan Carstensz, including his dates of birth and death, but he comes across in his journals as an ugly figure, with far more than his share of the racism of his age. Marching farther into the country, Carstensz and his men found 'great quantities of divers human bones, from which it may be safely concluded that the blacks along the coast of Nova Guinea are man-eaters who do not spare each other when driven by hunger'. (Carstensz thought he was in New Guinea, and that the Aboriginals were headhunters.) During this same trip, two hundred Aboriginals—having obviously been forewarned—set upon the shore party, which shot and killed one of them. The rest fled at the astonishing sound of the muskets. Invading the Aboriginals' 'wretched huts on the beach', the Dutch examined their weapons, which Carstensz refers to as mainly 'assagais' [spears]. The contents of the huts showed that they 'chiefly live on certain ill-smelling roots, which they dig out of the earth'.

In general, Carstensz wrote, 'the natives are ... utter barbarians, all resembling each other in shape and features, coal-black ... it may safely be concluded that they are poor and abject wretches'. Astonishingly, Carstensz goes on to make the claim that:

... in all the places where we landed, we have treated the blacks or savages with especial kindness, offering them pieces of iron, strings of beads, and pieces of cloth, hoping by so doing to get their friendship. But in spite of all our kindness and fair semblance, the blacks received us as enemies everywhere, so that in most places our landings were attended with great peril.

In this report—which was aimed at the council of the VOC—Carstensz is making excuses for the fact that he was not able to penetrate very far inland and learn anything about 'the population of [the land], and the nature of its inhabitants'. He seems oblivious to the fact that bringing ashore a party of armed men and then trying to kidnap Aboriginals while distracting them with

 'GOD WILL GUIDE THEM'

Fernández de Quirós (sometimes Queirós) was not what you might call your typical explorer of the seventeenth century variety—they tended to be men with visions, but men who nonetheless valued practicality and shrewdness. Not Quirós. He was Portuguese-born (in 1563) but entered the service of Spain as a young man and rose to become an expert navigator and seaman. He accompanied Mendaña de Neira on the latter's 1595 expedition to colonise the Solomon Islands and took over after Mendaña died and they were unable to find the islands again—in fact, he was credited with doing such a good job of saving the expedition that King Philip III of Spain supported another Quirós voyage to the Pacific, this time to look for the Unknown Southland. Quirós, a devout Catholic, convinced the king that 'among those hidden provinces and severed regions, [he was] destined to win souls to heaven and kingdoms to the crown of Spain'.

Fine, as far as that went, but ... something went awry in Quirós. He left Peru in December 1605 with a party of 160 men in three ships, instructing his navigators to 'put the ships' heads where they like, for God will guide them as may be right'. God brought them to the islands we now know as the New Hebrides. Quirós decided he had found the tip of the Southern Continent and called one island Austrialia del Espiritu Santu. There he founded a city, New Jerusalem, and created a 'new order of chivalry', naming all his seamen Knights of the Holy Ghost.

It was too much for even the most religious among the Spanish, and mutiny broke out. When the ships set sail again, Quirós, aboard his flagship, somehow managed to separate himself from the rest and sail all the way back to Mexico. He said he had been driven by a storm, but no one believed him and, in fact, he became an object of scorn and ridicule in Mexico and Spain. He spent the last seven years of his life rewriting the story of the voyage endlessly—he created fifty different memoirs, partially to offset critical stories told about him by his navigator Luis Vaez de Torres. He hounded the Spanish court to try one more voyage. In order to get rid of him, King Philip pretended to give him orders for a new expedition. He died on his way back to South America in 1615, happily unaware of the deception, ready for one last try.

BATAVIA'S GRAVEYARD

Francois Pelsaert's inadvertent and fleeting first contacts with Aboriginals on Australia's west coast came about because of one of the most horrific incidents in seafaring history—the bloody murder of two hundred men, women and children on a nameless island off the coast of Australia.

The instigator of the murder was one Jeronimus Cornelisz, one of history's nastiest sociopaths. An apothecary, he had shipped out aboard the VOC vessel Batavia *in the fall of 1628, heading from Amsterdam to Batavia (Jakarta). This was the* Batavia's *maiden voyage and it was the largest and proudest ship in the entire VOC fleet. Francois Pelsaert was the senior VOC official on board the vessel. During the lengthy voyage down the Atlantic and around the Cape of Good Hope, Cornelisz, possibly deranged because of the early death of his wife, plotted to take over the ship. As the* Batavia *sailed up from southern latitudes toward the Spice Islands, it ran aground on a desolate piece of land called Houtman Abrolhos, an island literally made of coral rubble and only 300 yards long and 500 wide (300 x 500 metres). There are some historians who believe Jeronimus Cornelisz caused the ship to run aground, although there is no way now of proving this.*

In any event, Francois Pelsaert ended up on a different small island with a group of experienced sailors, as well as women and children, and with both of the ship's small boats. Instead of going to help the 180 or so survivors on Houtman Abrolhos, he made the decision to try to get water or, failing that, to sail to Batavia to get help. It was a pragmatic decision, but it left the innocent passengers with a man who turned out to be filled with an insane bloodlust. Jeronimus Cornelisz quickly assumed dictatorial powers, gathered a force of young men around him and began slaughtering people with swords or drowning them, ostensibly because they had broken rules or stolen food. 'Who wants their ears boxed?' he would cry out, like a nasty bully in a schoolyard, except boxed ears now meant a horrible death.

In an amazing feat of seamanship, Francois Pelsaert was actually able to make it to Batavia, where he recruited a rescue party and came sailing back to Houtman Abrolhos, an island now known as 'Batavia's graveyard'. On a nearby islet, he found that a determined group of people had fought off Cornelisz and captured him. When he heard the full story, a horrified Pelsaert had the mutineers and Cornelisz executed. The crazed apothecary was hung after having his hand hacked off with a hammer and chisel. He died shouting: 'Revenge! Revenge!' while onlookers—the survivors of the crew—cheered.

trinkets was certainly not the best way to 'get their friendship'.

In 1616 another VOC captain, Dirk Hartog, became the first Dutchman to make landfall in Western Australia, in Shark Bay. This landmass was being called (naturally) New Holland, or sometimes the South-Land, although it was far from the fabled Unknown Southland mariners had been seeking. Hartog was followed in 1629 by Francois Pelsaert, the commander of a large VOC merchant vessel en route to Batavia (current-day Jakarta). He had survived a shipwreck (that would end in a blood-curdling series of murders) on a luckless atoll eighty kilometres (fifty miles) off the west coast. Setting off in a small boat with forty-eight men, women and children (including one infant), Pelsaert headed toward the coast of Australia, seeking water and shelter. They soon found land but, according to a contemporary English account of his voyage, 'the country was low, naked … and the coast excessively rocky'.

Sailing north along the coast, they saw smoke in the distance and finally forced their way through high breakers to the sandy beach. They spent the whole day searching fruitlessly for water; then, 'they saw four men, who came up very near, but one of the Dutch sailors advancing toward them, they immediately ran away as fast as they were able'. At a place farther up the shore, they found rainwater collected in the hollows of rocks and a 'savage' camp, with the remains of crayfish in the ashes of a cold fire. Now savage themselves with hunger, they ate the crayfish. Later, on a 'thirsty barren plain', while so plagued with flies that they could barely breathe, 'they saw at a distance eight savages, with each a staff in his hand, who advanced toward them within musket shot; but as soon as they perceived the Dutch sailors moving toward them, they fled as fast as they were able'.

A typical encounter for Europeans in Australia so far—mysterious strangers in a barren land try to make fleeting contact with shadows that move quickly away.

Abel Tasman

In 1642 Abel Tasman made the first serious attempt to discover just what New Holland was. Gradually, with landings in the northwest, west and southwest, this landmass was taking shape, but how far were the east shores and how far south did the land extend?

Abel Tasman, probably the finest explorer/navigator in the employ of the VOC, was the man to find out. Born in 1603 in The Netherlands, he had travelled back and forth as ship's pilot numerous times between there and Batavia, and had also made voyages to South America, China, Japan, the Philippines, and other islands in the Pacific. He left Batavia in August 1642 and sailed west to Mauritius rather than southeast toward New Holland. The reasons for this were twofold. He wanted to take advantage of the prevailing winds in the latitude of the forties, which blew east, and he wanted to try to dip far enough south to be able to clear the southern edge of New Holland—although, of course, he had no way of knowing where this might be.

Tasman had two ships, the *Heemskerk* and the *Zeehaen*, and they rode before gentle winds for days in the kind of weather seamen called 'flying fish weather', because the seas were calm enough for these creatures to skid across the decks of the ships with some regularity. As they coursed farther south, however, they came upon colder and stronger winds and huge seas. The little Dutch ships—called yachts, from the Dutch word *Jacht*, meaning 'hunting' or 'hunt'—were light and fast and rode atop the waves as their helmsmen wrestled to keep them on course. The biggest danger to Tasman's ships was floating icebergs, broken off from the Antarctic landmass, and his lookouts kept a sharp eye for the huge, glittering ice mountains.

Tasman worked his way north and on 24 November came within sight of the west coast of the island that would become known as Tasmania, about 200 kilometres (125 miles) south of Australia. He was the first European to spot Tasmania, which he called Van Diemen's Land after the governor-general of the Dutch East Indies. He had a hard time finding safe harbour but on 1 December, having worked his way around to the eastern side of the island, anchored there and sent a small boat ashore to reconnoitre. His journal captures what the crew said on their return:

> [They said] that they had found high but level land, covered with vegetation (not cultivated, but growing naturally by the will of God), abundance of excellent timber, and a gently sloping watercourse in a barren valley ... They [also] said that [they] had heard certain human sounds, and also sounds nearly resembling the music of a trump, or a small gong, not far from them, though they had seen no one.
>
> They [saw] two trees ... measuring from 60 to 65 feet [18 to 19 metres] from the ground to the lowermost branches, which trees bore notches made with flint implements, the bark having been removed for this purpose. These notches, forming a kind of steps to enable persons to get up the tree and rob the birds nests in their tops, were fully five feet [1.5 metres] apart, so that our men concluded that the natives here must be of very tall stature.

It is hard to know what music Tasman's men thought they heard coming from the underbrush, but it is almost certain they were being watched by Tasmanian Aboriginals, who had had the place to themselves for ten thousand years, since rising seas had separated Tasmania from mainland Australia. Tasman did not tarry in this remote, somewhat eerie place, and so the Aboriginals would remain undisturbed until the French landed and fought a skirmish with them in 1772. After that, Europeans would very quickly decimate their population.

Murderer's Bay

The ships of Tasman's era were difficult to control near land, especially in rough seas—there was always the danger of running aground or becoming 'embayed', stuck in narrow bays without the ability to tack out of them—and so Tasman moved on to the east over the rough waters of the Tasman Sea. Sailing east for two weeks, the Dutchmen suddenly sighted 'a large, high-flying land', which was the dramatic, mountainous presence of New Zealand rising from the ocean. They were the first Europeans to see it.

Working his way carefully along the west coast of the South Island, Tasman finally anchored at the entrance of 'a large open bay'—actually Cook Strait, which separates the islands of New Zealand. Tasman anchored off what is now known as Golden Bay, on the northern tip of the South Island, but to which he would give a far more descriptive name: Murderer's Bay. As Tasman was anchored there on the calm evening of 19 December, men in canoes came out to the Dutch vessels, blowing 'on an instrument that sounded like a Moorish trumpet'. Tasman wrote: 'This people apparently sought our friendship', and ordered his own trumpeter to sound a few notes in return. But, just to be on the safe side, he had the men stand double watches and ordered that the ship's guns be cleaned 'to prevent surprises'.

The next day, the local inhabitants—the Maori, who had inhabited the island for at least four hundred years and probably more, having first arrived as journeying Polynesians—paddled out again in a giant canoe that contained thirteen men. 'They called out several times, but we did not understand them, their speech not bearing any resemblance to the vocabulary given us by the Honourable Governor-General [apparently a Malay–Dutch translation book, which naturally the Maori would not have understood].' Tasman goes on to describe the Maori:

As far as we could observe, the people were of ordinary height; they had rough voices and strong bones, the colour of their skin being brown and yellow; they wore tufts of black hair right upon the top of their heads, tied fast in the manner of the Japanese at the back of their heads, but somewhat longer and thicker, and surmounted by a large white feather.

Waving white sheets and offering knives, the Dutch tried to get the Maori to come aboard, but the latter refused. Tasman then decided to send a boat with seven men ashore from the *Zeehaen*. When the boat was lowered, however, a twin-prowed Maori outrigger canoe, filled with seventeen warriors, 'began to paddle furiously toward it so that … they struck [it] so violently alongside with the stem of their prow that it gave a violent lurch, upon which the foremost man in this prow of villains with a long, blunt pike thrust the quartermaster Cornelis Joppen in the neck several times with so much force that the poor man fell overboard'. Then there was a melee:

Upon this, the other natives, with short thick clubs which we at first mistook for heavy blunt parangs and with their paddles, fell upon the men in the boat and overcame them by main force, in which fray three of our men were killed and a fourth

Tasmanian Aboriginals cross a river. They watched the arrival of Tasman's ships but remained hidden from the Dutch.

mortally wounded through the heavy blows. The quartermaster and two sailors swam to our ship, which had sent the pinnace out to pick them up.

Tasman's ships then opened fire on the Maori and the pinnace managed to recover the ship's boat with a mortally wounded sailor in it. The Maori lost at least one man who was killed and did not attack the ship again. Tasman then raised anchor and fled this place, which he would call *Moordenaersbay*, or Murderer's Bay.

Banished from memory

What happened at Murderer's Bay was a classic first-contact clash between two cultures. The Maori saw the Europeans arriving in their large ships—armed men (and men only)—as an obvious invading force. Thus they saw fit to attack without warning. Although Abel Tasman did not have any immediately malign designs upon the Maori land, certainly his

people intended to take it over eventually. Interestingly enough, when James Cook came to these waters over a hundred years later, the Maori living in the locale of Murderer's Bay had no oral tradition or had passed on no memory of the attack on Tasman, or even of Tasman's arrival—it was as if they had banished it from their collective memory.

For their part, the Europeans, too, seemed to banish Australia: not from memory, for it lingered in journals and charts, but from any exploration. Tasman's voyage had revealed precious little about the southern continent, or islands, whatever they might be, that would cause the mercantile-minded VOC to want to develop their interests there any further. It would be James Cook, a century later (see page 204), who would map the coastline of New Zealand and find the eastern reaches of Australia. After that, it was only a matter of time before first contact turned into overwhelming European presence.

The Maori were not shy of the Dutchmen, paddling out in their great war canoes and attacking when opportunity offered.

'VENUS IS THE GODDESS THEY WORSHIP'

Louis-Antoine de Bougainville in Tahiti, 1768

Louis-Antoine de Bougainville, the first Frenchman to circumnavigate the globe, was also the most fortunate of the great Pacific explorers. Unlike Magellan and Cook, he survived with his life (although his voyage was arduous in the extreme) and, in fact, he lived to the ripe old age of eighty-two, keeping his head when many others around him were losing theirs in the French Revolution.

Although he was not the first European to reach the island of Tahiti, his encounter with what he called 'the Indians' on that isle of fabled beauty—a place that he named New Cythera, after the birthplace of Aphrodite, the Greek goddess of love—lives on in history. He was the first to fully take advantage of Tahiti's charms and to make it famous for its 'ease [and] innocent joy'. Unfortunately, this flattering but incomplete portrait would be to the ultimate detriment of its inhabitants.

Mathematician, soldier, explorer

Bougainville was born in Paris in 1729, the son of a notary, and by the age of twenty-two had written a treatise on integral calculus that gave him an international reputation as a mathematician. But Bougainville was too restless for the academic life. Instead, he joined a famous corps of musketeers in the service of the king (the famous 'Black Musketeers', so-called because they rode black horses) and went off to North America to fight against the British during the Seven Years' War.

Bougainville became aide-de-camp to General Louis de Montcalm and played a somewhat controversial part in the siege of Quebec. When that city was under attack by the British under General James Wolfe, Bougainville was patrolling north of the city. Somehow he was unable to return quickly enough to come to Montcalm's aid and the city was lost.

Despite this, Bougainville fought on bravely, making a last stand on Saint Helen's Island, off Montreal in the St Lawrence River, before finally being forced to surrender to the British. He returned to France decorated and with the rank of colonel, and served as a diplomat, helping to forge the Treaty of Paris, which ended the Seven Years' War in 1763. Seeking new adventures—at a time when France's fortunes had fallen quite low—Bougainville colonised the Falkland Islands at his own expense but was disappointed when King Louis XV decided they were nearly worthless to France and sold them to Spain, with the understanding that France could use them as a stepping stone as it explored the Pacific.

However, the brilliant Bougainville soon had his reward. The king named him, aged only thirty-seven, as the head of a new expedition to explore the Pacific as well as circumnavigate the globe. Having lost its North American empire during the disastrous war, France now sought to find solace in the boundless reaches of the Pacific, and the multi-talented Bougainville was to be the point man. 'On his [Bougainville's] crossing to China', wrote the king, 'he will examine the Pacific Ocean as much of, and in the best manner he can, the land lying between the Indies and the western seaboard of America'.

Unlucky strangers

Bougainville's expedition consisted of two ships, the brand new 26-gun frigate *La Boudeuse* and a solidly built storeship, *L'Etoile*. He had with him eleven officers and four hundred men when the two ships departed Nantes, France, on 15 November 1766. The voyage was a tough one from the very beginning. Barely had they reached open sea when both ships were damaged by a storm, so much so that *L'Etoile* had to return to port and was delayed by many months.

La Boudeuse headed across the Atlantic to the Falklands, where Bougainville officially turned over his former island colony to Spain. By the time *L'Etoile* was able to join him and both ships started off for the Strait of Magellan, it was December of 1767 and Bougainville was impatient to find his way to the Southern Ocean. But his passage through the strait was to be difficult. Gales were blowing so hard that it took him four days merely to enter the strait, then another fifty-two to pass through it, sailing carefully through thick fogs and reef-strewn waters. Along the way, he encountered (as had Magellan before him) the Indians of Patagonia and, in particular, the Yaghan tribe on Tierra del Fuego, the island on the southern side of the strait. These people were, as James Cook would later write, 'perhaps as miserable a Set of people as there is this day on Earth'. They existed on a bare subsistence level, gathering shellfish along the windy and inhospitable coast and moving from temporary shelter to temporary shelter. The Spanish had dubbed their land Tierra del Fuego (Land of Fires) because of the fires the Yaghan had to constantly build in order to keep warm.

These luckless people were so happy to see the French that, as Bougainville later wrote, 'they embraced us and shook hands with us, continually crying, *shawa, shawa* …' Bougainville traded tobacco and red cloth for animal skins, and when his ships left the Yaghan were so distraught they ran out into the water shouting and waving after them. However, Bougainville and his men had a less enjoyable encounter a little farther through the strait, when they met a group of Indians who came on board for dinner and then began to eat everything in sight. They were the houseguests from hell, 'with an unsupportable stench about them' and 'rather difficult to get rid of', wrote Bougainville. Unfortunately, a small child ate some bits of glass that a sailor had innocently given him as a souvenir and went into convulsions, spitting blood. During the night, the French heard screaming from the camp of these Indians, and it was apparent that the boy had died. In the morning, the Indians could be seen racing into the rocky interior, fleeing 'from a place defiled by death and by unlucky strangers'.

'An immense horizon'

After nearly two months, however, the ordeal of *La Boudeuse* and *L'Etoile* was over. On 26 January 1768, they saw a sight treasured by all those who braved the Strait of Magellan: 'An immense horizon, no longer bounded by lands, and a great sea from the west, which announced a vast ocean to us'. It was the Pacific, at last, and with great joy Bougainville ordered that his ships set out across it. Blown by a southeasterly wind, the French experienced the headiest days of their voyage, sailing at a rapid clip across calm, deep blue waters, watching dolphins, whales and flying fish. The two ships sailed far

apart, just at the edge of the visible horizon, closing in together only as evening approached, in order to cover as much of the ocean as possible in their search for land. Bougainville, like James Cook (see page 204), was a firm believer in anti-scorbutics and managed to keep his men scurvy-free by dint of vinegar water and lemon drink made from citrus powder.

Bougainville was travelling across a Pacific still poorly known and relatively little explored and there was immense excitement aboard the ships when, in March, a sailor caught a tuna 'in whose belly we found some little fish, not yet digested, of such species as never go to any distance from shore'. The next day a small island group was sighted—Bougainville's first encounter with a Pacific island paradise:

The natives of Tierra del Fuego lived a miserable existence and were happy to see Bougainville's ships arrive in December 1767.

As we approached [one island], we discovered that it is surrounded with a very level sand, and that all the interior parts of it are covered with thick woods ... this verdure charmed our eyes, and the cocoa trees everywhere exposed their fruits to our sight, and overshadowed a grassplot adorned with flowers; thousands of birds were hovering about the shore.

Seemingly impenetrable reefs surrounded this island and others in the group, however. They also held men who were so tall and so light-skinned that Bougainville was certain they were shipwrecked sailors. Before he could decide on the risky course of trying to send a ship's boat over the reefs, however, the men brandished spears at the French vessels and made fierce cries, leading Bougainville to sail on. He called the islands the Dangerous Archipelago—they are the Tuamotu group—and he asked himself the question that almost every mariner in the Pacific in the next century would ask: 'Who can give an account of the manner in which they were conveyed hither?' Without knowing anything about Polynesian seafarers, Bougainville was puzzled that human beings could even be found on such remote, tiny islets.

'Their terror was indescribable'

Bougainville passed numerous other small islands over the course of the next several weeks, but none of them afforded safe landing. Scurvy began to appear among his men as he ran out of the supplies needed to combat it. Finally, in early April, they approached a beautifully rugged island with high hills covered with thick green vegetation, with waterfalls cascading down its sides and stunning black sand beaches. As the French sailed nearer, the island disappeared into a veil of mist, forcing the disappointed sailors to wait an entire day before approaching again. Reefs surrounded this island, too, but the French finally found an opening to take

their ships through, and as they did so they were surrounded by a fleet of canoes.

They had arrived at Tahiti—or O'tahiti, as its inhabitants called it. It is about 650 kilometres (400 miles) long and at its widest 45 kilometres (28 miles) across and was probably settled between 300 and 800 AD by Polynesian voyagers. The average temperature there is in the mid-twenties (mid-seventies Fahrenheit), it has lush rainforests, fast-flowing streams, panoramic views and fish-filled lagoons—it was literally a feast for the eyes of the exhausted French explorers who approached it.

Bougainville immediately understood that this was a far different place from others he had approached—there were no men brandishing spears at them, or poor beggars shouting pleas in freezing cold Patagonian waters. Instead, the canoes that surrounded the vessels contained mainly young women, 'most of them naked'. One of them made her way on board *La Boudeuse* and nimbly climbed the rigging while the sailors were lowering the ship's anchor. 'The girl carelessly dropped a cloth which covered her and appeared to the eyes of all beholders, such as Venus showed herself to the Phrygian shepherd ...' Bougainville suddenly understood how difficult it was going to be to 'keep at their work 400 young French sailors, who had seen no women for six months'.

Once on shore, Bougainville set up a camp and proceeded to fill water casks and re-provision his hold with fruit and wood. The Tahitians wanted to know just how long he was going to be staying—a sign, which Bougainville should have picked up on but did not, that Europeans had been there before. Bougainville laid out eighteen stones, indicating that he needed eighteen days. The Tahitians tried to take away nine stones, but Bougainville refused and they finally acquiesced, in part because Bougainville invited their leader and his family into his tent to dine. 'I had supper in my tent with the *cacique* [leader or chief] and part of his family, each kitchen having supplied its dishes; we did not eat much, his majesty and the princes of the blood having an appetite that we could not match.' After supper, Bougainville had twelve rockets fired off for his guests—'their terror', he wrote with some satisfaction, 'was indescribable'.

The Tahitians, however, had their revenge for this. 'Towards the middle of the night, there was a loud altercation between the king, his brothers and the people who appear to be their servants',

Bougainville wrote ruefully. '[It was] over some opera glasses that had been stolen from my pocket during the dinner. The king was accusing his subjects and threatening to kill them; the poor devils were, I think, less responsible for this theft than he was.'

A hymn to happiness

Despite this petty thievery—which the French would find was endemic in Tahiti—Bougainville

 ## THE BARING OF BARÉ

'*Yesterday*', *Louis-Antoine de Bougainville wrote in his journal on 29 May 1768, 'I checked a rather peculiar event on board the Etoile'. He was looking into rumours that a certain servant of his naturalist, Philibert de Commerson, was a woman. Not only was the servant beardless, unusually private in answering nature's call (a very difficult thing aboard a ship) and possessed of a high voice, but the Tahitians had reacted oddly to him. 'Hardly had the servant landed when the Cytherans [Tahitians] surround him, shout that he is a woman, and offer to pay her the honours of the island. The officer in charge had to come and free her.'*

Although this servant, one Baré, had performed all his duties, which included following the naturalist 'in all his botanizing' and carrying 'weapons, food, [and] plant notebooks with a courage and strength that earned for him from our botanist the title of beast of burden', it was Bougainville's duty, 'in accordance with the King's ordinances, to verify whether the suspicions were correct'. Called to Bougainville's cabin and questioned, the young man—or, really, woman—broke down and confessed. Her name, she said, was Jeanne Baré. Born in Burgundy, orphaned at a young age, she had fooled her various masters by appearing as a boy and had done the same to Philibert de Commerson. Why? 'She knew when she came on board that it was a question of circumnavigating the world and that this voyage had excited her curiosity … She will be the only one of her sex to go around the world.'

Bougainville was not much upset by this masquerade but knew that some superstitious sailors— especially since they were undergoing difficult times in the New Hebrides—might be, and so he took steps 'to ensure that [Baré] suffers no unpleasantness'. Commerson, too, was not upset—in fact, he dedicated the plant genus Baretia to her. The last record of her after the voyage had her living in the French countryside, a widow, in 1785. She was on a government pension, no doubt secured for her by Bougainville's largesse, for he greatly admired 'the indefatigable Baré'.

gradually began to realise that he was visiting a paradise. Or at least, this is the way he made it appear when in 1771 he published a portion of his journals concerning his visit. Beginning the day after his dinner with the royal Tahitians, 'several Frenchmen had cause to praise the country's customs', Bougainville wrote:

> *As they went into houses they were presented with young girls, greenery was placed on the ground, and with a large number of Indians, men and women, making a circle around them, hospitality was celebrated, while one of the assistants was singing a hymn to happiness accompanied by the*

Louis–Antoine de Bougainville's encounters with the Tahitians were to lead to the myth of their 'earthly paradise'.

> *sounds of the flute … Married women are faithful to their husbands, they would pay with their lives any unfaithfulness, but we are offered all the young girls. Our white skin delights them, they express their admiration in this regard in the most expressive manner.*

Bougainville described the Tahitians as a 'superb' race, the men being quite tall, with handsome features. 'They have a fine head of hair, which they wear in various ways. Several also have a long beard which they rub as they do their hair with coconut oil.' As for the women—they are 'very pretty … with the finest teeth in the world'. But then came the part that titillated the minds of people in Europe and America for generations to come:

> *These people breathe only rest and sensual pleasures. Venus is the goddess they worship. The mildness of the climate, the beauty of the scenery, the fertility of the soil everywhere watered by rivers and cascades, the pure air unspoiled by even those legions of insects that are the curse of hot countries, everything inspires sensual pleasure …*

'What a people!'

The besotted Bougainville did not find out certain home truths about Tahitian society—the practice of infanticide, the prevalence of incest, the strict caste system, which made social inequity commonplace, and the fact that the Tahitians often preyed on their neighbours, sending out war parties in huge canoes to destroy and enslave them. Quite happily, Bougainville claimed the island in the name of France, despite the fact that even before the Tahitians had heard the roar of the French rockets they had pointed at the ship's cannon, made bang-bang sounds and pretended to fall down dead. In fact, only eight months before, the English explorer Samuel Wallis had landed there and stayed six weeks, the first European to have found the island, which he had named after his own king, George III.

Bougainville was not the only person on board *La Boudeuse* to succumb to the charms of Tahitian women—Philibert de Commerson, a naturalist accompanying the expedition, waxed ecstatically about lovemaking on the island, which was almost always in public since Tahitian homes had no walls: 'Here, modesty and prudery lose their tyranny. The act of procreation is an act of religion; its preludes are encouraged by voices and songs of the assembled people; and its end is greeted by universal applause.'

But not everyone was charmed. Sailors who went off with Tahitian women found that they were pick-pocketed almost as a matter of course and that to leave a boat unattended on the beach was to come back to find every single nail removed. About eight days after Bougainville landed, an islander was murdered; a few days later, three others were bayoneted. Four Frenchmen were arrested and Bougainville nearly had one executed, but the chief of the Tahitians accepted an apology and the matter was closed. Still, it seemed to Bougainville that the time to move on had come, and on 15 April he sailed, taking with him a young royal Tahitian named Ahutoru, who wanted to see the land where the white men came from.

Even as he left, Bougainville could not restrain himself: 'What a country!' he exclaimed in his journal. 'What a people!'

'The location of hell'

Bougainville had been to paradise and now, perhaps fittingly, he was about to sample hell. Leaving Tahiti, the French ships sailed due west and came to another group of islands (Ahutoru was disappointed to find out that this was not France), which turned out to be Samoa. Bougainville did not tarry there, as the natives were not especially friendly, but kept on going. By the time the ships had reached the New

Hebrides, his men were suffering from scurvy again. He was forced to put ashore at one island to look for anti-scorbutic grasses but was attacked by natives who seemed to be suffering from some strange skin disease, hence the name Bougainville gave to the island, the Isle of Lepers. His men fired upon the natives, but the attack seemed a bad omen and *La Boudeuse* and *L'Etoile* moved on.

It was around this time, Bougainville wrote, that a 'rather peculiar event' happened on board *L'Etoile.* It was brought to Bougainville's attention that there were rumours that Philibert de Commerson's servant was a woman. These rumours were caused by this person's 'build, his caution in never changing his clothes or carrying out any natural function in the presence of anyone else'. When Bougainville confronted the servant, whose name was Baré, she tearfully confessed all and thus would become the first woman to circumnavigate the globe.

After this bit of excitement, the voyage settled down to a dull routine, but both ships were rapidly running out of supplies. The salt meat left on *La Boudeuse* was so dreadful that the men preferred to catch and eat the ship's rats. Bougainville sampled them and pronounced them 'very good'. One moonlit night in early June, a line of breakers appeared ahead of the ship. Bougainville steered away from them, but the next morning more and more shoals and coral reefs appeared; although some of the men with Bougainville 'were of the opinion there was a low land to the SW of the breakers', Bougainville himself could not be sure. He had just come upon the Great Barrier Reef off eastern Australia—if his men had indeed seen land, it would have been Australia itself, although this remains in doubt.

Bougainville, seeing coral heads breaking through the waves, changed course and headed north. The mountains of the island that would come to be known as New Guinea were sighted on

AHUTORU: THE NOBLE
SAVAGE OF PARIS

When Bougainville left Tahiti on 15 April 1768, he took with him a young royal Tahitian named Ahutoru, who was very eager to see the country 'where people knew how to build such large canoes capable of sailing across the ocean'. Ahutoru managed to survive the trials and tribulations of the rest of the journey and arrived in France in 1769, more or less intact. Bougainville then proceeded to introduce him to French royal society, where he was an instant hit, a tall, handsome man with glittering white teeth and a modest way about him.

He was, it seemed, living proof of the virtues of the 'noble savage', an idea that had been put forth by the philosopher Jean-Jacques Rousseau in 1750. Rousseau believed that man in his natural, Edenic state was good, but that civilisation (including religion, money, property and the like) corrupted him. This was such a popular idea that French aristocrats took to dressing like shepherds and shepherdesses, parading around with crooks and lambs in order to show their innocence.

Ahutoru, however, was the real deal and Parisian society was all over him. By all accounts, he was not corrupted by civilisation but enjoyed himself immensely, dining on fine food, drinking the best wine and attending the opera. In 1771, brimming with anecdotes, he headed back home aboard a French ship but caught smallpox—European diseases, even more than European civilisations, were the real destroyers of innocence—and died in Madagascar.

10 June, but as Bougainville tried to close with it, he was swept to the west by strong winds, toward what he thought was a large bay. The 'bay' was in fact the Torres Strait, which would have taken Bougainville safely into the Indian Ocean and homeward but, fearful that he might come upon more of the low-lying coral reefs, Bougainville made an almost superhuman attempt to beat back to the east against gale-force winds, with huge waves crashing over the vessels—the only way the ships could keep in touch was by the sound of signal cannons. Men became so hungry that Bougainville had to forbid 'the eating of that leather which is wrapped around the yards, and any other old leather, as it might have the most dreadful consequences'.

Finally, the ships beat around New Guinea's southern tip and headed north. They found themselves within a few days among the Solomon Islands, one of which, Bougainville, the French leader named for himself. He did not stay long. At one point, the French were attacked by the Melanesian natives of the area, who uttered 'horrible cries' and showered the ships with arrows and spears. Shortly thereafter, Bougainville found a canoe in which he discovered 'the jaw of a man, half-broiled'. Reaching the island of New Ireland, Bougainville ordered the ship's barrels filled with fresh water, but even here there was a problem—a huge earthquake occurred, making the sea flip and roll as if it were a carpet someone were shaking.

At this point, Bougainville departed again, vowing to make it to the Spice Islands and the Dutch colony of Batavia without stopping. It was mid-July. 'People have long argued about the location of hell', he wrote in his journal. 'Frankly, we have discovered it.'

Salvation—and fame

A few days after leaving the Solomons, men began dying of scurvy. Scenes on the voyage were horrific, with sailors literally crawling along the decks with their tongues lolling out, too weak to climb the rigging. A rumour began among the crew that Bougainville—who was naturally stout—had a store of food hidden, and even though this was not true, the men began to resent him. But finally, on 30 August 1768, the wafted smell of sandalwood and spices across the ocean—the starving men could smell the Moluccas, the Spice Islands, and the most horrible part of their journey was nearly at an end. The Dutch they met gave them a lavish supper—as Bougainville wrote: 'One must have been a sailor, and reduced to the extremities which we had felt for several months together, in order to form an idea of the sensation which the sight of greens and a good supper produced …'

Bougainville began to lose men to dysentery, however, and so ordered that both ships be taken to the French colony of Mauritius, in the Indian Ocean, where the vessels were refitted and the men recuperated further. After this, he sailed home, finally arriving back in France on 16 March 1769. Almost overnight, he became famous, becoming secretary to King Louis XV in 1772 and later leading the French fleet in support of the American Revolution. He was the ultimate survivor: when the French Revolution began, he managed to keep his head during the Reign of Terror, despite his close ties to King Louis XVI. Napoleon I awarded him the first Legion of Honour. He died in Paris in 1811, full of honours, married, with three children, all of whom served in the French army.

But what really kept Bougainville's legacy alive—and changed the life of every Tahitian— was his 1771 book *Voyage around the World* (*Voyage autour du monde*). In it, he described his vision of the earthly paradise of Tahiti, bolstering Jean-Jacques Rousseau's philosophy of the 'noble savage', which postulates men and women living in utopian primitive societies, protected by their innocence. Tahitians were far from innocent, of course, but the open sexual element of their way of life appealed to a great many people, most of whom were not philosophers, but rough sailors, adventurers and merchants.

After James Cook landed in Tahiti the following year—where already the women were demanding more and more payment for sex—the influx of Europeans really began. When Louis-Antoine de Bougainville had arrived, the population of Tahiti (including nearby, lesser islands) was estimated at about fifty thousand. Thirty years later, as a result of venereal diseases, alcoholism, typhus, influenza and smallpox, the population had dropped to only sixteen thousand. Bougainville's New Cythera had been destroyed by the very Europeans who had come to revere it.

Publicity, when it comes to Gardens of Eden, is never a very good thing.

THE VOYAGE OF THE ENDEAVOUR

James Cook and
terra australis incognita,
1768–1771

One day late in the fall of 1769, a group of Maori were gathering clams on the shores of a bay they called 'Gentle as a Young Girl', because its waters were so calm. They were on what is today known as the North Island of New Zealand, at a spot now called Mercury Bay. Suddenly, one of their number pointed and shouted. Something very strange had appeared on the ocean. It looked like a bird with giant wings or, some thought, a floating island.

Gradually, the Maori realised that the object was a large ship, far bigger than any they had ever seen. One of those present, a young boy named Te Horeta, lived long enough to be able to recount the story to white listeners in the next century. He said that as this massive ship approached, the Maori elders decided that it had come from the spirit world. This assumption was confirmed when a small boat was lowered from the larger vessel and

very pale beings began to row the boat toward shore. They had their backs toward land and so the elders said that they must be goblins of the spirit world, because they were paddling with eyes in the back of their head.

These goblins landed on shore and all the children fled into the woods while the Maori warriors watched warily. The pale spirit creatures seemed to mean them no harm. They gathered clams and oysters. Some of them put flowers and shells in small bags. Gradually, the children filtered out of the woods and came closer. They even dared to touch the goblins. 'We were pleased by the whiteness of their skin and the blue eyes of some of them', Te Horeta recalled. The goblins began to eat the fish and roots the Maori offered them, so perhaps they were not goblins after all. They offered the Maori food in return—fatty meat that Te Horeta thought might be whale meat, but the meat's 'saltiness ripped our throats' so that even the warriors in the clan could not stomach it and spat it out.

One of the goblins pointed a rod in the air and fired a shot out of it and a bird fell out of the sky, which puzzled the Maori—what had killed the bird? A little later some trading was going on and one warrior tried to make off with the coat of a goblin without giving anything in return. The goblin pointed his rod, there was the noise like thunder, and the warrior fell dead, a wide hole in his back. Now the Maori understood that these were weapons.

However, they did not blame the goblins for the warrior's death because he had been, after all, stealing. The goblins stayed in the bay for several days and one day Te Horeta and some others went on their ship. There they met a tall goblin who said little but examined the Maori closely. He patted the boys' heads and gave them small presents. Then he took a piece of charcoal, pointed to the shore and handed it to a Maori elder named Toiawa, who realised that this goblin wanted a sketch of the coast of the land they called Aotearoa, or the Land of the Long White Cloud.

The Maori drew the land for the tall goblin as best he could, including Te Reinga, the cliffs at the tip of the North Island where spirits flew into the next world. Toiawa lay down on the deck and pretended to be dead to illustrate this concept to the goblin—who, after all, should have gotten the point immediately.

However, the goblin did not understand them and finally the Maori left. A short time later, the ship sailed away and the Maori did not see them anymore. But before Te Horeta left the ship, the tall, quiet, kind-seeming goblin patted his cheek and blessed him with a gift: an iron nail, whose use Te Horeta did not understand for some years, but which he treasured as a sacred object for the rest of his life.

'A noble man'

The tall goblin Te Horeta was referring to could only have been James Cook for, as Te Horeta said, 'A noble man, one of high standing, cannot be lost in the crowd'. And certainly this greatest of British explorers was also one of the most intelligent and honest men to sail the Pacific Ocean during the great Age of Exploration. While it was his fate, like that of Magellan, to be killed by the indigenous peoples he made contact with, he also treated them far better than most Europeans of his day.

Cook, the son of a Scottish immigrant and farm worker, was born in 1728 in the village of Marton-in-Cleveland, England. Despite being born 'inland', as it were, the sea was somehow in young Cook's blood. He was desperate to work on board a vessel, and finally his father agreed—after about a year of pleading—that James could apprentice on a coal-carrying ship plying the North Sea. It was tough duty, but the eighteen-year-old Cook loved it. In his spare time, he taught himself mathematics and navigation and was soon appointed as mate.

In 1755 he volunteered for the British Royal Navy during the Seven Years' War and shipped off to North America to fight the French. Here he was instrumental in charting the shoals of the St Lawrence River, going out at night in a small boat, taking depth soundings in pitch darkness as French sentries paced above him on the cliffs of Quebec (where another great Pacific explorer, Louis-Antoine de Bougainville, was stationed—see page 195). At one point, Cook leaped out of the bow of his boat to save himself from French Indians jumping into the stern to try to kill him. His efforts were credited with allowing the British fleet to safely attack the French stronghold.

Cook's reputation was made by his sterling war service—which included charting lengthy parts of the rugged Canadian coastline—and furthered by his published account of the solar eclipse of 5 August 1766. Although he was still not even a lieutenant in the Royal Navy, he came to the attention of the British Admiralty and the Royal Society of London for the Improvement of Natural Knowledge, generally known as the Royal Society. The Royal Society was planning a grand expedition to the recently discovered island of Tahiti, in the South Pacific, in order to have scientists observe the transit of Venus, a rare but predictable astronomical occurrence in which Venus passes across the face of the sun. Using sightings taken from different parts of the globe, the Royal Society hoped to measure the distance from Earth to the sun.

'A Land of Great Extent'

James Cook finally received his commission as lieutenant for this voyage—the first of what would become three famous journeys of discovery—and set off from England in August 1768 aboard HMS *Endeavour*. The *Endeavour* was no cutting-edge and sleek new vessel, but instead a fat, squat, 360-tonne collier, or coal vessel, which was exactly the type of ship that Cook had cut his sailing teeth on. He had made sure the ship was well fitted for the voyage— with an extra layer of wooden hull to protect against the voracious tropical worms, twenty-two cannon, enough food for a year and extra cabins for all the scientific personnel on board, chief among them the brilliant naturalist Joseph Banks.

At this time, Cook was forty years old, tall, lantern-jawed, bluntly handsome and plain spoken. He was the kind of man who inspired instant trust and who also inspired men to follow him, despite occasional eruptions of temper that sent his officers scurrying away as fast as they could. He was perfect for this job he was publicly given—that of getting the scientists to Tahiti by 3 June 1769—and also for the job that was secretly bestowed upon him: to find *terra australis incognita*, the Unknown Southland, the southern continent that had long been rumoured to exist in the Pacific Ocean somewhere between New Zealand and the South American continent.

Scientists speculated that there needed to be a landmass below the Tropic of Capricorn in order to balance out the heavy northern continents of Europe and North America—without one, surely Earth would go spinning off its axis?

European peeks at Tasmania, New Zealand and present-day Western Australia had led people to think that this might be the southern continent, although many others still believed it was farther east and south—that its mountain peaks could even be seen, on clear days, from Tahiti. And so Cook's secret orders, once all the fussing about the transit of Venus was over, were to sail from Tahiti and proceed southward in order to find the 'Land of Great Extent' that some in the British government believed would provide a vast trading market for British goods 'sufficient to maintain the power, dominion, and sovereignty of Britain, by employing all its manufactures and ships'.

Tahiti and west

After stopping briefly in Rio de Janeiro, Cook took the *Endeavour* south, rounding Cape Horn and heading into the Pacific. He landed in Tahiti on 13 April and built a small fort while the scientists readied their instruments to take readings on the transit of Venus in June. Like Bougainville (see page 195) and Samuel Wallis before him, he was greeted enthusiastically by canoes full of shouting and laughing Tahitians offering to trade coconuts and fruit. The crew aboard—some of whom had been with Wallis—were looking forward to the Tahitian women especially, since a single nail from the ship could buy hours worth of pleasure—the Tahitians, as one historian has written, 'valued iron above virtue'. Cook understood this and had brought barrels of extra nails along, although not for trading for women, but for goods and food. Much to his men's dismay, he had drawn up a list of trading 'rules', which made it an offence punishable by flogging to trade for sex with the Tahitian women.

James Cook was a man who liked good order on his ship and knew how to enforce it—at least four seamen were given two dozen lashes with a cat-o'-nine-tails for breaking the rules, but some were punished because they had been harsh with the Tahitians. Many more, no doubt, found a way around the trading rules, although Tahitian women were perhaps not the great beauties they had all heard about—Cook, for one, wrote that he found them 'very masculine', perhaps because the royal princesses among them could weigh as much as 135 kilograms (300 pounds) and stand 1.8 metres (six feet) tall.

The day for the transit of Venus was 3 June and it could not have been more beautiful—hot and cloudless. Two telescopes were set up in the sand, while pieces of smoked glass were passed around so that people could look at the sun. At exactly twenty-one minutes and fifty seconds past 9 a.m., Venus began its journey across the sun, but the scientists watching saw 'a dusky shade around the body of the planet' that threw off their measurements. (It turned out that this shade was caused by the smearing of the image of Venus by turbulence in the Earth's atmosphere, which instruments in the eighteenth century were unable to correct for.)

While the scientists may have considered their expedition a failure, Cook did not. After bringing on new stores and repairing his vessel, he was off on what he considered to be his true mission: to seek the southern continent.

'We again launched out'

Heading south from Tahiti, Cook found himself among the beautiful, high and hilly islands he called the Society Islands, after the Royal Society. He wandered through these islands for a month, guided by a Tahitian priest named Tupaia, who had begged to come along and who, in fact, proved an able guide and translator. Once they departed from the Society Islands—'we again launched out into the ocean, in search of chance and what Tupaia might direct us to'—they sailed directly, following Admiralty orders, toward 40 degrees south latitude, which was where the southern continent was postulated to be. Two months passed by. Once they hit 40 degrees the weather turned cold and stormy, for they had arrived in the area known to generations of sailors as the 'Roaring Forties' where the wind blows around the southern part of the world without any large landmass to impede it.

'The seas ran mountain-high and tossed the ship upon the waves', wrote one of the scientists present. 'She rolled so much that we could get no rest, or scarcely lie in bed.'

Obviously there was no continent here, so Cook—'we had no prospect of meeting land', he wrote in his journals—now followed his secondary orders to turn west in order to seek the land found by Abel Tasman a century earlier, to see if this was part of a *terra australis*. After about a month or so, they began to see seaweed and driftwood floating by them, a sign that land was near. Excitement ran high and Cook offered a gallon (about 4.5 litres) of rum to the man who first spotted land.

It turned out to be a boy—a twelve-year-old named Nick Young—and he got not only the rum but a coastal bluff (Young Nick's Head) named after him. Cook had arrived on the east coast of New Zealand's North Island. New Zealand is made up of the North Island and the South Island, separated by a strait now known as Cook Strait, and it is one of the most isolated places on Earth, physically speaking, 2000 kilometres (1200 miles) from the nearest continental landmass, Australia. Thus it was one of the last large places on earth to be settled. The general consensus is that the islands were visited by Polynesian travellers in about 800 AD,

FOLLOWING PAGES The observatory set up by Cook on 'Point Venus' in Tahiti to watch the transit of Venus.

An English officer barters with a Maori for a crayfish (drawing by a crewmember of the Endeavour, *1769).*

perhaps drawn by the long white clouds that hang over New Zealand and can be seen far out to sea. The Maori peoples who were the descendants of those Polynesians developed in isolation for eight hundred years until Abel Tasman (see page 186) showed up and had his bloody encounter with them.

But that had been 127 years before and 500 kilometres (300 miles) away on the western side of the South Island. Not only did Te Horeta not know of this incident but, as Cook later discovered, even the descendants of the murderers at Murderer's Bay had completely forgotten it. So it was really as if Cook had dropped from the sky—no Maori had ever heard of or imagined white men.

'Black be the mark on it'

Before meeting Te Horeta's people, Cook and his men had had a far more deadly encounter with the Maori. Upon first sighting Young Nick's Head,

Cook had turned south to see if this land—he correctly assumed this was the same land whose west coast had been sighted by Tasman—was possibly connected to a southern continent and was perhaps a peninsula or part of an archipelago. Within a few days, he ran into trouble. The *Endeavour* anchored off the mouth of a river and Cook went ashore with a few boats to explore the banks of the river. While he did so, four Maori jumped from the woods and ran at one of the sailors guarding the boats; feeling threatened, he shot and killed one of them.

The next day, the British landed again to see the Maori performing a startling dance: 'With a regular jump from the Left to the Right and the Reverse, they brandish'd their Weapons, distorted their Mouths, Lolling out their Tongues and Turn'd up the Whites of their Eyes', wrote one ship's officer. Clearly, this was not a good thing. The British were seeing a Maori dance called the *haka*, an aggressive ritual performed before any encounter to pump up the warriors' spirits. The Maori were on the other side of the river and Cook, attempting to make peace, threw a nail into the water and then crossed over himself when a Maori warrior waded out to retrieve it.

The men touched noses in a ritual of friendship after Cook laid down his arms, and for a moment there was peace. It turned out that the Maori could easily understand Tupaia's Tahitian language, which differed from theirs only by a few words—both races, after all, had common Polynesian ancestors. Unfortunately, the moment of peace was shattered when a warrior stole a sword and the British shot and killed him.

The other warriors then ran away. Cook, always respectful even when he fought with indigenous peoples, placed beads and other trade goods around the body of the dead Maori, hoping his people would take them as a peace offering. Then he sailed off to another part of the bay—to which he gave the bleak name of Poverty Bay because of his inability to land long enough to replenish his vessel. Here there were seven men fishing from a canoe. Wanting only to scare them away—so that he could land for water and fruit—Cook ordered that his crew fire muskets over their heads. He immediately regretted this. 'Here I was mistaken', he wrote later, 'for they [the Maori] immediately took to their arms, or whatever they had in the boat, and began to attack us'. The enraged or frightened Maori threw rocks, lances and paddles at the *Endeavour* in a brave show of spirit. They even threw their fish at the boat. The British poured musket fire down upon them, killing several.

Cook wrote that night in his journal (in a passage that he later tried to cross out) that: 'I can by no means justify my conduct in attacking and killing the people in this boat who had given me no just provocation and [were] wholly ignorant of my design'. But, he went on, 'when we was once a long side of them we must either have stud to be knocked on the head or else retire and let them gone off in triumph and this last they would of Course have attributed to their own bravery and our timorousness'.

Joseph Banks stated the British regret bluntly: 'Black be the mark for … the most disagreeable day my life has yet seen', he wrote in his journal.

NEW ZEALAND'S MAORI: 'THE NATIVES OF THE COUNTRY ARE WELL MADE'

Despite some violent encounters with them, Cook was quite taken with the Maori people of New Zealand. He found them to be brave and intelligent, although their cannibalism took him aback. And he was curious about their tattoos.

Many of the old and some of the middle aged men have their faces mark'd or tatoow'd with black, and some few we have seen who have had their buttocks, thighs and other parts of their bodies mark'd but this is less common. The figures they mostly use are spirals drawn and connected together with great nicety and judgment … The manner in which it must be done must certainly cause intolerable pain.

The Maori actually used sharp bones or shells to prick their skin and then rubbed soot into the wounds, thus colouring the designs black. The tattoos were used as a form of identification, to show rank, genealogy or tribal history, as marks of beauty or to create the impression of ferocity.

Interestingly enough, one of the British sailors with Cook—a Mr Stainsby, and you cannot make up a name like that—elected to get tattooed, thus becoming the first in a long line of sailors to cover his body with designs.

The extraordinary circumnavigation

After leaving Poverty Bay behind, Cook sailed farther southward before reaching a point about eighty kilometres (fifty miles) from the southeastern tip of the North Island (something he did not, of course, yet know). With the coast looking bleak and waters boiling up with storms, Cook decided to turn around and head northward. He then engaged on one of the most extraordinary feats of his career—a 4000-kilometre (2500-mile) long counter-clockwise circumnavigation of New Zealand, along rugged coastlines, much of it in the Roaring Forties latitude.

Abel Tasman had only touched at this island. Now Cook was literally going where no European had gone before. The dangers in simply sailing the vessel were manifold—hidden reefs, sudden squalls, sudden shallows and treacherous bays where no anchorage could be found to hold. Once the lee yardarms of the *Endeavour* scraped against the side of a cliff. Yet Cook kept going on his way, patiently sounding shallows with knotted rope and sounding lead, carefully charting what he saw. He generally had better relations with the Maori he now met, as he had with Te Horeta's people, and he was able to gather supplies for his ship, including water, wood, birds and vegetables to treat scurvy. He rounded North Cape in late December (the crew managed to celebrate Christmas in traditional fashion, cooking a fat goose) and headed south along the coast of New Zealand, continuing to chart everything. When the ocean opened up again to his left into a strait 'broad and deep', he intended to make a turn to complete the circle—but then he saw, over the horizon, a blue-green and mountainous mass of land.

Perhaps this was the tip of the southern continent? Cook set out to explore it. He stopped in what he called Queen Charlotte's Sound, on the northern tip of the South Island, a beautiful spot where the crew was allowed to rest and the ship was hauled up and its bottom caulked and patched.

There, on 17 January 1770, Cook came into contact with Maori cannibals: 'Soon after we landed we met with two or three of the natives who not long before must have been regaling themselves upon human flesh, for I got from one of them the bone of the fore arm of a Man or Woman which was quite fresh …'

Cook wrote about this in a scientific manner, as did Banks, who even purchased—with a pair of his linen drawers—the head of one of the victims and then wrote that 'the flesh and skin were soft but they were somehow preserved so as not to stink at all'. For the rest of the crew it was, nonetheless, frightening. (During Cook's second voyage, ten crewmen from his second ship, the *Adventure*, were killed and eaten by Maoris, and afterwards cannibalism would not be viewed with such detachment.)

More amusing (although offensive to some of the British sailors) was the habit the Maori had of groping the chests and groins of the younger sailors and cabin boys, trying to see if they were women. They could not imagine men travelling without women—in fact, some of the hostility displayed toward the British was because the Maori assumed any group that contained only men had to be a war party. When certain British sailors made signs to the Maori to bring women to them so they could buy sex from them, the Maori brought boys, assuming this was what the British liked.

'*I do not believe any such thing exists*'

After resting at Queen Charlotte's Sound, Cook headed east through the strait that now bears his name, and then turned south to circumnavigate the South Island in a clockwise fashion, thus eventually describing a great figure-eight around New Zealand. His tour around New Zealand took him six months, but at last he was able to prove, as he wrote, that 'this country, which before now was thought to be part of the imaginary southern continent, consists of Two large Islands'. However, Cook recognised the value of what he had stumbled upon. 'Although it is a hilly, mountainous Country, yet the very hills and mountains are many of them covered with wood, and the Soil of the plains and Valleys appeared to be rich and fertile'.

However, he completely shut the door on the notion that *terra australis incognita* existed to the south: 'As to a Southern Continent, I do not believe that

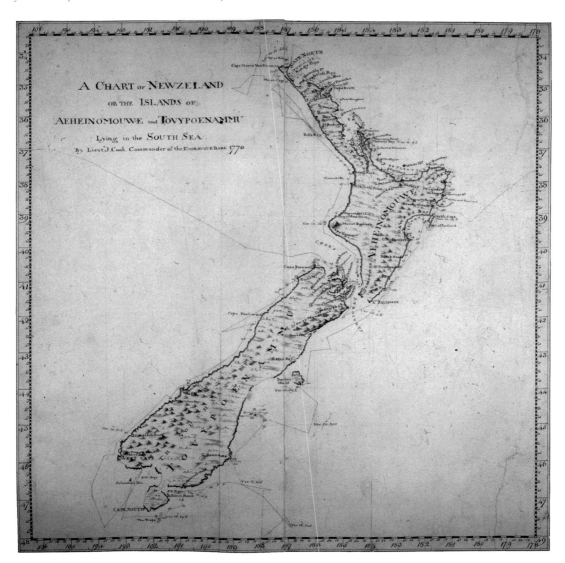

By following the coast closely, Cook was able to create an extraordinarily accurate map of the islands of New Zealand.

COOK AND SCURVY: 'THAT DREADFUL DISTEMPER'

Scurvy is disease caused by lack of ascorbic acid (vitamin C) and is characterised by swollen and bleeding gums, loose teeth, aching joints, anaemia and, finally (if it is left unchecked), haemorrhaging and death. After the discoveries of the fifteenth century, when long sea voyages became the norm, more and more men began to die of the disease—it was not unusual for a British ship in the eighteenth century to lose half its crew to scurvy.

The sad part was that it was easily cured by the introduction of fresh foods—lime juice, vegetables, certain types of grasses, even fresh meat—and this knowledge had been around for at least a century. James Woodall, a British military surgeon, knew how to treat scurvy as early as 1617 ('with Lemmons, Limes Tamarinds') but the knowledge seemed continually to get lost. James Cook, however, had done his homework and knew how to provide for his crew. He insisted that the men have sauerkraut and forced them to eat it, despite the fact that, as he wrote ruefully, 'Every innovation whatever, tho ever so much to their advantage, is sure to meet with the highest disapprobation from Seamen'.

Since much of the vitamin C content of sauerkraut was lost in boiling it, it is probable that Cook's crew did not get scurvy because of his frequent stops for fresh food. In any event, on his first voyage he did not lose a single man to 'that dreadful distemper the Scurvy'.

any such thing exists, unless in a high latitude.' Cook now decided to head home (his men, he said, 'were sighing for roast beef'), planning to head west for the Cape of Good Hope. He knew that Van Diemen's Land, discovered by Abel Tasman, was to the west but he was not daunted by the prospect of a large landmass between himself and home. He would simply sail west and see what he found. However, winds drove him a bit north of west, and after nineteen days at sea, on 20 April 1770, he found land. At first he thought this was Van Diemen's Land, but then he realised his error, since Tasman's discovery should have been farther south.

In fact, Cook had become the first European to spy the eastern coast of the continent of Australia. It was a momentous occasion for the British,

although Cook did not as yet realise it. He set sail north along the coastline, surveying as he went, until he found Botany Bay (which was first called Stingray Bay for the large numbers of those creatures that could be seen dashing through the waters), so named because of the large number of plant specimens gathered there. In its relatively calm waters, the *Endeavour* anchored and Cook and his scientists and crew went ashore. They spent a few days there collecting specimens and Cook claimed the area for the British crown.

Cook's encounters with the Aboriginal peoples were far less dramatic than the contacts the British had made in New Zealand. As soon as he landed at Botany Bay, Cook saw 'natives and a few huts' and he approached these people with Tupaia, hoping that the Tahitian could communicate with them as he had with the Maori. But these Aboriginal people were very, very different, and quite strange to the eyes of Cook and his fellows. The British seemed to make little impression on these people they called 'Indians'. Fishermen fished, barely raising their heads to look at what must have been the amazing spectacle of this European vessel. They 'looked at the ship but expressed neither surprise nor concern, to all appearance totally unmoved by us'.

Cook wrote that these people had 'skin the Colour of Wood soot or of a dark Chocolate'. The men had bushy hair and beards and were usually completely naked except for 'White paist or pigment' daubed in thick bands around their foreheads and waists. The women were completely naked. Their huts were poor, their canoes 'the worst I think I ever saw'.

Cook tried to throw nails to the Aboriginals as a peacemaking gesture, but they took it as a threat and one warrior hurled a spear at the British, which caused Cook to respond by shooting a musket loaded with small shot, meant to scare rather than do serious injury. Gradually, the people drifted away, shouting the only words they had spoken— *Warra warra wai*, which the Europeans later found out meant 'Go away'. And, indeed, Cook wrote with some puzzlement, 'all they seemed to want was for us to be gone'. Which they were, within nine days, continuing north and mapping the coastline at a slow pace.

'An alarming and terrible circumstance'

Cook sailed north without a problem for a month or so, until, on the evening of 11 June, near a point that he would call Cape Tribulation—'because here', as he wrote, 'began all our troubles'—shoals were spotted dead ahead. No problem—Cook ordered that the *Endeavour* be pointed farther east, out to sea—to avoid them. There should not have been any problem, because, even though night had

fallen, it was a clear one, with good visibility and calm water. But at about 11 p.m., the *Endeavour* shuddered and came to a halt with a scraping bang. They had hit a coral reef where, reasonably speaking, there should have been none.

Cook raced up onto deck and began shouting out orders.

We went to work to lighten [the ship] as fast as possible, which seemed to be the only means we had left to get her off ... throwed over board our guns, Iron and stone ballast Casks, Hoops, staves, oil Jars, decayed stores, etc ... All this time the Ship made little or no water.

Fifty tonnes of jettisoning later, the *Endeavour* was still stuck fast, and the tide was going out, pushing it deeper into the sharp coral. The next morning, 12 June, saw the tide rise again, but the ship was leaking badly, 'an alarming and I may say terrible circumstance', wrote the horrified Cook, who loved his *Endeavour* as much as he loved anything in the world.

Finally, through luck—a piece of the coral broke off and acted as a plug in the ship's hull, stopping the leaking—the *Endeavour* was floated off and taken to the mainland for repair near the mouth of a river that Cook named after his rescued ship. He spent seven weeks there, patching the ship up again and making it seaworthy. During that time, Cook and his men became the first Europeans to spot a kangaroo—'except the head and ears, which I thought was something like a Hare's, it bears no resemblance to any European Animal I ever saw', Cook wrote. The local Aboriginal people did show up—this is how Cook knew to call the animal a kangaroo—but became upset that the Europeans were capturing the turtles they themselves regularly hunted in the river and tried to set a fire to scare them off—a situation Cook resolved by firing small shot from his muskets.

'THUS FELL OUR GREAT AND EXCELLENT COMMANDER!'

After returning from his unsuccessful attempt searching for a Northwest Passage north of the Bering Strait, James Cook brought his two vessels, the Resolution and the Discovery, to the Hawaiian Islands, landing there on 17 January 1779. He was looking forward to some much-needed rest—for both himself and his men—while his ships, battered by ice in northern waters, were being repaired.

A year earlier, on his way to North America, Cook had become the first white man to arrive at the Hawaiian Islands (Cook called them the Sandwich Islands). The natives took him for a god: 'The very instant I leaped ashore, they all fell flat on their faces and remained in that humble posture til I made signs to them to rise.'

Despite the fact that the British accidentally killed a man during their stay there, the Hawaiians literally treated them like royalty, and thus it was natural to expect the same when the Resolution and the Discovery returned a year later. The Hawaiians had by this time even identified which god Cook was—Lono, the god of good times and no war, a god who had been exiled long ago from Hawaii but had promised to return. Cook was carried off the ship in reverence, red cloth wrapped around him, his limbs massaged with coconut oils, a piece of pork placed in his mouth. But after a while, feeding such a large crew as well as Lono himself became too much for the Hawaiians—they were running out of provisions themselves.

Realising this, Cook decided to sail on 4 February, but unfortunately a gale broke one of the masts of the Resolution and he was forced to return. The Hawaiians were not happy to see him—once Lono left, he was supposed to be gone for another few centuries. Gradually, they began to steal from the British, and if there was one thing Cook hated in all his explorations, it was indigenous peoples stealing from his men. He tried at first to ignore the thefts but finally, on 13 February, when the Hawaiians stole the ship's boat from the Discovery, he flew into one of his rare but volcanic rages, went ashore with a squad of marines and tried to take the king hostage. This was a fatal error, for a crowd of angry Hawaiians mobbed him.

Cook was carrying one pistol filled with small shot, which he discharged at a warrior, but the pellets merely bounced off the man's wooden shield. He laughed at Cook—at the great Lono—and pulled out his dagger, at which point Cook discharged another pistol, which had a real round in it, and the warrior went down, mortally wounded. Enraged, the crowd began stoning Cook and a general melee ensued, killing four of Cook's marines and numerous Hawaiians. Cook's guns were empty at this point, but as long as he faced the Hawaiians, they did not dare attack him. However, as soon as he turned his back to signal his boats to come in, he was stabbed and then the crowd tore him to pieces with their knives.

It was, perhaps, a fitting fate for a god who failed to disappear. The British were so shocked that they did not even take revenge on the Hawaiians and, in fact, the Hawaiians were quite sorrowful afterwards. But it was too late. As James King, one of Cook's lieutenants wrote: 'Thus fell our great and excellent Commander'.

The *Endeavour* finally set sail again early in August. Unbeknown to him at the time, Cook had encountered the first signs of the Great Barrier Reef, a treacherous coral maze that extends 2000 kilometres (1250 miles) along the northeastern coast of Australia. As he progressed north, he realised how difficult this maze was. He sought and finally found a passage outside the reefs, but then found himself blown by the trade winds back toward the sharp edge of the coral—'between us and destruction was only a dismal Valley, the breadth of one wave', Cook wrote on one occasion. Finally, however, on 21 August 1770, the ship reached Cape York, the northern tip of Australia, where Cook claimed for Britain the country whose coast he had just traversed: 'I now once more hoisted British Colours and in the name of His Majesty King George the Third, took possession of the whole Eastern Coast ... by the name of New South Wales'.

'An instinct for discovery'

James Cook made his way back to England by way of the Torres Strait, the Indian Ocean and the Cape of Good Hope. He stopped to provision in the Dutch colony of Batavia, where, tragically, malaria was raging. Ultimately, Cook lost twenty-nine of his men to this disease or dysentery, including several scientists, the talented illustrator Sydney Parkinson, whose sketches captured so much of the voyage, and the adventurous Tahitian, Tupaia. This was especially vexing to Cook, because he had not lost a man to scurvy for the entire voyage, a record at the time. But the *Endeavour* finally returned to England in triumph, arriving on 13 July 1771. Cook had been gone almost four years, had travelled 8000 kilometres (5000 miles) and had made, as he wrote with pardonable pride, a voyage 'as complete as any before made to the South Seas'.

He had not found *terra australis incognita* but had, in fact, explored the real Australia and claimed it for the king. Despite this fact, he was sent back to sea on a second expedition within eighteen months— leaving his poor wife, Elizabeth, behind to care for the five children they had at the time (one more would come later). The Admiralty still wanted Cook to find *terra australis incognita* and this time he navigated the waters near Antarctica, proving conclusively that there was no continent in the southern Pacific. His third voyage, beginning in 1776, took him in search of another chimera, the Northwest Passage and, once again, Cook became a man who discovered a great deal while not discovering his goal, for he charted much of the western coast of North America while sailing up into the ice-clogged Bering Strait.

It was on his return voyage that he stopped in Hawaii and was tragically and unexpectedly killed while attempting to regain a ship's boat stolen by natives. In his last journal entry, describing Hawaiians swimming around his ship 'like shoals of fish', Cook wrote: 'We could not help but be struck with the singularity of the scene.' It was the search for such scenes, and such people, that made James Cook one of the most famous men of his age, a man with, as one historian has written, 'that essential quality of all great explorers, an instinct for discovery'.

PART 5

FATEFUL
ENCOUNTERS
IN THE HEART
OF AFRICA

Henry Morton Stanley in a photograph
commissioned by the New York Herald
before his 1871 expedition to find
David Livingstone.

AN ENGLISHMAN WITH THE IMBANGALA

The strange adventures of Andrew Battell, 1589–1610

On a warm July day in the summer of 1610, the residents of the English fishing village of Leigh, in Essex, were startled to see a strange apparition strolling their main street—a gaunt, sunburned man, walking with a slight limp, carrying a seaman's bag over his shoulder. Walking a little behind him was a young black boy, perhaps twelve years old. The man said hello to a few shopkeepers who came out to stare, but they merely looked at him blankly, until he introduced himself.

'I'm Andrew Battell', he said.

And, peering closely, they knew him as the very young man who had left Leigh more than twenty years before and had long been presumed dead. Battell told them that he had been enslaved by the Portuguese and then lived with a fierce tribe of African warriors who routinely killed their own young and cannibalised their enemies. The black boy with him had been held captive by gorillas;

Battell had rescued him. It is possible that many of the good burghers of the village turned away in disbelief, while others listened, fascinated. It is also possible that Battell's family flocked to him, hugging him to them. Or perhaps they were now all dead. We do not know. A curtain now closes over the scene.

History fails to record what became of Battell, not even the date of his death, or the fate of the black boy who accompanied him. Our consolation prize, however, is that Battell spoke often about his trials in Africa with Samuel Purchas, a vicar in a neighbouring village and a compiler of exotic travel stories. After Battell's death, a manuscript he had written about his adventures was given to Purchas, who edited and published it in a volume entitled *The Strange Adventures of Andrew Battell, of Leigh in Essex.*

It is the first truly reliable eyewitness account of a European in the African interior, a man who went where no white man had gone before—deep into the Congo and Angola—and, what is more, returned.

'We burned the village'

We do not know how old Andrew Battell was when he shipped out of England with Captain Abraham Cocke on 20 April 1589, but he was certainly old enough to know he was sailing with a pirate. Or perhaps a privateer—the line could be thinly drawn in those days. Cocke left England with two vessels, the *Dolphin* and the *May-Morning*, to prey upon Portuguese shipping off the coasts of Africa and Brazil—there was a war on with Spain (the Spanish Armada had been defeated less than a year before) and Portugal, having been annexed by Spain, was considered fair game.

They headed down the coast of Africa until they were in the Gulf of Guinea, intending then to head west across the Atlantic to Brazil, but the wind dropped, they were becalmed and the sailors began to suffer from scurvy. Needing to get them fresh fruit and water, Cocke directed that they sail to a small island called Iheo das Rolas (Turtle-dove Island), a densely wooded little spot of land inhabited by sick slaves sent from the African mainland by their masters to recover or die.

There was no naturally occurring water on the island, and its inhabitants were dependent on water from cisterns, or palm wine. Battell landed with the rest of the pirates. 'Having refreshed ourselves with the fruit of this island', he writes, 'we burned the village', apparently not caring what happened to the sick slaves within it, simply because it was Portuguese. They paid for this act of destruction when they sailed by the large island of St Tomo (São Tomé), fortified by the Portuguese, and had to dodge cannonballs sent their way from the fortress.

Even then, Cocke attempted to land on another part of the island to replenish his water casks from a small river, but the Portuguese ambushed them and killed one pirate, at which point Cocke decided to try his luck in Brazil.

Captured by Indians

After thirty days of sailing west-south-west, the two ships (led by a shoal of leaping dolphins) raised the Brazilian coastline. They stopped at an uninhabited island to take on wood and water and captured a Portuguese merchantman unlucky enough to pause there on the same errand. The captain of that vessel told Cocke that 'great stores of treasure' were transferred overland from Peruvian silver mines and taken to the Rio de Janeiro. Cocke then hatched a daring plan.

He decided to take the *May-Morning* (with extra sailors from the *Dolphin*) down the coast to the Rio de Janeiro—a journey of over a month. Once there, the pirates hid on a small island off the coast, living on seals, 'in great distress of victuals', as Battell puts it. Then, Battell writes, the plan was 'to run up to Buenos Aires, and with our light-horseman [small boat] to take one of the pinnances that rid [road] at the town'. However, when the attempt was made, a storm arose and drove the pirates back to their island.

At this point, apparently unable to exist on a steady diet of seal, the pirates took up anchor and went back north to the island of San Sebastian. While Abraham Cocke lay off the shore in the *May-Morning*, Battell and four others went into the woods to gather fruit, 'for we were in all manner famished'. But, as Battell relates:

> There was at that time a canoe fraught with Indians, that came from the town Spiritu Sancto [Espirito Santu, which is on the coast of Brazil]. These Indians landed on the west side of the island, and came through the woods and took five of us, and carried us to the River of Janeiro [Rio de Janeiro].

There was, of course, no loyalty among pirates. Battell writes: 'After this mishap our captain, Abraham Cocke, went to sea, and was heard of no more'.

Although Battell mentions no dates—in fact, aside from the date his vessel left England, there are no dates in his entire journal—his capture by Indians hired by the Portuguese probably occurred at the end of 1589, or possibly in 1590. Battell was now going to pay for his sins as a pirate. He was held in Rio de Janeiro for four months and then, to his horror, sent to Angola, in Africa.

'Here I lived a most miserable life'

Africa was a particularly fearsome place at the end of the sixteenth century. The Portuguese, the first European power to come into extensive contact with Africans, were heavily involved both in slave trading and in bloody wars with African coastal nations. Battell landed in hell. He was sent 200 kilometres (130 miles) up the steaming Kwanza River and placed in a pestilential prison, but after two months the governor's pilot died and so he functioned in that position until he himself became ill, probably with malaria: 'For eight months I lay in a poor estate, for they hated me because I was an Englishman'.

Finally, Battell recovered and the governor apparently trusted him enough to send him in a small pinnace to trade red cloth for 'elephant's teeth [tusks], wheat, and oil of palm' on the 'River of Congo, which the natives call Zaire'. Battell did

The Portuguese were the first European power to prosper in east Africa, supplying slaves to their New World settlements.

well, and the governor promised him his freedom if he continued to serve him well on a number of such trading missions, but two and a half years went by and no end to his servitude was in sight.

Around this time, Battell met a friendly Dutch sea captain who promised to help him escape on his vessel, and he even got so far as to secretly stow himself away on the ship, but 'I was betrayed by the Portugals which sailed in the ship', Battell writes bitterly, 'and was fetched to the store by sergeants of the city and put in prison, and lay with great bolts of iron for two months, thinking the governor would have me put to death'.

For some reason, this did not happen. Instead, the governor banished him 'for life' to the Portuguese fort at Massangano, where he was forced to serve, along with 'Egyptians' (actually, gypsy convicts who had been exiled from Portugal) and 'Moriscoes' (captured Moors or Arabs), in attempting to conquer the tribes of the region and take them as slaves. It was hard, dirty, vicious work, among men who had been toughened and depraved past belief, and for six years, Battell writes, 'I lived a most miserable life … without any hope to see the sea again'.

Another escape

Unable to take it any longer, Battell told one of the gypsies that 'it was better for us to venture our lives for liberty than to live in that miserable place', and together the two of them fomented an escape of a dozen convicts. They overpowered guards, stole twelve muskets and found a canoe to take them down the Kwanza River. After they were far enough away from Massangano, they sank the canoe and struck off overland, heading for the coast, where they hoped to find a ship to take them away. After seven days, they got close enough to hear 'the surge of the sea' and they could see the buildings of the Portuguese capital of São Paulo (modern Luanda), but then they were attacked by a force of Portuguese

horsemen and armed slaves and driven into some woods. Numerous of Battell's fellow escapees were killed, and he finally decided to give himself up, at which point he was taken to São Paulo and placed back in its horrible prison, with an iron collar around his neck.

Batell was released from prison as experienced fighters were once again needed, and he was sent deeper into the jungle with hordes of captive fighters—fifteen thousand, if he is to be believed—to defeat the local kings. One battle pitted Battell and his fellow slaves and soldiers against twenty thousand men of a tribe Battell calls the Ingombe. After a pitched battle, the chief of the Ingombe surrendered, and Battell visited his stronghold in the mountains, a paradisiacal town filled with oranges and lemons and through which a sparkling stream ran. But, filled with bloodlust, as Battell writes, 'we marched up into the country and burned and spoiled for the space of six weeks', after which Battell, wounded in his leg, was sent south on a frigate to found a small settlement in a bay near the mouth of the Congo River. He ventured far inland to trade with the locals, but found them 'very treacherous … as well as very simple'. The men wore skins and beads wrapped around their heads, and carried 'darts of iron, and bows and arrows in their hands'. The women, Battell added, 'wear a ring of copper about their necks which weigheth fifteen pounds at the least', as well as clinking copper bands about their arms and legs. Moreover—if Battell is to be believed—the tribe had 'men in woman's apparel, whom they keep among their wives'.

Shortly after this, on a short trading voyage up the coast, Battell and his companions saw a large camp on the shore. They sent a boat in and were greeted by five hundred warriors. 'We asked them who they were', Battell writes, 'and they told us they were the Gagas … that came from Sierra de Lion [Sierra Leone]. The Great Gaga, which is their chief, came down to the waterside to see us, for he had never seen white men before'. These Gagas had slaves with them, hundreds of them, whom Battell and his men bought surprisingly cheaply. They were getting ready to leave when the chief of the Gagas asked them to ferry his men across the river, for they wanted to attack the land of the Benguelas. This Battell and the others did, and they then watched a pitched battle ensue, in which the Benguelas were destroyed and their women and children taken captive. A hundred heads were tossed in front of the chief of the Gagas and, to Battell's horror and astonishment, 'the men, women and children that were brought in captive alive, and the dead corpses that were brought to be eaten, were strange to behold. For these Gagas are the greatest cannibals and man-eaters in the world ...'

'I determined to live'

Unbeknown to himself, Battell had fallen in with a marauding tribe known as the Imbangala, who arose in the sixteenth century from the central highlands of present-day Angola and swept with great ruthlessness west across Africa. They were as destabilising a force as the Huns or Vandals, crashing into established West African kingdoms in frenzies of killing, rape and anarchy. By the time Battell encountered them, they had become an important part of the slaving business, for the slaves that the Imbangala—known as the Jagas, although Battell spells it with a 'G'—captured they sold to Europeans for export.

Leaving the Jagas to rampage as they wanted, Battell and his fellows went back to their fortress, but they returned three times to buy more slaves from the Jagas. The fourth time they came back, the Jagas had moved farther inland, and so eager were the Portuguese for these cheap slaves that they followed the Jagas into the unknown interior. They did not immediately find them, but Battell entered a land 'where they never saw a white man before, nor guns'. These people threatened the Portuguese

with death unless they gave them trade goods, of which the Europeans had very little. So the Portuguese left and promised to return in two months with more. As surety of their promise, they forced Battell to remain behind. When they did not return, the chief of the tribe Battell was living among wanted to have him executed and even stripped him of his clothes prior to cutting off his head. But then the chief thought better of it—deciding that the Portuguese would surely come, bringing gifts with them—and decided to keep Battell alive a little while longer.

Realising that this was not a safe place for him, Battell waited until nightfall and ran away 'purposing to go to the camp of the Gagas'. After stumbling through nearly impenetrable jungle all night long, he came upon the town of a Jaga lord named Cashil. It is a sign of how desperate Battell had become that he was 'very glad to see' the Jagas and immediately joined them. His initial depiction of their camp is chilling:

> In the middle of the town there is an image [statue], which is as big as a man, and standeth twelve feet [3.5 metres] high; and at the foot of the image there is a circle of elephant's teeth, pitched into the ground. Upon these teeth stand a great score of dead men's skulls which were killed in the wars. [The Jaga] used to pour palm oil at [the feet of the statue], and kill goats and pour their blood at his feet. This image is called Quesango, and the people have great belief and swear by him; and do believe that when they are sick that Quesango is offended with them.

It is hard to know what this image actually looked like—*Quesango* is probably a corruption of *Kisangu*, which means fetish—but the sight of all those heads on ivory tusks was a sobering one. Battell was actually in a temporary camp and was soon taken farther into the country to the land of 'the Great

Gaga' himself—the man he had met while the Portuguese were buying slaves near the shore. Here, Battell writes, 'I determined to live, hoping in God that they would travel so far to the westward that we should see the sea again; and so I might escape by some ship'.

'They will not sow'

We know nothing of Battell beyond what he tells us, but reading between the lines we can see that he is a determined survivor, ready to do anything in the hope of finally escaping. Many people, faced with the circumstances Battell found himself in, would give up hope, but Battell never did. This does not mean that he did not do unsavoury things. For the next sixteen months he ranged across West Africa, fighting with the rampaging Jagas. 'I was so highly esteemed by the great Gaga because I killed so many negroes with my musket that I had anything I desired from him', wrote Battell; he even led Jagas into battle.

He became an expert on their military organisation. The Jagas were led by a general named Imbe Calandola, who held sway over twelve captains, who in turn commanded smaller groups of warriors. Calandola, according to Battell, worshipped 'the Devil' and could see into the future. He believed that the only way he would die was in battle; otherwise, he was immortal. He would not tolerate cowards: 'Those that are faint-hearted, and turn their backs to the enemy, are presently condemned and killed for cowards and

 TRIAL BY ORDEAL

According to Andrew Battell, many African tribes practised forms of trial by ordeal, not unlike the trials that suspected witches and wrongdoers were forced to go through during the Middle Ages in Europe. The Jagas, predictably harsh, would take a heated hatchet blade and press it against a suspected criminal's skin—if he screamed, he was guilty and they beheaded him.

Another tribe, the Luongo, tried something a little different. If they could not find a person to admit to committing a crime, a witch doctor took a powdered root called Imbondo and scraped it into water. Battell told Purchas that this root 'made the water bitter as gall (he tasted it) and one root will serve to try one hundred'. Those who drank the water and were able to urinate were considered innocent. However, some people drank it and 'it striketh up into the brain, as though he were drunk, and he falleth down, as though he were dead. And those that fall are counted as guilty, and are punished.'

The flaw in this system is that obviously the witch doctor was putting more of the poison into the drink of the person he suspected of committing the crime. These trials took place, according to Battell, almost continuously. As with certain tribes in New Guinea (see page 293) 'none of any account dieth but that they kill another for him'—meaning, almost any death is considered an act of sorcery and witchcraft. It was not unusual for Battell to see as many as five hundred people line up for the poison after the death of a prominent person.

their bodies eaten'. Every night, to stir the Jagas up to fever pitch, Calandola made 'a warlike oration upon a high scaffold'.

The Jagas seemed to be driven as much by their love of palm wine as by warfare and they were typically destructive in the way they got their favourite tipple. Battell describes the Jagas coming into an area of palm groves and—instead of climbing to the top of these tall trees to milk palm wine—simply cutting the tree down and draining it dry over the course of a month, so that it was useless to anyone else. After a month's time, the Jagas would move on: 'In that little time', Battell wrote, 'they spoil the country'. In fact, the Jagas 'will not sow, nor plant, nor bring up any cattle, more than they take by wars'.

This martial people could not be slowed up by children, either. Battell writes: 'The [Jaga] women are very fruitful, but they enjoy none of their children; for as soon as the woman is delivered of her child, it is presently buried quick [meaning, alive] so that there is not one child brought up in all this generation'. The Jagas survived as a people by taking captured children as their own. 'These little boys they train up in the wars and hang a collar about their necks … which is never taken off til he

 ## 'HAVING UPON EACH SIDE OF HIM A MAN-WITCH'

One of the things that disturbed Andrew Battell the most about the Jagas was their propensity for human sacrifice. Whenever the general Calandola was about to go to war against the inhabitants of a country, he would make a sacrifice to an entity that Battell called 'the Devil' on the morning of the day the venture was to begin.

'He sitteth upon a stool, having upon each side of him a man-witch', Battell wrote. 'Then he hath forty or fifty women which stand round about him, holding in each hand a zebra or wild horse's tail, wherewith they do flourish and sing.' In front of Calandola was a large earthen pot, which was filled with white powders, over a great fire. As drums played and the women sang louder and louder, the witches would anoint Calandola with these powders—'forehead, temples, thwart the breast and belly, with long ceremonies and inchanting terms'. This spectacle would go on until sundown. 'Then,' writes Battell, 'the witches bring his Casengula, which is a weapon like a hatchet, and put it in his hand, and bid him be strong against his enemies: for his mokiso [or brave spirit] is with him'. A captured boy was brought before Calandola, and Calandola would kill him with the hatchet. Then four men were dragged in front of the great chief. Two of them he would kill; two he would command be killed outside his fort. At this point a veil falls over these ceremonies, since, according to Battell, the witches made him leave—as a Christian, he could not be present when the Devil arrived.

Other human sacrifices occurred when a Jaga nobleman or chief died. He was buried in a sitting position and two of his wives, their arms broken, were put alive into the grave on top of him.

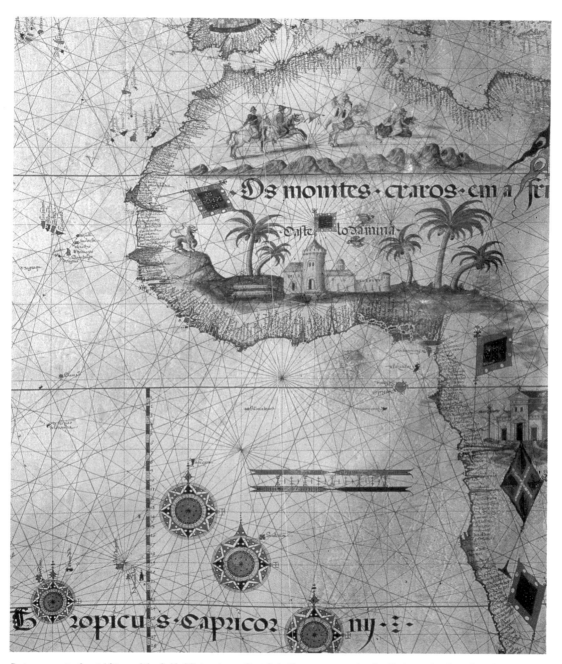

Portuguese map of west Africa and the Gulf of Guinea in 1558, with the Portuguese capital at São Paulo, modern Luanda, at bottom right.

proveth himself a man, and brings his enemy's head to the General.'

After this point, a boy was freed of his collar and became a warrior. Battell writes that in the camp he was in, only the general and his captains were 'natural' Jagas—all the other warriors had begun as captured boys.

'As white as any white man'

As the first white man many of the Jagas had seen, Battell was the object of intense curiosity and not a little hostility. He had the backing of the king, but he was forced to prove himself in dangerous combat over and over again. He led a brutal life,

A Jaga warrior with shield and weapons. Battell fought with the Jaga until he could stand their brutal life no longer.

travelling through the jungles, mountains and dry savannas of Africa, fighting off natural beasts—such as crocodiles, hippopotami and elephants—while often being the only European for many kilometres around. It was hard, too, to be surrounded by so much cannibalism. The Jaga chieftains kept their skin soft by rubbing it with human body fat, much as we might use a moisturiser cream. Prisoners were routinely slaughtered and prepared for dinner, as were the corpses of those who had died in battle or been executed as cowards. Battell hints that on more than one occasion he was forced to partake.

Finally, it became too much for him. When the Jaga war machine swung again to the west, he escaped and made his way back to Massangano, where a new Portuguese governor promised him clemency if he would go to work for him. This Battell did for some months, serving as a sergeant in the ceaseless fighting against the Africans, but once again the governor broke his word, causing Battell to run away again. He lived in the jungle alone for six months, with a musket and a hundred rounds of ammunition, but when he tired of this life of misery, he found a small boat and made his way to the kingdom of Longo, farther up the coast, where he stayed for three years, hunting for the king.

Longo was a far more typical African nation than that of the Jagas, run by a potentate with ten houses, 150 wives and 400 children. He claimed the right to execute anyone who looked at him while he was eating; even so, he was not so completely a psychopath as a Jaga ruler. Battell found his time there much easier. Although this nation had had little contact with whites, he wrote, 'here are sometimes born … white children, which is very rare among them, for their parents are negroes'. Presumably these were albinos. 'And when any of them are born, they are presented unto the king and are called *Dondos*. These are as white as any white man. These are the king's witches, and are brought up in witchcraft, and always wait on the king. There

THE APE-MONSTER PONGO

Andrew Battell was most impressed, and frightened, by a 'monster' known as Pongo *(probably* Mpungu*) that lived in the jungle. 'This Pongo', Battell wrote, 'is in all proportions like a man, but that he is more like a giant in stature than a man; for he is very tall and hath a man's face, hollow-eyed, with long hair upon his brows. His face and ears are without hair, and his hands also. His body is full of hair, but not very thick, and of a donnish colour'.*

Battell is obviously describing a gorilla here. The Carthaginians had encountered similar creatures, possibly in the same area of West Africa (see page 14), many years before. While Battell is treating the great apes as if they were mythological beasts, he actually describes them quite well—it is possible he saw one or two while out in the woods:

> [The Pongo] goeth always upon his legs, and carryeth his hands clasped upon the nape of his neck when he goeth upon the ground. They sleep in trees and build shelters from the rain. They feed upon the fruit they find and upon nuts, for they eat no kind of flesh. They cannot speak and have no more understanding than a beast.

Battell goes on to write, with probably less accuracy, that the gorillas 'go many together and kill many negroes that travel in the woods. Many times they fall upon the elephants, which come to feed where they be, and so beat them with their clubbed fists and pieces of wood that they will run roaring away from them'.

Perhaps most amazingly, Battell claims that he found his 'negro boy'—the one he returned to Leigh with—after the boy had been taken by Pongos and actually lived with them for a month. Samuel Purchas, recording this story after Battell's death, wrote that Battell told him the Pongos 'hurt not those which they surprise at unawares, except [unless] they look at them, which the boy avoided. He [Battell] said that their height was like a man's, but their bigness twice as great'.

is no man that dare meddle with these *Dondos* ... for all men stand in awe of them.'

Escape and return

Finally, around 1609 or 1610, Andrew Battell made good his escape from Africa. Exactly how we do not know. Out of the reach of the Portuguese, but with a friendlier tribe for whom his white skin was a talisman, he was probably able to find his way to the coast and pay his way aboard a Dutch ship with ivory or other trade goods. Once in The Netherlands, it would have been an easy matter to find his way back to England, and Leigh.

What his emotions must have been like when he returned to his village after twenty long years, it is difficult to say. He had been scarred by his first encounters, in this case much more so than the indigenous peoples he met, since he had been forced into violence and probably cannibalism simply to survive. Twenty years of almost unrelenting war and privation changes a person—and yet, Battell did bring back with him—whether as slave or free servant we do not know—the young boy he had supposedly saved from the gorillas, which presumably meant he had risen above some of the horrors he had been forced to endure.

The Strange Adventures of Andrew Battell are strange, indeed, but nonetheless extraordinarily valuable as an intimate portrait of Africa at the moment of first contact.

'A CAT-EYED DEVIL DIPPED IN MILK'

Mungo Park's travels in Africa, 1795–1805

By the late eighteenth century, Europeans had spread out across the world—into North and South America, the Pacific Ocean, Oceania, Australia and the Spice Islands—dramatically changing the lives of millions of human beings on the face of the Earth. But European armies, trading vessels and settlements had made only the barest of dents in the mysterious continent known as Africa.

The coastline of Africa had been known to Europeans since the fifteenth and sixteenth centuries when the Portuguese pioneered the trading route around the Cape of Good Hope to the Spice Islands in the Indian Ocean. However, very few white men had pressed farther into the interior of Africa in the way that they had explored North and South America.

There are a couple of reasons for this. Firstly, Africa's topography essentially consists of a central plateau falling into relatively narrow coastal areas filled with dense forests. The only way for large groups to make their way through these jungles was by river, but the great waterways leading into the interior of Africa were blocked quite near the coast by shallows, waterfalls and rapids, making them impractical for merchant vessels. Secondly, the main reason Europeans haunted the coast of Africa was for slaves to sell abroad—in Britain, the West Indies and America—and they had no need to venture far inland because slave traders conveniently captured slaves for the Europeans and brought them to the trading centres established along the west coast of the continent.

Even so, Africa had long been a powerful goad to the European imagination, a land of 'every kind of beast under heaven', as a medieval chronicler wrote—for distorted images of the crocodile, the elephant and the hippopotamus had made their way out of the continent. Africa was home to the mythical King Prester John, who kept a court where unicorns killed lions and rivers flowed with precious stones. At the same time, the mysterious continent was thought to be the home of Gog and Magog, evil biblical demons or giants who had sired a race of fierce cannibals.

By the 1790s, Europeans had long ceased to believe in Prester John, but the exploration of Africa was only a matter of time, especially for the British. This was because a rapidly industrialising Britain was seeking new areas to which to export manufactured goods. And there was another reason, one without a profit motive. Britain contained the most powerful antislavery movement in the world, one that would see the full emancipation of Great Britain's slaves by 1838. It was extraordinarily important for these abolitionists to work to suppress the African slave trade and open up the continent to Christian missionaries, who could convert and protect the indigenous peoples.

The African Association

In 1788 the African Association was founded by Sir Joseph Banks, the distinguished naturalist who had accompanied James Cook on his first voyage to the Pacific (see page 204). Banks and other gentlemen with humanitarian impulses—as well as a scientific fascination with the unknown people, flora and fauna that might be found—decided to fund some worthy explorer on an expedition into Africa and thereby help open up the continent. The target of this expedition was to be the Niger River.

The Niger held great fascination for Europeans; some thought it might even be the source of the Nile River. Some 4000 kilometres (2600 miles) long—it is the third largest river in Africa, after the Nile and the Congo—the Niger arises out of the forested Guinea highlands, runs northeast and then swings back south and west before exiting the continent into the Gulf of Guinea in the Atlantic Ocean. At the time the African Association was

formed, Europeans knew almost nothing about the Niger, except stories that a massive river flowed through the West African savanna. They did not know the river's source or end, or even in which direction it flowed.

If it could be properly mapped and charted, the Niger could be used as a highway for British missionaries and merchants. The African Association sent several explorers after the mystery of the Niger. The first died of disease and the second was thwarted by hostile tribes. The third, Major Daniel Houghton, left Gambia in western Africa in November of 1790 and a year later sent a pencilled note back that said that he was well and getting closer to where he thought the Niger might be. Then—silence. Much later, it was discovered that he had been robbed, stripped and murdered by thieves. His body was never found.

Obviously, the search for the Niger did not belong to the faint of heart. In 1794, as the association was casting about for yet another intrepid soul to make the journey, it was approached by a tall, bearded and engaging young Scot named Mungo Park who, in his own words, 'had a passionate desire to examine into the productions of a country so little known; and to become experimentally acquainted with the modes of life, and character of the natives'.

'A young man of no mean talents'

Mungo Park was born in 1771 near Selkirk, Scotland, the seventh of thirteen children of a fairly well-to-do farmer. He was apprenticed to a local surgeon and, in 1788, went to Edinburgh to study medicine. He became particularly passionate about botany (then taught as part of a medical curriculum) and through his brother-in-law James Dickson, a self-taught naturalist, met Sir Joseph Banks, who was impressed by Park and befriended him. After Park successfully took his oral examinations to become a surgeon, Banks pulled strings and got him a job aboard a British merchant ship heading for the East Indies in the early winter of 1793.

With this foreign experience under his belt (and a few rare plants he had brought back to give to his patron, Banks), Park arrived back in England in May 1794, ready for new adventures. Although trained as a surgeon, the mundane life of a Scottish village doctor was not for him. With Banks's encouragement, Park applied for, and received, a grant from the African Association to explore the Niger River. The members of the association were impressed by his enthusiasm and credentials. They found him 'a young man of no mean talents, who had been regularly educated in the medical fields … [and] sufficiently instructed in the use of Hadley's Quadrant to make the necessary observations, and geographer enough to track out the path through the wilderness, and not unacquainted with natural history'.

All these things Park would need to be to brave the wilds of Africa. Twenty-four years old, he set off from Portsmouth in May of 1795, reached West Africa and then travelled up the Gambia River about 300 kilometres (200 miles) to a trading post at Pisania, which was the last outpost of British civilisation. He stayed there for most of that autumn. This was partly to 'season' himself against the malarial fevers of the region; although he did come down ill, he recovered under the care of Dr Laidley, who as well as being the only doctor for hundreds of kilometres (Park himself excepted) was also the chief British slave trader of the region—not the last time that Park would rely upon the kindness of those in the slave trade. He also spent his time at the remote post learning Mandingo (or Malinke) the main language the tribes he would encounter would be speaking—and a language Park would become quite proficient in.

Mungo Park started off on his exploration on 2 December 1795, carrying only two days' provisions and 'a small amount of beads, amber and tobacco, for the purchase of a fresh supply'. This was because he had learned that Major Houghton had been robbed and killed because he was carrying large amounts of trade goods with him, and Park hoped to avoid the same fate. With a touch of the eccentricity that would mark future British explorers, Park also took with him an umbrella, as well as a top hat. He wore the latter for much of the first part of his journey and thus made an unusual sight travelling through the scrubland of the upper Senegal Basin.

'My painful and perilous journey'

It was Park's idea to cross overland toward where he thought the headwaters of the Niger might be, and then to explore the river in order to find where

Mungo Park, as depicted in his book Travels in the Interior Districts of Africa.

it debouched into the ocean. He had with him two natives to act as guides, both given to him by Dr Laidley. One was a servant named Johnson; the other a slave named Demba, who had been promised his freedom in return for taking Park on this journey and acting as interpreter. Park rode on a horse, while the other two men were on mules. As a courtesy, Dr Laidley and a few friends accompanied Park for the first few days of his journey and then bade him farewell—'I believe', wrote Park, 'they secretly thought they should never see me afterwards'.

Park was now alone with his guides, searching an unknown country for a river no white man had ever seen, embarking on what he called 'my perilous and painful journey'. It was a daunting prospect. 'I now had before me a boundless forest, and a country, the inhabitants of which were strangers to civilized life, and to most of whom a white man was the object of curiosity or plunder. I reflected that I had parted from the last European I might probably behold, and perhaps quitted forever the comforts of Christian society.'

Park was travelling through a volatile and dangerous region. The peoples of the area through which he initially rode—an undulating and relatively open savanna—were mainly farmers living in villages of thatched huts, growing cotton, tobacco and assorted vegetables. They had no writing but were fine ironworkers, making weapons and cooking and ceremonial implements from the red iron ore that dotted the area. Some of them had been converted to Islam by Moorish traders—they were called *Bushreens*, Park noted. Most were pagans, however, worshipping the old gods of West Africa, and these the *Bushreens* called *Kaffirs* (unbelievers) or *Sonakies* (drinkers of strong liquor).

MUNGO PARK AND THE ABOLITIONISTS

While Park's Travels in the Interior Districts of Africa *was a great success with the London reading public, it caused some problems with British abolitionists because of his relationships with slavers such as Dr Laidley and Karfa Taura, who trafficked in human misery and yet had saved his life, more than once. Park also differed from the abolitionists on key points of antislavery doctrine. The abolitionists felt that if the British government patrolled the African coastline and stopped slaves from being shipped out (as, indeed, it would begin to do), slavery in Africa would wither on the vine.*

But Park, with far more practical experience, wrote that slavery was an institution that predated the Atlantic slave trade and would continue after its demise. He estimated that slaves in West Africa outnumbered free people by three to one and that slavery was far too embedded in the economy to go away very easily, even if Africa stopped exporting slaves. If asked, Park wrote bluntly, 'the effect which a discontinuation of that commerce would produce on the manners of the natives, I should have no hesitation in observing that, in the present unenlightened state of their minds, the effect would be neither so extensive or beneficial as many wise and worthy persons fondly expect'. And in fact this turned out to be the case, with slavery continuing throughout the nineteenth century on the African continent.

The people of these communities turned out to stare at Park as he went, but not, as he first assumed, because they had not seen a white man before. In fact, as the king of one tribe told him, they had—Major Houghton. This king beseeched Park not to continue on his way, telling him 'that the people of the east had never seen a white man and would certainly destroy me'. Notwithstanding the king's pleas, Park went on his way, taking with him a few more guides to help probe the land ahead. He was a little disconcerted to note that these guides insisted on stopping along the way and preparing spells or incantations against the danger that lay ahead. This was done by spitting on a stone and throwing it some distance ahead, then picking up the stone, repeating the procedure, and throwing it again. Thus protected against misfortune, Park proceeded.

'The request of an African prince'

By January, Park began to near the Senegal River; beyond the Senegal lay the semi-arid country just south of the Sahara. Travelling through a hilly land covered with woods, where hyena lurked in the shadows as they passed, Park and his procession reached a large African town and were summoned to the presence of its king, one Almani—'a Moorish name', Park wrote, 'though I was told that he was not a Mohomedan, but a Kafir, or Pagan'. Park became alarmed when he was forced to walk through a labyrinthine palace guarded by sinister men with muskets. When he finally met the king, the man treated him civilly but expressed great interest in Park's umbrella, opening and closing it over and over again. He then began to admire Park's coat, particularly its yellow buttons. He asked Park to give the coat to him as a present, explaining that whenever he wore it he would tell people that the white man had given it, and such generosity would speak well of Park's nature and gain him a good reputation wherever he travelled.

Park was not won over by such empty cajolery but was forced to comply. He wrote: 'The request of an African prince in his own dominions, particularly when made to a stranger, comes little short of a command. It is only his way of gaining by gentle means what he can, if he pleases, take by force'.

After this unsettling visit, the king told Park that his harem, who had never before seen a white man, were very interested in meeting him and thus Park was led before 'ten or twelve' women 'most of them young and handsome, and wearing on their heads ornaments of gold and beads of amber'. They gathered around Park, paying close attention to 'the whiteness of my skin and the prominency of my nose. They said that both were artificial. The first, they said, was produced when I was an infant, by dipping me in milk; and they insisted that my nose had been pinched every day til it had acquired its present unsightly and unnatural conformation.'

This encounter put Park in a better humour, and he wrote: 'On my part, without disputing my own deformity, I paid them many compliments on African beauty. I praised the glossy jet of their skins, and the lovely depression of their noses'. The women then sternly told Park that flattery—they called it by the apt expression *honey-mouth*—was not allowed in their kingdom, but one gets the impression they were pleased with the young Scot nonetheless. As Park was leaving, one woman looking at him appraisingly and then called him 'a cat-eyed devil dipped in milk'.

'Fancy had placed me'

Within a few more weeks, Park reached the Senegal River and began to pass through an area that was more arid and rocky than those he had previously traversed, although he found it a place where 'the air and climate are, I believe, more pure and salubrious than at any of the settlements towards the coast', perhaps because of the absence of disease-bearing mosquitoes.

This was the kingdom of Kajaaga. Across the Senegal lived a fairer-skinned people who spoke Arabic (or possibly Berber) and, unlike the people of the savanna, were all devout Muslims. They were not farmers, but cattle-herders, and they also spent much of their time raiding the people of the savanna for slaves, whom they took across the Sahara and sold on North African slave markets or as labour for salt mines.

Park settled into a village in Kajaaga, where he viewed a celebration and then went to sleep for the night. At about two o'clock in the morning, however, ten horsemen came thundering into the town and surrounded the place where he was sleeping. One of them, while Park feigned sleep, attempted to steal his musket but was unable to extricate it and thus went away. The next day, however, ten more horsemen arrived and surrounded Park, Johnson and Demba. These men, Park was told, came from the king of the country, one Batcheri. Park had offended Batcheri by entering his kingdom without paying tribute to him. Accordingly, all of Park's goods were forfeit and he must come and see the king at his palace at Maana, a short distance away.

Park was advised by his host that he should under no circumstances go to Maana, and so he bribed the king's men into letting him go and he and his men went on. In a few days, they crossed the Senegal River, but here things began to get even dicier. Every 'king' who put Park up for a night demanded tribute from him, and there was a war going on between two tribes, which made travelling difficult. To make matters worse, Moors constantly raided the country, looking for slaves. These men were in the employ of the King of Ludamar, Ali.

One day in early March 1796, Park and Demba (Johnson had refused to go farther and so Park had sent him back toward Gambia with a progress report) spent an afternoon with a tribe of 'poor Negroes', who nonetheless provided them with 'a

fermented liquid made from corn … and better I have never tasted in Great Britain'. Park started to relax. 'I flattered myself that all danger from the Moors was over', he wrote. He even indulged in fantasy: 'Fancy had already placed me on the banks of the Niger and presented to my imagination a thousand delightful scenes'. But then, with striking swiftness, 'a party of Moors unexpectedly entered the hut and dispelled my golden dream'.

These men told Park that they were there to take him to see King Ali, at his camp at Benown. Park was immediately 'struck by surprise and terror', even though the Moors told him that the only reason Ali wanted to see him was because his wife, Fatima, had never seen a Christian before and was desirous of meeting one. After she interviewed him, the men told Park, the king would let him go and give him protection for the rest of his journey. Park did not believe this, for as he travelled with the Moors they guarded him closely, literally sleeping outside his hut at night. It was all he could do to keep up with them, as they raced across the desert on their horses, touching neither food nor water until nightfall.

Enslaved

When Park was a day's journey from Benown, he was first taken to meet one of the king's sons, who brusquely handed him a broken flintlock musket and told him to fix it and to dye its stock blue. When Park told him he had no idea how to do this, the man said that Park should 'give him some knives and scissors immediately'. Demba, acting as interpreter, stepped in to say that Park had no such items, at which point the king's son 'snatched up a musket that stood by him, cocked it, and putting the muzzle close to the boy's ear would have shot him dead on the spot, had not the Moors wrested the musket from him'.

That night the loyal Demba, who had chosen to accompany Park into the land of the Moors, tried to escape but was prevented from doing so by the Moors. The next day they reached Benown, which was a collection of dirty huts surrounded by herds of goats, cattle and camels. The moment the Moors brought Park into camp, people stopped whatever they were doing, 'threw down their buckets or jumped on their horses, and, men, women and children, came running or galloping towards me. I soon found myself surrounded by such a crowd that I could scarcely move'.

The people pulled the buttons of his waistcoat and took off his hat and shouted at him, for he was the first white man they had ever seen. Moving with some difficulty, Park's Moorish guards took him into the tent of King Ali, who turned out to be 'an old man, of the Arab cast, with a long white beard;

he had a sullen and indignant aspect'. He was sitting on a black leather cushion clipping hairs from his upper lip while a member of his harem held a mirror in front of him. He spoke once, to ask the Moors with Park if Park could speak Arabic. When they answered in the negative, he lapsed into silence again. In the meantime, Park was surrounded by the crowd in the tent, most of them women. These 'inspected every part of my apparel, searched my pockets, and obliged me to unbutton my waistcoat, and display the whiteness of my skin; they even counted my fingers and toes, as if they doubted whether I was human'.

As evening prayers commenced, Park was given a mat to lie down upon and fed a little corn. The next day, he was conducted to a hut, which he was

Mungo Park watches from the bank as his party crosses the Black (Bafing) River in present-day Mali, in late 1795.

MEDICINE IN AFRICA

One would expect that, as a surgeon, Park would be disdainful of African medical practices, but far from finding witch doctors practising spells over patients, he discovered medicine that he admired and wrote about in his journal:

On the whole, it appeared to me that the Negroes are better surgeons than physicians. I found them very successful in their management of fractures and dislocations and their splints and bandages are simple and easily removed. The patient is laid upon a soft mat and the fractured limb is frequently bathed in cold water. All abscesses they open with the actual cautery; and the dressings are composed of either soft leaves, shea butter or cow's dung. Towards the coast, where a supply of European lancets can be procured, they sometimes perform phlebotomy …

Park observed the prevalence of illness in Africa, particularly some horribly disfiguring diseases such as elephantiasis and leprosy, which African healers could do little about, but for everyday matters they did as well as most surgeons in London at the time.

at first grateful for, since it provided relief from the broiling sun, but then he realised that his roommate was a pig tied to a stake—a derisive joke, since the Muslims felt that unclean animals like pigs and Christians deserved each other. The pig and Park then began to suffer in tandem. Moor after Moor visited the hut. After beating the pig with a stick, they insisted that Park partially disrobe to show his white skin.

'I was employed', Park wrote, 'dressing and undressing, buttoning and unbuttoning, from noon till night'. It was no wonder he developed a dislike of his captors: 'I was a *stranger*, I was *unprotected*, and I was *Christian*; each of these circumstances is enough to drive every spark of humanity from the heart of a Moor. But when all of these were combined in the same person … the reader will easily imagine that I had something to fear'.

'My acknowledgements to the lady'

Demba was immediately taken from Park and put to work as a slave, but the Moors seemed to have some problem figuring out employment for Park. He was at first set to work as a barber, King Ali having discovered he was a surgeon, but in cutting the hair of one of the king's sons Park proved so shaky with the razor that it was taken away from him. In the meantime, much to his surprise, his servant Johnson showed up, having also been captured by the Moors. They brought with Johnson all the supplies Park had entrusted to him; thus, the Moors had now captured everything Park owned.

Within a few days, the Moors held a council to decide what to do with Park. It seemed to be a choice, Park was informed by one of Ali's younger sons, between death or mutilation. Some favoured the former, some the latter, versions of which included cutting off Park's right hand, or possibly putting out his eyes, which were said 'to resemble those of a cat'. Ali, however, apparently decided to wait until Queen Fatima arrived before making a decision. In the meantime, Park suffered different persecutions, ranging from Moors pointing (fortunately empty) pistols at him and pulling the trigger to women (their fingertips stained saffron, for what reason Park could not ascertain) visiting him and demanding to see if he was circumcised. (Park deflected this request, or so he says in his published journals. However, he later told the poet Walter Scott, whom he befriended back in Scotland, that he had suffered even worse physical abuse, which may have included being sodomised.)

Despite the danger that he was in, Park never did lose his sense of humour. As he waited in the camp day after day in order to find out his fate, he witnessed a wedding ceremony, replete with much dancing and singing. Feeling sleepy, he returned to his hut and had nearly dozed off when he was awakened by an old woman carrying a bowl, whose contents she said were a gift from the bride. She then 'discharged the contents of the bowl full in my face', the stunned Park wrote. It turned out to contain the bride's urine, which was always thrown in the face of a young unmarried man at a wedding, as a kind of nuptial benediction. Once he ascertained this, Park said, 'I wiped my face and sent my acknowledgements to the lady'.

Weeks passed and still Park was held captive. He did meet Queen Fatima ('a remarkably corpulent lady'), who seemed to look with favour upon him and even gave him a bowl of milk, but still Ali kept him captive. He was given little food and less water and, degree by degree, was weakening, despite Demba's attempts to keep him alive. Park began to dream feverishly of the crystal clear rivers and streams of his native Scotland. Finally, in the June of 1796, the Moors made ready to move and Park was roughly told that 'the boy' (Demba) would be kept

as a slave, along with everything Park possessed, except Park's horse. Park was then free to go and he could take with him 'the old fool'—Johnson. Despite Park's best efforts, he was unable to change the Moors' minds about Demba. In the meantime, Johnson refused to accompany him, and Park was sure that the Moors would change their minds about letting him go if he stayed around any longer.

And so, after waiting for the Moors to fall asleep one night late in June, Park slipped out of their camp with his horse and the clothes on his back. But within kilometres, to his horror, he realised that he was being followed by four Moors on horseback. These men at first told him that he must return to Ali, but then began to ransack his meagre belongings and he realised that they were there to rob him. Park was sure he would die there like Major Houghton, but after taking everything but his horse, the men left him, alone and destitute, in the wilderness.

Geo affili

The American poet Theodore Roethke was to write: 'Out of nothing, all beginnings come', and such would be the case for Parks, who now began a period of wandering absolutely alone through a foreign wilderness, with no food or water, and with only a compass. Terrified of becoming prey to some wandering band of Moors, he travelled onward in the blazing heat through a desert of sandy hillocks and brush. His thirst was 'insufferable' and he began to feel he would die. What appeared to be the darkening of the sky prefatory to a thunderstorm proved to be a sandstorm that filled his eyes and nostrils with grit. At one point, he lay down on the sand, 'affected with sickness and giddiness', and prepared to die. 'Here must the short span of my life come to an end', he thought.

FOLLOWING PAGES Park's depiction of a caravan of slaves as it passes a village in the African hinterland.

But somehow he found the strength to get up and drag his horse onward. He began to travel at night to avoid the Moors, but at one point stumbled into a camp and startled some women, who screamed and Park raced off into the woods. At last, he heard the sound of frogs croaking—'heavenly music to my ears'—and followed it to a shallow muddy pool so full of the creatures he had to shove them aside to drink.

Wandering onward, he began to enter African villages and begged for assistance from the people who lived there. 'Knowing that, as in Europe, hospitality does not always prefer the highest dwellings', he begged at the door of humble homes and was rewarded, more often than not, with a

meal. Moving farther to the south and east, Park was now in less danger from the Moors and was able to enlist the aid of the Africans he met, with whom he could speak Mandingo, and some of them accompanied him on his journey—a good thing, since the forests he was beginning to enter were home to lions and other dangerous creatures. To Park's rueful amusement, many of the people he met, seeing his deeply sunburned countenance, took him for a Moor—'He has been at Mecca', one of them said.

But all of his hardships were driven from Park's mind when, on 20 July, a man from whom he had purchased some corn with one of his buttons told him that he was a day's journey away from a great

 THE FATE OF MUNGO PARK

In 1805 Park returned to the Niger with a much larger expedition, which consisted of thirty soldiers of the Royal Africa Corps already stationed in Gambia, as well as his brother-in-law Alexander Anderson and four boat builders who would construct a boat when the party reached the Niger.

Stubborn to a fault, Park refused to wait out the rainy season before setting out from Gambia and soon his men began to die of dysentery. By the time Park's party reached the Niger, only seven of the original Europeans were alive. The party now rested for two months but, even so, two more men died, including Alexander Anderson. Park pressed ahead. After sending his journals back to the slave trader Dr Laidley, Park, with an alcoholic lieutenant named Martyn and three soldiers, set off down the Niger in a canoe, which Park had dubbed the HMS Joliba. With so many dead in the party, each man was extremely well armed (fifteen muskets apiece) but they had little in the way of other supplies.

Having travelled about 1500 kilometres (1000 miles) on the river, Park and his party reached the Bussa Rapids, where they were attacked by local natives. They managed to fend them off, but the boat became stuck in a cleft in some rocks, midstream. With the Africans attacking again, Park and his white companions jumped into the river to try and save themselves, but all drowned. Only one slave lived to tell the tale of the end of Mungo Park. Even so, his family never quite believed that the larger-than-life Park was dead. In 1827 his son Thomas, thinking his father might be held as a prisoner, landed in Africa intending to follow Park's trail, but he died of a fever before getting very far.

river, called the *Joliba*, meaning the 'great water'. Park knew that this was the African name for the Niger. The next day, he met some men who agreed to take him to their king. As they rode through a marshy area, one of the men turned to Park and casually said: *Geo affili?*, which meant 'See the water?'

Park followed his gaze.

Looking forward, I saw with infinite pleasure the great object of my mission—the long sought for majestic Niger, glittering in the morning sun, as broad as the Thames at Westminster, and flowing slowly to the eastward. I hastened to the brink and having drunk of the water, lifted up my fervent thanks in prayer to the Great Ruler of all things for having thus far crowned my endeavours with success.

'Omens follow those who look to them'

Park was the first European to lay eyes on the Niger, and the first to note which way it flowed—rather startlingly, to the east instead of west toward the Atlantic (it would eventually loop back to the west on its way to the Gulf of Guinea). Park gazed happily at the river he had dreamed of for so long and then continued along its bank, following the course of the Niger east for some 150 kilometres (100 miles) or so, travelling as far as Ségou. But by this point, Park had almost reached the end of even his considerable energies. He was, in his own words, 'worn down by sickness, exhausted with hunger and fatigue, half naked, and without any article of value with which I might procure provisions, clothes, or lodging'. To make matters worse, in early August, during the height of the rainy season, he reached the area of the Niger where the river spreads out into a vast delta or marshland. 'The country was so deluged that I was frequently in danger of losing the road, and had to wade across savannahs knee deep in water.'

But even getting home presented its difficulties. Park was robbed again, by three bandits, and left without even his horse, 800 kilometres (500 miles) from the nearest European settlement. As it happened, a slaving caravan, or *coffle*, came along, led by the Muslim slave trader Karfa Taura, who befriended the sick, destitute and depressed Park and cared for him for seven months, until he was well enough to make his way back to Pisania—and even then Taura took him there personally, refusing to relinquish him until he was in European hands. Park then made his way back home via the West Indies (on a slave ship) and finally arrived in Great Britain on 22 December 1797.

His return caused an instant sensation, because everyone thought Mungo Park was dead. He quickly published his book, *Travels in the Interior Districts of Africa*, which was a huge success—one of Park's biographers says that 'London devoured the book' and that it was reprinted three times in three months, earning Park a quick £1000 in royalties, which allowed him to set up a medical practice in Selkirk, near his birthplace, and marry Alice Anderson, the daughter of the surgeon to whom he had been apprenticed.

The peaceful life was not for Mungo Park, however, and in 1805 he decided to prepare for another expedition to the Niger. This caused some concern among his family and friends, especially Walter Scott, who had grown close to Park and admired the younger man greatly. As they were bidding their farewells in Scotland, Park's horse stumbled in a ditch and nearly fell. Half-jokingly, Scott told him: 'I'm afraid, Mungo, that's a bad omen'.

Park merely looked over his shoulder and kept on riding. 'Omens follow those who look to them', he called back. Scott's, as it turned out, was prescient—Park would never return to Scotland—but it could never be said about the cat-eyed devil, Mungo Park, that he was afraid of an omen or two.

FIRST ENCOUNTERS ON THE 'JOVE-DESCENDED NILE'

*John Hanning Speke and the quest
for the Great River, 1857–1864*

Of all the great rivers that nineteenth century explorers lusted to explore in Africa, the Nile, even more than the Niger or the Congo, was considered the ultimate prize. The Nile fed the ancient civilisation of Egypt—more than fed it, sustained it—and yet, for thousands of years, no one knew from whence it arose. In the mid-nineteenth century, the source of the Nile was, as one historian has written, 'the greatest geographical secret after the discovery of America'.

It was not as if no one had tried to discover it. The Greek historian Herodotus had travelled up the river a short way around 460 BC, but he had been stopped by waterfalls at Aswan and ended up bringing back only the vague theory that the Nile arose from four fountains deep in Africa. Even the Emperor Nero tried, sending a Roman legion commanded by two centurions, but they found their way blocked by impassable swamps. And it was

long known that the shorter Blue Nile (so-called because during the flood season its waters are blue-black), which flows from the southeast, originated in Lake Tana in Ethiopia and joined the main stream at Khartoum—the explorer James Bruce discovered this in the 1770s.

But the source of the White Nile, named for its greyish-white colour, was a deep mystery. It was known it must, of course, originate somewhere to the south, deep within Africa, but the heart of Africa was full of wild tribes who had never seen Europeans and whom no one dared to confront. As far as everyone was concerned, even in the 1850s, the Nile was, as Homer called it, 'Jove-descended', meaning it flowed from the sky.

Burton and Speke

Between 1815 and 1857 numerous white explorers, mainly British, poured into Africa, the number increasing after quinine was discovered to be effective against the malaria that routinely killed a third of European travellers who entered the region for any length of time. The greatest of these explorers, whose unlikely partnership would result in the discovery of the source of the Nile, were Richard Francis Burton and John Hanning Speke.

Burton, born in England in 1821, was the son of a wealthy ex-army officer. He was probably one of the most brilliant Britons of the nineteenth century, a linguist who mastered thirty languages and was fluent in many others. After an unsteady stay at Oxford (where he considered that he was far too bright for his fellow students, an attitude they naturally resented), Burton joined the army and went to India for eight years, where he perfected his linguistic skills, particularly in Arabic. At the age of thirty-two, he undertook the adventure that made him famous—disguising himself as a devout Muslim pilgrim, he made the *haj*, or pilgrimage to Mecca, claiming to be the first European to do so.

While resting from his journey in Cairo, Burton met a missionary who had been to East Africa and who had barely escaped with his life from the tribes of the region. Burton listened to his stories but, far from being discouraged, formulated a plan to penetrate that region in search of the 'fountains of the Nile'. To toughen himself up for such an undertaking, he decided to take an expedition into Somaliland (present-day Ethiopia) in 1854. When one of the members died before the expedition set forth, Burton consented to take along a British army lieutenant on leave, one John Hanning Speke.

Speke, at twenty-seven years old, was some six years younger than Burton and a very different personality indeed. Born to an old English family, he was tall, with blue eyes and a pale complexion, and had an air of seemingly imperturbable calm about him. He was far from an intellectual and had none of the questing intelligence of Burton—in

fact, Speke's main love in life was hunting, especially up and down the Himalayas. On furlough from his regiment, Speke travelled with the idea of undertaking a two-year hunting expedition in the mysterious Mountains of the Moon (the modern Ruwenzori Mountains) in central Africa, where legend had it that the Nile arose.

Speke joined Burton's expedition to Somaliland (although Burton went off on his own for much of it) and they were together at their camp on the coast when Somali tribesmen attacked one night at midnight and a furious fight began. In fighting them off, Burton was stabbed through the left cheek with a spear, thereafter carrying a jagged scar, while Speke was wounded some twelve times and captured, although he managed to escape. Despite the fact that Speke would claim that Burton accused him of cowardice during the fight, the two agreed to join in a further, epic exploration of Africa two years later: a concerted search for the source of the Nile.

The wondrous lakes

Burton and Speke landed in Zanzibar—the island, some thirty kilometres (twenty miles) off the African coast, from whence all expeditions set forth in those days—in late December 1856 and set about raising an expedition of some 154 men, necessary to carry their load of supplies and because the desertion rate was so high. Burton and Speke landed on the African mainland in June of 1857 and followed an Arab slaver caravan route that stretched through the flat scrubland of the coast and then slowly wound its way up onto Africa's central plateau. They were heading toward some rumoured lakes—three of them, at least—from which they felt the Nile might arise.

Burton and Speke were already entering territory few Europeans had ever visited and their men were heavily armed, with muskets and cavalry sabres. The local inhabitants flocked to see these

John Hanning Speke, adventurer and hunter, who discovered Lake Victoria and identified it as the source of the White Nile.

men with their strange white skin, making such a nuisance of themselves (at least from Burton's point of view) that he wrote a sardonic entry in his memoirs that detailed the twelve different types of stares he received.

Theirs was not an easy journey. Although they possessed quinine, figuring out just how much to take was an inexact science and Burton and Speke both became ill with malaria and recurrent fever. Some disease of the eye blinded Speke, at least temporarily, while Burton suffered from ulcerated legs. As the expedition climbed into the mountains, they were so weak that they often had to be dragged up by their men. To make matters worse, as they got farther and farther into the interior, more and more men began to desert, afraid of hostile tribes. But, at last, on 13 February 1868, they climbed a hill and saw a huge lake before them—or at least Burton saw it, since Speke was nearly blind. 'The whole scene suddenly burst upon my view', Burton wrote, 'filling me with admiration, wonder and delight … An expanse of the lightest and softest blue, in breadth varying from thirty to thirty five miles [fifty to fifty-five kilometres] … truly it was a revel for the soul'.

Burton and Speke had become the first Europeans to look upon Lake Tanganyika, which Burton was almost instantly convinced was the source of the Nile, although Speke had his doubts. The two men journeyed in canoes partway around the shore of the lake, but fear of hostile tribes kept them from circumnavigating it (this would have to wait for Henry Morton Stanley's expedition a decade later; see page 254). Instead, the two returned overland to the caravan village of Tabora, to rest before heading back to the coast.

'I no longer felt any doubt'

After their arduous expedition together, the differences between the two men were becoming more and more pronounced. Speke was a hunter—

almost anything else bored him. Burton, who was head of the expedition, disliked Speke going off to hunt because it wasted time but could himself sit for hours chatting with Arab traders, while Speke paced restlessly and resentfully. Burton was intellectually curious to the point of absurdity (at one point he lived with thirty monkeys in order to try to put together a monkey vocabulary) but was also a racist when it came to Africans, especially, writing page after page about their supposed laziness, drunkenness and stupidity. Speke disliked books and had no such intellectual curiosity, but he was not inclined to be harsh in his judgements about the native peoples he was meeting. Although he had none of Burton's stunning arrogance or extraordinary appearance—Burton, with his jagged red scar and glittering black eyes, made people think of the devil—he was nonetheless his equal in ego. Burton wrote—accurately though bitingly—that beneath his 'modest aspect' Speke possessed 'an immense fund of self-esteem, so carefully concealed, however, that none of his intimates suspected its existence'.

As Burton tarried in Tabora, chatting with Arab traders, Speke grew more and more impatient. He finally proposed to Burton that he, Speke, should go off on a sort of side expedition—a 'flying trip'—to the north, where he had heard rumours of a lake even larger than Lake Tanganyika: the Nyanza, about three weeks' journey away. Burton, heartily sick of Speke, told him to go ahead. This, as it turned out, was a crucial, even life-changing, mistake on Burton's part.

Speke set off with a small group on 10 July 1858. Three weeks later, he stood on the shores of a vast lake, obviously larger than Lake Tanganyika, a lake 'so broad you cannot see across it', Speke wrote, 'and so long that nobody knew its length'. With the lake breeze blowing in his hair, standing on a beach of yellow sand, Speke was stricken with an intuitive certainty 'that the lake at my feet gave birth to that interesting river, the source of which has been the subject of so much speculation, and the object of so many explorers'.

The Nile, in other words. 'I no longer felt any doubt', Speke added. Spending only three days at the lake—which he named Victoria, after the queen—he turned and headed back to Tabora. When he told Richard Burton of his find, Burton wrote scathingly (and jealously) in his journal: 'We had scarcely … breakfasted [upon Speke's return] before he announced to me the startling fact that he had discovered the sources of the Nile … The fortunate discoverer's conviction was strong; his reasons were weak'.

Speke, for his part, wrote that Burton grumpily listened to him and did not contradict him outright, although he could see that Burton was not happy with this news. 'Burton is one of those men', Speke later wrote, 'who never *can* be wrong, and will never acknowledge an error'.

With that breakfast, a famous feud had begun.

'Always eager to kill something'

Speke returned to England two weeks ahead of Burton and immediately went to the Royal Geographical Society to tell them of his find. His enthusiasm so excited Sir Roderick Murchison, president of the society, that Murchison agreed to fund a return trip to Africa so that Speke might further explore his find. When Burton arrived in London, he protested in vain that Speke and he had agreed not to speak to the society until Burton showed up (something Speke denied). By once again letting Speke go ahead of him, he had become the odd man out.

In April of 1860 Speke journeyed to Africa once again, this time to prove the certainty that he intuitively felt. He took with him as second-in-command Captain James Grant, a capable but self-effacing man who was about as un-Richard Burton-like as he could get—exactly what Speke wanted.

Speke's plan was to find the outlet river that he was sure ran from Lake Victoria and would flow into the Nile, and then go down it. He arranged for John Petherick, an ivory trader and British vice-consul at Khartoum, to come up the river and meet him with supplies as he descended.

Speke followed his previous route—from Zanzibar to Tabora and then north to Lake Victoria—and when he arrived he set about fully exploring the region that is now Uganda. He was the first white man to do so. Arabs had penetrated south close to the shores of what would become Lake Albert and Lake Victoria, but they had been turned back by Bunyoro people who lived north of Lake Victoria. To the south, right around the northern shores of Lake Victoria, was the fearsome empire of Buganda, and on the western shore of the lake were the Karagwe people, who were quasi-vassals of the Bugandans.

When Speke and Grant arrived in this territory, they were, therefore, forging new ground in encountering the native peoples. Speke, whose eyes still bothered him, wore grey-tinted glasses but had to take them off because they so astonished the tribespeople he met that they were constantly peering into his face to look at them. Speke headed around the western side of the lake first. Without Burton present, there were no checks on his hunting. As he wrote in his journal: '… always eager to kill something, either for science or the pot, I killed a bicornis rhinoceros … and I also shot a bitch fox. This was rather tame sport, but the next day I had better fun'—at which point he recounts killing numerous buffalo during a hunt that he initiated, simply wading in among the beasts and shooting them. Finally, however, he got to Karagwe, on a pleasant plateau filled with open country that gently sloped down toward the lake. He was welcomed by Rumanika, the king, and feasted royally, and then wrote about some of the strange customs of the land—customs that titillated Speke's Victorian readers when he published his *Journal of the Discovery of the Source of the Nile*, but also scandalised them.

Speke wrote that obesity was much prized in Karagwe, and the royal princesses were force-fed to the point where they could no longer walk but could barely crawl along on all fours through their huts. Speke decided that he wanted to measure one young woman and was given permission as long as he showed her the flesh of his arms and legs—unlike his face, which was burned by the sun, his limbs were startlingly white and thus an object of great curiosity. In any event, Speke got the woman to 'sidle and wriggle into the middle of the hut', then

 ## THE EXTRAORDINARY BAKERS

Samuel White Baker was born in England in 1821, a child of such wealth and privilege that he never had to attend school—a private tutor was afforded him. Like John Hanning Speke, Baker developed a taste for hunting and shooting early in life, revelling in what he called 'whole hecatombs of slaughter'. His favourite way of killing stags at bay in Scotland was to plunge a 12-inch (30-centimetre) hunting knife into their hearts.

He married and went to work managing the family properties in Ceylon, but his wife died of typhus in 1855 after giving birth to four daughters and this seems to have set off the wanderlust in Baker. He spent much time hunting all over the world. One day in 1860, he was passing through the Balkans on his way to Turkey when he stopped in a small town to view slaves being sold, not an uncommon sight in the Ottoman Empire. His eye was taken by a pretty seventeen-year-old girl from Hungary and, on a whim, he purchased her. Her name was Florence von Sass—she was an orphan whose parents had died when she was seven. Against the odds, the two married and became the love of each other's life.

Baker knew that the society circles he moved in back in England would never accept Florence, so at this point he decided to fulfil a long-held dream of becoming an African explorer. He and Florence travelled to Africa in 1861 and decided to search for the Nile River, enduring numerous hardships, including charging rhinoceroses, malaria, hostile tribes, native kings who lusted after Florence, and meals of crocodile flesh ('nothing can be more disgusting than crocodile flesh', wrote Baker, since it combined the flavours of 'bad fish, rotten flesh, and musk'). Fortunately, as Baker wrote, Florence was not 'a screamer' and put up with all this with equanimity.

Tipped off by Speke that there was another, undiscovered lake north of Lake Victoria, the Bakers trekked there and found the magnificent body of water they named Lake Albert, after the recently deceased Prince Consort. An exhausted Baker rushed into the water and 'drank deeply from the sources of the Nile' but, of course, the largest source was Lake Victoria, discovered by Speke, which fed into Lake Albert. Nonetheless, Baker was met back in England with some acclaim and was even knighted by Queen Victoria—who, however, would never receive Florence at court.

took her dimensions—her bust was 132 centimetres (52 inches), each thigh 79 centimetres (31 inches).

The land of Mtesa

Since James Grant was now unable to walk because of an ulcerated leg, Speke decided to go off on his own northward around the lakeshore to the kingdom of Buganda, which was the most powerful and advanced kingdom around Lake Victoria. The houses of the Bugandans were fifteen metres (fifty feet) high, conical structures made of woven reed or cane. Music filled the air from drums and flutes and trumpets, and Bugandan warriors travelled in

elaborately carved war canoes, some of them as much as twenty metres (seventy feet) long. Most of the men dressed, according to Speke, 'like prophets of the Old Testament' or ancient Romans, with long togas tied with a knot at the shoulder and white sandals. Noblemen often draped capes made of brushed antelope over their shoulders. Food was plentiful—fish, meat, chicken, sweet potatoes and maize—coffee beans were chewed as digestives, and *pombe*, the African banana beer, was drunk plentifully by both men and women.

The ruler of all of this, as Speke arrived, was one King Mtesa, a twenty-five-year-old tyrant with

Speke watches as King Mtesa of Buganda, a powerful kingdom on the northern shore of Lake Victoria, reviews his troops.

great, liquid dark eyes and a stiff-legged walk that was meant to imitate that of a lion. When Speke was first summoned to the royal court, he found out later, the king's advisors were telling Mtesa to kill him—surely, with his white skin, Speke was a sorcerer. But Mtesa was curious to have the white man around for a while, and thus we have a fascinating image of a long-vanished kingdom in its first encounter with European civilisation.

What stands out most is the cruelty. The punishment for almost *anything*—from forgetting to wear your sandals at court to touching the king's body—was death. While Speke was there, he got used to seeing summary executions every day. One day a girl spoke too loudly in the king's presence; she was dragged off screaming to have her head chopped off (with the pounding of drums masking the actual moment). Attending Mtesa's court (a daily compulsory occurrence) was dangerous for his subjects. Cowardly soldiers were sentenced to be castrated, 'drilled with a red hot iron, until they are men no more'. Other culprits, Speke wrote—'perhaps guilty of showing an inch of naked leg whilst squatting' before Mtesa— might find themselves drowned, burned alive or mutilated. If a particularly prized minister of Mtesa died, the king often sentenced the man's wives to be buried alive with him.

Speke witnessed all this and much more, but he only raised his hand once, to stop the execution of a young girl who had accidentally touched the king while handing him a piece of fruit. Speke was criticised for this when his memoirs came out but, in fact, there is almost nothing he could have done to stop most of these executions. However, he can be faulted for giving Mtesa a rifle as a present—the first firearm the king had seen. Naturally, Mtesa was delighted, as Speke reports:

The King now loaded one of the carbines I had given him with his own hands, and giving it full-

cock to a page, told him to go out and shoot a man in the outer court: which was no sooner accomplished than the little urchin returned to announce his success, with a look of glee as one would see on the face of a boy who had robbed a bird's nest ... The King said to him: 'Did you do it well?' 'Oh, yes, capitally.' He spoke the truth, no doubt, for he dared not have trifled with the king: but the affair created hardly any interest. I never heard, and there appeared no curiosity to know, what individual human being the urchin had deprived of his life.

'Old Father Nile'

James Grant, finally healed, showed up in Mtesa's court in July of 1862, and ten days later Speke and he moved out, heading to the east, where they had heard that a mighty river flowed out of Lake Victoria. But before he left, Speke created further scandal— for Victorians, that is—by accepting the gift of two young girls from the Bugandan queen mother. Speke had an odd relationship with this woman. In her mid-forties and greatly overweight, she held many parties in her huge house, during some of which she was so drunk she had to drink her *pombe* on all fours out of a wooden trough. She complained of stomach and liver ailments; Speke dosed her with quinine, but also sensibly told her she should quit drinking so much, advice she ignored.

However, she was quite curious as to what the children of Speke and a Bugandan girl might look like, and sent the young women over to Speke to 'carry his water', as he writes euphemistically (Speke is the king of indirection in his journals, even referring to his own trousers by the Victorian euphemism 'unmentionables'). Speke appears to hint that he had sex with the girls and then passed them on to his head porters, and this part of the journal angered many of his readers—it was taken for granted that men might dally in foreign climes, but writing about it made one a 'cad'. However, several modern historians feel that Speke was a repressed homosexual who had no interest in the women and was merely writing as he did in order to appear a red-blooded male.

In any event, he and Grant now began to close in on the river that flowed out of Lake Victoria. Before they got there, Speke sent the loyal Grant off on a side mission of little importance—it is apparent that he wanted to be the lone one to discover where the Nile began flowing. And on 28 July 1862, he found it, a waterfall pouring into a wide river:

> Here at last I stood on the brink of the Nile; most
> beautiful was the scene and nothing could surpass
> it. It was the very perfection of the kind of effect
> aimed at in a highly developed park: with a
> magnificent stream, 600 to 700 yards [600 to
> 700 metres] wide, dotted with islets and rocks …
> I saw that old Father Nile, without any doubt rises
> in the Victoria Nyanza and, as I had foretold,
> that lake is the great source of the holy river which
> cradled the first expounder of our religious belief.

By which he meant Moses. In a rather telling moment, he told one or two of his men that they should 'shave their heads and bathe in the holy river, the cradle of Moses', but one of them replied that, since he was a Muslim, 'we don't look on these things in the same fanciful manner as you do'.

Fanciful manner or no, it was time to move on. Speke named the falls Ripon Falls, after the well-known British politician George Robinson Ripon.

With Grant rejoining him, the two men made their way down the Nile, finally arriving at the trading village where they were supposed to rendezvous with Petherick. In fact, Petherick was not there, which angered Grant mightily, but Samuel Baker and his wife, Florence, who had been forging their way up the Nile, were. Baker was disappointed that Speke had arrived before him but was happy to set off in search of another great lake Speke had heard about, the lake Baker would name Lake Albert.

'The Nile is settled!'

Speke and Grant arrived back in London in 1863, Speke having first sent a famous telegram: 'The Nile is settled!' Of course, this only enraged supporters of Richard Burton, and Speke further angered the Royal Geographical Society (which, after all, had sponsored his expedition) by refusing to publish his results in their journal, since it might interfere with commercial publication of his journals. When he finally showed his topographical figures, he was ridiculed because—sloppy in his calculations—he had the Nile River running uphill.

Finally, in 1864, it was agreed that a debate between Burton and Speke might settle the matter, once and for all, but on the day before it was to happen, Speke died mysteriously. Still, Speke, it would turn out, was correct about the headwaters of the Nile and would go down in history as the first European to view them, and the first European to meet the extraordinary tribes of the central African basin. He was not a pleasant man—great explorers seldom are—but he was right.

WAS JOHN HANNING
SPEKE A SUICIDE?

After Burton and Speke returned from Africa, and Speke then travelled there again with Captain Grant, debate raged fiercely between the two men and their supporters as to whether or not Speke had discovered the true source of the White Nile. Burton's supporters claimed that Speke was 'muddled and confused', while Speke himself accused Burton of 'incompetence, cowardice, malice and jealousy'.

This public argument being quite unseemly, it was decided by the British Association—a group that sponsored debates on scientific issues—that Burton and Speke should debate to settle the matter in September 1864, in Bath, England, with David Livingstone acting as mediator and monitor. The two men sat stiffly on the debate platform on 14 September, during an initial session while other areas of Africa were discussed—their debate was to take place the next day. But at about 1.30 in the afternoon, Speke stood up, exclaimed to himself, 'Oh, I can't stand this any longer', and left the room.

After walking out of the hall, Speke went hunting partridges with his cousin George Fuller. Fuller, about sixty metres (two hundred feet) away, heard him fire twice at birds. Then came a third shot. Fuller turned around to see Speke standing atop a low stone wall—and then his cousin suddenly toppled over. Fuller raced over to see Speke lying on the ground, his chest a mass of blood. 'Don't move me', Speke said. Fuller raced to get help, but by the time he returned Speke was dead.

Burton, unaware of this, showed up at the hall the next day for their debate, but his wife felt that they were being 'shunned' by the others present. Only then was Burton apprised of the terrible news, at which point he cried: 'By God, he's killed himself!'

But had he? The coroner returned a verdict of accidental death—it was felt that Speke had been climbing over the stone wall and pulling his gun by its barrel after him when it went off. While it is hard to believe so experienced a hunter as Speke would have made such a mistake, it is also difficult to believe that Speke would have committed suicide before debating an issue that mattered so passionately to him. Perhaps, as the historian Frank McLynn has written, he was 'an unconscious suicide'. However it happened, public opinion now turned against Burton, and the obituaries lionised Speke. There were many who hinted that Burton had hounded him to his death. As Burton himself wrote sardonically to a friend: 'The charitable will say he shot himself, the uncharitable that I shot him'.

'THE RIVER THAT SWALLOWS ALL RIVERS'

*Henry Morton Stanley explores
the Congo, 1874–1877*

Like many great Victorians, Henry Morton Stanley provides a veritable feast for modern-day psychoanalysts. Born illegitimate, abandoned by his mother, raised in a Dickensian workhouse in his hometown, he literally renamed and reinvented himself and went on to a career of the sort even the boldest novelist would not dare to invent. At the same time, while longing for the simple connection and love that only his lost mother could give him, he was unscrupulous, aggressive (sometimes murderous), private to the point of paranoia, and extraordinarily vain. When asked to describe his role on his famous expedition to find David Livingstone, he called himself 'the vanguard, the reporter, the thinker, and the leader'.

But for all this mixture of pomposity and neurosis, Stanley has to be appraised as the greatest of all the Victorian African explorers. He was the man who in one great journey traversed the unknown centre of Africa, circumnavigated two of the greatest lakes in the world and went the length of the ancient and much feared Kongo River. The Europeans called it the Congo—and it is now the Zaire—but the meaning of the name did not change: 'The river that swallows all rivers'. The Congo arises in southeastern Africa, 1600 kilometres (1000 miles) below the Equator and 1600 kilometres from either coast, and ultimately heads for the Atlantic Ocean in a journey that takes almost 5000 kilometres (3000 miles) and sees the river head north, loop up over the Equator, and then finally turn west and southwest. The Congo attracted explorers like flies to honey and was second only to the Nile as an object of their fascination.

The epic three-year adventure of Stanley was even more important because he was traversing unknown territory. His journey down the Congo was extraordinarily violent because he was the first white man any of the cannibal tribes of the region had ever seen. They did not want him or his men there, except as dinner, and they made this very clear, at one point lining the riverbank, brandishing their spears and shouting: *Niama! Niama!*, which meant 'Meat! Meat!'

Yet Stanley persevered and returned to Britain, an old man at the age of thirty-seven, his hair turned white, to find at the moment of his greatest triumph that he had been abandoned once again by a woman he loved desperately.

John Rowlands

Henry Morton Stanley was born John Rowlands on 28 January 1841, in the small town of Denbigh, Wales. His mother, Elizabeth Parry, was nineteen years old and would go on to give birth to four more illegitimate children. Rowlands's father was, supposedly, John Rowlands, Jr, son of a local farmer, but there is some doubt as to whether this is true— he may have been a Denbigh lawyer named James Vaughn Horne. Who his father was, as Rowlands was growing up, was less important to him than the fact that his mother simply refused to have anything to do with him, despite the fact that she raised her other illegitimate children. This is as puzzling to historians now as it was then to Rowlands, who was raised until the age of five by his maternal grandfather, with almost no contact with his mother. When this kindly old man died, Elizabeth Parry's family placed Rowlands in the care of a local family, but when they stopped paying for his upkeep, the people taking care of him simply took him and dumped him on the doorstep of the local poorhouse, the St Asaph Union Workhouse.

Rowlands stayed at St Asaph's until the age of fifteen. At one point when he was ten, he had the unnerving experience of seeing his mother, Elizabeth, down on her luck, arrive with two of her other children to stay at the workhouse. He wanted to approach her but saw 'that she was regarding me

with a look of cool, clinical scrutiny' and so he never did. After leaving St Asaph's he went to Liverpool, got a job as a butcher's boy on the docks and was impressed by the sailors striding to and fro on the waterfront, telling swaggering stories of the sea. One day, while making a delivery to an American ship in the harbour, he fell into conversation with the captain. The Yankee skipper promised him five dollars a month pay if he would sail to New Orleans as the ship's cabin boy. It turned out the man had no intention of paying him, but Rowlands had no intention of sticking around, anyway. Once he arrived in New Orleans, in February 1859, he jumped ship and set off to seek his fortune in America.

Henry Morton Stanley

Rowlands now underwent a rather profound transformation—an attempt to erase his past— which he was to record in his memoirs and in numerous interviews. Walking along the New Orleans waterfront, knowing not a soul, he came across a wealthy gentleman sitting outside a general store and asked the man if he could have a job. The man was taken by the eighteen-year-old Welsh boy and not only offered him a job, but eventually became so close to him that he insisted on adopting him. The man proved a loving surrogate father to Rowlands, even giving him his own name: Henry Stanley. (Stanley added the 'Morton' himself.)

The only problem with this story is that it is a fantasy. Recent biographers of Stanley, notably Tim Jeal, in his book *Stanley: The Impossible Life of Africa's Greatest Explorer*, have proven fairly conclusively that Stanley applied for a job at the modest grocery store of one James Speake and worked there until Speake died the following October. He grew close to Speake but was out of a job after his death and was forced, once again, to fend for himself. There was a Henry Hope Stanley in New Orleans at the time, a wealthy cotton trader. Stanley never met him but appropriated his name and invented the story in order to fulfil a long-held desire to have a father and benefactor.

Stanley's transformation now continued. He left New Orleans, travelled to St Louis, and finally ended up with a job as a grocer's clerk in a small store in Arkansas. He worked to lose his Welsh accent and began telling people he had been raised in the South. This was perhaps not wise, since the Civil War was then beginning. Stanley quite naturally felt that, as a foreigner, the fight was not his, but when someone anonymously sent him a lady's petticoat in the mail, he understood that he was being called a coward. Goaded by his pride, he joined the Fourth Arkansas Infantry in time to be marched into the front lines at the bloody battle of Shiloh, in April 1861. Stanley charged into battle wearing flowers in his cap but lost his innocence as 'the patter, snip thud and hum of bullets' whizzed by him, 'raining death' upon his friends.

During the horrible fighting that followed, Stanley was captured by the Union Army and imprisoned outside Chicago, in a POW camp rife with typhoid and dysentery. Men died daily, to be wrapped in old blankets and dumped into mass graves. Feeling 'doomed', Stanley felt there was no alternative but to join the Union Army, but he deserted as soon as he could and was finally able to sail out of war-torn America and back to Britain in November 1862.

'Dr Livingstone, I presume?'

An amazing adventure for someone not yet twenty-two years old, but more was to come. After spending the next few years seafaring between Britain and the Continent or Britain and North America, Stanley returned to America in 1864 and, incredibly, joined the Union Navy, changing his name slightly so that he would not be identified as a previous deserter. After deserting yet *again*, Stanley, a wide reader and strong writer, decided to become a journalist and began writing articles for papers such as the *Missouri*

Democrat and the *Chicago Tribune*. After travelling through the American West, he went to Turkey, where he and his friends were robbed and nearly put in jail by corrupt police officials, until Stanley talked his way out of the situation—showing the persuasiveness that would become his hallmark.

In December of 1867, back in America, he walked with no introduction into the offices of the *New York Herald*, America's largest daily newspaper, and talked his way into seeing its owner, James Gordon Bennett Jr. There was going to be war soon between a native king in Ethiopia and Great Britain, Stanley told him, offering his services as a foreign correspondent to cover the conflict. Bennett finally agreed to allow Stanley to write for the *Herald*, as long as he paid his own way. Stanley scooped the opposition on this story, and Bennett put the twenty-six-year-old permanently on staff.

Not bad for a Welsh boy raised in a workhouse. Stanley, as he began to enter his prime, was described as short (about 165 centimetres, or 5 feet 5 inches), with a square jaw, big moustache, intense eyes and a 'ferocious loquaciousness'—when he wanted to talk, he talked. He was bold, courageous and intensely ambitious, but there was something a little pathetic about him, particularly in his attempts to find love. Around this time he became infatuated with a sixteen-year-old Greek girl named Virginia, as well as a young Welsh girl named Katie Gough Roberts, and he even proposed marriage to the latter, but neither of these relationships went anywhere. This is partly because Stanley had just received the biggest assignment of his life: in 1870, James Gordon Bennett tasked him with finding the revered missionary/explorer David Livingstone, who had been missing in Africa for some five years.

Actually, Livingstone was not lost at all, but searching for the source of the Nile in central Africa—he did not believe John Hanning Speke's contention that it arose from Lake Victoria (see page 244). However, rumours floated through the world that he was dead, or a hostage of hostile tribes. Numerous search expeditions were funded but, with typical dash and aggressiveness, Stanley was determined to get there first—despite the fact that he had been in Africa only once before.

Arriving in Zanzibar on the east coast of Africa, Stanley set off with a massive expedition consisting of 170 porters, seventy-one cases of ammunition, two collapsible boats, Champagne and a bathtub. Two hundred and thirty days later, having lost eighteen kilograms (forty pounds)—as well as numerous porters and expedition members to disease—he arrived at the village of Ujiji on the shores of Lake Tanganyika, where Livingstone had actually just arrived himself. It was either late October or early November 1872 (both Livingstone

and Stanley had lost track of time). Stanley was taken to the famous explorer and greeted him with the words 'Dr Livingstone, I presume?'

'*To fire me with a resolution*'

Or did he? These lines have became as famous as *Et tu, Brutus?* but it is unlikely that Stanley uttered them. He *claimed* that he did, in his first articles on the momentous encounter for the *Herald*, but in fact neither Livingstone nor Stanley recorded such an utterance in their diary accounts of the meeting. Such a stilted line is the way Stanley, ever the workhouse boy, thought gentlemen should address each other, and so, as was the case with so much else in his life, he invented it. Later he appears to have regretted this, because the line was instantly parodied and made him a bit of a laughingstock,

Henry Morton Stanley and David Livingstone explore the Rusizi River after their momentous meeting at Ujiji in late 1872.

particularly among the high society he so wished to impress, but he was stuck with it.

Stanley spent four months with Livingstone and came away impressed—in fact, awed—by the man. Livingstone became something of a father figure for the young Welsh reporter. Stanley listened eagerly as Livingstone expounded his pet theory: that the headwaters of the Nile were not Lake Victoria, nor Lake Albert, but were in fact 'four full-grown gushing fountains' as first postulated by the Greek historian and traveller Herodotus. These mythical fountains turned into four flowing rivers, which turned into the Lualaba River and became the mighty White Nile.

THE JOURNEY OF LIVINGSTONE'S BODY

David Livingstone had made many journeys in his lifetime, but none was stranger than the one his body took after his death. Early on the morning of 1 May 1873, Livingstone's long-time African servants Susi and Chuma entered his tent and found him kneeling in prayer, his head pressed against the covers of his cot. They approached quietly and realised that he was, in fact, dead, probably of a combination of malaria and dysentery. They were 1500 kilometres (1000 miles) from the coast of Africa, but it never occurred to them to simply bury Livingstone there. They decided to take him home, as they thought he would have wished.

This was a dangerous thing to do, since they would have to pass through the territory of numerous tribes, carrying a corpse that could get them killed as witches. But they were determined. One member of Livingstone's African party had worked for a doctor, so he made an incision in Livingstone's abdomen and took out his heart and internal organs, which were buried. Then a large quantity of salt was placed inside the body, as a preservative, and the body was exposed to the sun for two weeks, with Susi and Chuma taking turns guarding the corpse and changing its position so that the sun could do its work.

Finally, with the body at least partially mummified and wrapped in waterproofed canvas, they set forth, making an arduous journey through dangerous territory, hiding what they were actually carrying from the tribes they encountered. In October 1873 they came upon a British expedition—led by Verney Lovett Cameron—that had come in search of Livingstone. To Cameron's literally feverish astonishment, he realised that these men had been carrying Livingstone's corpse for five months. Cameron urged them to bury Livingstone then and there—he was anxious to be on with his own explorations—but the two faithful servants refused and pressed on to the coast, where a British warship finally picked up the corpse of the famous explorer.

The Royal Geographical Society would, a year later, strike medals to award Susi and Chuma, but by that time they and the other men of Livingstone's party were scattered throughout Africa and they never received them.

Livingstone was certain that he had been no more than two or three hundred kilometres (100–200 miles) from these fountains and refused to come out of Africa with Stanley—he needed to finish his work, he said. These fountains, of course, existed only in Livingstone's, by now, too-fervent imagination, but Stanley was so impressed that when he left he promised to send back a supply-filled caravan for Livingstone's use in carrying out further explorations.

Stanley then returned to London, where he found that his discovery of Livingstone had made him famous. He was presented to Queen Victoria, had a wax dummy created after him in Madame Tussaud's, and was awarded the gold medal of the Royal Geographical Society. After this, he returned to New York and resumed work as a journalist for the *Herald*.

But something was missing in all this acclaim, or so Stanley felt—respect. He was well known now to the general public, but other explorers laughed at him. Certain British adventurers (jealous that Stanley, considered an American, was the first to encounter their countryman Livingstone) claimed, with some veracity but a good deal of cattiness, that Livingstone 'discovered Mr Stanley' and not the other way around, since Livingstone was not lost to begin with. Even more painful for Stanley, who hero-worshipped Livingstone, many felt that Livingstone's 'Four Fountains' theory about the source of the Nile was simply balderdash.

Then something happened to change everything. Livingstone, on yet another expedition, died deep in the African bush on 1 May 1873. After his body was brought to London for an extraordinary state funeral on 18 April 1874, Stanley, who acted as one of the pallbearers, was in a state of shock. But the cumulative effect of Livingstone's passing was to, as Stanley wrote in his diary, 'fire me with a resolution to complete his work, to be if God willed it, the next martyr to geographical science'.

'We solemnly pledge to be faithful'

And so Henry Morton Stanley, upstart and relative newcomer to African exploration, sat down in a London hotel room to plan the most ambitious African exploration of the nineteenth century, one that would settle some weighty issues once and for all.

Firstly, Stanley would circumnavigate Lake Victoria, which Speke had claimed (correctly) was a single body of water and the source of the White Nile. However, since Speke's death some seventeen years before, many had postulated that Lake Victoria was actually five or six different lakes fed by different rivers. Circumnavigation would prove or disprove this once and for all.

Secondly, Stanley would also successfully circumnavigate Lake Albert, discovered by fellow explorer Samuel Baker, and Lake Tanganyika, discovered by Sir Richard Burton. Each of these men claimed *their* lake was the source of the Nile. By circumnavigating them, Stanley would see what, if any, outlet they had.

Finally, and perhaps most importantly, Stanley would then strike westward and follow the course of the Lualaba River to see if it became the Nile, as Livingstone had postulated, or the Congo. This would be the most dangerous part of the trip, as it would take Stanley into territory where no white man had ever been—where even Arab slavers were afraid to venture, a place filled with savage tribes of cannibals, or so it was rumoured.

Stanley knew that such a daring and audacious venture would require extensive funding. Using his considerable powers of persuasion, he got London's *Daily Telegraph* and the *New York Herald* newspapers to share the cost. Stanley then feverishly threw himself into preparations. He was naturally impatient to be going, but he had another reason to hurry—the young British explorer Verney Lovett Cameron was already in Africa (had been for some time) and was heading for the Lualaba on the same mission as Stanley. After putting an ad in the newspaper for assistants (some 1200 replies were received), Stanley picked brothers Edward and Frank Pocock, who were capable boatmen, and, rather puzzlingly,

Frederick Barker, a hotel clerk whose chief qualification seemed to be his unremitting desire that Stanley should take him along.

Stanley left England on 15 August 1874, but not without first having fallen in love. This time

Map of Africa to show the areas explored by David Livingstone, Verney Lovett Cameron and Henry Morton Stanley.

the object of his affections was seventeen-year-old Alice Pike, the daughter of a wealthy American businessman. Alice seemed to return the feeling. In July, both wrote and signed a declaration that read: 'We solemnly pledge to be faithful to each other and to be married to one another on the return of Henry Morton Stanley from Africa'.

The Great Lake

Six weeks after leaving Great Britain, Stanley arrived in Zanzibar and there assembled what he called 'the best organized and best equipped [expedition] that ever left the seacoast of East Africa'. On 17 November he set off from present-day Tanzania, with eight tonnes of supplies, 356 porters and soldiers, and a portable barge that he had designed himself, had broken down into pieces for easy reassembly and dubbed the *Lady Alice*. Anxious to beat Cameron, he maintained a literally killing pace. At a certain point, instead of taking the more indirect but well-trodden caravan route to the town of Mpwapwa and from there to Lake Victoria, the impatient Stanley decided to forge a new route overland. This was not a good idea. Travelling through rough country—an arid plain called Ukimbu—exhausted the men and they became sick and died or deserted. Edward Pocock succumbed to typhus in January. Hostile tribesmen attacked with spears, killing stragglers, and at one point engaged the column in a pitched battle that lasted three days and cost the lives of twenty-two men.

On 22 February 1875, Stanley reached Lake Victoria, having covered 1000 kilometres (700 miles) in 103 days—a record—but only 166 men out of 356 were left. No European had seen the lake since Speke had arrived so many years before, and its 70,000 square kilometres (27,000 square miles) had never been mapped. Assembling the *Lady Alice*, Stanley set out to do just that, although he had trouble finding men to journey on the lake with him, since most of his porters were terrified of the

tribes they might encounter. Finally, Stanley ordered eleven porters to accompany him. Leaving Frank Pocock and Frederick Barker behind with the remaining porters to guard their supply camp, he set off on a counter-clockwise navigation around the lake. Lake Victoria was no millpond—storms crashed over the *Lady Alice* as the crew gamely rowed (or sometimes sailed) around the shores. There were other dangers, as well. 'We were frequently chased by hippopotami; crocodiles suddenly rose alongside and floated for a moment side by side, as though to take the measure of our boat's length.'

When the men rowed, the people who lived along the lake laughed at them, because they rowed backwards. But when they raised their sails, the natives 'ran away in terror', because they had never seen such a thing before. Stanley kept going, despite dire warnings of cannibals ahead. He passed the Ripon Falls, through which the waters of Lake Victoria spill out and eventually form the White Nile and then, on the northern shores of the lake, came to the kingdom of Buganda (present-day Uganda), which was led by the fearsome King Mtesa. John Hanning Speke had met him in 1862 and described him as a cruel despot, much given to human sacrifices. However, Mtesa (whose lineage would rule the area until the 1960s) had mellowed with age and gave Stanley a warm welcome.

Departing on 15 April, Stanley continued along the western shores of the lake until he got to Bumbire Island, where he put in to trade for supplies and received a warm welcome of quite a different sort on 28 April. All of a sudden, two hundred warriors surrounded the *Lady Alice* and, with brute force, pulled it up on the shore. Stanley attempted to parlay with them and tried to bribe them with cloth and beads, but the men, their faces painted black and white, grew ever more threatening, and Stanley realised that he had only a short time before he was attacked. He told his men to grab the boat and, when he gave the signal, push it back into the water. They did, as the warriors attacked. The warriors had taken away the oars, but Stanley's men ripped up planking from the deck and used it to pull frantically away from the shore, while Stanley fired his gun, killing three or four of the attackers.

Shaken, the crew of the *Lady Alice* brought the ship around the western shore and back to their starting point, and Stanley had proved that Lake Victoria was only one lake after all. Unfortunately, in his absence Frederick Barker had died of malaria and, when he returned, Stanley himself came down with it, bringing his weight down to 50 kilograms (110 pounds) and exhausting him.

'A secret rapture'

Stanley next planned to head north to Lake Albert and circumnavigate that body of water. Instead of going overland, he took the expedition in canoes provided by King Mtesa. However, on the way back around the western shore, he decided to teach the natives of Bumbire a lesson. Bringing 250 men together in a fleet of canoes, he sailed around the western side of the island as the sun was setting (so its brilliant rays would be in the eyes of the defenders) and demanded an apology for the attack on him in April.

When none was forthcoming, Stanley 'ordered [his men] to fire as if they were shooting birds'. The spears and stones of the natives were no match for modern firearms—Stanley killed forty of the natives and wounded perhaps a hundred.

This massacre—for so it was—represented Stanley at his most ruthless and caused a stir back in London when the story (told by Stanley himself in dispatches to the *Herald* and the *Telegraph*) was first heard a year later. There were even cries that Stanley should be tried for murder. He could never understand this. 'The savage only understands force, power, boldness and decision', he wrote. And he pointed out that rumours of his attack spread along the lakeshore, causing other tribes to bring him gifts and allow him to pass unmolested.

Reaching the Buganda again, Stanley received an escort of two thousand warriors from King Mtesa and set out across country for Lake Albert in January of 1876. Unfortunately, he did not get closer than about 150 kilometres (100 miles) from it. Every step the expedition took was dogged by hostile tribesmen—the Wanyoro—who frightened even Mtesa's warriors. 'These men take no prisoners', one of Mtesa's generals warned. Finally, Stanley turned around and went back to Lake Victoria. He was not unduly upset, since he had already decided that Lake Victoria was the source of the White Nile. By June of 1876, he had headed south and launched the *Lady Alice* on Lake Tanganyika. By the end of August he had circumnavigated it and come to the conclusion (correctly) that it had no northern outlet and could not be the source of the Nile.

Pausing at Ujiji, where he had first met Livingstone, Stanley was quite disappointed to find that no letters had arrived from Alice Pike—he had been away now, after all, 'a few days short of twenty-five months', as he wrote her. Still, his love for her was strong, he said: 'You are my dream, my stay and my hope, and my beacon'. Then, having heard that Verney Lovett Cameron had reached the town of Nyangwe on the Lualaba—the farthest point any European had gone on the river—some two years before, Stanley hurried northwest from Lake Tanganyika and, on 17 October, first beheld the mighty river. 'A secret rapture filled my soul as I gazed upon the majestic stream', he wrote later. 'The great mystery that for all these centuries Nature had kept hidden away from the world of science was waiting to be solved ... My task was to follow it to the Ocean.'

Heart of darkness

When Stanley arrived at Nyangwe he received goods news and bad news. The good news, from his point of view, was that Cameron had given up on the idea of heading down the Lualaba River, and thus it remained unexplored by Europeans, its potential connection to the Congo unknown. The bad news was that Stanley faced the same problems that Cameron had, namely, he could get none of the local Africans to go with him down the river, to provide canoes and labour. The locals said that the land that lay ahead 'was a country of large mountains wooded to the summits, and valleys filled with such dense forest that [one could] travel four or five days in succession without seeing the sun'.

Also, the tribes there were cannibals who were very fierce and warlike and used poisoned arrows, so that a scratch would kill a man in the space of three or four minutes. Despite these fears, Stanley, typically, found a solution by using a combination of bribery and dishonesty. He paid a local slaver—

THE UNKNOWN VERNEY LOVETT CAMERON

The name Verney Lovett Cameron is not one that springs immediately to mind when one thinks of the great British explorers of the nineteenth century, yet his contribution was real and important. V.L. Cameron was born in Great Britain in 1844 and began his career as a naval officer working to stymie the East African slave trade. In 1872, at the age of twenty-eight, he was sent by the Royal Geographical Society to give whatever aid was possible to David Livingstone. He set out from East Africa to try to find Livingstone with a party that included three other white men, including a nephew of Livingstone's by marriage.

Unfortunately, they were hit by malaria, which made them half-blind and crazy with fever (one of Cameron's companions ended up committing suicide). This was the shape Cameron was in when he received a note from an African saying: 'Your father died of disease beyond the country of Bisa'. The 'father' in question was Livingstone, whom the Africans believed to be an honorary father to all Britons, but Cameron was so delirious he thought it was his own father.

When they finally realised the truth, his companions turned back for the coast, but Cameron was determined to go forward. After reaching Lake Tanganyika, he explored the southern portion of the lake and found the river that was its outlet. He then proceeded on to the Lualaba, which he was rightly convinced was the main river that fed the Congo but, unfortunately, he was unable to acquire canoes to follow the river, or history would have been changed. (Stanley would later have the same problem but, with more resources and more perseverance, would be able to overcome it.)

Even so, Cameron had a marvellous adventure, trekking all the way across Africa to the Atlantic and becoming the first man to cross the continent at the Equator from coast to coast. He went on to a life of writing, editing and further adventures in Africa, a life that was cut short at the age of fifty when he died after being thrown from his horse.

a prominent Arab from Zanzibar named Tippoo Tib—the staggering sum of five thousand dollars to provide an armed escort for the first leg of the journey. This was partly to protect Stanley and his men from tribes who had been attacked by slavers and were hostile to any newcomers to the area, but also partly to keep Stanley's own men from deserting until they were far enough away from Nyangwe that it would be too dangerous to do so.

With this arrangement in place, Stanley set off up the river on 5 November 1876. Stanley's men numbered about 150, while Tib's forces were about seven hundred, although three hundred of these would depart on a separate slaving expedition within a few days. Still, it was a large and well-armed force. For the first several weeks of the journey, Stanley and his men went overland, 'crawling, scrambling, tearing through the damp, dank jungle'. A python three metres (ten feet) long crawled across Stanley's path. Sometimes it was so dark in broad daylight he could barely read his notebook. Finally, on 21 November, he assembled the *Lady Alice* and launched her with an advance force of fifty men—thirty in the barge and another twenty in some canoes he had stolen (thus ensuring the enmity of the locals). The rest of the party crossed to the west bank, where the forest was less heavy, and continued overland.

They were passing through the land of the Wenya, where it appeared that the rumours about cannibalism were true—Stanley landed at a deserted village that had two hundred skulls stacked up in front of it. When an old man appeared from the woods and tried to take back the canoes Stanley's men were stealing, they shot him dead and things began to go from bad to worse. A few kilometres farther, as Stanley camped for the night, spears were hurled out of the darkness, fortunately missing everyone. It was the first attack of many.

Just after Christmas Day, Tippoo Tib told Stanley that he and his men were leaving the expedition—many of his people (including three of his concubines) had died of disease so far. Stanley reluctantly went on, with 143 people, including women and children belonging to some of his porters. They now had twenty-three canoes as well as the *Lady Alice*, so the entire expedition was on the water. He was beginning a new year by entering what Joseph Conrad would later call 'a heart of darkness'.

'A murderous world'

The river began to carry the men along at such a rapid clip that many of the inexperienced natives (who habitually smoked marijuana during the trip) were unable to control their canoes. There were now signs they were reaching an area where no white men had ever gone before. Previously, locals had yelled out *Wasambye*, meaning 'slavers', as they went by. Now the natives had no word for them. Stanley tried to make peace, but the warriors hid in the bushes, bows at the ready, until the expedition got into their boats again, at which point the warriors would leap into their canoes and attack. One time, forewarned of Stanley's coming, they stretched a large net across the river and tried to snare the expedition. 'They considered us as game to be trapped, shot or bagged on sight', Stanley wrote angrily. Each time the expedition was attacked, they answered with their rifles—which these tribes had never before seen—and killed men, blowing them out of their canoes.

Still the attacks continued, and something more chilling—one of Stanley's interpreters heard the warriors who pursued them in their canoes saying to each other: 'We shall eat meat today!' And they cried *Niama! Niama!* ('Meat! Meat!') at the expedition as it passed. This caused Stanley's men to shoot as many of them as they could, surprising the tribes with the explosive power of their guns. In early January, a new challenge presented itself. Stanley heard a roar ahead and realised they were coming

Stanley supervises from the bank as his men begin the laborious task of carrying their canoes overland to bypass falls on the river.

STANLEY'S WOMEN

Henry Morton Stanley had trouble with women all his life, beginning with (and perhaps stemming from) his abandonment by his mother. He and his mother were able to effect a partial reconciliation later in life—when Stanley became successful, his mother became more interested in him—but the great explorer was to spend most of his days trying to figure out how to deal with the fairer sex.

'The fact is,' he said, 'I can't talk to women. In their presence I am just as much a hypocrite as any other man'.

He sought other women after being jilted by Alice Pike but had little luck until he met Dorothy Tennant, a Victorian neoclassic painter of some talent. He married her in 1890 when he was forty-nine and she thirty-five, and they lived relatively happily together, with Tennant protecting Stanley from the eyes of a prying press and encouraging him to run for Parliament (and in so doing reclaim his British citizenship, which he had abandoned when he became an American citizen in 1885). Even after Stanley died, she protected him by burning early letters and diaries that contradicted his 'official' version of his life.

upon rushing rapids, a series of seven cataracts that would become known as the Stanley Falls. It took him three weeks to traverse these, cutting a path overland and dragging the boats over rocks, under constant attack by tribesmen hiding in the brush.

But by the end of January, they were back on the river and Stanley began to note that the Lualaba was flowing westward, not to the north. This, and the volume of water rushing them along, led him to suspect that this was indeed the Congo, not the Nile, the very thing he had wanted to prove by travelling the river. Yet there was no time yet to congratulate himself. In early February, the mighty Aruwimi River joined the Lualaba, creating a river that was turbulent and almost five kilometres (three miles) wide. Here they were attacked by at least twenty native canoes (Stanley inflated the number to some fifty or so in his memoirs) and fought a pitched, two-day battle on open water that had the characteristics of a naval engagement, with

canoes attempting to cut off and surround Stanley and his men, and Stanley blowing them away with his superior firepower.

By mid-February, Stanley counted twenty-four pitched battles with the local tribes, to whom these men were apparitions from hell. He described 'the canoes darting forward impetuously to the attack, while the drums and horns and shouts raised a fierce and deafening roar'. Only thirty of his men, by this time, remained unwounded. 'Our blood is now up', Stanley wrote. 'It is a murderous world and we feel for the first time we hate the filthy, vulturous ghouls who inhabit it.' Stanley then did again what he had done on Lake Victoria—aimed a retributive attack on a village the expedition was passing, attacking and burning it to the ground.

'You may not know me by name'

By the middle of March, the Congo—a peaceful tribal chief Stanley met had confirmed for him that

266

this was indeed 'the river that swallows all rivers'—had turned from northwest to west to southwest and was very obviously heading for the Atlantic Ocean. After eight more battles with local tribesmen, Stanley now entered an area inhabited by peaceful tribes, but the river itself became the battle, as it plunged into a series of waterfalls, whirlpools and rapids. The men hauled the *Lady Alice* and the canoes overland, at one point negotiating a 350-metre (1200-foot) mountain, but for the next five months the journey was hell, with more and more men dying of disease. Most grievous to Stanley, Frank Pocock, his last English companion, drowned in one boiling cataract.

Stanley had been determined to take the expedition all the way to the ocean, now a relatively short distance away, but his men were on their last legs. Accordingly he struck out overland for the European trading post at Boma, fighting his way through the Crystal Mountains, until at last his 116 ill and emaciated men could go no farther. He sent a note on to Boma that was addressed 'To any Gentleman who speaks English', in which he begged for supplies for him and his men, who 'are in a state of imminent starvation'. He signed the note 'H.M. Stanley', but added a PS: 'You may not know me by name; I therefore add, I am the person that discovered Livingstone in 1871'.

And, with this odd but characteristic bit of insecurity, Stanley's 11,000-kilometre (7000-mile) journey through Africa ended on its 999th day. Supplies reached him in time and he and his men were rescued. As he had promised them, Stanley then took his men home (by boat) to Zanzibar. Only 116 were left of the 356 who had started the journey. And in Zanzibar, Stanley finally received word from his beloved Alice. Her note began: 'I have done what millions of women have done before me, not been true to my promise'. In fact, Alice had married after only a year. She tried to soften the blow, telling Stanley: 'You are so great, so honoured and so sought after that you will scarcely miss your once true friend and always devoted admirer'.

It was a bitter disappointment for Stanley, who had gone through 'the mouth of hell and the jaws of death' with Alice's iconic image wavering before his feverish eyes, but soon a wave of fame spread over him. His journey was acclaimed even at the time as the most comprehensive expedition in Africa, tracing the major watersheds of the central part of the country for Europeans. Unfortunately, Stanley's discoveries set the scene for what one historian has called 'the most vicious colonial exploitation in Africa's history'—that of King Leopold of Belgium, who subjugated and despoiled the Congo for his personal profit after Stanley helped, beginning in 1879, to open up a safe route along the Congo River.

In many ways, Stanley was as innocent as many of the tribes he had met for the first time along the Congo, for, focused only inward, he had not seen the future coming. He died in 1904, knighted by the British government and full of honours. Afterwards his wife burned many of his early papers, so that only Stanley's official version of his life would exist for future generations.

PART 6

FIRST CONTACT IN THE TWENTIETH CENTURY

*Warriors in full regalia take part in a
ceremony at Mt Hagen, in the central
highlands of Papua New Guinea.*

STRANGER-WOMAN AMONG THE YANOÁMA

The story of Helena Valero, 1932–1956

The hundreds of kilometres of heavy jungle on the border between Venezuela and Brazil was one of the few unexplored areas in the world in 1932 and remains so to some extent today. 'Since the time of the conquest', wrote the anthropologist Ettore Biocca in the late 1950s, 'all efforts to penetrate the interior of this forest have been useless'. It was here, rumours had it, that a great salt lake existed, on whose banks rose the golden city of El Dorado, guarded by woman warriors, the Amazons.

Although numerous rivers ran through this area, few who had followed one in ever came back out. Those straggling survivors who did return to civilisation spoke of a fierce tribe of people who did stand sentinel over the area, not the Amazons but a group anthropologists now call the Yanoáma, which means simply 'those of the village'. Actually, this group comprised a number of different tribes—the Waka, the Shiriana, the Guaharibo, the Shirishana,

as well as others—who were often at war with each other, but who were united in their desire to keep out the *napë*, which means 'strangers'.

What Biocca calls the 'obstinate hostility' of the Yanoáma guarding the riverine pathways into their land kept the conquistadors and their deadly guns and, even better, diseases from reaching the Indians in this pristine area of rugged mountains and forests filled with jaguar, anaconda and tapirs. The first real scientific explorers approached at the beginning of the nineteenth century and had brief encounters with the Yanoáma but were then turned away. Some of them disappeared forever. Some, like the American explorer Hamilton Rice in 1921, had violent encounters with the Indians—Rice shot and killed three Yanoáma because they were standing on a riverbank shouting at him and tapping their teeth, a sign that he thought meant they were going to eat him. (Despite certain funerary rites in which they ingest the ashes of their dead, the Yanoáma are not cannibals.)

Many of the Yanoáma had never seen a white person. Many had heard of white people, as a taboo race of *napë*, but none of them had any idea of the world beyond their few square hundred kilometres of it. They lived as they had for centuries, as they had when the Inca reigned in Peru and even before that, their customs unadulterated by outside influences. White people who lived on the fringes of their territory—missionaries, loggers, scientists, government officials—knew these Indians only as a vague and sometimes dangerous presence. When the Yanoáma showed themselves openly, it was usually with violence in mind, and this is exactly what happened on a remote river on a day in 1932, to a young girl named Helena Valero and her family.

'Don't shoot us!'

Helena Valero was twelve years old in 1932, living in a remote region of the great Amazon basin between Brazil and Venezuela. Her father was Spanish; her mother was a local Brazilian woman. Helena had been studying at a Catholic mission near the Uaupés River, but one day the head priest wrote to her father and asked him to come and get her, saying (ironically, in light of what was to happen) that his mission was to teach Indian children, not 'civilised' girls like Helena. Her father fetched her and brought her back to the family home at the village of Marabitanas, on the Negro River, a tributary of the Amazon. Helena's family was poor and now suffered a tragedy when Helena's older sister died of illness, leaving her and her two brothers.

Her mother's brother offered them the use of two small houses he had built on the Dimiti River, a remote tributary of the Negro, 'a small river in the forest', as Helena said when she related her life story to anthropologist Ettore Biocca. It was the kind of quiet, lost river the Indians called an *igarapé*. Helena and her mother, father and brothers left to canoe

there in a huge dugout canoe, carrying with them almost all their belongings, as well as plant seedlings, for they intended to begin a large garden in the forest. The journey took them several days. Early one morning as they were approaching the small huts that were their destination, Helena's father noticed white smoke hanging low over the river ahead of them. He thought perhaps that some huntsmen might have used Helena's uncle's house to smoke meat, and so he landed the canoe just short of the houses and walked up the bank of the river, machete in hand.

Within a few minutes, he came running back, pale, clutching an arm down which blood was streaming. He seemed to be unable to speak for a moment, but then finally managed to get out that some Indians had shot him with a poisoned arrow. Frantically, he piled everyone into the canoe and pushed it away from shore. They threw out all their plant seedlings to lighten their load. Helena's father, still in a state of shock, began rubbing salt on his wound, to inhibit the spread of the poison. They all paddled frantically back down the small river but then noticed that nearly naked Indians had appeared on the banks, bows drawn. Arrows one and a half metres (five feet) long whizzed by the boat. Helena's father yelled at the children to lie down, but it was too late—one arrow had entered the skin of Helena's belly and pierced her thigh at the same time, so that her stomach was stapled to her upper leg.

Sobbing, her mother frantically broke the arrow and pulled it out; she used her teeth to pull out the arrowhead buried in Helena's thigh. When Helena raised her head, there were Indians standing on a large rock above where the river narrows. Some of them were painted black; others had red streaks down their bodies. In terror, Helena's mother cried out in a local dialect: 'Don't shoot us, we'll be friends, don't shoot us'. But the current pulled them inexorably toward this rock, and the Indians began shooting. Eight arrows hit Helena's father, but he managed to pull them all out. Finally, the family abandoned the canoe, diving into the water and swimming to the opposite bank. Once they made it to land, Helena related, 'my father took me in his arms and began to run like a drunken man towards the woods'.

But Helena began to pass out as a result of loss of blood from her arrow wound. She said to her father, 'Leave me, I'm dying'. Concerned for the safety of his younger son, Luis, her father did so and ran off through the woods. Helena fainted.

Napëyoma

When Helena awoke, she thought she was dreaming. It was night, she was in the forest, and a fire was burning. She gradually realised that the dark figures flitting around her were Indian warriors. They had their penises tied up in penis sheaths. Their lower lips seemed grotesquely extended—she later realised that this was because they were in the habit of stuffing huge wads of tobacco into their mouths. The men had hair cut in a bowl cut, with a shaven spot on top. There were women there as well. A woman was sitting next to her and for a bright moment of hope, Helena thought she was her mother. When Helena reached to her, the woman turned and Helena realised it was an old Indian woman. The girl began to cry in terror. The woman offered her some water, but Helena would not be comforted. When her crying continued, Indian warriors stood in front of her tapping arrows together in a threatening gesture. Helena stopped crying but became even more terrified. That night, she tried to run away into the forest, but they caught her and brought her back.

Many years later, Helena was to learn that her parents had continued their mad flight into the forest and become separated, her mother and father finally finding each other after two days. They went back to look for Helena but she had disappeared, so

her family returned down the river and told the authorities. Soldiers came back to look for her but, being afraid of the Indians, they did not venture too far into the jungle, and Helena was given up for lost, even though the Yanoáma, for that is who they were, remained in the area with Helena for a month. In fact, they sent warriors down the Dimiti as far as the Negro River in order to find and kill her father, so he could not exact revenge on them, but they finally gave up and took Helena back with them to their main village, a journey of some eleven days. By this time, Helena was beginning to understand some of their language. They called her *Napëyoma,* which means 'stranger-woman', and there seemed to be a tug of war over her. While the Indians at first all seemed the same to her, Helena realised that they were from different tribes of the Yanoáma, and that one of these groups, the Karawetari, wanted to take her. But the tribe that had captured her, the Kohoroshiwetari, refused to give her up, and the two groups parted on bad terms.

In the meantime, though she cried bitterly, the women around Helena insisted on cutting her hair and shaving the top of her head. They took her clothes and painted her body with red streaks. Shortly after this happened, another group of Indians entered their camp with a captive, a white boy of about ten years old, with startlingly blue eyes. At first he would not talk and simply cried; however, he grew to trust Helena a little and told her, in Portuguese, that he wanted to go home. Shortly afterwards, his captors took him away. 'I have never heard anything about him since', Helena related. 'I have never seen him again.'

'You must be tired'

Helena lived for a short time in the Kohoroshiwetari *shapuno*, or village, but one terrifying morning arrows began to fall all around. It was an attack by the Karawetari, who were shouting that they were going to take Helena and all of the other women.

The men of Helena's village fled in terror, while the women and children climbed a rocky hillside, Karawetari warriors scrambling behind them. Helena was thin and weak; she could not, at this point, eat the monkey or wild boar meat the Indians prepared (such meat was simply boiled and eaten half raw) and was subsisting on a diet of wild roots.

She and some other women piled into a small cave but the Karawetari warriors, painted black, surrounded them and forced them out. Then, in an unimaginably savage scene, the Karawetari began killing the children who were with the women. Helena reported: 'One man took a baby by his feet and bashed him against a rock … They picked up his tiny body, which had turned purple, and threw it away. I wept with fear'. Other whimpering children, from toddlers to those about ten years old, were lined up and killed one by one. The Karawetari stabbed them with the ends of their sharp bows or took the youngest by the feet and smashed them

A small village on one of the tributaries of the Amazon. It was from one such village that the Valeros set out on their trip upriver.

TRYING TO KILL RAHARA

One of the most extraordinary scenes in Helena Valero's life among the Yanoáma—a scene that opens a window on the struggles of primitive tribes with the elements—is the time when she went with some Indian warriors and women to a shallow part of a local river in order to fish. On the bank of the river was a huge anaconda—the carnivorous, non-venomous South American snake that can grow up to nine metres (thirty feet) long and kills its prey by squeezing it to death in its powerful coils.

This snake was asleep, having earlier swallowed a deer—the outlines of the animal could be discerned within the reptile's belly. One of the Yanoáma warriors approached and hit the snake as hard as he could on its head, with an axe. The serpent stiffened and shook and the Indians decided to leave it to its death throes. Bad weather kept them from going back to the river for three days, and when they got there the snake was lying dead on the riverbank.

Or so they thought. While the others were fishing, Helena approached the creature—which had a huge chasm in its head from the warrior's axe—and when she neared, it turned and put out its tongue at her. In terror, she ran back to the Indians and told them this, but they did not believe her until a warrior went over and poked the snake with his bow and it began to move. The Indians then made a concerted effort to kill it by repeatedly beating it over the head. The snake's response was to spit out pieces of decaying deer, including antlers. The Indians thought the anaconda was dead and decided to tie vines around it and haul it over a tree branch in order to cut it up and dry its meat in the sun. With enormous effort, they hoisted the huge creature high in the air and began cutting pieces of flesh from its tail.

When they got to the midsection of the snake, one woman stuck a sharpened bamboo into its intestine and the snake gave a huge heave, wrenched itself, thrashing, off the tree and fell back into the pond. The water churned with blood and foam and Helena and her companions ran away in fright. A few days later, one man returned to the pond. Afraid to get too close, he climbed a nearby tree. The anaconda, as he reported back to the tribe, was basking in the pond, alive, as though nothing had happened.

'It's the nephew of Rahara', the Indians told Helena—Rahara being an immortal serpent of their mythology. Their shaman forbade the tribe to return to the pond, and no one ever did.

against trees and rocks. They threw the dead bodies into the woods, shouting 'Stay there, so that your fathers can find you and eat you'.

As the mothers of the dead children wept, the Karawetari shouted insults at the Kohoroshiwetari warriors, who were hiding in the forest: 'Cowards! Cowards! Come and avenge yourselves and kill us'. But they did not get an answer and finally went away, shadowed by one or two Kohoroshiwetari who wanted to try to get their women back. It was, in fact, the Kohoroshiwetari women who showed the greatest courage, many of them attempting to escape on the way to the Karawetari village.

Once at the Karawetari village, an older woman once again took charge of Helena, warning everyone not to touch her until she came of age as a woman. Then she told Helena, as if the girl had not just witnessed scenes of awful carnage: 'You have a rest; you must be tired after such a long walk'.

The wild Shamatari

Living with the Karawetari, Helena began to learn something of the rhythms of Yanoáma life. There were about a hundred men, women and children in the group Helena stayed with and they spent much of their time seeking food. The men went out to hunt; the women searched for food closer to home. One day, Helena and the others went out searching for butterfly grubs, caterpillars that lived on the branches of certain trees. The grubs were carefully packed in leaves and then roasted after being rubbed between stones to removed their hairs, which prickled on the tongue. This all had to be done at a certain time of the year, just before the caterpillars fell off the trees, buried themselves in the ground and formed cocoons.

Women and men both hunted small fish in the local *igarapé*, wading through the water toward the shore and splashing, knowing that the fish would seek refuge in piles of rotting leaves at the bottom of the water. The women would then scoop up the

leaves and toss them on the bank. It was at this same *igarapé* that Helena witnessed the attempted killing of the largest anaconda she had ever seen, and this only underscored how primitive the conditions were under which she was living.

Helena was extraordinarily adaptable and protected, to some extent, by her youth. Had she been a fully grown white woman, the Yanoáma women might have killed her out of jealousy but, as it was, they took care of her. Many of them had never seen a white person before and were curious about her, but they also felt sorry for her, since she did not have a mother or father to protect her. They helped her paint red designs on her body with small seeds and gathered around her when warriors came to stare at her, men who said things like: 'Is this Napëyoma? I thought she was a grown and beautiful woman. Napëyoma's reputation comes from afar'.

Helena had begun gradually to forget the scenes of horror she had witnessed and become used to living with the Karawetari when there was another cataclysmic event in her life. While visiting another tribe, she and the Karawetari came under attack from another group of Yanoáma called the Shamatari. In fact, the other Indians called them the 'wild Shamatari', because they were considered so unpredictable and so savage. Once again, arrows rained down on the village Helena was in, black-painted warriors flocked in, and Helena was a prisoner on a forced march. She was now about to begin the most nightmarish period of her existence in the wild.

'Kill Napëyoma'

The Shamatari took Helena and the other Karawetari women far away from the village, so much so that Helena began to lose her bearings completely and had no idea where she was. The Shamatari warriors shouted *Au, au, au!* as they marched and bragged about the men they had just killed. One of them said: 'I fell stunned. I have shot eight arrows and all of them have hit human flesh … I feel soft in my body'. The Shamatari believed that when one of them killed an enemy, their body felt soft. Later on the march, Helena watched a Shamatari warrior sit down suddenly and snort white worms out of his nose—this was a sign, according to the Shamatari shaman, that the man he had killed had not yet been cremated.

The talk of the Shamatari, all the way to their village, was obsessively about death. One man said his breath smelled bad and another told him he must have killed a woman with his arrows—killing women turned one's breath putrid. When Helena finally reached the Shamatari village, she found that numerous women were jealous of her, because

of the attention she received from the men and because, since she was still weak and thin, she was unable to carry a full load and some of the warriors had been finding her special food to eat.

Helena stayed in the village for some months. One day, she went out with some of the Shamatari while they hunted toads. They captured one, cut off its head and pulled out its claws with their teeth. They then squeezed the veins of the creature to get out the poison it carried. One woman—a woman who had been jealous of Helena—wrapped the toad in some leaves along with its eggs and told her to take it back to the village and eat it for dinner. Helena, not suspecting anything, went back to the hut she was staying in and cooked the toad. She tried a bit of its flesh and one of the eggs, but spat

Amazon warriors. Some tribes succeeded in maintaining their isolation for many years.

EPENA: HALLUCINOGEN
OF THE GODS

Epena is a powdery substance made of the resin found beneath the bark of certain types of slender trees in the western Amazon basin. It causes hallucinations when snorted and a snuff made from it was a staple of the Yanoáma's spiritual life. The Yanoáma ingested it by either snorting it themselves or having a friend blow it through a long tube into their nostrils.

Epena took the Yanoáma on spiritual journeys, putting them in touch with their dead and with the mystical creatures they believed lived in the forests surrounding them; it also helped shamans heal the sick by allowing them to wrench the illness out of the sufferer's body and take it to the spirit world. However, epena was not saved simply for ceremonial occasions but was used by almost all males above the age of thirteen or so, sometimes on a daily basis. Helena learned that when the males started drinking all the banana mingau in sight, they were about to snort epena, since under the influence of the drug 'someone will go almost mad and will run about and knock over the big bark vessels with the mingau in them'.

Although it was taboo for women to take the drug, Helena and another young woman sampled some in a scene reminiscent of Western teenagers sneaking into their parents' liquor cabinet. Helena's friend was preparing the powdery substance for her father and said, 'Let us inhale to see what it smells like'. Helena then said: 'I think I inhaled it four times, then I sat down ... When I stood up, my feet would not move properly. I said to my friend, "If I take any more, I shall not stand up again"'. Her friend, who inhaled a good deal more than Helena did, said, 'The shapuno is moving all around me'.

Then they went swimming, but Helena was too high to go into the water. She simply sat on the bank, in a daze. After this, she never tried the drug again, although her friend urged her to.

them out, finding them foul tasting. But a little girl wandered in and ate all the eggs. Immediately, she felt unwell, vomited and then shortly thereafter died in her mother's arms. It turned out that the toad's eggs were poisonous, something that the woman who gave them to Helena knew very well. No matter how much Helena protested her innocence, the dead child's mother shouted: 'Kill Napëyoma! Kill Napëyoma!'

That night, Helena was awakened by a woman friendly to her and warned that warriors were preparing poisoned arrows to shoot her with. She needed to get out, right now. Helena ran into the forest and hid nearby. In the morning, she could hear weeping from the village—they were hanging up the little girl's body in a tree. This was the usual burial custom among the Yanoáma. When the flesh rotted off, the bones of the dead were burned and the ashes mixed with *mingau*, a pap-like drink made from bananas. Then every member of the tribe drank them, as a way of ingesting the spirit of the dead person and absorbing it back into themselves.

Helena wandered through the woods, weeping, for a couple of days. She climbed a high hill, hoping to see where she was, but she saw no familiar landmarks, no rivers, only 'the great mountains and the forest, beautiful, blue and green here, blue and green there'. At night she dreamed that jaguars were coming to kill and eat her. She began praying to God, asking him why he had forsaken her in this wilderness, among these savages. Finally, starving, she went back to the Shamatari village, hoping that she could explain what happened, but as she was out gathering wood for the evening fires, the father of the child who had died shot her with a poisoned arrow, piercing her leg through. She raced into the woods, trying to pull the arrow out, feeling her leg go numb.

Finally, unable to walk, she lay down among some rocks and hid herself with leaves and branches. She heard the Shamatari warrior looking for her and passed out.

Alone

When she came to, the man was gone, but her leg had turned purple and was aching. She dragged herself over to a huge tree and hid in its cavernous roots. After a while, a group of Shamatari women walked past, and she heard them saying: 'Napëyoma is dead!' She managed to contact an old woman

FIGHTING TO BE FRIENDS

While many disputes among the Yanoáma could turn out deadly, they had another way of settling matters akin to a staged prizefight. Helena Valero saw this happen numerous times. When two Yanoáma men got into a heated dispute, one might say: 'You are upset, we are upset, we must calm ourselves'. At this point they would engage in a contest of blows. Sometimes the blows would be with the closed fist— a man might strike his opponent four times in the arm or chest and then await his turn to be struck himself. This would go on until their anger was satisfied or exhausted.

However, if using fists did not accomplish this, they would cut heavy branches from trees and take turns clubbing each other, first in the chest and then on the shaven spot on the top of their heads. This would often make the men's knees buckle and cause them to bleed from the nose. After the sticks, the men would often turn to a set of axes they had stolen from some rubber workers a long time before. Using the blunt end of the axe, they would club each other repeatedly in the chest and arms.

Helena's husband Fusiwe got into such a clubbing battle with another man, each taking a turn, until, as she related, 'Fusiwe sat down and vomited warm blood from his mouth'. At this point, his opponent said: 'We have beaten you hard, and you have beaten us hard. Our blood has flowed, we have caused your blood to flow. I am no longer troubled, for our anger has passed'.

This method was not perfect—clubbing could result in the occasional and accidental fatality, which would mean that revenge must be taken by the dead man's relations—but, brutal as it may seem to us, it was a fairly effective way to stop disputes before they reached epic proportions.

who had been kind to her, and this woman gave her some food and had her husband lead her farther away into the jungle. After this, Helena was on her own. She was looking for the trail that the Shamatari had taken from the land of the Karawetari, for the only thing she could hope for was to return to those people, who had been relatively kind to her.

Thus began a seven-month sojourn alone as she wandered, naked and without weapons, through the jungle. It would be an incredible tale of survival for an adult, let alone a girl barely into her teens. She was without fire and lived by following monkeys and eating the fruit they dropped half eaten (anything the monkeys would not eat, she did not touch). When there was no other food, she ate small crabs, shrimps, ants and ants' eggs. She stayed for a while in an abandoned Shamatari hut near an old patch of cultivated ground. She found seeds and painted herself red, for to be without paint seemed to her now to be naked. She became one with nature, another animal in the forest. On one of her first nights in the hut, she heard a jaguar walking by with her son. 'The mother called *hua, hua* … and the son answered. In the morning I went to see where they had been; the mother had vomited some wild boar flesh, which was still fresh.'

One day on the banks of a dry river, she thought she heard someone calling her name. She thought perhaps she was saved and stood up on a rock to look. What she saw was hallucinatory: two enormous snakes making their way together down the riverbank, making a whistling noise as they glided along next to each other. She ran away and hid, and then followed them. She convinced herself that someone had trained them, that they were going back to the man who was their master. But as the sun went down, the snakes entered a large, dark cave and stayed there. Indians later told her that the snakes made this whistling noise to attract the attention of small rodents, the *agouti*, which they then ate.

Helena stayed in the abandoned hut until a jaguar began to prowl nightly around her, coming closer and closer. Frightened, she moved on. Wandering through the forest, she found a trail and began to follow it, and at last saw human footprints. These she followed until she saw some Yanoáma men and women near a riverbank. She followed them as they wandered through the forest. By this time, Helena's hair had grown out and hung long and straight, midway down her back; she tied it with liana vines pulled from trees.

When she saw the Yanoáma she paused to paint herself with red streaks—'I wanted them to know that I was human like them', she said—but they recoiled when they saw her materialise from the forest. They thought she was Poré, the spirit of the dead, who frightened them greatly. One of the men went to get his arrows to shoot her and she ran away, but then she entered the village again that night and sat down by the fire in one of the huts. Most of the people were terrified, and Helena herself began to cry, thinking they would kill her, but then a woman approached her and peered at her closely.

'But it really is Napëyoma,' she told the others. 'They had said that the worms had eaten her all up; how can she be alive?'

'We lived happily in those days'

Helena had found a tribe called the Namoeteri and it was with these people that she would spend much of the rest of her time in the wilderness. She had become a beautiful young woman and many of the men tried to have her as their wife, some even trying to kidnap her from her hut. But she made what turned out to be a love match, becoming the fourth wife of a man named Fusiwe, who was headman of the Namoeteri. From the day that she met him, Helena later said, 'I stayed with the Namoeteri. From that day on I never escaped. Fusiwe was tall and strong'.

Helena Valero helps Father Bortoli at the mission school at Uaupés River where she found sanctuary after her return to civilisation.

Helena now began to truly settle into Yanoáma life, learning from Fusiwe a great deal about the lives and myths of these Indians, which had never heretofore been imparted to a white person. Fusiwe told her everything, from the way curare and *epena* were made to legends such as the story of how the hummingbirds were once men, which is why they steal cotton fibre from the Yanoáma in order to make their nests. Whenever there was a thunderstorm far off over the jungle, he told her it was the dead, moaning and screaming in the forest.

She learned a great deal about the marital habits of the Yanoáma—how some women were faithful to their husbands but others not, and how all the men were afraid of their mothers-in-law, who carried large sticks with which to chastise them if need be. Sometimes husbands who did not have

children arranged for other men to go with their wives, so that they might conceive. Because of close living conditions, men and women were modest and went into the forest by themselves in the evening to make love.

'We lived happily in those days', Helena remembered. She had two sons by Fusiwe, and even for a time forgot her real heritage, since she was so satisfied. Despite numerous wars with the Shamatari and other tribes, the Namoeteri thrived, partially because of Fusiwe's strong leadership. But then one morning, he awoke and told Helena: 'I have had such a bad dream. I have dreamed that these people had taken boiling ashes and were rubbing them on my face'. That day, in a battle with another tribe, Fusiwe was hit in the shoulder by a poisoned arrow. Holding onto one of their children, he said, 'It grieves me to leave my sons', and then he died.

The wicked white men

Although she lived among the Yanoáma for another five years or so, the death of her husband effectively meant the end of her happiness. The tribe who had killed him was afraid that her sons were going to grow up and take revenge on them, as was the Yanoáma tradition, and so they made several attempts to kill them. Terrified, Helena moved far away to another tribe, where she met and married a man named Akawe. But, although she had a son with Akawe, he treated her badly and sometimes beat her; he was almost murderous in his rages. Then the tribe that had killed Fusiwe moved nearby and began renewing their threats. To Helena, this was the last straw. She had now moved into an area where there was a fast-flowing river and where white men were occasionally seen. One of them, a German scientist, had built a hut near the river. She was able to approach him and ask, in broken Spanish, where she was, and he told her: 'Venezuela'. But Akawe pulled her away before she could give him her name.

Finally, as the tribe that threatened to kill her children came closer, she learned that white men in a motorboat sometimes passed by on the river, and she took her children, followed by Akawe, to the banks. When the boat came by she flagged it down and explained, as best she could, who she was. The man who ran the boat, as it turned out, knew her father, who was still alive, and this man and his wife took Helena, her children and Akawe on board. As the boat moved off, Helena recalled, 'I saw the bank drawing away from us. I felt a great happiness'.

It was 20 October 1956. Helena Valero had been away from the white world for over twenty years. The boat took her to the town of San Fernando, some seven days' journey away, but Helena's happiness was not to last for long. When she finally met her father, he reproved her and told her that she should have stayed in the forest— he was ashamed and embarrassed that she had become an Indian, had Indian children and an Indian husband. Her brothers felt the same way, although gradually they and her father warmed to her. Her mother was the only one who welcomed her with open arms. Akawe went back to his people, alone, and suddenly, as Helena said, she was in 'the wicked world of white men'. She was not trained for any work and no one would help her. Newspapers wrote about her ordeal, but the government would give her neither a job, nor food, nor education for her children—because they were considered Indians.

Despite the violence of Yanoáma existence, it was considered a sacred duty not to let anyone go hungry. Not so, Helena discovered, in the white world. Finally, she was helped by missionaries, who gave her food and helped get her children an education. Realising that her life had been irrevocably changed, she decided to go back to the mission school in the wilderness at the Uaupés River—where she had been as a girl before being asked to leave for not being 'Indian' enough— where she could work and be close to the Indians as well as keep in touch with the white world. After telling her story to Ettore Biocca, she lived in peace for another forty years, dying in the late 1990s, part Yanoáma, part white, an absolutely brave and unique woman.

In the meantime, Yanoáma territory has shrunk considerably, under inroads made by government infrastructure, gold miners and factories. White diseases finally attacked the previously protected Indians; tuberculosis and viral hepatitis have become endemic in some Yanoáma tribes. Part of the Yanoáma territory in Venezuela has been named a Biosphere Reserve but, for the most part, the society that the captive young Helena Valero knew has now disappeared forever.

THE BLANK SPOT ON THE MAP

Mick Leahy prospects
New Guinea, 1930–1935

Michael J. Leahy—but everyone called him 'Mick'—had a love for unknown wild places bred into him from a very early age. Born in 1901 in Toowoomba, in the Australian state of Queensland, he was the fourth of nine children of Irish immigrants. The family did not have much money, but Mick had a happy childhood wandering the hills of the Great Dividing Range, the mountains that dominate eastern Australia's landscape.

'The blue haze of distance over the scrub-covered ranges towards the coast always fascinated me', he wrote in his classic book *Explorations into Highland New Guinea*. 'With barefooted friends and a few dogs, we hunted wallabies and hares and trapped the small, beautifully marked finches that abounded ... My experience fuelled my enthusiasm and my urge to see what was on the other side of the haze-shrouded ranges.' He would soon have his chance.

After leaving school, Mick worked for a time as a clerk with the Queensland Railways, but soon found this indoor job restricting and quit to roam the forests of the eastern slopes of the ranges, cutting timber to be used for sleepers for railroad tracks. One day in 1926, as he was hauling wood blocks to the sawmill in a Model T Ford truck, he heard the news that there was a gold strike in New Guinea. 'I left my truck by the side of the road', Leahy wrote, 'teamed up with a group of men who, like myself, knew nothing about gold mining or about the country into which we were so impulsively heading, and caught the first steamer to New Guinea'.

The blank spot on the map
New Guinea is the second largest island in the world—only Greenland is larger—roughly 2500 kilometres (1500 miles) from end to end, the distance

from London to Moscow, although not quite so civilised a journey. The island has more mountains per square kilometre than any country in the world—a spine of rugged peaks runs the entire length of New Guinea, topping out at 4500 metres (15,000) feet. Areas of these central highlands are known to aviators as 'broken-bottle country' because, from the air, the chalky cliffs appear like the shards of huge bottles smashed into the landscape. Some peaks are snow-capped and there are active volcanoes. Clouds enshroud the deep valleys etched down from these mountains by fast-moving rivers.

New Guinea is a country that holds its secrets well. Settled for at least forty thousand years, it was only discovered by Europeans in 1526, when a Spanish sea captain sailed by and named it *ihas dos Papuas—papuas* from the Malaysian word for 'frizzy-

 NARMU AND THE SEA

During one of his expeditions to the highlands in 1932, Leahy and his brother Dan managed to convince a young man, Narmu, who had just seen his first white men, to come with them as they trekked out—they wanted to bring him back to civilisation, treat him well, and then take him home to show his tribe that they meant no harm.

They walked for eleven hours with Narmu to a rough landing strip cut into the grass of a mountain plateau. During their trek, several local tribes tried to 'rescue' Narmu, since they assumed he was being held against his will, and had to be forced back by gunfire being shot over their heads. When they got to the landing strip, Narmu was placed in the back of an open Gypsy Moth biplane—quite a feat of courage for someone who two weeks earlier did not suspect the existence of anyone outside his valley—and it took off. Narmu apparently looked down only once, and then got his head inside the plane for the entire trip to the coast.

Once there, he was taken to the sea, which he had never seen and which he approached only with the greatest trepidation, leaping back as if the waves were attacking him. However, all this changed when he realised that the water was salt water. Salt was a scarce commodity in the highlands and what little could be grubbed from the soil around mineral springs was of poor quality. Narmu immediately filled up as many empty beer bottles with salt water as he could. To him, wrote Leahy, 'the sea represented an endless supply of probably the scarcest and most valuable commodity the inland natives know … Murders and wars and changes of ownership often occurred near inland mineral springs'.

Happily, Narmu got into the Gypsy Moth to return to his people with his beer bottles full of salt water—although two were all he was allowed to carry, because of weight restrictions in the plane. Once back in his village, he dipped straws in the precious liquid and gave everyone a taste, thus forever cementing his fame among his people.

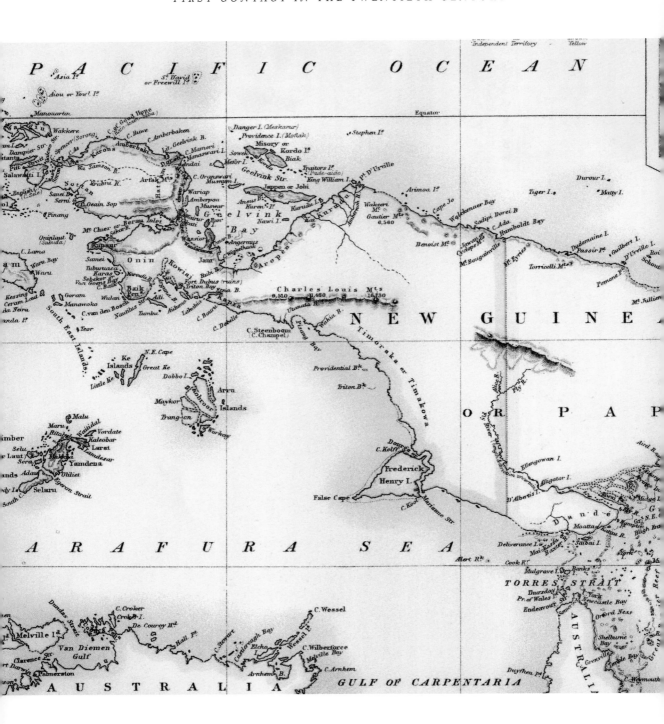

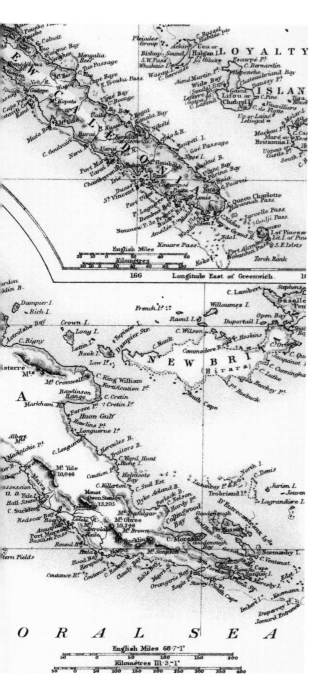

haired', after the natives' wild hair styles. A subsequent Spaniard called the island New Guinea because the islanders reminded him of natives from Africa's Guinea coast, but in fact the inhabitants of New Guinea are unlike any others, divided into numerous warring tribes without any of the inherited chieftainships or hierarchies usually found in such peoples. Instead, power went to those who displayed what social anthropologists call 'aggressive individualism'.

No one got too close to New Guinea for centuries: the terrain was rough and the natives unpredictable—headhunting and cannibalism were endemic there. But by the late nineteenth century, Europeans decided to carve up the island, which had gradually become a strategic pawn in the ever-expanding world power game of nation against nation. The western half (now Indonesian territory) was owned by The Netherlands, while the eastern half was divided between Germany, in the north, and Britain, in the south. After Germany's defeat in World War I, both the eastern territories were administered by Australia, with the northern part known as the Mandated Territory and the south as Papua.

A map of New Guinea from the early twentieth century shows a well-defined coastline and numerous river systems, like branching trees, but all of these precisely etched lines simply stop as they approach the centre of the island, where there is a massive blank spot. Sometimes such blank spots on maps were marked 'Uncharted' or 'Unexplored', but more often they were simply left empty. Throughout the nineteenth and early twentieth centuries, blank spots had disappeared from maps of Africa, North and South America, the Arctic and Australia, but the tantalising emptiness at the centre of New Guinea's map remained.

Map of New Guinea in the 1870s, with the 'blank spot' that would remain unmapped well into the twentieth century.

Gradually, in the 1920s, gold prospectors began to mine the country's swift rivers, getting closer and closer to the unknown territories in the country's central highlands—a place, as Mick Leahy wrote, that was considered to be 'a jumbled mass of unpopulated, timber-covered mountain ranges'. His first major expedition, in 1930, would drastically change that perception.

'Very hungry spirits'

By 1930, Leahy had been in New Guinea for four years and had not yet struck it rich—the wealthy Edie Creek mines, a walk of some eight days from the northeast coast of the country, were crowded with miners trying their luck. Determined to find 'another Edie Creek', Leahy set off on 24 May 1930 with another prospector, Michael Dwyer, and a group of sixteen New Guinean porters, to head up the Ramu River from the north coast. They had heard rumours of gold inland from solitary miners. Soon they arrived at the foothills of the Bismarck Range that bisects northern Papua New Guinea but found, to their surprise, that they had difficulties finding local guides to take them over the mountains—that people were terrified of being attacked by strange tribes who lived on the other side.

Leahy eventually found an old man who would guide them to the top of the range. From there, he reported an astonishing sight in what should have been an empty wilderness: 'From a small clearing we gazed into a vast area of steep, timber-topped, grass-covered ranges and high mountain peaks. There were fenced gardens in straight rows and smoke curling up from barricaded villages'. This was certainly not a 'blank spot' on a map. Leahy and Dwyer and their men bedded down somewhat uneasily that night and the next day made contact with natives who had never seen white men before. 'We found that first contact with whites was always quite a shock to the natives. They gave no thought to [offering us] food until they saw us picking up

pieces of sugarcane and sweet potato skins, when they seem to have realized that although we were spirits of some of their dead relatives, we were also very hungry spirits.'

The natives Leahy met were covered with pig grease, wore string belts but little else, and carried huge shields and bows and quivers of cane arrows. They pierced their noses in as many as five places, filling the holes with pieces of bone, pig tusk and quartz. This weight caused, as Leahy wrote, 'a continual snuffling' noise, quite noticeable when dozens of natives were present. After getting over their surprise, these people gave the expedition food in return for trade goods, especially steel knives and axes. Leahy and his men set off in canoes they had brought and reconstructed, paddling along the Ramu—here a fast-moving stream 1500 metres (5000 feet) above sea level that runs through steep, grassy hills and then out into a vast open valley populated by 'thousands of Stone Age natives living in barricaded villages with compact gardens nearby'. These tribes were constantly warring with each other, but the appearance of the expedition was so astonishing that they often stopped fighting and flocked to see the white men.

After two weeks of travel, as the river continued and widened, Leahy and Dwyer realised that they were, in fact, no longer on the Ramu (which should have narrowed to its upland source) but on a completely new and undiscovered river, heading downstream through a land that flickered at night with thousands of fires. The natives they met, wrote Leahy, 'endowed us with supernatural powers and associations', but Leahy also noted that this sense of awe only lasted so long and then the tribes they met began to show an unseemly interest in the fabulous belongings of the white men. Leahy was only too aware that, as far as the New Guineans knew, they were unarmed—they carried no bows, only their guns, which the tribes took to be mere sticks.

'The most treacherous cannibals'

Leahy had entered this country for a limited journey, but this new river was sweeping them along at a rapid clip and he felt woefully unprepared, especially with only two .12 gauge shotguns, two .22 rifles, two .32 rifles and two .45 pistols. He felt that if the party turned back and returned the way they had come, that the natives would have time to get over their superstitions and possibly attack—and that would be a fight the expedition could not win.

They were indeed in a savage country. The natives often buried their dead sitting up, with their heads above ground. The dead of enemy tribes, however, were either eaten or left to rot on the ground. Body after body floated down the river, victims of tribal wars higher in the mountains; when they washed up on the sandy banks, giant iguanas came out from the jungle to tear at their putrid flesh. But, without really knowing it, Leahy and Dwyer had become the first Europeans to cross the highland divide in Papua New Guinea. Exhausted, they left the river they were on—which turned out to be the Purari—and made their way down from the mountains to Port Romily, on the Gulf of Papua. Leahy and Dwyer had revealed a country teeming with heretofore unknown people and Leahy, for one, could not wait to go back.

Early in 1931, Leahy was hired by a company called New Guinea Goldfields Ltd to explore the headwaters of the Watut River, which flows through the northern slopes of the Owen Stanley Range. This time he was better prepared. He hired a small plane to take him over the country into which he was going to be walking, to check out the population

 LOSING A DIGIT

Mick Leahy noticed that wherever he went in the New Guinea highlands, people were missing fingers and sometimes entire hands. This was not due to warfare or accidents while farming, but to mourning. Whenever a loved one died, a surviving spouse, relative or friend would cut off a finger or two to show how much they missed the dead one.

Leahy witnessed this procedure once and he never forgot it. First the grieving man's hand was given a rough kind of anaesthesia by hitting his funny bone with a club, which somewhat numbed his nerves. Then an axe was brought out. As Leahy noted, however, these were Stone Age axes—'the cut was more a mash than the severing that a steel knife or tomahawk would make possible'. Once the finger was torn off, the wound was wrapped in a bandage created by warming two leaves over a bed of coals and then tying them on with a vine. If the wound healed without sepsis setting in, the amputee could consider himself or herself lucky.

Leahy also noted another side of this custom, however. If his expedition was in an area where the people enjoyed their presence and did not want them to leave, the warriors would pretend to be in elaborate grief and would grab their stone axes and claim they were going to cut their fingers off. However, Leahy soon realised that he was supposed to protest and tell the grievers not to go to such lengths, at which point the men gladly desisted.

and to look for flat, grassy areas where landing strips could be built so that the expedition could be resupplied by air (no strips existed in the rugged, mountainous territories).

On 24 March the expedition set off. Leahy had again brought along Michael Dwyer, as well as his own brother Pat and numerous native bearers. They walked along spiny, wooded ridges in the northern part of the Owen Stanleys, through territory whose indigenous peoples, the Kukakukas, had never seen white people before. 'The Kukakukas', Leahy wrote, 'have established a reputation for being the most treacherous cannibals in New Guinea and are said to stalk the ingredients of their meals with the same impersonal single-mindedness that a cat shows in pursuit of a mouse'.

Leahy, his brother Pat and Dwyer, as well as their terrified bearers, were themselves followed by the Kukakukas, who would crowd closely around them until Leahy got in the habit of stringing fishing line around their camps and refusing to let anyone come through it. Things were not helped any when the expedition came upon the empty camp of a German prospector, Helmuth Baum, who had preceded Leahy into the region. When Leahy decided to follow Baum's trail, they were stopped by Kukakukas, who kept making the strange gesture of bowing their heads and pouring water over their necks. Leahy took this to mean there was an impassable waterfall ahead, and turned back. Still, this bothered him, as it should have— for he found out only later that the Kukakukas

Michael Leahy with his dog, Snowy, and members of the expedition.

had attacked, killed and eaten Baum: the strange gesture was meant to show that the German had been beheaded.

Leahy did not know this when he camped a short time later and, therefore, he did not keep as close a watch as he should have. Just before dawn, a commotion broke out—shots were fired and he could hear his porters yelling and screaming. Leahy grabbed his .45 and ran outside into the dim light. A black man was standing a short distance away from him and Leahy thought he was a porter. 'Where are the bastards?' he said to him. Simultaneously, he turned and saw a Kukakuka warrior crossing a stream not ten metres (thirty feet) away. He fired with his .45 and then the world exploded around him. When he regained consciousness he was lying on the ground, with blood pouring down his head. The man he had spoken to was a Kukakuka, who had brained him with his stone 'pineapple' club. Leahy's life had been saved by a porter, armed with a bow and arrow, who had shot the warrior as he moved in to administer the *coup de grâce*.

Leahy could barely see, but he finished out the battle leaning against a tree and firing at the shadowy figures who flitted through the woods near the camp. When the battle was over, he went to check on his brother, who had received two arrow wounds, one to the chest, but had pulled out the arrows and kept on fighting. After this, the wounded expedition staggered back to civilisation, where Leahy learned the story of Baum's death and learned, as well, that the bush pilot with whom he had overflown the territory had died in a plane crash, his severed head rolling down onto a mountain trail where it was found by some hunters.

Sobered by these experiences, Leahy would never underestimate New Guinea again.

'Undisguised awe and terror'

In 1932 Leahy returned to the bush, this time to the New Guinea highlands, to an inland area called Bena Bena, which contained tribes of the same name. He brought with him his eighteen-year-old brother Dan, as well as a geologist from New Guinea Goldfields Ltd. Much better prepared this time, Leahy was able to stake several gold claims and cut out an airstrip that was used in the future both by colonial administration officials—who were beginning to take more of an interest in the area now that so many thousands of people had been found—and by gold miners.

Now something of an 'old pro' at first contact, Leahy wrote the following:

> First contact usually elicits undisguised awe and terror ... followed by stunned silence and tears, dances of what appeared to be joy, and loud, windy speeches by stone-axe-wielding old men who eventually give all and sundry their visions of the encounter.

At this point, plentiful food would be given to the expedition—the omnipresent pigs, sweet potatoes, sugarcane and bananas—and some serious trading would go on, with these inland people bargaining fiercely for discarded cans and bottles, empty rifle cartridges, even the coloured labels from food tins. 'The natives considered anything associated with our party to be impregnated with the spirits and magic that apparently protected us as we travelled amongst their neighbours and hereditary enemies.'

However, if the expedition stayed too long in any one place, the local people began to covet their possessions. Leahy punished even minor incidents of theft by threatening to shoot the miscreants, feeling he could not show the slightest weakness. In his memoir of those days, it is clear that he feels justified in doing so, and calls the tribes treacherous for their attacks on his party and for their ongoing attempts to steal the expedition's stores—but Leahy had a frankly old-fashioned and somewhat racist mindset when it came to the indigenous peoples he met in New Guinea. He never seems to have asked himself what he might do, back home in Australia, if a large party of heavily armed black men had camped out on the property that had been in his family for centuries, spending a good deal of time scooping dirt from streams and examining it closely.

'We shall surely die'

In March of 1933 Leahy and his brother Dan made an expedition into the area around Mount Hagen and discovered the huge and heavily populated Waghi Valley. As was now their habit, they overflew the area first and were astounded to see:

> ... a great, flat valley, possibly twenty miles [thirty kilometres] wide and no telling how many miles long ... with a very winding river meandering through it ... Below us [was] a continuous patchwork of gardens, with oblong grass houses in groups of four or five dotted thickly over the landscape. Except for the grass houses, the view below us resembled the patchwork fields of Belgium as seen from the air.

Leahy and his party hiked into this previously unexplored area, which was full of people 'who had never seen or heard of white skins before'. The people were fascinated by anything having to do with the white men, including their two dogs, from whom they plucked hairs until the animals howled, and also including the animals' faeces, which the locals took home rolled in leaves for leisurely examination around the fireside. Despite the civilised-seeming nature of their cultivated landscape, Leahy understood that these people were at constant war with each other. Every house had a secret escape tunnel, and Leahy passed numerous burnt-out villages. Refugee groups wandered the land; with no one to take them in, they lived a poor life of near-starvation in the forests.

Despite some of his attitudes toward the people he met, Leahy understood that he was making history and was careful to make a record of it for posterity. He took over five thousand 35-mm still photographs and several hours of 16-mm movies during the course of his journeys through the backcountry of New Guinea. Much of the film was developed right there in the field. These pictures provide us with an invaluable peek into a Stone Age way of life just as it was about to change—we can see the cultivated Waghi Valley, with its fenced-in gardens and straight pathways, the warriors with their greenstone axes and the woman who wears her late husband's jawbone around her neck as a sign of mourning.

For their part, the people did not know what to make of Leahy and his group. Anthropologists in the Mount Hagen area many years later asked those who had first seen Leahy's plane fly over what they had thought, and they replied that they had told each other: 'If we look at this thing, we shall surely die'. They gathered closer when he carved out a simple grass landing strip for resupply planes to land, but when the plane came in they would throw themselves on the ground in terror. One pilot, named Grabowsky, was 190 centimetres (6 feet 3 inches) tall and wore a brilliant white flying suit, a white leather skullcap and large green goggles. When he stepped out of the plane, the tribal people moaned in awe and horror.

Working with Jim Taylor, an official of the Australian colonial administration, Leahy and his brother Pat began to open up others of the hidden mountain valleys in Papua New Guinea—the land of the Goroka, Chimbu and Wabag. Each time, they were the first white men into the valley. 'People could not decide', Leahy wrote, 'whether to laugh or cry' when they saw him. There was only one more attempt at an attack, with an enraged

THE DEATH OF
BROTHER EUGENE

During his last journey through New Guinea, Mick Leahy befriended a Catholic missionary named Brother Eugene, who had been appointed by his bishop to open a mission in the newly created district of Mount Hagen, an area that Leahy had explored on his travels.

Brother Eugene, Leahy wrote, was so excited by his appointment 'one would have thought he had won a lottery ... He had no thought of any comfort or remuneration other than the privilege of serving God and the Catholic church and saving his own soul. Men and women must be born with such an outlook. I know I would not last very long as a missionary'.

In late 1934, just as Mick and his brother Dan were preparing to leave for the coast after learning from the Fox brothers that the area they wanted to prospect was bereft of gold, Brother Eugene approached and asked if he could borrow a .22 rifle. He was making a trek back to mission headquarters on the coast, he said, and wanted the gun to shoot small game. Leahy offered him a more powerful rifle in case he was attacked, but he refused it—he was certain he would not have any trouble.

In early January 1935, Leahy learned that both Brother Eugene and his superior, Father Morscheuser, had been killed by a band of Chimbu natives as they journeyed down to the coast. As Leahy pointed out, their killing was almost incidental—robbing them of their goods was the main motive. Leahy became concerned when some time passed without the colonial administration seeking to bring the perpetrators to justice. He knew that the Chimbu would see this as weakness and might exploit other white people in the area. So he, his brother Dan and the Fox brothers decided to mount an expedition of their own to the area to catch those who had killed the clergymen. Just before they set off, they heard electrifying news—a native had arrived claiming that a white man was wounded near the Chimbu River and in need of help.

Leahy set off at once with a heavily armed group of white men and black bearers and had arrived within one day of where the attack had occurred when a messenger arrived with a note from administration officials—he must turn back his impromptu expedition and allow the authorities to handle the situation. Reluctantly, Mick turned his men back—they had decided, in any event, that Brother Eugene could not possibly be alive. Bearers who had escaped the attack insisted vehemently that he had been killed. Much to Leahy's horror, he learned a few weeks later that Brother Eugene had, in fact, survived—wounded by eight arrows—in a hut near a river, cared for by two old Chimbu men. The administration patrol found him and brought him in, but he died in a field hospital. Had Leahy kept on going—rather than surrendering, for once in his life, to authority—he might have saved Brother Eugene's life.

warrior throwing a spear into the camp to signal a massacre, but Leahy put a stop to this by stopping the charging warrior dead in his tracks with two soft-nosed bullets.

'Our principal interest in life'

The strange thing for Mick Leahy was that he never did find any gold—in fact, by 1935 it began to seem almost beside the point. Once, staring from a ridge into unknown country, to 'alpine grass-covered mountaintops brightened by the long rays of the rising sun ... [and] dark, cloud-filled narrow valleys and gorges', Leahy reflected that he would have been 'mortified to have a new gold field stop us up before we had a look beyond the ranges in front of us'.

A hunger for contact and new people was what was driving Leahy, not gold. He made a final expedition in 1934 and then a quick foray into the bush in early 1935 to find the killers of a missionary he had befriended, but by that time the Fox brothers, Tom and Jack, had gone all the way to the border of Dutch New Guinea without finding any gold. 'When we heard this,' Leahy wrote, 'Danny and I walked back to the base camp in almost total silence, both of us feeling that we had been robbed of our principal interest in life'. With no evidence of gold, Mick's ventures into the backcountry would no longer be underwritten by companies seeking to mine the precious ore, and he would no longer be able to explore new vistas.

For the next five years, Mick Leahy prospected for gold in areas he had already discovered, but he found very little. In 1935, enraged that colonial administrators were claiming that one of their own had discovered the source of the Purari River in mountains Mick and Michael Dwyer had explored on their first journey, Leahy flew to London, where he forced the Royal Geographical Society to hold a hearing in which he could defend his claims. He was so convincing that the society awarded him its prestigious Murchison Grant and published his reports.

In 1940 Leahy got married and settled down on the New Guinea frontier, just in time for the Japanese invasion during World War II. After his wife was evacuated, he melted into the New Guinea highlands and helped a group of European refugees be airlifted from the Mount Hagen area. He then went to work for the United States Fifth Air Force, pinpointing sites for bomber fields in the wilds of New Guinea.

Leahy lived until 1979, a respected although sometimes controversial figure. While his expedition was not as bloody as those of Jack Hides (see page 293) or the Fox brothers, many excoriated him for his willingness to shoot to kill. Others believed that he shot only when necessary.

Leahy himself held the opinion that he and his men had survived for three reasons: 'Our presumed magic, our superior mentality, and our firearms, in that order'. What no one could doubt was Leahy's bravery and the fact that he had opened up for the world one of the least known places on Earth.

THE STRICKLAND–
PURARI PATROL

First contact in New Guinea's
southern highlands, 1935

In 1935, with gold prospectors like Mick Leahy and the Fox brothers moving into the wild areas of New Guinea, the Australian Colonial Service in Papua decided that it behoved them to mount an expedition into the southern highlands to see what type of people, country and resources lay there. This expedition, which was to be known as the Strickland–Purari Patrol for the river systems it came to explore, can be considered almost the last of the nineteenth century European-style expeditions that headed out into the great unknown with porters, guns and a large dose of *sang-froid*—the latter to make up for the lack of aerial reconnaissance, radio communications or advance supply dumps, all the niceties employed by subsequent expeditions.

Much of the *sang-froid* on this expedition would be provided by an extraordinary fellow named Jack Hides.

Skill and pluck

Jack Hides did not quite make it to the age of thirty-two before keeling over from alcoholism and a failed sense of mission, but he is legendary in New Guinea. In some ways Hides cut a figure straight out of a movie, the Indiana Jones of Oceania. At the time he became simultaneously famous and notorious, he was twenty-nine years old and had been a government officer in the Papuan Service of the Commonwealth of Australia for some nine years. Hides was born in 1906, the son of the jail warden in the then tiny town of Port Moresby, on New Guinea's southeastern coast. He was a boy who was raised with Papuan children and spoke Moru, the local dialect, as well as he spoke English. He grew into a tall, handsome young man with more than a passing resemblance to the actor Errol Flynn (who was actually living in New Guinea at the time and with whom Hides once got into a bar-room brawl).

As a young government officer, Hides had the unenviable task of conducting 'murder' raids into the interior from his remote outpost at Mondo, in the Papuan mountains. The lives of the natives of New Guinea revolved around an endless cycle of revenge killings; in an attempt to curb these, Hides, accompanied by native police, would make night-time raids deep into the jungle, creeping up on the huts of those responsible for the latest killing, calling out their names and then capturing them as they stumbled out into the dark. Dangerous work, but Hides loved it, despite the fact that he and his group were often attacked by angry kinsmen of those captured—they would send arrows whizzing in their direction and follow them through the jungle, shouting threats.

By 1935 Jack Hides, although impulsive and sometimes imprudent, was known as the premier figure in the Papuan Service—a superb jungle trekker, a man other men would readily follow and someone not afraid to take on a dangerous mission against the odds. He had, as his admiring superior wrote in the understated lingo of the service, both 'skill and pluck', as well as a romantic's vision of exploring—there was always something fascinating, he thought, over that next ridge, just around the bend of that new river.

Finally, Jack Hides loved the people of Papua and wanted to do his best for them in every way—to bring them forward into the light of civilisation, as he perceived it. It was a paternalistic, almost Victorian view, and it would clash with the reality of the unknown country he was about to enter.

Leaving civilisation

The Strickland–Purari Patrol consisted of Jack Hides, a fellow patrol officer named Jim O'Malley, ten Papuan policemen and thirty Papuan supply carriers. O'Malley, some six years younger than Hides, had become a close friend when he joined the Papuan Service and he accompanied Hides on some of his more dangerous patrols. Born and bred in Papua like Hides, O'Malley was stocky and well built, even-tempered where Hides was impulsive, and brave and unflappable—the perfect second-in-command.

The patrol set out up the Fly River by motor launch from the Gulf of Papua on 1 January 1935. The plan was to move roughly west-north-west up the Fly before turning almost due north up the Strickland River. The idea at that point was to find a tributary of the Strickland they could then follow east and south, before trekking overland and returning to the coast by travelling down the Purari River.

As they motored up the Fly, the patrol towed four dugout canoes filled with supplies, as well as steel knives and axes for trading with the tribes they might meet. Hides and O'Malley had no idea what they might run into, but they knew that all newly encountered tribal groups in New Guinea loved steel tools.

While he brought instruments for peaceful trading, Hides made sure his patrol was heavily armed. The police carried bolt-action Martini-Enfield .303 rifles and Hides and O'Malley also had .303 rifles, though of a different make. O'Malley carried a .45 pistol, as well, and there was a stockpile of perhaps three hundred rounds of ammunition, as well as the twenty rounds each man carried.

The group made its way up the Fly and then up the Strickland, covering some 550 kilometres (350 miles) before the river narrowed and they were forced to leave the motor launch behind and proceed by canoe. They were travelling through land that had only been sparsely charted and were now looking for a river that would take them eastward into unknown territory. They found one on 29 January and began to follow its course, winding between high sandstone banks, and travelled down it, now literally going where no white man had gone before.

'We meant them no harm'

As the days went by Hides saw, off in the distance, a large extinct volcano surrounded by a cluster of jagged peaks. The sandstone banks of the river gave way to heavy tropical jungle; the sense of being hemmed in by trees and underbrush made the men grip their rifle stocks tightly and scan the banks more closely.

They had as yet seen no people, but one day Hides spotted a dirt trail that led through the bush and decided to follow it with four policemen. Creeping along slowly, they reached a clearing, where they saw what Hides would later call a 'peaceful but savage scene'—a group of native women and girls making sago paste. They were guarded by men with long bows and arrows. On an impulse, Hides stepped from hiding, holding up a knife and a piece of cloth as presents, smiling in a friendly fashion.

One girl ran into the forest when she saw Hides, but the other women stood frozen to the spot as he advanced. The men unslung their bows but also stood stock-still, so that it seemed to Hides, for a moment, that all might be well. But as he took one more step into the clearing, all hell broke loose. There was a loud crash in the woods to his left, the men turned, bows at the ready to face the

Jack Hides and the patrol before setting out from Rona to travel up the Fly River and into the southern highlands of New Guinea.

sound, and then three shots rang out and one of the natives pitched forward, blood spouting from his chest. The others disappeared into the woods. Racing into the clearing, Hides found that one of his native policemen had been trying to enter the clearing from another path but had become stuck in the mud. A native bowman had advanced on him, shooting two arrows that nearly impaled him. The policeman, after firing warning shots, had had to kill the bowman, whose body now lay in the quiet clearing where even the voices of the birds were stilled.

Horrified, Hides left a shiny new steel tomahawk and a steel knife tied to a broken arrow, meant to signify peace, next to the dead man's body. He understood that his police constable had had to defend himself, but wondered if the natives

'understood afterwards that we meant them no harm'. It is unlikely that they did—fatal misunderstandings of this sort would plague his mission in the months to come.

The Great Plateau

A few weeks later, around 18 February, Hides and O'Malley found that the river they were on was rapidly narrowing and would soon become impassable, even for canoes, so they made the decision to strike out overland to the east and south. The first thing they did was destroy their dugout canoes, so that the porters would understand that there would be no return this way. Then Jack Hides climbed a tall tree to get his bearing and saw, spreading out before him, a sight no white man had ever seen: the Great Papuan Plateau.

 ## AT THE HEART OF A WITCH HUNT

Members of the New Guinea tribes, even more than most people, had an uneasy relationship with death, and this was particularly true of the Etoro, the first major tribe Jack Hides and his patrol made contact with. There was no death, including deaths from old age, accident, illness or combat with other tribes, that was considered 'natural'. All deaths, or so the Etoro thought, were the work of witches.

This was one of the reasons why life in Etoro communities was so precarious. When someone died of malarial fever, his relatives looked suspiciously around the community to see who could have cast a spell on him. Witch hunts almost always targeted people who lived in the same longhouse as the victim, since it was thought that they would be more easily able to curse him. One way of deciding if a person was a witch was to cook a cob from a pandanus plant from the victim's garden, along with one from the suspected witch's private plot and a hair from the victim's head. If the pandanus was firm, rather than mushy, after the usual cooking time, then the accused must be a witch.

If a person was identified as a witch, the punishment was swift. Relatives of the dead person usually ambushed and killed him. After he was dead, a further test would be taken to confirm his guilt or innocence. The murderers would cut him open and examine his heart. If it was flabby, with yellow deposits of fat, then he was indeed a witch. However, a normal heart of dark red colour meant that the accused was not a witch, and that the victim's relatives would now be open to retribution themselves.

The Great Plateau is midway up to the highlands, a vast step, as it were, before one reaches the limestone outcroppings and ridges of mountainous central Papua. It is about 3000 square kilometres (1200 square miles) of heavy tropical forest, with an average climate of 27 degrees (80 degrees Fahrenheit) and an average rainfall of over 5000 millimetres (200 inches) a year. When Hides and his patrol entered what was to them a wilderness, they were entering the homeland of three different ethnic groups: the Bosavi, the Onabasulu and the Etoro. These tribes, numbering perhaps three thousand in all, lived in tiny villages in communal longhouses, farmed sweet potatoes, raised pigs and warred constantly with each other. They believed firmly in witchcraft; in fact, like many New Guinea tribes, they felt that no death was natural, that even sickness was brought on by evil spells cast by witches. The people of the Great Plateau were cannibals and believed in eating their dead enemy as well as consuming dead relatives—the latter custom is known as 'affectionate' or mortuary cannibalism, a way of incorporating the dead back into the tribe.

'To save these people from their fear'

The inhabitants of the Great Plateau knew only the plateau. The world outside their borders was inhabited by the spirits of their dead, but also—or so their creation myths had it—by light-skinned people who had long ago been chased from these lands. If these light-skinned people returned, it would mean the return to what was called 'the Origin Time'. And this rejoining of light and dark people would mean the end of the world.

Cautiously moving through the plateau, steering by compass, Hides and his men were aware of being watched nearly constantly, although those watching were mere fleeting shadows in the bush. Around 20 March they came upon a village and found it abandoned, but they discovered, next to a still-warm cooking fire, human skulls and cracked human bones. Inside the village longhouse two human arms hung from the ceiling. Despite this gruesome find, Hides wrote in his journal of the beauty of the cultivated landscapes around the village, where sweet potato crops were planted next to cultivated flowers, there 'simply to add beauty to the landscape'. At night, they could see torches in the distance and hear singing, music of an otherworldly, almost ethereal variety 'that rose in volume in delightful harmony'.

Hides surmised that the people who lived in the village had seen them and were singing to make themselves brave, and he was right. Interviewed many years later by social anthropologists, a man who had been a small boy at the time described how Hides's patrol had suddenly emerged from the forest without warning. 'We jumped', he said. 'No one had ever seen anything like this before or knew what it was … these must be spirit people coming openly, in plain sight.'

Not only might they be spirit people, come to bring about the end of the world, but Hides and his patrol had unwittingly come from a direction in which the natives believed a recent plague of sickness had arisen, and so they were viewed with double suspicion. There was no way Hides and his men could begin to understand either of these perceptions on the part of the natives. When he came on an Etoro longhouse atop a hill, he climbed toward it; this time warriors came out to meet him, men with wild, bushy hair, bones or sticks through their noses, the jawbones of dead enemies slung around their necks, and tall bows with arrows 1.2 metres (four feet) long. Hides advanced up the hill, carrying steel axes as presents, but here the differences in the two cultures again led to tragedy. As an Etoro who was present remembered long afterward, their usual gesture of peace was to offer valuable objects or food, but unlike the coastal tribes, these Stone Age men had never seen steel before and so simply did not know what it could possibly be.

Pushed forward by the spirit medium of the tribe—a kind of shaman—the warriors began to shout and advance on Hides's men, who responded by opening fire over the heads of the Etoro, causing them to flee. But when two Etoro men shadowed the patrol as it continued on its way, Hides shot and killed one of them, who may have been about to fire an arrow at him. Hides later wrote: 'I deeply regret the shooting of this native, for I was prepared to risk a lot to save these people from their fear … but it all happened so fast'.

Once again, a dead body was left behind as the patrol made its way deeper into the wilderness. The man with a deep love of exploring and the

Huli warriors in full regalia cross a tari, a handmade wickerwork bridge.

Papuan people was leaving more and more cold corpses in his wake.

'People like sand'

Knowing the propensity of the New Guinea natives for revenge, Hides had his patrol hurry away from the area of the Etoro longhouse, cutting a new trail. Because of his need to move quickly, he made a fateful decision to leave at least half his stores of food behind.

Leaving the Great Plateau, the patrol climbed through a region of limestone crags and geological faults, with huge blocks of rock tossed upon each other as if by some giant's hand. After the fecund greenery of the Great Plateau, it was eerily empty: 'a silent and desolate land where only bandicoots and pythons could find a home', wrote Hides. Because low cloud cover and fog kept him from seeing ahead, Hides had a hard time guiding his men through the area, and it was twenty days before they found their way to the end of the limestone. By this time, his men were on half-rations and some were suffering from the beginnings of beriberi.

As the limestone ended, Hides, O'Malley, the patrol and the carriers limped painstakingly through a dense forest. On the fourth day in the forest they came to an opening in the trees and stared open-mouthed, stopped dead in their tracks. What they saw was a series of huge rolling valleys, stretching as far as the eye could see. Not only that, but almost every inch of the land in front of them was cultivated—it was as if they had stumbled upon a bit of England or Scotland hidden in New Guinea, with neatly marked out fields, drainage ditches, hedges and copses of trees—everything laid out with 'mathematical exactness', according to Hides.

Who had carved such a sophisticated and extensive agricultural system in what should have been a vast wilderness wasteland—a blank space on the map? 'These people', one of Hides's police corporals said, in an awed voice. 'They have plantations. What people are they?'

The people were, in fact, the Huli, a Stone Age people who lived in one of the most fertile high valley areas of New Guinea. As with the Great Plateau, temperatures averaged about 27 degrees, but the average rainfall was only half that experienced by the Etoro and other plateau peoples, so that the land, while well watered, was not jungle. The Huli were farmers—sweet potatoes, mainly—who kept herds of pigs that were not only food but were also used as currency. An interesting feature of the Huli land was the deep ditches that traversed the farming squares and were used to keep pigs from despoiling crops when they were being herded, but they were also called 'fighting ditches' because warriors employed them to sneak through to attack their enemies in distant villages.

For, more than any other tribe they had met so far, the Huli were warlike and aggressive— 'cantankerous individuals', as written by one social anthropologist, whose cycles of killings and revenge killings went on for decades. The Huli warrior was a stunning sight: tall, carrying bow and arrows and a shield, he also wore a huge wig, usually bedecked with flowers.

Jack Hides and his men emerged from the forest into this cultivated wonderland on 21 April 1935 and were immediately confronted by a group of men with bows and arrows, who stood watching them from about 100 metres (330 feet) away. In the 1980s one of these men, now quite elderly, was interviewed by social anthropologists and spoke of his first encounter experience. The man's name was Telenge. He thought of the patrol as 'men' but they materialised almost as spirits would. Some of them were carrying wooden sticks (their rifles) and most had black skin. But two of the men had skin so pale it seemed to glow with an otherworldly light, so that Telenge thought they must be *dama*, extremely powerful spirits of the dead.

The Huli nearby thought the same thing and they backed slowly away. But the two white-skinned *dama* approached and, making signs, asked Telenge and a friend to cut stakes for them, so that they might use them to pitch their tents. In shock, the Huli complied. When they were done, one of the *dama* gave them a steel axe, but Telenge later recalled: 'I gave it back. It was the first time and we were very frightened. We didn't know what this stuff [steel] was then'.

Jack Hides took his patrol through the land of the Huli but now found himself in serious trouble. Surrounded by plenty, the men were beginning to starve. He had blithely assumed, in leaving half his supplies behind, that he could trade for food with the natives he met, but he had failed to realise that the people he was making contact with simply did not know what steel was and, therefore, had no use for it. What they liked and treasured—and what was usually brought up from the coast by native traders and passed along even to these remote tribes—was pearl shell, which they used as prized ornamentation. And Jack Hides had brought no pearl shell.

Death at Dumi Creek

The next day, as Hides and his men awoke in their camp, they were greeted by a man whose name was Puya. Puya was a 'Big Man', one of the aggressive individuals who could influence a number of Huli groups. While he brought them bananas, he was suspicious of the white men, just as Hides and his native police were suspicious of his air of authority and the arrogant disdain with which he looked at them.

In fact, Puya's arrogance hid a good deal of fear. Later reports from among the Huli indicated that he was certain these men were spirits of the dead—in fact, he thought he recognised his dead brother among the native police. While it appears he was not going to immediately attack them, he wanted

them out of his land and so insistently pointed them to a route he wanted them to take. It was not, however, the route Hides would employ—'a child could see that such a route to the east was impossible', he later wrote, since it would lead back into the limestone area they had just exited. Hides and his men instead set off farther north into the valley, walking in the fighting ditches and followed everywhere by crowds of armed natives, who had the disconcerting habit of yodelling loudly—Hides thought it was to signal those ahead that the white men were coming.

Hides, hungry and growing increasingly wary, crossed a river and continued on deeper into Huli territory. Warriors followed the expedition everywhere, sometimes brandishing bows, other times simply staring in wonder. The high yodelling began to tell on the nerves of the men. More than once, Hides, at the head of the column, would hear a shot ring out and would race back to find that one of the native policemen had fired over the head of a Huli who had danced too tauntingly close. While all this was going on, their reserves of rice continued to diminish and they were thwarted in their attempts to trade for pigs and sweet potatoes. When they asked for food, the tribespeople waved their arms dismissively and replied *Nahai! Nahai!*, meaning 'there is none'. Yet Hides, O'Malley and their men could see fields of plenty all around them. Hides became increasingly alarmed because he knew that in the Papuan tribes closer to the coast hospitality was a main hallmark of their encounters with strangers. But then, those tribes did not believe that the white men were dead spirits, or sorcerers, as the Huli did, and that these objects they offered in trade would surely enchant any who touched them.

In such a fraught situation, it was almost certain that another scene of violence would occur and it did, on 27 April, as the patrol prepared to break camp and cross Dumi Creek, a fast-moving stream that incised a deep valley. Marching toward the

THE TIME OF DARKNESS

Located in the Bismarck Sea 650 kilometres (400 miles) northeast of New Guinea, Long Island is an uninhabited mass with two volcanic peaks, which in the mid-seventeenth century produced an explosion that became an integral part of a Huli myth.

When researchers first explored the beliefs of the Huli, they were struck by the story of the time of darkness (mbingi), which had happened, according to Huli elders, in the distant past. The Huli people were experiencing a period of agricultural decline and dwindling pig herds—as well as social chaos—when, one day, a cloud of darkness spread over the sun and dark sand began falling from the sky. The Huli hid in their houses until the sand stopped falling and the sun returned, and then they went back outside. The sand from the sky covered everything—the farmlands, the forests and the houses—and at first there was a period of starvation.

But then the Huli replanted their crops and were astonished to find amazing harvests in their gardens; not only that, but their pig population, fed on newly grown plants, rebounded. Thereafter, whenever the Huli experienced a period of poor crop growth, they performed a sacred ritual associated with bringing back mbingi. Interestingly enough, geological evidence indicates that the explosion of Long Island in the seventeenth century—nearly as powerful as the eruption of Krakatoa—caused several centimetres of volcanic ash to settle on Huli lands, thus bringing on mbingi. The ash also settled at other places in New Guinea, but the Huli, with their intensely cultivated lands, were the ones to mainly benefit from this rich volcanic fertiliser.

water, the patrol was followed by hundreds of warriors. The Huli were fearful as these spirits moved deeper and deeper into their land but, typically, were not organised enough to pull off a coherent attack—had they been, the patrol certainly would have ceased to exist, then and there. Instead, they shouted at the white men, shook their bows and generally acted in an angry and provocative manner.

Hides was certain they were going to attack. He sent O'Malley to the rear with five policemen and took five policemen himself in the front, sandwiching the carriers between them. As they approached the creek, O'Malley heard three shots ring out from behind him and turned to see that the police had fired at attackers, one of whom had shot an arrow that pierced a police officer's uniform. Two natives now lay dead and the rest dispersed.

'Something very strange approaching'

The patrol, which had started off in such high spirits of adventure and goodwill, was now falling apart. Shortly after the shooting at Dumi Creek, one porter died of beriberi, while others were beginning to show the bleeding gums and swollen limbs that are harbingers of that disease. Hides, who was beginning to feel ill with what would soon

THE FOX BROTHERS AND THE
FOOT OF THE RAINBOW

Although it is not clear whether the Huli that Jack Hides's patrol met knew this, another European patrol had arrived in a different part of the sprawling Huli world some five months earlier, in November 1934.

This patrol had a very different mission from that of the Strickland—Purari Patrol. It was led by two gold-mining brothers, Tom and Jack Fox, who brought along with them sixteen carriers on an unauthorised search for gold in the streams of the southern highlands. The Fox brothers were tough, hard-nosed, brave but amoral, not unlike many of the other independent prospectors hovering around the fringe wilderness areas of New Guinea, in search of a big gold strike like the ones that had occurred in Australia.

The Fox brothers were gone for six weeks and returned to the coast in December. 'We've been clear to the foot of the rainbow and there's not a pot of gold anywhere', Jack Fox told a friend. 'But there are plenty of natives, all of them full of beans and ready to fight.'

It is hard to know where the Fox brothers went, since they kept no notes of their journey, but they apparently reached some of the same areas as Jack Hides, since a later account left behind by both brothers has them in an area of 'sunken roads' among warlike natives wearing flower-bedecked wigs. Since they were not supposed to be there, the Foxes denied killing any men, but the Huli interviewed later said the Fox brothers were the cause of numerous deaths: 'They came, killing men as they came', said one Huli warrior. In a radio interview that took place in 1973, Jack Fox's callousness was apparent: 'We were looking for gold, you see … We weren't really interested in the natives. They were just there because they were there'.

become life-threatening dysentery, decided to abandon his journey north and strike out eastward, back in the direction of the Purari River. Finding a valley that ran south-southeast, he entered it, unwittingly finding new peoples, the Wola and the Nembi, who had not yet heard of their approach. A Wola man much later recalled that, when the patrol arrived in their territory, people said, 'Oh, there's something coming, something very strange approaching from over there. They say that it is ancestor spirits arrived to eat us'.

The Wola, like those Papuan tribes closer to the coast, were not cannibals and so were horrified at the thought of these ghosts coming to devour them. This impression was fostered by the carriers' black teeth (from chewing betel nuts), which made them look as if they had devoured the skin of other black creatures. But the patrol now could barely limp along—had the Wola been able to see past their fear, they would have seen a hungry, exhausted and frightened group of men. Unfortunately, this made them even more dangerous. Hides's patrol was, in a sense, like a combat squad that has probed deep into enemy territory, taken losses, pushed itself to the edge— and was now at the edge. When a Wola man tried to barricade a path leading to his home, should these ghosts try to come down it, one of the native policemen simply shot him.

Forcing two Wola men to act as guides, the patrol continued. Gradually the people began to lose their fear of this ragged band, particularly as they came begging for food, which the Wola would not give them (although they did trade a little for the pearl buttons from Hides's shirt).

On 11 May, a week after entering Wola country, the patrol entered a ravine, followed by hundreds of shouting and yodelling warriors, men who hurled taunts that the white men could not understand (perhaps just as well, because later ethnologists would translate Wola curses such as 'We will skin your penis!' and 'Go drink your mother's menstrual fluids!'). It was the same threatening display they had been treated to in the past, but this time, according to Hides and his men, they were attacked. Arrows flew into the column. Standing together, Hides and O'Malley fired as rapidly as they could load. 'I fired at a number of men rushing at me with stone axes; I also turned and fired at the men behind me.'

The native policemen were under even fiercer attack. One later testified: 'Then another man came and pulled his bow at me and I fired and I shot him. I shot this man but the others no run away. I said [to my friend]: "Like this and we shall all be dead"'.

Within a few minutes, it was all over. Hides figured that they had shot and killed eight Wola, although the Wola themselves would count fifteen dead. The Wola also said that they had not provoked the white men in any way and had merely been shot because of their curiosity in following them. The truth will never be fully known, but after the fight, Hides told his men to break into a native farm, kill pigs, uproot sweet potatoes and feed themselves, something he had vowed never to do. He and his patrol were now on the very edge of survival.

Finding their way home

As Hides began to feel serious effects from his dysentery—stomach cramps, fever, debilitating diarrhoea—O'Malley took over more of the day-to-day running of the patrol as it headed east and south, seeking streams that might flow into the Purari. They found one likely waterway and built makeshift rafts to float down it, but they reached unexpected rapids and were overturned. Soon, another carrier died and was buried in the bush.

The patrol now made little effort to trade for food, simply taking what they needed, which caused more friction with native groups. In one violent episode, they were attacked by warriors of the Semin-al, another Stone Age tribe, and had to hole up in an old farm hut and make a concerted stand to drive them off in a battle that lasted five hours and killed eight natives. The patrol moved on the next day, leaving the tribe to mourn its dead and wonder how they could take revenge on an enemy who had rapidly disappeared.

Finally, the patrol crossed the limestone barrier that separated these highland valleys from the Great Plateau and began to wend their way back to the coast, gradually entering an area that was familiar to Papuan Service patrols, where friendlier people provided them with food. Finally, on 18 June, they reached a white settlement not far from the coast. Hides and O'Malley were gaunt and dressed in rags. 'These two officers', wrote a government administrator a few weeks later, 'seemed to be bordering on a state of nervous breakdown'. Hides had to be hospitalised.

FOLLOWING PAGES Urama warriors of the southern highlands line up outside a large thatched temple reserved strictly for initiated men.

On hearing that the patrol had killed, conservatively, thirty people (possibly as many as fifty) during the course of its journey, the resident magistrate opened up an inquiry into the affair. It cleared the patrol of misconduct and, in fact, lauded them for coming through 'a very difficult situation' intact. But, within a year, another patrol found its way through an area near those explored by Jack Hides's patrol and came back without having killed one native, something that reflected badly on Hides. There were explanations for this—the chief one being that the subsequent patrol had taken along pearl shell to trade for food and so did not have to operate in a state of near-starvation—but doubts were cast on Hides's accomplishment.

Hides himself, in the meantime, had become a celebrity in Australia, lionised by the press, and soon wrote a bestselling book, *Papuan Wonderland*, that turned him into a hero. When he returned to work in New Guinea he was resented by many members of the Papuan Service, who would not speak to him. Hides began to drink a good deal and to fall into depression. He resigned from the Papuan Service in 1937 and went to work for a prospecting company seeking gold in New Guinea. He even took an expedition into the mountains at the headwaters of the Strickland River, but when the mineral expert who accompanied him took sick Hides abandoned the trip and dashed back to the coast in an unsuccessful attempt to save the expert's life.

Despondent and drinking heavily, Hides returned to Australia, where he died of pneumonia in June 1938.

To finish us all off

It cannot be disputed that the Strickland–Purari Patrol was an extraordinary one, opening up a vast territory of rivers, mountains, plateaus and tropical rainforest that had previously been unexplored. It also showed great courage and determination on the part of Hides, O'Malley and their men.

At the same time, these first encounters, like so many that occurred between European civilisations and native ones, were fraught with violence that came from deep cultural misunderstandings. The patrol and the native tribes they encountered met, but they did not come to know each other in any substantial way. For white civilisation, Jack Hides and his patrol represented romance, adventure and the triumph of Europeans over natives—the same triumph that had been occurring for centuries. Naturally, tribes like the Etoro, Huli and Wola had a different point of view. As one elderly Wola man was to report into the spinning tape recorder of a European researcher in the 1980s: 'We didn't know where these creatures came from; we wondered if they had come from the sky, from under the ground, or from inside the water ... We were very scared of them and thought that eventually many of them would come back and finish us all off'.

THE END
OF UNKNOWN
PEOPLE

*Are there any first
encounters left?*

The Earth is shrinking and it has been since 1492, a process as inexorable as death and taxes. As frontiers vanish, so too do first encounters. Where are the contemporary versions of the painted Britons shouting from their white cliffs, the Taino Indians gazing with wonder at Columbus's sails, the Maori watching James Cook's 'goblins' fill their bags with shells and flowers, the New Guinea highlanders who thought they were seeing their dead walk again? The answer is that a few such tribes *may* be out there.

In June 2008, Brazil's National Indian Foundation (FUNAI) released astonishing photographs and video of uncontacted Indians in the Amazonian rainforest, clustered around a small group of huts, firing arrows at the aeroplane from which the pictures were being taken. Some of the Indians are painted black or red, a sign of aggression (see the story of Helen Valero, page 270). A few months earlier another group of uncontacted Indians was

photographed gathering turtle eggs along the banks of the Las Piedras River in Peru's southeastern Amazon, their temporary grass huts erected on the beach just behind them.

Whenever such photographs and stories appear, they cause great excitement and controversy. A group called Survival International estimates that there are a hundred uncontacted tribes in the world, and that half of them live in the Amazonian rainforest and are being rapidly pushed to their last hiding places by logging and oil exploration. Like any uncontacted people, these tribes are especially vulnerable to outside diseases, to which they have no immunity, and their primitive weapons are no match for guns and hand grenades.

'It's like the Loch Ness monster'
When the uncontacted tribe along the Las Piedras River was spotted in late 2007, a lawyer representing

THE GENTLE TASADAY?

In July 1971, in the tangled and murky rainforest of South Cotabato Province, on the island of Mindanao in the Philippines, a tribesman led a Filipino official named Manuel Elizalde to a group of twenty-six primitive people living deep in the jungle.

Much to Elizalde's astonishment, as he later reported, he had found a Stone Age people who had not had previous contact with the outside world. At a time when a large-scale war was being fought in Southeast Asia, with bloody and disastrous consequences for the entire region, the world was happy to hear of the people the American author John Nance called 'the gentle Tasaday'. They were captured in their Stone Age innocence by the cameras of the respected National Geographic magazine, which wrote several stories about them—detailing how they lived in caves deep in the jungle, wore clothing made of leaves, had tools of stone, and had no word for 'weapon', 'war' or 'enemy'. They also called Manuel Elizalde, 'Great Man, God of the Tasaday'. One of the Tasaday explained: 'Our ancestors told us never to leave this place of ours. They told us the god of our people would come. These words have been proven true by the coming of [Elizalde]'.

In an effort to protect these people, Philippines President Ferdinand Marcos established a protective area of thousands of hectares around them and had it protected by soldiers. Anyone who wanted to contact the Tasaday had to do it through Manuel Elizalde, and he approved not scientists, but certain journalists and celebrities such as the aviator Charles Lindbergh. Although some scientists were a bit sceptical—there were rumours of Tasaday seen smoking cigarettes and wearing modern clothing—the matter stood this way until Marcos was ousted in 1986 and the area was opened up for unrestricted visits by journalists and scientists. A Swiss writer and scientist named Oswald Iten arrived unannounced to visit the Tasaday and found their caves deserted. They were, in fact, living in modern huts and wearing modern clothing.

It is, of course, possible that any group contacted by a more advanced civilisation would trade leaves for cotton and caves for huts, but further investigation seemed to indicate that the Tasaday had been a hoax perpetrated by Elizalde from the beginning. Why were their caves so clean? How did so small a group survive without showing the effects of interbreeding? Why did scientists never observe them actually gathering food? One Tasaday told a journalist: 'We didn't live in caves, only near them, until we met Elizalde … Elizalde forced us to live in caves so we'd be better cavemen'.

Elizalde, who had become rich through a foundation he set up for the Tasaday, decamped for Costa Rica and died in 1997, a drug addict. One scientist went so far as to call the Tasaday 'rain-forest clock punchers', but the controversy continues. There are numerous social scientists who believe that the Tasaday did, in fact, live in total isolation for several centuries, even if they were not quite in that state when Elizalde came across them. Unfortunately, the combination of Marcos's deliberate isolation of the tribe and Elizalde's exploitation of them will probably keep us from ever really knowing the truth.

Peru's oil and gas leasing agency told a newspaper: 'It's like the Loch Ness monster. Everyone seems to have seen or heard about uncontacted peoples, but there is no evidence'. Peruvian President Alan Garcia echoed this, claiming that uncontacted tribes are fictions concocted by environmental groups (like Survival International) in order to stop oil and natural gas development.

However, American oil companies take the situation seriously; one recently issued a manual to employees entering the region for the first time, ordering workers to treat such Indians peacefully. One section of the manual gives advice on how to make contact, instructing the worker to say: 'We are people like you; We are workers passing through;

We aren't going to stay; We have women and children far from here; We have houses and farms far from here'.

But what does 'uncontacted' mean in this day and age? Survival International feels that most of the 'uncontacted' tribes in the Amazon basin have had traumatic contacts with white people, perhaps as long ago as the nineteenth century, and have therefore shunned all such encounters. John Hemmings, author of *The Conquest of the Incas* and an expert on the region, says that after generations pass, such contact becomes a taboo, although the actual experience may fade from individual memory or be transformed into legend.

 ## 'A PLACE MAN HAS NEVER TOUCHED'

Perhaps even rarer than first contact in the twenty-first century is finding a land where no human beings have ever lived at all, but this is exactly what happened in 2006. On an expedition into unexplored territory around western New Guinea's Foja Mountains, scientists discovered what they termed a 'lost world' of species never before seen by humans.

The territory, in Irian Jaya, covered over 200,000 hectares (500,000 acres) and scientists found hundreds of previously unknown flowers and plants, 150 different kinds of butterflies, forty new species of animals, including a tree kangaroo and a spiny anteater, sixty new species of frogs and 225 new species of birds. 'It's as close to a Garden of Eden as you're going to find on Earth', said Bruce Beeher, who was co-leader of a team of eleven American, Indonesian and Australian scientists who spent a month in the area. The wildlife in the area was remarkably unafraid of human beings, possibly because even indigenous tribes living nearby had never ventured there—game is plentiful lower down the mountain slopes and the tribes would have had no reason to make the arduous climb. Several species of egg-laying amphibians allowed scientists to pick them up and take them into their camp, while a rare bird of paradise performed a mating dance right in front of their astonished eyes. 'What was amazing is the lack of wariness of all the animals', Beeher told a news conference. 'This is a place with no roads or trails and never, as far as we know, visited by man. This proves that there are still places that man has not touched.'

And, since tribes in the Amazon tend to split apart into separate groups once they get too large and exhaust the resources in a certain area, it is quite possible that there exist splinter groups who really do have no knowledge of the outside world. It is unlikely that any Indian with any real contact with white people would bother firing arrows at an aeroplane. However, it is also possible that the Indians who were photographed do fully understand the dangers posed by aeroplanes and are sending a warning shot across the bow of the twenty-first century.

'We thought they were stars'

First contact could still be made as the twentieth century began, but opportunities were fading fast. New Guinea was a prime example, a place filled with peoples about whom the outside world had no knowledge and who themselves knew nothing about the outside world. Even after the discoveries of Mick Leahy and Jack Hides, tribes were still being contacted for the first time. World War II moved over the island, and Allied troops stationed there discovered valley after valley filled with tribes with no knowledge of other races or ways of life but their own.

Uncontacted people remained in the Amazon, but these were rapidly suffering the depredations of white people who saw the area's rich natural resources. There are numerous Indian groups, especially in western Amazonia, who have hidden since the rubber boom swept through the Amazon in the late nineteenth century—during the period beginning in 1845 a large population of truly uncontacted Indians, left unmolested after the Spanish conquest, was massacred or press-ganged into tapping rubber. A second rubber boom, which ended around 1912, also contributed heavily to the deaths of uncontacted people. Many of the 'uncontacted' people of today fled deep into the forest after this period.

A clue to how primitive peoples view the machines used by white people comes from a member of a tribe of Ayoreo Indians who lived in the scrub forest south of the Amazon basin and who had been on the run for a number of years. When at last this man came down with tuberculosis, he was brought in for medical help and he told of running from bulldozers, thinking they were living: 'We thought the bulldozer could see us. We had planted many crops in the garden because it was summer time. We thought that the bulldozer had seen our garden and came to eat the fruit—and eat us, too'.

This man's view of aeroplanes was similar. 'We have always seen aeroplanes, but we did not know that it was something useful of the [white people]. We also saw long cloud behind the planes, which frightened us because we thought something might fall on us. When we saw these big planes with this white smoke behind, we thought they were stars.'

The man knew of the existence of white people, but he was wary of them and thus avoided contact for as long as possible.

The Sentinelese islanders

Other groups of uncontacted people did not hide but have remained as hostile as possible in order to make sure they are not bothered. This was the tactic of the Yanoáma; it is also the approach of the Sentinelese islanders of the Andaman Islands in the Indian Ocean. These are some of the most remote people on Earth, people thought to be descended from the first human populations to emerge from Africa. They have probably lived on North Sentinel Island for sixty thousand years. From the very beginning of European and Arab exploration, the Sentinelese have refused to be assimilated and have violently fought any type of encroachment on their territory.

This is an extremely primitive tribe about whom we know very little. It is thought that they number

The Tasaday in front of their cave in the jungles of Mindanao, in the Philippines. The controversy over these 'Stone Age' people continues.

as many as a hundred, but their number could be as low as twenty. The tsunami that swept the Indian Ocean in 2004 may have decimated the tribe, but they reacted with great hostility to any attempt to contact them. (In 2006, two fishermen who got too close to Sentinelese fishing grounds were killed with arrows and the helicopter sent to retrieve the bodies was also driven off.) The Indian government, which controls the islands, has backed off a previous approach of attempting to contact the Sentinelese and now leaves them alone—which is what they apparently desire. If any 'uncontacted' tribe will survive well into the twenty-first century, it is probably this small band.

First contact

Do any tribes with no knowledge of the outside world exist today? The chances are slim but, if they do, they probably live in Irian Jaya, the Indonesian half of the island of New Guinea. It is here that

 ADVENTURE TOURISM: FIRST CONTACT IN NEW GUINEA

Of course, it had to happen. In an age when tourists have literally climbed the highest mountain in the world and plumbed the depths of the oceans, someone had to come along to take the adventurous among us into jungles where they might make first contact with indigenous tribes.

That someone is a controversial American named Kelly Woolford, who runs an outfit based in Irian Jaya that takes tourists into the wilds of the region in search of tribes who have never had contact with civilisation. His website calls them 'pockets of humanity who have had no contact with the outside world … people who have never experienced anything from our modern world, who have never seen or used metals'.

These 'first contact' expeditions are limited to only four people—because Woolford says 'extreme sensitivity' must be shown to the people contacted in such a way, and a larger expedition might frighten them—each of whom pays thousands of dollars for the privilege. Guided by New Guinea locals, Woolford goes deep into the backcountry, following stories of local contact with tribes who supposedly live in the rainforests.

Reports on Woolford's results are mixed. One member of a group that was threatened deep in the bush by tribesmen brandishing bows and arrows felt the whole thing was a hoax. But others who have accompanied Woolford feel that they did make contact with truly primitive tribes. The question is whether it was first contact, and the answer is it probably was not—these people had had some connection, even if only through trade, to the larger world.

There are questions of ethics involved in Woolford's expeditions—such as the fact that even the common cold, brought by a visitor, could destroy an unprotected people—but there is no shortage of tourists willing to risk hardship and expense for a glimpse of a fast-vanishing world.

scientists have recently discovered a so-called 'lost valley', filled not with unknown people, but unknown species. It is also here that controversial 'adventure tours' take rich tourists in search of unknown tribes. There are still vast unexplored areas in western New Guinea that are too rough and remote to attract industry and here, somewhere, may be people who have lived their lives in the same way for centuries, oblivious to the turbulent world swirling around them. Most scientists feel that this is not the case, but scientists, as we know, do sometimes get it wrong.

If such people exist, should they be contacted? Even though Rousseau's image of 'the noble savage' has long been discredited, we still hold romantic images in our minds of simpler, more innocent ways of life. We forget the murder and mayhem that occurs in primitive society, the infant mortality, the times of starvation. But people all over are alike in some essential ways. If we found ourselves faced with a more advanced society that practised the art, say, of instant teleportation, we can be sure there would be an instant demand for this new, energy-efficient miracle of transportation. It is the same with many primitive peoples. In 1984 a group of Pintupi Aboriginals who were living in the Gibson Desert in Western Australia were tracked down and brought to the settled area. The Pintupi Nine, as they are known, are thought to have been the last uncontacted tribe in Australia. They had been grubbing out a typical survival living in the desert, but when they saw the availability of food and water in civilisation, they beat their relatives with sticks, asking why they had not told them about this bonanza earlier.

So we have a lot to offer an uncontacted primitive tribe, as long as we contact them in the right way—without guns and bulldozers, with caution, and bearing in mind the idea that all of us are, in some essential way, alike.

BIBLIOGRAPHY

Biocca, Ettiore. *Yanoáma: The Story of Helena Valero, A Girl Kidnapped by Amazonian Indians.* Kodansha International, New York, 1996.

Bjerre, Jens. *The Last Cannibals.* Drake Publishing, New York, 1974.

Cabeza de Vaca, Alvar Nunez. *The Narrative of Cabeza de Vaca.* Edited, translated and with an introduction by Rolena Adorno & Patrick Charles Pautz. University of Nebraska Press, Lincoln, Nebraska, 1999.

Clark, William R. *Explorers of the World.* The Natural History Press, Garden City, New York, 1964.

Crittenden, Robert & Schieffelin, Edward L. *Like People You See in a Dream: First Contact in Six Papuan Societies.* Stanford University Press, Stanford, California, 1991.

Dando-Collins, Stephen. *Caesar's Legion: The Epic Story of Caesar's Elite Tenth Legion and the Armies of Rome.* John Wiley & Sons, Inc., New York, 2002.

Dor-Net, Zvi. *Columbus and the Age of Discovery.* William Morrow & Co., New York, 1978.

Duncan, David Ewing. *Hernando de Soto: A Savage Quest in the Americas.* University of Oklahoma Press, Norman, Oklahoma, 1996.

Editors, Reader's Digest. *Mysteries of the Ancient Americas.* The Reader's Digest Association, Inc., Pleasantville, New York, 1986.

Fischer, David Hackett. *Champlain's Dream.* Simon & Schuster, New York, 2008.

Fitzhugh, William W. & Ward, Elizabeth I. *Vikings: The North Atlantic Saga.* The Smithsonian Institution Press, Washington, DC, 2000.

Forbath, Peter. *The River Congo. The Discovery, Exploration, and Exploitation of the World's Most Dramatic River.* Harper & Row, New York, 1977.

Hemming, John. *The Conquest of the Incas.* Harcourt Brace Jovanovich, New York, 1970.

Horwitz, Tony. *Blue Latitudes: Boldly Going Where Captain Cook Has Gone Before.* Henry Holt & Co., New York, 2002.

Hudson, Charles. *Knights of Spain, Warriors of the Sun: Hernando de Soto and the South's Ancient Chieftains.* The University of Georgia Press, Athens, Georgia, 1997.

Humble, Richard. *The Explorers.* Time-Life Books, Alexandria, Virginia, 1978.

Jeal, Tim. *Stanley: The Impossible Life of Africa's Greatest Explorer.* Yale University Press, New Haven, 2007.

Johnson, Donald S. *La Salle: A Perilous Odyssey from Canada to the Gulf of Mexico.* Cooper Square Press, New York, 2002.

Josephy, Alvin M., Jr. *America in 1492: The World of the Indian Peoples Before the Arrival of Columbus.* Alfred A. Knopf, New York, 1992.

Kelso, William M. *Jamestown: The Buried Truth.* The University of Virginia Press, Charlottesville, VA, 2006.

Leahy, Michael J. *Explorations into Highland New Guinea, 1930–1935.* University of Alabama Press, Tuscaloosa, Alabama, 1991.

McLynn, Frank. *Hearts of Darkness: The European Exploration of Africa.* Carroll & Graf Publishers, Inc., New York, 1992.

MacQuarrie, Kim. *The Last Days of the Incas.* Simon & Schuster, New York, 2007.

Mann, Charles C. *1491: New Revelations of the Americas Before Columbus.* Alfred A. Knopf, New York, 2005.

Marriott, Edward. *The Lost Tribe: A Harrowing Passage into New Guinea's Heart of Darkness.* Henry Holt & Co., New York, 1996.

Milton, Giles. *Big Chief Elizabeth: The Adventures of the First Engliash Colonists in America.* Farrar, Straus and Giroux, New York, 2000.

Moorehead, Alan. *The White Nile.* Harper & Row, New York, 1960.

Morrison, Samuel Elliot. *Samuel de Champlain: Father of New France.* Atlantic Monthly Press, Boston, 1972.

Paige, Paula Spurlin. *The Voyage of Magellan: The Journal of Antonio Pifagetta.* Prentice-Hall, Inc., Englewood Cliffs, NJ, 1969.

Park, Mungo. *Travels in the Interior Districts of Africa.* Wordsworth Editions, Hertsfordshire, 2002.

Parkman, Francis. *The Discovery of the Great West: La Salle.* Rinehart & Company, New York, 1956.

Price, Donald A. *Love and Hate in Jamestown: John Smith, Pocahontas, and the Heart of a New Nation.* Alfred A. Knopf, New York, 2003.

Resendez, Andres. *A Land So Strange: The Epic Journey of Cabeza de Vaca.* Basic Books, New York, 2007.

Rice, Edward. *Captain Sir Richard Francis Burton: The Secret Agent Who Made the Pilgrimage to Mecca, Discovered the Kama Sutra, and Brought the Arabian Nights to the West.* Charles Scribner's Sons, New York, 1990.

Sale, Kirkpatrick. *The Conquest of Paradise: Christopher Columbus and the Columbian Legacy.* Alfred A. Knopf, New York, 1990.

Sandler, Corey. *Henry Hudson: Dreams and Obsessions.* Citadel Press, New York, 2007.

Schama, Simon. *A History of Britain: At the Edge of the World, 3000 BC–AD 1603.* Hyperion, New York, 2000.

Scullard, H.H. *Roman Britain: Outpost of the Empire.* Thames and Hudson Ltd, London, 1979.

Smith, Anthony. *Explorers of the Amazon.* Viking, New York, 1990.

Stefansson, Vilhjalmur. *Great Adventures and Explorers.* The Dial Press, New York, 1947.

Villiers, Alan. *Captain James Cook.* Charles Scribner's Sons, New York, 1967.

ACKNOWLEDGEMENTS

I want to thank the whole Murdoch crew for making *First Encounters* such a delightful encounter—Diana Hill acquired the book then waited patiently while I coursed uncharted waters, while Emma Hutchinson helped it sail smoothly through editing and photo research. Thanks also to Christine Eslick for her sharp copyediting pencil, and to Hugh Ford and Susanne Geppert for their handsome and evocative design.

IMAGE CREDITS

AKG Images: page 107

Australpress / Granger Collection: Back cover, pages 7, 171, 184, 194, 276

Corbis: Front cover, pages 2, 11, 51, 60, 103, 121, 142-143, 163, 169, 200, 219, 222, 228, 233, 269, 298, 304-305, 311

Getty Images: pages 67, 137, 180, 208-209, 265, 280

Library of Congress, The: page 131

National Library of Australia, The: pages 288, 295

Photolibrary.com: pages 5, 9, 16, 26, 29, 34-35, 41, 44-45, 85, 115, 119, 126-127, 147, 156, 173, 193, 197, 210, 213, 227, 237, 246, 250, 257, 260, 273, 284-285

Picture Desk / Art Archive: 54, 72-73, 78, 89, 92, 96, 113, 240-241

INDEX

First published in 2009 by Pier 9, an imprint of Murdoch Books Pty Limited

Murdoch Books Australia
Pier 8/9
23 Hickson Road
Millers Point NSW 2000
Phone: +61 (0)2 8220 2000
Fax: +61 (0)2 8220 2558
www.murdochbooks.com.au

Murdoch Books UK Limited
Erico House, 6th Floor
93–99 Upper Richmond Road
Putney, London SW15 2TG
Phone: +44 (0) 20 8785 5995
Fax: +44 (0) 20 8785 5985
www.murdochbooks.co.uk

Publisher: Diana Hill
Project Manager: Emma Hutchinson
Editor: Christine Eslick
Cover designer: Hugh Ford
Internal designer: Susanne Geppert
Text copyright © Joseph Cummins 2009
Design copyright © Murdoch Books Pty Limited 2009

National Library of Australia Cataloguing-in-Publication Data:
Author: Cummins, Joseph.
Title: First encounters : epic true stories of cultural collision and conquest / Joseph Cummins.
ISBN: 9781741961430 (pbk.)
Series: Lost and found in history.
Notes: Includes index.
Bibliography.
Subjects: First contact of aboriginal peoples with Westerners.
Cultural relations—History.
Adventure and adventurers.
Explorers.
Discoveries in geography.
Dewey Number: 904.7

A catalogue record for this book is available from the British Library.

PRINTED IN CHINA.